POWER OVER PROPERTY

CHINA UNDERSTANDINGS TODAY

Series Editors: Mary Gallagher and Xiaobing Tang

China Understandings Today is dedicated to the study of contemporary China and seeks to present the latest and most innovative scholarship in social sciences and the humanities to the academic community as well as the general public. The series is sponsored by the Lieberthal-Rogel Center for Chinese Studies at the University of Michigan.

Resisting Spirits: Drama Reform and Cultural Transformation in the People's Republic of China
  Maggie Greene

Going to the Countryside: The Rural in the Modern Chinese Cultural Imagination, 1915–1965
  Yu Zhang

Power over Property: The Political Economy of Communist Land Reform in China
  Matthew Noellert

POWER OVER PROPERTY

*The Political Economy of Communist
Land Reform in China*

Matthew Noellert

UNIVERSITY OF MICHIGAN PRESS

Ann Arbor

For questions or permissions, please contact um.press.perms@umich.edu

Published in the United States of America by the
University of Michigan Press
Manufactured in the United States of America
Printed on acid-free paper
A CIP catalog record for this book is available from the British Library.
Library of Congress Cataloging-in-Publication data has been applied for.

First published September 2020

ISBN: 978-0-472-13211-9 (Hardcover : alk paper)
ISBN: 978-0-472-03798-8 (Paper : alk paper)
ISBN: 978-0-472-12710-8 (ebook)

To the people of Shuangcheng

Preface

This book is meant to be "a brick put out to attract jade" (引玉之砖). It uses novel data and methods and makes new claims about modern Chinese history that don't quite fit into common understandings. For many readers, therefore, this book may appear rather crude and brick-like. But by publishing it, I hope it will attract more people to study the experiences of China in the twentieth century, because in the course of that century more than half of the people on this planet went from living in predominantly family-based agrarian societies to living in corporate-based industrial societies, and China comprised roughly one-third of these people. Of course, Chinese society has been an important subject of study over the past century, but this book suggests that we still have a lot to learn.

How I came to study Shuangcheng County and write this book is also somewhat unusual, like "following a stem to discover a melon" (顺藤摸瓜). This stem began when I served as food steward at a residential co-op in Ann Arbor and my regular contact with farmers at the market inspired me to learn more about agriculture. After finishing an MA in Chinese Studies at the University of Michigan, I spent a year working on family farms in various parts of rural Japan. When I returned to graduate school at the Hong Kong University of Science and Technology, I told my adviser, James Z. Lee, that I was interested in farming, and he told me that his former student, Shuang Chen, wrote her dissertation on the late Qing history of Shuangcheng, a rural county in Northeast China that is now home to one of the largest Nestlé milk powder factories in China. James described how "Swiss boys" went out to the countryside every day to collect milk from thousands of small producers, and he was sure that I would fit right in. When I first arrived in Shuangcheng in the summer of 2010, all the proverbial Swiss boys were already gone, but I was still able to go out to the countryside twice a day with local Nestlé supervisors to observe milk collections and interview farmers. In the meantime, I began exploring the county archives where Shuang Chen had left off in the Republican period. I soon discovered the "Liberation period" archives dated between 1945 and 1949, which quickly proved rich enough to be the sole focus of my PhD dissertation and now this book.

The cover of this book displays my name as the sole author, but this means only that I take sole responsibility for any errors and problems in the pages that follow; the cover should not be misunderstood to mean that this book is purely the product of my own individual ability. In this respect my name is used only as shorthand to represent the sum of all the teachings, support, and encouragements of my teachers, friends, and family who over the past decade have contributed to the information, ideas, and effort that have gone into this book. Some of my more notable teachers include, but are in no way limited to, Hilda Hsi-Huei Tao, Henry Em, David Rolston, William Baxter, and James Robson from the University of Michigan; Ma Jianxiong, Li Bozhong, He Wenkai, and David Chang from the Hong Kong University of Science and Technology; James Watson from Harvard University; John Shepherd, Ira Bashkow, Frederick Damon, and Joseph Miller from the University of Virginia; Enatsu Yoshiki from Hitotsubashi University; Joseph Esherick from the University of California San Diego; Xing Long from Shanxi University; and Andrew Walder from Stanford University. I also especially thank the two anonymous reviewers invited by Stanford University Press and three anonymous reviewers invited by University of Michigan Press for their close readings and helpful suggestions on earlier versions of the manuscript.

This book is also a product of the Lee-Campbell Research Group, a group of students and scholars who collaborate on diverse historical Chinese big data projects with professors James Z. Lee and Cameron Campbell at the Hong Kong University of Science and Technology. James and Cameron taught me how to respect and analyze historical archives and have shepherded me on the straight and narrow path of a professional historian. Shuang Chen's research on the first century of Shuangcheng's history, especially, was the starting point for my excursions into the villages and archives of the county, and I look forward to continuing to work with and learn from her. Our dedicated research group coders, Sun Huicheng, Xiao Xing, and Guo Jiyang, spent one year transcribing into Excel most of the archival data used in this book. I have also depended on the intellectual and moral support of Dwight Davis, Byungho Lee, Liang Chen, Dong Hao, and all the other research group members, past and present.

The research in this book has been carried out thanks to generous funding from numerous sources. This project began with the Hong Kong Research Grant Council's (RGC) PhD Fellowship scheme, which kept me well funded during my PhD research from 2010 to 2014 and tolerated my long international forays to the University of Virginia, Hitotsubashi University, and Shuangcheng. Then I was able to make a first round of revisions to my manuscript and continue further research supported by a China Postdoctoral Fellowship at Shanxi University from 2014 to 2016 and a Hong Kong RGC General Research Fund #16602315, "Fanshen Revisited: New Perspectives on Land Reform and Rural Collectivization in North China, 1945–1965," from 2015 to 2018. After my first unsuccessful attempt to publish the manuscript, I applied for and was awarded a Postdoctoral Fellowship from the Henry Luce Foundation/ACLS Program in China Studies, which together with support from the University of Iowa gave me a free academic year from 2017 to 2018 to make a second round of revisions to my manuscript and submit it to the University of Michigan Press.

Above and beyond all of these acknowledgments, however, are the personal debts of gratitude that I owe to my family and friends who have supported me over the past decade. First and foremost, thanks are due to the boundless hospitality and generosity of the Shuangcheng County archivists and the friends and foster family(s) whom I have met during my annual visits to Shuangcheng, especially Jiang Mingshan, Yin Wenhua, Guan Guoqing, Ge Yunbo, Li Guoqing, Zhang Ying, Aunt Dong and all of their extended families. They have all helped make Shuangcheng my second hometown and have taught me most of what I know about Chinese society, despite all of the trouble I know I have caused them as a "good-for-nothing son" (败家子). For them this book is little more than the gift of "a single blade of grass trying to pay back its debt to the spring sun" (寸草春晖). Next, thanks are due to the close friends and classmates from Michigan, Beijing, Hong Kong, Tokyo, Virginia, Shanxi, and Iowa who have entertained my intellectual wanderings throughout much of my academic career. Last but most important, are the thanks due to my parents, wife, and children, to whom I owe everything I have.

Contents

Digital materials related to this title can be found on the Fulcrum platform via the following citable URL: https://doi.org/10.3998/mpub.11601496

List of Figures

List of Tables

List of Maps

CHAPTER 1

China's Land Reform

Land reform, defined as "the redistribution of property or rights in land for the benefit of small farmers and agricultural laborers," was the primary social platform of the Chinese Communist Party (CCP) and the founding myth of the People's Republic of China (PRC).[1] Between 1946 and 1953 the CCP redistributed 47 million hectares of farmland to 300 million peasants, making the CCP land reform one of the largest redistributions of property and power in history.[2] The founding myth of the PRC is that to achieve social and political equality, land reform had to first equitably redistribute landed property. This book argues that in practice, the opposite occurred: land reform required first redistributing political power, which then enabled a more egalitarian or fair distribution of property within rural communities. This seemingly simple reversal has profound implications for our understandings of modern China.

Accepting the premise that property rights determine social and political rights generally implies that property rights, or relations to property, are the key to understanding Chinese society both before and after land reform. Marxist historians naturally subscribe to this view, but even most non-Marxists and modern economic historians would agree that property rights play a primary role in the modern world. From seventeenth-century England to the twentieth-century United States, a central feature of the modern nation-state was its role in promoting and supporting private property rights, which are often claimed to be fundamental to the development of industrial capitalism, democracy, and many other features believed to define the modern world.[3] But in such nation-states, it was really only the "means of production," or the property of established landowners and bourgeois merchants and capitalists, that these states protected. In 1917 the Russian Revolution provided an alternative model in which the state claimed to protect the labor of industrial workers rather than the production capital of the owners. As a result, the ultimate question of the twentieth century was no longer whether or not the role of a modern state was to enforce property rights but what kind of property rights it should enforce.

This property-based modern state was one outcome of a longer historical process of commercialization. William McNeill marks the year 1000 C.E. as a turning point when "trade and market-regulated behavior"—that is, economic relations—started to gain influence vis-à-vis "command systems," or political relations, in societies around the world.[4] This process culminated in seventeenth-century England, where R. H. Tawney writes that the Tudor dynasty "made the command of money more important than the command of men," marking "a transition from the medieval conception of land as the basis of political functions and obligations to the modern view of it as an income-yielding investment."[5] As part of this transition, beginning in the sixteenth century with the enclosure movement, the English gentry began consolidating and laying private claim to previously communal lands in the name of agricultural improvement and economic progress. Ultimately, this gentry played a pivotal role in the English Parliament, and together with other economic elites, they used the economic wealth and power they acquired through the commercialization of agriculture to take over the English state in the civil wars of the seventeenth century. Through this triumph of economic interests over royal and political interests, English enclosures helped pave the way for private property rights and economic power to dominate modern state building in the West.[6]

Ironically, despite being one of the last major nations to establish a "modern" state in 1949, McNeill saw China as the earliest catalyst of this global process of commercialization. He writes that "the upsurge of market-related behavior that ranged from the sea of Japan and the south China seas to the Indian Ocean and all the waters that bathe the coasts of Europe took decisive impetus from what happened in China."[7] However, despite the fact that "the rise of a massive market economy in China during the eleventh century may have sufficed to change the world balance between command and market behavior in a critically significant way," it was still unable to change this balance within China.[8] China's marketization was powerful enough to transform Europe and beyond, but it was still not powerful enough to overcome the Chinese state, and most private accumulations of wealth in China would continue to be invested in or controlled by the state, not the market.[9]

One of the primary institutions through which the Chinese state continued to subordinate economic interests in society was the civil service examination system. In contrast to Europe, where political power was rooted in hereditary landed property, in China from at least the eighth century C.E. political power became rooted in education and civil service degrees directly controlled by the state.[10] According to Etienne Balazs, this all-powerful bureaucracy comprising a class of scholar-officials was one of the most enduring and definitive features of Chinese society.[11] Thus, in contrast to Europe, where commercialization transformed land from a political object into an economic object, in China the same transformation did not directly affect the roots of political power. As a result, as the economy commercialized, much wealth continued to be invested in education and officialdom rather than capital and markets.[12]

At the community level, generational seniority and social relationships, not property, have also been identified as the primary sources of political power and status in late Imperial China. Two major comparative studies have brought this contrast between Chinese and European sociopolitical organization into clearer focus. Tommy Bengtsson and his colleagues (2004) use historical demography to demonstrate that when the price of grain increased in eighteenth and nineteenth century European rural communities, all individuals in households with less property would be more likely to die. In contrast, when the price of grain increased in a similar Chinese context, women and kin with more distant relations to the household head would be more likely to die, in all households regardless of property holding. Based on these and other findings, Bengtsson and his colleagues therefore conclude that in Europe property was a more important source of power over the allocation of family resources, while in China social relationships, gender, and seniority were more important.[13] Taisu Zhang also arrives at similar conclusions, arguing that customary laws regarding rural property rights in late Imperial China were shaped by local elite whose power and status derived from generational seniority in the community or lineage, not property holding.[14] As a result, these laws protected the rights of poorer households much more than corresponding laws in England, which, in contrast, were shaped by property-rich local elites.[15] Thus, from rural communities up to the central state, by the nineteenth century Chinese society had developed a set of institutions in which power derived more from generational seniority and educational/political attainment than property or landed wealth.

I refer to this social dynamic in the past millennium of Chinese history as "power over property."[16] This phrase embodies a dual meaning in the sense of both political relations being more important than property relations in structuring society, and political power being used to redistribute and redefine entitlements to property. One premise of this book is that China's historical development is the exact opposite of what happened in Europe, which can be characterized as "property over power."[17] In Europe the market came to dominate the state, and the result was capitalism and industrialization. The development of "power over property," in which the state and relations to it continue to dominate social and economic organization, has been defined as "backward," in contrast to the European mode defined as "modern." Another example of this dichotomy appears in Eric Hobsbawm's trilogy, in which he identifies the years 1789 to 1848 as "dominated by a dual revolution: the industrial transformation pioneered in, and largely confined to, Britain, and the political transformation associated with, and largely confined to, France." The year 1848 marked the failure of the political transformation in Europe, and henceforth "the (British) industrial revolution swallowed the (French) political revolution."[18] As such, Hobsbawm also explicitly links the social revolutions of 1848 to twentieth-century socialist and communist regimes, like China, in which their political revolutions dictated their industrial revolutions.

The century of reform and revolution that preceded CCP land reform can be understood in terms of Chinese local elites struggling to adopt and adapt European models of "property over power" to create a modern China. In this narrative, land reform's attack on rural elites violently reversed a European-style process of modern development.[19] From a Western perspective, such a reversal was counterproductive and for most of the twentieth century could be conceived only in terms of a Soviet-style communist takeover. From the Chinese perspective, however, the century of "property over power" reforms that began after China's defeats in the Opium Wars led to increasing social fragmentation and disorder, suggesting that such reforms were incompatible in China.[20] In this alternative narrative, therefore, land reform can be seen as a return to a historically more typical model for China, that of "power over property."[21]

The founding myth of CCP land reform, by asserting that the redistribution of property was the means to solving China's social problems, rewrites or even erases the thousand-year-long historical trend in China described above. In addition to the CCP's own vested interests, there are a few more global reasons why this truly revolutionary rewriting of history has been taken for granted in the first place. First, as mentioned above, one of the effects of the Russian Revolution and later Cold War was the creation of a world in which the triumph of "property over power" is a universal given, and the only question is whose property should have priority. Second, the CCP's initial allegiance to the Soviet Union made it easy to define the PRC in Soviet terms. Third, underlying all of this was the general conviction that modern social revolutions, both capitalist and communist, were capable of such transformative reversals of history, as exemplified by the French and Russian revolutions, for instance. The crucial distinction, however, is that European revolutions were in line with what Karl Polanyi has called the Great Transformation, the political and economic processes associated with the transition from power to property, while in China the long-term trend was the reverse. Perhaps the real power of the CCP's revolutionary narrative, therefore, is that it was capable of both assimilating China into this "modern" world, on the one hand, and assimilating this "modern" world into Chinese society, on the other hand.

This brief comparative history provides the context for this book, which demonstrates that the process of CCP land reform, no matter how much it emphasized property in word, was in fact accomplished largely by and because of relations to power. While this book is concerned with the details of such power struggles in rural communities, some general features stand out. First, land reform, which lay at the heart of the Chinese Communist Party's social revolution, helped create a modern party-state but did so through a traditional alliance of the state (an organization of ruling elites) and the farming majority against local political middlemen.[22] As such, it was primarily a revival of state power rather than a fundamental transformation of the state's role in society based on a new alliance with local leaders and their property. Second, through land reform the CCP state reasserted its dominance over economy and society (through the redistribution of wealth), established new categories of political entitlement (social class labels), and consolidated a new class of political elites (CCP members). Third, the implementation of land reform did not involve a struggle for land between propertied and unpropertied social classes but a struggle to realign relations of power between the state and the village in a political hierarchy in which power flowed down from a singular source (in this case the CCP Central Committee).[23] The equal redistribution of land was a consequence, not a cause, of the equal redistribution of this power.

A central finding of this book is that the CCP's revival of state power and overhaul of the political hierarchy was not a completely top-down, state-centric process but was dependent on the revival of local village power and organization.[24] In other words, my understanding of the process of land reform involves what Philip C. C. Huang describes as the "societalization of the state" and the "state-ification of society," which basically means that both the central state and local communities adopt similar strategies to negotiate their contradictory interests.[25] Land reform was successful, therefore, insofar as it established a common platform through which the central state and local communities could both get what they wanted. And after a century of social and political instability, what they both wanted was a strong state—strong in the sense of being able to effectively organize and enforce a fair distribution of resources for all.[26] In many ways this is also precisely where concepts of state and society break down, because in order to build a strong state, the CCP needed to build strong villages, and in order to build strong villages, local communities needed the organizational strength of the CCP.

Just as land reform was the culmination of over a century of reforms in China, so this book has as a foundation the accumulation of half a century of scholarship on the CCP's social revolution. Many of my basic findings have precedents in previous studies but have rarely been presented in the context of a comprehensive narrative of an entire county. In this context these findings stand out in greater relief and reveal deeper currents and broader understandings of modern China than have been previously possible. In the following chapters I relate specific findings back to some of the earliest observations of land reform; here I highlight only the main historiographic trends. CCP land reform and China's rural revolution have been central to understandings of twentieth-century China since the journalist Edgar Snow visited CCP headquarters in Yan'an in the 1930s.[27] Before the 1980s, the rise of the CCP was overwhelmingly viewed as a communist takeover by a powerful Marxist-Leninist party-state. The main question was how the CCP won popular support in the countryside, and the main answers were either through socioeconomic appeals or through organizational power and coercion.[28] As a result of ideological biases and a lack of access to source materials, much scholarship in this period focused on high-level national politics.[29] Written during the ongoing revolution, this earlier scholarship was dominated by political scientists, whose methods helped widen the rift between China's recent past and its revolutionary present.

Beginning in the 1980s, the end of the Maoist era and a renewed political focus on local interests ushered in a new period of scholarship with access to new sources and an eye for complicating previously monolithic narratives of the CCP revolution. In this period, studies focused on local contexts, increasingly incorporated theories of comparative revolution, and generally agreed that the revolution was a political process rather than an outcome of structural factors or revolutionary conditions and consciousness.[30] After 1989 the bulk of the Western research agenda on China shifted to the study of post-socialist society, and the study of the politics of rural revolution shifted from political science and sociology to history. Western historical scholarship has continued to drill down into the political processes of the revolution. Some of these fundamental processes, such as mass mobilization, class struggle, and the restructuring of power relations in the countryside, have become the subject of increasingly specialized studies drawing on increasingly diverse sources.[31]

Scholarship within China on the CCP revolution has also taken off in the twenty-first century, likewise due to the historical distancing of the events from current affairs. Here studies range from new comprehensive historical accounts of land reform and the revolution to focused analyses of the distribution of land, mass mobilization, and rural politics.[32] Other Chinese scholars have produced county-level studies of land reform similar to this book, but access to primary sources remains a challenge.[33] Outside of history and social science, literary studies have also provided important challenges to understandings of the revolution and its narratives, based on a rich body of novels set in prerevolutionary and revolutionary China.[34] Perhaps the most important trend in Chinese scholarship, however, has been toward the large-scale accumulation of local and unofficial archival sources and data, which provide new grassroots perspectives and have the potential for more systematic analysis.[35]

Ultimately, however, political interpretations of land reform have yet to go beyond the CCP regime to focus on other deeper elements within Chinese society. Joseph W. Esherick writes that "the revolution was not a Liberation but (for most) was the replacement of one form of domination with another," but he goes on to suggest that the new form of domination was purely a function of Soviet influences and Leninist tactics, with little relation to China's indigenous political culture.[36] In other words, the PRC is totalitarian only to the extent that it is "communist" or socialist, not because of any inherent features of Chinese social and political organization. Similarly, Edward Friedman and his colleagues conclude that "a castelike system, not liberating equality, resulted from class-struggle land reform," but the primary implications of their narrative highlight the repressive side of the CCP state and its ultimate similarity with the Soviet Union in subordinating the needs of society to those of the state.[37] In contrast, for example, few studies have made explicit comparisons highlighting the fact that the only viable alternative to the CCP—the Chinese Nationalist Party (KMT) under Chiang Kai-shek[38]—was just as totalitarian and hierarchical as the CCP.[39] In terms of "power over property," one study of the KMT regime in the 1920s and 30s even suggests that "the Shanghai capitalists, the most powerful economic group in China, had failed to convert their economic power into political power."[40]

The primary contribution of this book, therefore, is to demonstrate that the politics and power struggles of land reform are rooted in a more enduring trend of "power over property" in Chinese society and cannot be adequately explained by the twentieth-century rhetoric of modern political regimes.[41] In describing Imperial China's scholar-official state, for example, Balazs writes, "The world 'totalitarian' has a modern ring to it, but it serves very well to describe the scholar-officials' state if it is understood to mean that *the state has complete control over all activities* of social life, absolute domination at all levels. . . . Nothing escaped official regimentation."[42] I argue that to see the PRC as simply a modern authoritarian state ignores Chinese realities and ultimately implies that someday China still has a chance to become "modern," in the Western sense of "property over power." Deng Xiaoping's market reforms after 1978 and China's rapid rise to global prominence in recent decades have helped keep this chance alive, but China today seems to be moving in the opposite direction yet again. Instead of seeing this trend as another deviation from "modern" norms, however, this book suggests that it is time to start entertaining the idea of a truly alternative modern world of "power over property."[43]

In other words, I argue that Chinese state authoritarianism is born out of the political organization of local Chinese society in which the primacy of interpersonal power relations creates a society that is organically oriented toward centralized state governance.[44] Instead of trying to conceptualize land reform in terms of state and society relations, I follow more recent literature that sees state and social actors as "not always unitary and antagonistic—they often form alliances with each other and against other political groups, and there can be conflict within both state and society."[45] In this conceptualization, I reframe earlier understandings of "oriental despotism" or totalitarianism in ways that do not assume that such state control exists in opposition to society but is instead an extension of social organization itself, or what in traditional Chinese terms is called "All under Heaven is one family" (天下一家).[46]

This book demonstrates that the dynamics of "power over property" have deeper roots in Chinese society through an empirical analysis of two years of CCP land reform in Shuangcheng County, Heilongjiang Province. The novel source materials and methods of analysis that form the core of this book make it possible to peel back multiple layers of interpretation and reveal some of the basic social processes that shaped, and were shaped by, individual experiences of land reform. Until now, virtually all source materials used to describe the events and experiences of land reform have come from a scattered selection of village case studies, personal interviews, and CCP work team reports from throughout China.[47] In contrast, this book is based on a relatively complete collection of county archives, including more than seventy village land reform work reports, seven thousand individual records of property expropriation and violence, and eighty thousand household records of property allocation, which describe two complete years of land reform in an entire county of over five hundred village settlements. By describing a complete county, therefore, this book represents one out of two thousand county experiences of land reform in China, rather than one or a dozen out of roughly eight hundred thousand village experiences.[48] The more complete picture afforded by these sources challenges some of our deepest modern assumptions.

These data describe a land reform that was not only a struggle for power but also a struggle waged *through* relations of power. As outlined above, at the national level this meant that the state controlled the market. Likewise, at the village level this meant that village leaders controlled all village resources. The question was not whether these leaders should have control over everything but whether they were socially/morally responsible in their exercise of control. The clearest sign of irresponsibility was the private accumulation of wealth at the expense of villager welfare. As I will show, this was the most common grievance expressed by villagers and suggests a strong moral element of power. This is also the point in our story where property and power become interchangeable. The CCP chose to emphasize property, perhaps because this was the only comprehensible rhetoric in the twentieth century. But based on the closer reading that I attempt in this book, I argue that almost all CCP discourse can be interpreted in a way in which property holding was used as a symbol or symptom of the abuse of power rather than the source of power.

The CCP's solution to abusive relations of power was to use party discipline to secure village leaders' obedience (or loyalty) to the state, and use collective decision making to ensure village leaders' attention to village welfare. This book focuses on the latter, because it is more closely related to the final outcome of land reform—the equal redistribution of rural wealth. Insofar as the unequal distribution of wealth before land reform was a function of village leaders abusing their power and appropriating village resources, so too the equal distribution of wealth was a function of equal, or democratic, decision-making power within the village. The common denominator is entitlements to village resources. One traditional role of the Chinese state is to guarantee fair entitlements to subsistence, and in this ideal, village leaders were morally bound to use their power to guarantee subsistence to everyone in the village.[49] When this moral bond broke down over the course of the early twentieth century, the CCP's solution to guaranteeing fair entitlements was to give every villager a role in the decision-making process rather than relying on a single leader. This made sense in principle and sometimes worked in practice for a limited time, such as in the final campaign of land reform in 1948 when village assemblies meticulously determined every individual's entitlement to a piece of village land. However, in the everyday management of village affairs and at levels above the village, it was difficult to attain consensus, and most decisions continued to be made by a village leader or small group of cadres. Because the state and these village leaders still monopolized control over village resources, the story of modern China continues to be a story of managing power, not property.

This book fleshes out these practices through four different perspectives on one county's experience of land reform in the late 1940s. Chapters 3 and 4 focus on the perspectives of state actors, and chapters 5 and 6 focus on the perspectives of village actors. Chapter 3 views land reform as a process of integrating state and village interests. Similar to other modern nation-states, the CCP intensified administrative control over society in part to be able to better represent local interests. The common logic behind this integration was a unification of state and village interests—what was good for the people was good for the state, and vice versa. In contrast to modern European states, however, these interests were conceived not in terms of economic opportunity but of political entitlement.[50] In rural China the common interest took the form of a hierarchical system of entitlements to "fair" shares of resources, in which fairness was based on natural inequalities in experience, moral character, and productive ability.

Chapter 4 focuses on land reform work teams as embodying the relationships between state and village, theory and practice. Work teams played a key role in a process that incorporated local interests into fundamentally top-down policy making. This chapter uses spatial analysis to trace the complete process from central policy, to work team experimentation, to general local implementation, and back again as it occurred in an entire county over the course of two years. In the terms of this book, work teams and the reports they created are the mediums through which property-based theory was translated into power-based practice, and vice versa. A close comparative reading of one work team's draft reports in chapter 4 demonstrates how land reform theories stayed true to Marxist-Leninist principles of class struggle while in practice the struggle for village power was waged in purely political and moral terms.

Chapter 5 is about the main event of land reform—the redistribution of land and other property. Contrary to popular belief, the CCP's redistribution of rural property was neither violent nor equal. I argue that there were few bitter struggles over land because land in itself was not the source of political power. Most people in rural China expected the state to manage the distribution of land (through local leaders), and its unequal or inefficient distribution was a problem of political control, not capitalist accumulation. The most violent period of land reform in Shuangcheng was a result of natural disaster and state misappropriation, and the lines of violent conflict were drawn between village communities, not between social classes. In the end, land was allocated fairly on a per capita basis, but fair did not mean equal. Villagers used class and moral rankings to ensure an unequal allocation that villagers nevertheless regarded as fair. The best land went to the most-wronged individuals, and the worst land went to the most-despised individuals in the community.

Chapter 6 is about another central feature of land reform: violence. Land reform violence is typically depicted as a staged performance orchestrated by the CCP and targeting wealthy landlords. This is viewing violence through the eyes of a work team or the state. I argue that from the perspective of villagers, they were condemning politically and morally corrupt local strongmen who had prioritized personal interests above community interests. Struggle meetings, at which local strongmen and their accomplices were publicly humiliated, were public performances of good overcoming evil. The CCP always made sure they were on the good side, even when the victim was a CCP cadre. This violence targeted all corrupt villagers, regardless of wealth or class status. Even when the victim was a stereotypical wealthy landlord, he was punished for his abuse of political power, which was seen as the cause, not consequence, of his accumulated wealth. This was not state violence but local retributive justice. The CCP was able to motivate villagers to exile, humiliate, beat up, and sometimes kill local strongmen because in the past these villagers had been on the receiving end of the same kinds of violence.

The remainder of the present chapter and chapters 2 and 7 provide the context and framework for understanding these stories. The following sections introduce the historical context of CCP land reform and the novel sources that make this book possible. Chapter 2 then introduces the historical context of Shuangcheng County and the actors and actions that comprised Shuangcheng's land reform. Chapter 7 concludes my narrative by generalizing my findings from Shuangcheng County to suggest an alternative understanding of PRC history and political economy, which begins with land reform.

Land Reform in Time and Space

As a single event, CCP land reform is best known as one of the largest redistributions of wealth in history. But the CCP had been experimenting with agrarian reform programs since the 1920s, and nationwide land reform began in 1946 in North China and ended seven years later and two thousand kilometers away in South China. This was a complicated process carried out across vast amounts of time and space, the details of which have yet to be fully described.[51] In this section I provide an overview of the nationwide land reform movement, a series of policies carried out between 1946 and 1953 designed to equally distribute landholding rights among rural populations throughout China. Then I focus on the first two policies of this land reform, carried out between 1946 and 1948 in much of North China, that comprise the context of this book.

The CCP had already redistributed over one-half of the nationwide land reform's total 47 million hectares, affecting one-third of China's rural population, before the founding of the PRC in October 1949 (Table 1, Map 1). This first stage of land reform took place in North and Northeast China, an area larger than France, Germany, and the UK combined, which the CCP occupied following the surrender of Japan and the end of the Sino-Japanese War in 1945. Acting as a revolutionary government in the context of civil war with the Chinese Nationalist Party (KMT), the CCP effectively

Table 1. Rural Land and Population Affected by CCP Land Reform, 1946–1952

Time Period	Land Redistrib- uted (mill. ha)	%	Rural Pop. Affected (mill. persons)	%
By Apr. 1946	0	0.0	0	0.0
By June 1949	25	53.2	125	33.3
By Apr. 1950	—	—	150	40.0
By Apr. 1951	—	—	250[a]	66.7
By Aug. 1952	47	100.0	375	100.0

Sources: Chang Yen, "China's Land Revolution: A Brief Review," *People's China* 2, no. 2 (1950): 32; Shaoqi Liu (Liu Shao-chi), "On the Agrarian Reform Law," *People's China* 2, no. 2 (1950): 5–9; Yibo Bo (Po Yi-po), "Three Years of Historic Achievements." *People's China* no. 20 (Oct. 16, 1952): 10–15; Sidney Klein, *The Pattern of Land Tenure Reform in East Asia After World War II* (New York: Bookman Associates, 1958); Runsheng Du, «中国的土地改革» (北京: 当代中国出版社, 1995).

[a] Based on Shaoqi Liu's 1950 schedule (not actual).

Note: "Rural population affected" refers to the total rural population in the areas where land reform was conducted, in contrast to the actual number of persons who received land, which is often not recorded.

reallocated 25 million hectares of land (more than the combined total arable land in France and the UK) to 100 million landless and land-poor peasants in the span of four years.

In between the founding of the PRC in October 1949 and the announcement of the first national Agrarian Reform Law in June 1950, the CCP expanded land reform to another 25 million rural inhabitants living near major cities in the north. The policy regulating land reform in these areas was passed in January 1950 by the PRC's Government Administrative Council and was unique in explicitly stating, "In the interest of municipal construction and industrial development, [the lands to be confiscated] shall be placed under state ownership and be administered by the people's municipal governments. They shall be distributed for the use of peasants with little or no land."[52] The peasants in these areas were therefore given "State Land Usage Deeds" rather than the standard "Land Title Deeds" implying private ownership that were issued in most rural areas of North China.[53]

In preparation for the Agrarian Reform Law of June 1950, Liu Shaoqi laid out a schedule for expanding land reform to the remaining 250 million rural inhabitants in the remainder of the country. Speaking in June shortly before the announcement of this Law, Liu said that over three hundred counties with a total rural population of about 100 million had already

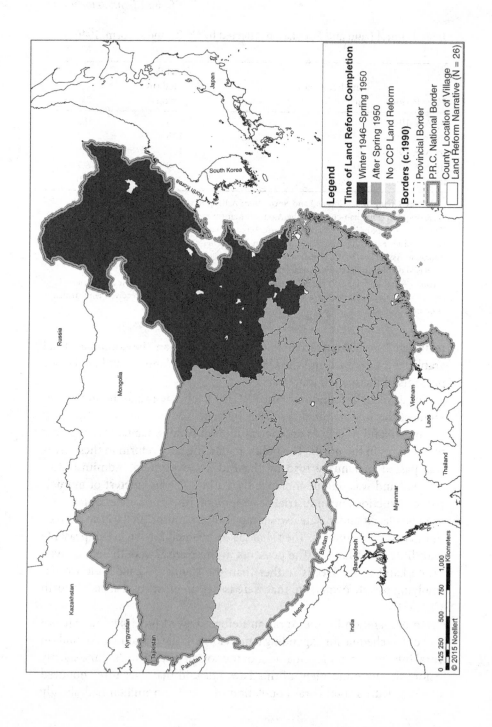

Map 1. National map of CCP land reform, 1946 to 1953

Sources: Chinese Academy of Surveying and Mapping—CASM China in Time and Space—CITAS—University of Washington, and Center for International Earth Science Information Network—CIESIN. China Dimensions Data Collection: China Administrative Regions GIS Data: 1:1M, County Level, 1990 (Palisades, NY: NASA Socioeconomic Data and Applications Center [SEDAC]), 1996. http://dx.doi.org/10.7927/H4C24TCF. Accessed September 14, 2014); World base map from DIVA-GIS, Global country boundaries, 2011. http://www.diva-gis.org/Data. Accessed September 14, 2014.

Note: I drew this map by overlaying a stylized map illustrating the different stages of CCP land reform (from Limin Guo and Jianying Wang eds., 《中国新民主主义革命时期通史地图集》 (北京: 中国地图出版社, 1993), 74) onto a 1990 county-level GIS map and approximating the area to the nearest county-level division. Since the total number of counties ca.1950 was approximately 2,050, excluding Tibet, the number of counties experiencing land reform before 1950 would have been significantly smaller, or roughly 600, but still represented about one-third of China's counties. Central Intelligence Agency, *China: Provisional Atlas of Communist Administrative Units* (Washington, DC: US Department of Commerce, 1959), plate 4, v; James Pinckney Harrison, *The Long March to Power: A History of the Chinese Communist Party, 1921–1972* (New York: Praeger, 1972), 371–72). See also a more detailed but still stylized map, the "schedule of agrarian reform," in Liu Shao-chi (Liu Shaoqi), "On the Agrarian Reform Law," *People's China* 2, no. 2 (1950), 7.

A land reform policy was not implemented in the Tibet Autonomous Region until September 1959, following the "Decision on Abolishing Feudal Land Ownership System and Implementing Farmers' Land Ownership." See Information Office of the State Council of the People's Republic of China, "Fifty Years of Democratic Reform in Tibet" (The Central People's Government of the People's Republic of China, March 2, 2009). Accessed September 19, 2014, http://english.gov.cn. Since this was independent from the 1950 Agrarian Reform Law, I follow the map from Guo and Wang in labeling Tibet as an area where it was "temporarily decided not to implement land reform" (as of 1993). There were also numerous minority areas in Southwest China that did not directly implement the 1950 Agrarian Reform Law; see, for example, Yunnan sheng wei dang shi yanjiu shi, 《云南土地改革回忆录》 (云南民族出版社, 2008).

made requests to carry out land reform in the winter of 1950, pending National Committee and Central People's Government approval. There remained an area with about 150 million rural inhabitants, the greater part of which Liu said could carry out land reform after the fall of 1951, while it was still impossible to decide when land reform in national minority areas with a total population of as much as 20 million would be carried out.[54] As Liu's report makes clear, land reform was to be "carried out under guidance, in a planned and orderly way, in complete accordance with the laws and decrees promulgated by the Central People's Government and the people's governments at various levels, and the principles, policies and steps decided by them."[55]

The earliest areas to complete land reform began implementing policies in the fall of 1946 and finished by the fall of 1948. During this time the CCP released two central policy documents. The first central CCP policy, the "Directive on the Land Question," was an internal-party document circulated on May 4, 1946, and thus commonly known as the May Fourth Directive. This directive called on the CCP to support the "masses" in taking land from landlords, combating "Han traitors" (汉奸), settling accounts with landlords, and reducing rent and interest. The policy thus focused on large landowners, was lenient toward rich peasants, and sought above all to gain support from as many social groups as possible.[56] The implementation of this directive focused on prominent former officials and criminal local elites and took place in contexts of tenuous CCP control.

Almost one and a half years later, a more definitive "Outline Land Law" was passed by a CCP National Land Committee and announced on October 10, 1947. This law clearly stated that "the land system of feudal and semi-feudal exploitation is abolished. The land system of 'land to the tillers' is to be realized," and prescribed the equal per capita allocation of all village land.[57] Initial attempts to implement this new law in the winter of 1947/48 resulted in widespread violence against virtually all landlords and rich peasants and many middle peasants. This led to further refinements at the local level, but the Outline Land Law would remain the central guiding policy until the 1950 Agrarian Reform Law, which retained much of the same basic text.

Both the May Fourth Directive and the Outline Land Law were brief documents consisting of general guidelines or principles for redistributing land and other property, while more concrete measures were expected to be developed at local levels to fit particular circumstances. The "Resolution on the Chinese Communist Party Central Committee's Promulgation of China's Outline Land Law" explicitly declares, "It is hoped that the democratic governments of all areas . . . will discuss and adopt this [Outline Land Law], and furthermore will work out concrete methods appropriate to local conditions."[58] These concrete measures came in the form of local campaigns and were dependent on leadership abilities at every level, which led to a diversity of practices even within a single county. Even in later land reform policy documents after 1949, exceptions and allowances for local decision making are common. This kind of decentralized policy implementation was not a consequence of lack of experience or control, however, but characterized a salient feature of Chinese political economy that combined centralized guiding principles with localized administrative practices, an issue discussed throughout this book.

In Shuangcheng County the implementation of the first two central policies of land reform can each be split into three campaigns, as illustrated in Figure 1. Beginning in the fall of 1946, the CCP County Committee organized work teams to experiment with implementing the May Fourth Directive through an "Anti-Traitor and Settling Accounts" (反奸清算) campaign.[59] In this campaign, work teams visited villages and tried to identify the most-hated local elites, mobilize villagers to publicly accuse and denounce them, confiscate and redistribute their land, and then organize a peasant association (PA) and local militia to protect villagers' property from vengeful local elite and bandits. Most of the targets of this campaign were former officials of Manchukuo, the Japanese state established in Northeast China from 1931 to 1945, and "settling accounts" referred to a kind of retributive justice in which villagers demanded that these local elites pay back what they had illegitimately appropriated from the community.

By the winter of 1946, however, several shortcomings of the Anti-Traitor and Settling Accounts campaign were brought to the attention of regional leaders, who then initiated an "Eliminate Half-Cooked Rice" (煮夹生饭) campaign. In November 1946 the Northeast Regional Bureau issued a directive on the "half-cooked" problem of land reform, stating that "mass work" in the majority of areas was incomplete. In other words, most local CCP leaders failed to effectively implement the May Fourth Directive, local elites still held power, villagers were not politically mobilized, and land had not been effectively redistributed, if at all.[60] For the time being, however, the CCP Central Committee left it up to regional and lower levels of government to figure out how to solve these problems.[61] One important change in tone, however, was that while the May Fourth

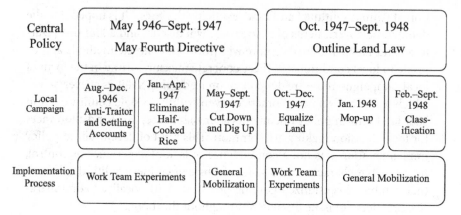

Central Policy	May 1946–Sept. 1947 May Fourth Directive			Oct. 1947–Sept. 1948 Outline Land Law			
Local Campaign	Aug.–Dec. 1946 Anti-Traitor and Settling Accounts	Jan.–Apr. 1947 Eliminate Half-Cooked Rice	May–Sept. 1947 Cut Down and Dig Up	Oct.–Dec. 1947 Equalize Land	Jan. 1948 Mop-up	Feb.–Sept. 1948 Class-ification	
Implementation Process	Work Team Experiments		General Mobilization	Work Team Experiments	General Mobilization		

Figure 1. CCP land reform policy structure in Shuangcheng County, 1946–1948. Adapted by the author from information recorded in Shuangcheng work reports. See Appendix E.

Directive emphasized redistributing land, from the winter of 1946 onward, CCP reports placed greater emphasis on mass political mobilization and organizing a majority of villagers to take active control of village affairs. In other words, redistributing land first did not lead to political change, so politically empowering peasants soon took priority.

In the summer of 1947, a new campaign to "Cut Down Big Trees and Dig Up Wealth" (砍大树挖财宝) superseded the Eliminate Half-Cooked Rice campaign. At a Songjiang provincial meeting of county party secretaries in June 1947,[62] leaders summarized the past six months of land reform work and continued to push for eliminating "half-cooked rice," which required that: "1) the political and economic power of landlords is completely swept away and all fruits of struggle are expropriated, and 2) the 'basic masses' take power and cadres have good class backgrounds."[63] "Cut down big trees" and "dig up wealth" were figurative references to the first point. This new campaign suggested significantly more extreme measures than those originally laid out in the May Fourth Directive and called for the mobilization of villagers to confiscate and redistribute all local elite property, including housing, grain, domestic animals, clothing, jewelry, and other household belongings, in addition to land. The message now was that land was not enough, and as long as the local elite still held some economic power, they could assert political power. Through the course of this campaign, moreover, CCP work teams discovered that villagers were more enthusiastic about confiscating household belongings than they had been in the past ten months trying to confiscate land.

It was amid these local land reform developments that the CCP called a national land committee to draft a new central policy, the Outline Land Law, which both legitimated the intensifying summer campaigns and called for the complete egalitarian redistribution of all village land as well as other non-landed property of landlords and rich peasants. Although in principle the Outline Land Law called for a much more radical redistribution of rural property than the May Fourth Directive, in practice the campaigns that followed appeared like the continuation of the process of intensification that was already under way by the summer of 1947. In Shuangcheng, CCP work teams carried out an "Equalize Land" (平分土地) campaign from November to December 1947, shortly after the Outline Land Law was announced, which expanded land reform work into new areas within the county. In this campaign, work team reports continued to emphasize the persistence of local elite influence and the need for the Outline Land Law's more thorough redistribution, partly because CCP work teams were working in new, previously unvisited villages. Despite nearly eighteen months of continually intensifying land reform campaigns many CCP work teams at the end of 1947 continued to encounter resilient local elite resistance and poor peasant apathy.

In their attempts to carry out the Equalize Land campaign, CCP work teams discovered a new strategy to once and for all mobilize the masses and completely sweep away local elite power in what became known locally as the "Mop-Up" (扫荡) campaign. Spreading throughout the county in January 1948, the Mop-Up campaign marked the climax of land reform violence and had to be called off by the CCP county government within the month. This campaign was described as more of a mass movement than a CCP policy and involved bands of poor peasants going from village to village to help other villages attack and confiscate the property of their local elites. Originally encouraged by the CCP as a united class movement of poor peasants against their oppressors, the campaign quickly devolved into inter-village rivalries and feuds over village property in which village solidarity often took priority over class solidarity. As we will see in chapter 5, widespread famine also played an important role in motivating inter-village violence over grain and other resources.

After the chaos of the Mop-Up campaign, CCP damage control seemed to put everything in order again, and it was time for the closing land reform campaign, variously labeled as the "Classification," "Rectification," or, more colloquially, the "Line Up" (站队排号) campaign. This campaign lasted from February to August 1948, during which time all 559 village PAs in the county led multiday village conferences at which every single household in the village was systematically assigned a class label, ranked within their class, and accordingly allocated a fair share of land per capita. Extant household registers recording this allocation among all of the more than eighty thousand households in the county were compiled between April and July 1948, and preparations for issuing land deeds appear to have been made by October 1948.[64]

In each of these campaigns, ad hoc CCP work teams organized by various levels of government played a crucial role in putting policy principles into practice. Local adaptation was accomplished by work team–led policy experiments in select villages, which always preceded general mobilization throughout the county or subcounty district. Then, in the course of general mobilization, which involved issuing directives and holding district and village meetings of PA representatives, work teams continued to operate in a supervisory capacity to inspect and assist particular villages. In terms of extant archival evidence, the Anti-Traitor and Settling Accounts and Eliminate Half-Cooked Rice campaigns were dominated by work team experiments and inspections (reports), while the Cut Down and Dig Up campaign was characterized by more widespread PA activity (victim register recording). Then, under the Outline Land Law, the Equalize Land campaign was dominated by work team experiments, while the Mop-Up and Classification campaigns were characterized by more widespread PA activity (classification register recording) (see Figure 1 above).

Although the local campaigns to break down these central policy directives into stages of local experimentation and implementation had unique names to reflect their vernacular origins, similar local campaigns unfolded almost simultaneously throughout North China. Detailed village and campaign narratives exist from at least ten counties in North China, plus another sixteen counties in the south (see Map 1).[65] Broadly speaking, therefore, the development of land reform in Shuangcheng between 1946 and 1948 described above occurred around the same time in at least five hundred other counties and represents the CCP's first attempt at carrying out a national-scale land reform program. While the central policies and local adaptations were broadly similar, however, two crucial differences allow for endless comparisons of land reform practices between localities: every locality had a different leader as well as a unique social and historical background. These differences allowed for variations in land reform practices as divergent as the compensation of landlords in exchange for their land to the targeting of individuals who may have been poor at present but had wealthy ancestors.[66] But at least until June 1950, all of these experiences were subsumed under the Outline Land Law.

The overarching feature of most land reform experiences in China is that political needs were always prioritized over economic needs. The increasing intensification of campaigns that characterized Shuangcheng's land reform, for example, should not be seen solely as the result of the need for more land but the need for more political participation. This point is even more obvious in a county like Shuangcheng in Northeast China, where the average land per capita was several times larger than in the other old liberated areas of North China. As mentioned above, by the end of 1946 it was already clear that it was more difficult for the CCP to mobilize a village majority than to confiscate land or attack landlords. Land was a static object, but politics and power relations were always in flux, and likewise so were CCP land reform practices. Outsiders tend to view such changes in terms of CCP fiat or opportunism. Instead of arguing for consistency, however, this book suggests that on the ground we can find even more variation than previously imagined and that this variation is an important factor in the CCP's success.

New Data and New Perspectives on Land Reform and Rural Society

This book presents a new approach to studying and understanding not just CCP land reform but Chinese rural society in general. Since the beginnings of rural social surveys in the early twentieth century, social research in China has predominantly relied on methods of surveying "typical" (典型) communities.[67] The main goal of this approach is to balance limited time and resources with the ability to generalize findings, to say more with less. Taken to the extreme, one implication of this approach is that one detailed, representative data point is sufficient to understand the rest. One of the premises of this book, however, is that in rural China, one family, village, district, or county cannot represent another.[68] The method employed in this book seeks not to generalize but to particularize and to complicate our picture of Chinese society in order to gain a deeper understanding of it. Something as complex as CCP land reform cannot be understood by studying a single village or a single policy.

The single village community has long been the traditional unit of social analysis in China, for, from an anthropological perspective, the village is a self-contained social microcosm.[69] But at the same time, every single village is embedded within a larger context. Even at the scale of a single county, studying one village to understand the county is like studying one household to understand the village. However, in the past century of research on twentieth-century rural China, perhaps only one study—G. W. Skinner's (1965) study of village marketing structures in Sichuan—has systematically described and analyzed larger organizations of Chinese society.[70] Of course, any Chinese administrator above the village level has to be aware of and personally involved in these larger organizations.[71] In April 1947, almost one year after the first land reform policy was announced, Liu Shaoqi, then secretary of the CCP Central Working Committee, challenged the leaders of the Jinsui liberated area (Northeast Shaanxi and Northwest Shanxi), saying:

> According to a report from the 6th regional committee, five counties altogether containing over 1,500 villages had mobilized over 900 villages, and over 200 villages have already redistributed land to the peasants. But these 200 villages are spread throughout five counties, and do not form a single mass. As such, until now they have not solved the land problem in a single county, and not even in a single district. The regional committee sent a powerful work team to spend one or two months solving the land problem in a single village but were unable to use this village as a starting point to expand the movement to neighboring villages. They were unable to reform the district government, county government, or other units, and depend on these government units to systematically mobilize the masses of an entire district or county from the top down to solve their land problems. They only completed work in a single village without touching neighboring villages and government units. This village is thus like a lone island in the middle of the ocean, completely isolated.[72]

An isolated village cannot support a larger political organization. Most of the CCP's efforts in land reform involved building these larger units, not simply mobilizing isolated village communities. A large part of this book, therefore, is devoted to exploring land reform in Shuangcheng from multiple levels.

What makes possible a more comprehensive understanding of the political economy of land reform are virtually complete county archival

Table 2. Distribution of Land Reform Sources over Time, Shuangcheng County, 1946–1948

Time Period			Sources			
Start Date	Central Policy	Local Campaign	Victim Registers (persons)	Classification Registers (households)	Work Reports (*tun* mentioned)	District Statistics (districts)
May 1946	May Fourth Direc-tive	Anti-Traitor and Settling Accounts			43	
Jan. 1947		Eliminate Half-Cooked Rice			35	
May 1947		Cut Down and Dig Up	7,246		26	11
Oct. 1947	Outline	Equalize Land			34	
Jan. 1948	Land	Mop-Up			75	
Feb. 1948	Law	Classification		82,603	43	10

records describing thousands of individual and household land reform events in Shuangcheng. I divide these records into three levels: nominative individual- and household-level data, village-level reports and surveys, and district-level aggregate statistics. Table 2 illustrates the coverage of these sources over the course of land reform in Shuangcheng.[73] In general, these three levels of data were also recorded by three different levels of authors. The individual- and household-level registers were primarily recorded by PA and administrative village cadres, the village-level reports and surveys were produced by district and county work teams, and the district-level statistics were compiled by district and county government offices. In Shuangcheng these historical archives cover a special time period, called the "Liberation period," and are distinct from the Manchukuo archives that end in 1945 and the PRC archives that begin in late 1949. They therefore document a critical time of transition and are an important source for studying Chinese state building. The nominative individual- and household-level register data covering the entire county have been entered into Excel spreadsheets by a dedicated team of coders, combined into a data set, and analyzed using Stata and QGIS software packages.[74] In addition, I have transcribed nearly two hundred thousand Chinese characters of village-level work team reports and surveys, representing all legible text contained in more than seventy such extant documents dated between July 1946 and April 1948.

Some of the first-ever studied nominative data describing the patterns and practices of CCP land reform for a complete county come from what I refer to as Shuangcheng's victim and classification registers. Table 3 summarizes the four sets of victim registers and one set of classification registers that form the core of this book. The four sets of victim registers were primarily compiled in the summer of 1947; they record over 6,000 individuals who had their land expropriated; 2,000 who were struggled against; 750 who escaped; and 300 who were killed.[75] The set of household classification registers was compiled in the summer of 1948 at the completion of land reform in Shuangcheng; they record the entire county population of over 80,000 households, including the urban county seat, and the amount of land and livestock allocated to each household. Together, these registers represent the most systematic data on CCP land reform ever studied.

As records of the entire county population at the completion of land reform, the household class registers form the foundation for our picture of Shuangcheng.[76] As described in Table 4, these registers record a rural population of more than 370,000 persons living in 70,000 households, plus the county seat population of more than 50,000 persons living in 11,000 households. Although titled "Classification" registers, in addition to recording household class status, these registers record the amount of land and number of draft animals allocated to each household, demonstrating the relationship between class status and property entitlement. These registers show that 87 percent of the county population lived in villages, while 90 percent of the population was engaged in agriculture (i.e., classified as landlord or peasant). Furthermore, despite being official and final registers of the land reform, they record at least thirty-seven unique class labels, which have been simplified into class categories in Table 4.[77] As registers compiled by tun (屯, a regional name for "natural village") PAs, such a diversity of class labels demonstrates both the localization of land reform categories and a lack of simple class standards even at the completion of a movement that is typically seen as the epitome of class struggle. Nevertheless, as we can see in Table 4, Shuangcheng society had unusually high proportions of landlords, rich peasants, and hired laborers, making it much more polarized than typical communities in North China. Nearly 15 percent of rural households were categorized as landlords and rich peasants, and nearly 70 percent were poor peasants and hired laborers (compare with chapter 2, Figure 2).

Compared to other forms of registration at the time, the classification registers demonstrate the CCP's basic interest in property as a symbol of

Table 3. Summary of Land Reform Register Data from Shuangcheng

English Title	Chinese Title Original Document	Chinese Title Archive Cover	Dates of Compilation	Volumes	Coverage	Unique Individuals	Contents
Registers of persons whose land was expropriated	被分地人登记表	各村屯:被分地主、富农,中农土地登记表	May–Aug. 1947	10	10 rural districts, 91 *cun*, 591 *tun*	5,900	Name, crime, family size, class, originally held land, redistributed land, and kept land
Registers of escaped landlords	任逃地主登记表	各村屯土改时地主、富农外逃登记表	May–Aug. 1947	2	10 rural districts, 81 *cun*, 566 *tun*	734	Name, date of escape, family size and conditions, crime, and current location
Registers of persons struggled against	被斗争人员登记表	各村屯对运动中的斗人斗争情况	May–Aug. 1947	2	10 rural districts, 61 *cun*, 401 *tun*	579	Name, class, reason for struggle, method of struggle, and official opinion
Registers of executed criminals	被处置人犯登记表	在运动中对坏人处置情况登记表(包拒枪杀)	May 1947– Feb. 1948	2	10 rural districts, 65 *cun*, 472 *tun*	290	Name, class, crime, supervisory unit, method of execution, public reaction, and the offender's family situation
Land Reform Classification Registers	土地改革阶级划分表	土地改革时期观划分级档案	Apr.–Aug. 1948	34	11 districts, 91 *cun*, 559 *tun*, and 35 urban precincts	82,514 households (423,759 persons)	Name of household head, class and rank, number of males and females in household, amount of land allocated (4 grades), and number of draft animals allocated

Sources: Shuangcheng County archives 129-3-1 through 129-3-10; 129-1-20 through 129-1-25; 129-3-12 through 129-3-45.

Table 4. Shuangcheng County Population, Land, and Livestock, by Class
Category, Summer 1948

Class Category	Rural House-holds %	Urban House-holds %	Total % House-holds	Persons	Allocated Land %	Allocated Livestock %
Landlord	6.6	5.1	6.4	7.5	7.2	2.7
Rich Peasant	8.2	2.0	7.3	9.7	10.5	6.7
Middle Peasant	15.7	6.7	14.5	17.7	19.0	18.5
Poor Peasant	27.1	9.8	24.7	24.4	26.6	29.6
Hired Laborer	41.5	9.1	37.0	32.0	36.0	41.4
Urban Bourgeoisie	0.1	2.7	0.4	0.4	0.01	0.1
Urban Semi-Proletariat	0.3	11.8	1.9	1.6	0.02	0.1
Urban Proletariat	0.2	47.3	6.7	5.6	0.3	0.7
Other Status	0.1	0.7	0.1	0.1	0.04	0.02
Missing	0.4	4.8	1.0	0.9	0.3	0.3
Total	100.0	100.0	100.0	100.0	100.0	100.0
N	71,165	11,349	82,514	423,759	230,159	38,447

Source: Author's own calculations based on the classification registers.
Notes: Land unit = hectares; Allocated Livestock includes horses, oxen, donkeys, and mules.

rural control. The contents of the classification registers, as well as other
archival evidence, suggest that one of the main purposes of these registers
was to record the allocation of rural property.[78] Between April and August
1948, however, at the same time that village PAs were recording the classification registers, the Public Security Bureau began a parallel process of
population registration in the county seat and the compilation of *hukou*
registers, which included more detailed information on every member in
each household. *Hukou* registration of the rural population, however, did
not begin until September.[79] In other words, the recording of rural land
took priority over the recording of rural people, even though more than
80 percent of the county population lived in the countryside.

Because of the novelty of the four victim registers, it is worthwhile to
critically review their major features one by one. Starting with the covers of the victim registers, over time the historical registers themselves
became more radicalized. With the exception of the escape registers, the
original titles of the Songjiang provincial forms that comprise the victim
registers do not mention anything about classes or other characteristics
of the victims but simply state "persons" whose land was expropriated or

who were struggled against, or "criminals" executed. The covers of the extant archival volumes, however, which appear to have been compiled in the 1960s, specifically identify the victims as landlords and rich peasants or simply "bad persons" (see Table 3).[80] At the time these registers were created, the height of land reform, class status appears to have played a minor role in defining the targets of land reform struggle. As we will see in chapters 5 and 6, the contents of these registers further support this argument.

Since the victim registers were recorded by PA cadres from all over the county, actual recording practices greatly varied. These registers were originally recorded by *tun* PAs, but for some villages the only extant registers are products of *cun* (村, or "administrative village") or district government recording, or district work teams.[81] The land expropriation registers, for example, which are compiled by district in the county archives, demonstrate a number of district-level variations. By looking at the notations and forms used, we can see that in most districts the extant registers were compiled by *cun* or district governments (Districts 2, 3, 4, 7, 9, 10, and 11). In Districts 5, 6, and 8, however, the forms are much more heterogeneous, and many of them have the original seals of *tun* PAs, while parts of Districts 5 and 9 were also registered by district work teams. The execution registers from District 7, which contain distinct district, *cun*, and *tun* records, further demonstrate that these registers passed through multiple levels of local administration. In this case, over the course of four days the *tun* forms were received by the *cun* governments, who compiled summary tables, and then the district government received these materials and compiled their own summary tables for the entire district.[82] Like many of the forms, these summary tables were hand drawn and had their own distinctive formatting.

In addition to being recorded by various agents, victim register data were recorded at various times. The blank forms for all four registers are printed with the words "Created by the Songjiang Provincial Committee, May 1947," which gives us the earliest possible time of recording. Furthermore, a number of forms were hand dated in June, July, and August, and many others consist of a wide variety of undated, handmade copies of the original forms on random sheets of paper. Some of the execution registers are also dated November 1947 or February 1948, which most likely provide the latest possible time of recording, since by early 1948 a new wave of campaigns following the Outline Land Law had already begun. Although the majority of forms are not hand dated, we can assume that they were most likely recorded between June and August 1947. The limited hand-dated forms available suggest that District 6 recorded their registers in June, Districts 5 and 10 recorded their registers in July, and District 9 recorded their registers in August.[83] Five of the remaining districts have no hand-dated forms, and District 11 has hand-dated forms from all three months of June, July, and August for different villages.

These victim registers were originally recorded as part of the 1947 summer campaign of intensified struggle in Shuangcheng (the Cut Down and Dig Up campaign), and for the majority of villages without work reports they represent the first records of land reform events. According to my calculations, all of the extant work reports in the county archives dated on or before August 1947 mention by name a total of around one hundred villages (*tun*). In contrast, the victim registers record data on over five hundred villages. These registers thus represent the first evidence of the general mobilization of a land reform campaign—that is, the administrative mass mobilization of PAs to carry out struggle against landlords and other enemies. Some of the forms are also signed by work teams, but many more are stamped with the seals of PAs or administrative village government offices (see chapter 3, Figure 5).

These victim registers record select village events from before the end of the Second Sino-Japanese War, in 1945, to one of the final campaigns of land reform in February 1948. The earliest records are of villagers who escaped in the months before August 1945. The death registers record executions of persons related to events that took place as early as December 1945, executions that took place in June 1946, and deaths during the land reform's Mop-Up campaign in January/February 1948.[84] A number of crimes recorded in the land expropriation registers are also related to a counterrevolutionary uprising in June 1946, although again when the expropriation of these persons' lands actually took place is not clear. Land expropriation registers from District 9 record rent reduction activities and expropriations that took place in the fall of 1946.[85] Finally, in the struggle registers at least one village notes that the persons who were struggled against served as village cadres in 1946.[86] Thus, although we know that the victim register forms were not printed until May 1947, the actual coverage of events could vary tremendously between villages, possibly because some villages experienced more events or because of local idiosyncrasies in recording practices. In either case they represent local understandings of land reform, which, as we will see throughout this book, were often very different from official ideals.

The events of land expropriation, struggle, escape, and execution recorded in these registers were explicitly modeled on the major types of rural political struggle that Mao had observed as early as 1927. Mao's 1927 *Hunan Investigation* lists nine types of political struggle against land-lords: (1) settling accounts, (2) fining, (3) asking for donations, (4) interrogation, (5) demonstrating, (6) parading in a tall hat, (7) detainment, (8) banishment (escape), and (9) execution.[87] Shuangcheng's land expropriation registers record types 1–3, the struggle registers record types 4–7, and the escape and execution registers match types 8 and 9. At the June 1947 Songjiang provincial meeting to organize the summer campaign, the provincial leader's report directly quotes from and recommends the county secretaries in attendance to study Mao's 1927 *Hunan Investigation*.[88] Although land reform of the late 1940s is generally considered to be a period of experimentation when compared to the early 1950s, in reality the CCP was already drawing on nearly two decades of experience in rural mass mobilization.

Although the original instructions printed on the victim register forms explain that at least three of the four separate registers were designed to be complementary, in practice there was often little overlap between them. The instructions for filling out the land expropriation registers are as follows:

1. All persons who have had their land expropriated, regardless of their class status or if they did not experience struggle, should be recorded, but cases of the expropriation of public land should not be recorded here.
2. Whether or not an individual experienced struggle in the process of expropriation should be annotated in the notes field.
3. Persons who escaped or were sentenced to death in addition to having their land expropriated should also be recorded here.
4. If a landlord has escaped and his land has not been expropriated, he should be recorded in the registers of escaped land-lords.[89]

Given common conceptions of class struggle, in which we would expect that many landlords either escaped or were killed when their property was confiscated, one might assume that there was a lot of overlap between the expropriation registers and the escape and death registers. However, preliminary linking across these registers demonstrates that of the individuals who were expropriated, only 7 percent are recorded as escaping and less than 3 percent are recorded as being killed. Of the individuals who escaped, only 44 percent are recorded as being expropriated. Of the individuals who were killed, less than 10 percent are recorded as being expropriated.[90] In other words, as of the summer of 1947, the majority of recorded individuals experienced only one of these forms of punishment, suggesting a salient disconnect between violence and the struggle for land. This disconnect is the focus of chapter 5.

In addition to expropriation, escape, and death, the struggle registers are unique in being the only register designed to record non-class enemies—that is, corrupt village CCP cadres. The instructions for filling out the struggle registers state:

1. Landlords who are struggled against are not to be recorded on this form. Record them in the land expropriation form.
2. District and administrative village cadres who are struggled against should be recorded on this form, but their position must be specified in the notes field.
3. Persons already sentenced to death are not to be recorded on this form. Record them in the form of persons to be executed.[91]

Over 90 percent of the individuals recorded in these struggle registers were class allies—middle and poor peasants and hired laborers. Many of these individuals were from the first batch of PA cadres, who may have been poor but were often landlords' lackeys (狗腿, or 走狗, literally, "running dog") and not necessarily willing or able to "serve the people." As such, these registers represent some of the earliest records of cadre rectification in Shuangcheng, a systematic cleanup of village cadres that took place eight months earlier than the rectification of 1948 that is the subject of William Hinton's *Fanshen* and other land reform studies.[92] Moreover, these registers demonstrate that this attack on non-class enemies was not only a product of local politics but also originally part of provincial government policy. These registers are analyzed in chapter 6.

These nominative data are complemented by a relatively complete collection of village work reports that document CCP work team activity and provide an important source of descriptive data on mass mobilization practices in Shuangcheng. As listed in Appendix E, the county archives preserve seventy-one reports and related documents in ten archival volumes. These documents are dated between July 1946 and April 1948 and describe the campaigns and events of land reform in seventy-two out of ninety-one *cun* in the county. Altogether, these reports mention by name just over two hundred *tun* communities, spread out unevenly across both space and time. As I mentioned earlier, these work reports can be categorized into the two national policies of the May Fourth Directive and Outline Land Law or even further into local subcampaigns. For each national policy, work teams began experimenting with policy implementation first, to be followed by general mobilization and work team inspections. These reports often reveal just as much about the CCP policies and work team objectives of a given campaign than they reveal about the village communities they describe. While the nominative registers described above provide an extensive view of land reform from the perspective of villagers, CCP work reports provide intensive views of mass mobilization at select locations, as well as intimate looks at CCP–village interactions. Only by combining these work reports with register data can we get a complete picture of land reform that illustrates mass mobilization at multiple administrative levels and continuously over time at the same localities. This picture is described in chapter 4.

In addition to these nominative and village-level data, the Shuangcheng archives also have important district-level aggregate data on property confiscation and violence from both the May Fourth Directive and Outline Land Law periods of land reform in Shuangcheng. The first collection of data was compiled in October 1947 in a volume of numerical tables titled "Statistics of the Fruits of Struggle by District and Administrative Village for the Entire County." As recorded in a number of the tables, many of which are hand dated July 1947, these statistics summarize the amounts of property expropriated and persons struggled against over the previous year, divided into two periods: 1946 to May 1947 and "after the intensification of struggle beginning in June 1947." The specific items expropriated varied from place to place but generally included land, housing, draft animals, carts, grain; money (gold, silver, and cash); and household items such as clothing, blankets, wardrobes, trees, and pots. Although only district-level expropriation data is complete for the entire county, a number of districts also include complete *cun*-level data (Districts 5, 7, 9, 10, and 11), and a few *cun* include *tun*-level data (in Districts 5 and 6). The format of these data (together with a few references to recording practices in work reports) suggests that, similar to the victim registers, PAs originally recorded registers of confiscated property at the village level and then submitted them to their superiors at the administrative village and district levels. The victim registers also record confiscated land and struggle victims for every rural district, but these district statistics are the only extant source recording all the non-landed property confiscated in the first year of land reform in Shuangcheng.[93] These statistics demonstrate, for example, that although CCP policy did not explicitly target non-landed property until the summer of 1947, many PAs had already confiscated more property before the summer campaign than during it.

The second collection of district-level data was compiled in March 1948 in two volumes of numerical tables originally titled "Population, Livestock, and Land Statistics for Each District and Class" and "Statistics of Landlord's and Rich Peasant's Confiscated Means of Production and People Beaten, Killed, and Detained by District for the Entire County." The former volume contains a summary table for each district recording the total number of households, persons, and livestock broken down into twelve class categories, plus the total landholding for each of these class categories before and after the Equalize Land campaign. Each district also records the total numbers of middle and poor peasants and hired laborers who participated in the campaign, or were struggled against, and how many received confiscated property or not.

The latter volume contains similar tables for each district, summarizing in more detail the number of households, persons, and confiscated property (land, housing, draft animals, farm implements, and household belongings) for four categories of landlords (large, medium, small, and managerial landlords) and two categories of rich peasants (rich peasants and rich tenant peasants). Each district also tabulates counts of beatings, killings, and detainments, divided into three campaign periods, for all class categories, including middle and poor peasants and farm laborers. Together these statistics summarize the events that took place from the implementation of the Outline Land Law beginning in November 1947 up to March 1948. The statistics of violence further divide this five-month period into three campaigns: the Equalize Land campaign (c. November to December 1947), "Pre-Mop-Up" (c. January 1948), and "Post-Mop-Up" (c. January to March 1948).[94] Similar to the previously mentioned sources, these statistics record the persons and property affected by land reform, formatted according to the objectives of particular local campaigns. Unfortunately, however, unlike the earlier period, for which we have both individual and aggregated data, for the Outline Land Law period these district-level statistics are the only source of information describing county-wide mobilization in Shuangcheng.

With all of these novel sources as its foundation, this book seeks to first document and analyze what CCP land reform was before trying to interpret its meanings and implications. In the process we will discover previously unexplored or understudied features, such as the spatial features of work team activity, escaping landlords, and victimless struggle meetings, which stand out in Shuangcheng's relatively complete data. As such, the greatest contribution of this book may be the questions it raises, not the answers it suggests. Although this is fundamentally a case study of a single county in Northeast China, we will see that, on the one hand, we are still just "blind men feeling an elephant" («瞎子摸象»), for despite a much more complete picture there are still many unknown details. While on the other hand, we will see how the practices of small village communities can have profound global and historical implications.

CHAPTER 2

Land Reform in Shuangcheng County

This chapter introduces the historical and social contexts of the subject of this book, Shuangcheng County.[1] Shuangcheng has its own unique history, but from 1946 to 1948 it carried out the same land reform policies as hundreds of other counties in North and Northeast China. What was the relationship between Shuangcheng's social and historical background and experiences of land reform within the county? On the one hand, Shuangcheng's past is more feudal, colonial, and commercial than many other parts of China and more closely fits classic preconditions of social revolution. While on the other hand, the total absence of a self-conscious rural proletariat in the county's CCP sources stands in stark contrast to the historical claims of the CCP's revolutionary program.[2]

The actors who play prominent roles in Shuangcheng's land reform story can be divided into those whose primary interests aligned with the village community and those whose primary interests aligned with the CCP state. In terms of Chinese society, the former group comprises previous local elites and rural non-elites, and the latter group comprises career bureaucrats and local officials. The relationships between these groups remained relatively constant before and after land reform, but their social composition was radically altered through the process of land reform. Through land reform, career bureaucrats allied with rural non-elites to neutralize local officials and elites in order to centralize power, unify CCP and village interests, and strengthen the nation.[3]

CCP land reform is typically conceived in terms of mass mobilization and struggle. Mass mobilization was fundamentally a process of political education in which work teams taught villagers to understand Chinese society and their relationships to state power in new ways. By struggling against and condemning abusers of power, villagers were able to personally experience their new role in a new order. The CCP aspired through such mass mobilization and struggle to achieve a new level of social integrity characterized by personal investment and self-control rather than formal compliance.

Historical and Social Contexts

Shuangcheng's institutional and social history, from its establishment as a state farm settlement in the early nineteenth century up to the early twentieth century, makes it an ideal place to study CCP land reform. As Shuang Chen describes in *State-Sponsored Inequality: The Banner System and Social Stratification in Northeast China*, the Qing imperial state (1644–1911) organized Shuangcheng society around different state-defined categories of settlers. At the top of the social hierarchy were six hundred metropolitan banner households from the imperial capitals of Beijing and Rehe (present-day Chengde) who settled in 40 central villages. Below them were three thousand households of rural bannermen from nearby Jilin and Liaoning provinces who settled in 120 villages organized into twenty-four groups of 5 villages each, surrounding three administrative offices (Map 2). And below these rural bannermen were another three thousand households of unsponsored bannermen migrants to the area.[4] Similar to land reform, each population category had different entitlements to landed property. The main difference was that while nineteenth-century Shuangcheng was designed based on inequality between categories, land reform in Shuangcheng was designed to achieve equality between categories.

By the mid-nineteenth century, nearly one hundred years before land reform, Shuangcheng had already become an important center of commercial agriculture on the northeast frontier. From 1903 the Chinese Eastern Railway—the primary transport artery of Northeast China—ran directly through the heart of the county, linking its economy to Harbin in the north and the port of Dalian in the south. From 1931 to 1945 Shuangcheng was part of the Japanese puppet state of Manchukuo, making it one of the longest formally colonized parts of mainland China. Its location also made Shuangcheng a strategic point on the front line of the KMT-CCP civil war struggle for the Northeast (1946–1948), a region that by then had become an industrial center of China.

Once the Shuangcheng settlement was established, fertile land and a constant flow of immigrants ensured a prosperous future. Favorable ecological conditions meant that Shuangcheng, much like the American Midwest, was ideal for farming. Within the county borders as of 1985, the

Table 5. Distribution of Crops Sowed in Shuangcheng, by District, 1947

District	Crop as % of Cultivated Land							Amount of Cultivated Land (ha)
	Soy-beans	Sorghum	Millet	Corn	Wheat	Other	Total %	
2	20.5	13.3	24.7	26.9	9.5	5.1	100.0	21,773
3	16.9	16.7	23.0	28.3	5.3	9.8	100.0	23,706
4	19.9	17.1	22.6	21.7	9.3	9.5	100.0	25,767
5	12.4	17.0	26.7	22.4	6.0	15.5	100.0	22,842
6	13.8	18.1	23.2	28.8	3.5	12.7	100.0	21,013
7	9.7	13.3	26.2	36.1	4.1	10.7	100.0	23,160
8	16.9	18.2	23.1	25.8	1.5	14.4	100.0	20,922
9	21.6	9.5	24.3	18.3	11.3	15.0	100.0	24,842
10	20.5	12.1	24.8	26.6	5.8	10.1	100.0	23,793
11	15.8	18.6	19.5	23.9	2.6	19.5	100.0	19,686
Total	16.9	15.3	23.9	25.8	6.1	12.1	100.0	227,504

Source: 129-1-31, 26–27 (Sept. 1947).

elevation ranges from only 120 to 210 meters above sea level, and over 90 percent of cultivatable land has a slope of less than two degrees (Map 2).[5] In addition, according to a 1959 soil survey, over 70 percent of land in the county was composed of rich chernozem (black earth) and prairie soil.[6] Despite some alkaline and low-lying micro-environments in certain patches of the county, the majority of Shuangcheng consists of extremely flat and fertile soil. By 1921 Shuangcheng was exporting 80 percent of its total marketed grain and soybeans, not including such locally processed exports like grain alcohol and soybean oil and oil cakes.[7] In 1944 the Manchukuo state extracted an annual grain quota of 190,000 metric tons from Shuangcheng County alone, while in 1946 the Songjiang CCP provincial government (which included Shuangcheng and thirteen other counties) set a total provincial grain quota of only 136,000 metric tons.[8] Such a highly productive county had high priority in the provincial land reform program.

Agriculture in Shuangcheng at the time of land reform focused on grain and soy. Table 5 summarizes the distribution of crops sown in 1947, by district.[9] More than 80 percent of the county's cultivated land at that time was planted with a relatively equal ratio of soybeans, sorghum, millet, and corn—all of them dryland crops with similar growing seasons and production processes. Furthermore, across all ten rural districts, these four crops ranged from 74 to 85 percent of all cultivated district land, exhibiting a high level of agricultural uniformity both between districts and within each district. Previous studies seeking to complicate our understanding of China's rural revolution have often pointed out the important role of local environmental factors in shaping revolutionary outcomes, but here in Shuangcheng we can take this argument a step further to show that even within the same environmental conditions, local sociopolitical factors could play just as important a role in shaping different land reform experiences.[10]

By the early twentieth century most of the space between the original 120 banner settlements was settled by immigrants from all across North China. These settlers often founded villages colloquially called "shacks" (窝棚, or 窝堡) (e.g., "Wang family shack" 王家窝棚), because they grew out of the temporary shelters that farm laborers set up near the fields they worked on the vast prairie. Moreover, this immigration accelerated after the Chinese Eastern Railway connected Shuangcheng to the port of Dalian after 1903. In 1890 the Shuangcheng government recorded a population of about 8,000 households, less than one quarter of which were non-bannermen.[11] Twenty years later a census in 1910 recorded a population of over 60,000 households, an eightfold increase.[12] The Shuangcheng County gazetteer also records that in the Republican period (1912–1931), in addition to the 120 original banner villages, there were at least 200 civilian villages in the county, which is perhaps a clearer sign of the impact of recent immigration.[13]

The county's relatively recent settlement on a fertile prairie and its heterogeneous and mobile frontier population make it unique from typical rural communities in either North or South China.[14] By the time of land reform, Shuangcheng's agricultural population, despite having a higher land/population ratio than practically anywhere south of the Great Wall, was characterized by large proportions of absentee landlords and hired laborers, and small proportions of owner-cultivators and tenants. In theory the greatest social divide was between the 120 original banner villages and over 400 later village settlements. Both of these populations can be further subdivided as well. Of the 120 original villages, the central 40 included urban settlers sent from the Qing imperial capitals of Beijing and Rehe, while the outer 80 were settled by rural bannermen migrants from other areas in Northeast China. The new village settlements can be divided into roughly three different areas: those located within the original banner settlement boundaries, those located in the northwest of the county, and those located in the west/southwest.[15] In practice, however, I have yet to find any archival evidence suggesting that these differences mattered to CCP land reform workers.

Table 6. Notable National Elite Property Investors in Land Reform–Era Shuangcheng

| Background | Name | | Positions held in the Republic of China (ROC) and Manchukuo (MCK) (1912–1945) |
	Pinyin	Chinese	
Native descendants of Shuangcheng bannermen	Mo Dehui	莫德惠	ROC Governor of Fengtian (present-day Liaoning Province), State Council member (post-1945)
	Cai Yunsheng	蔡运升	ROC Mayor of Harbin; MCK Minister of Economic Affairs, State Council member
	Zhai Wenxuan	翟文选	ROC Head of Jilin provincial police department, Governor of Fengtian
Native of Shuangcheng	Yu Chencheng	于琛澄	MCK Minister of Security, High-ranking General
Bannerman descendant	Ma Ziyuan	马子元	Head of the Harbin branch of the Bank of China
Descendant of Qing Imperial Clan	Xi Qia	熙洽	MCK Minister of Finance, Minister of the Interior
Native of Liaoning Province	Zhang Jinghui	张景辉	ROC Head of the Eastern Provinces Special Administration Region (1923–1932); MCK Prime Minister
	Lü Ronghuan	吕荣寰	ROC Vice Chairman of the Fengtian Provincial Assembly; MCK Minister of Industry, Minister of Civil Affairs

Sources: SCXZ, 154, which is sourced from TDGGYD, 2:23; Youchun Xu, ed., «民国人物大辞典» (河北人民出版社, 2007, 1121 (Mo Dehui), 2227 (Cai Yunsheng), 2387 (Zhai Wenxuan), 31-32 (Yu Chencheng), 1853 (Zhang Jinghui), 2307 (Xi Qia); Majia shi zupu «马佳氏族谱» (京华印书局, 1928), 序言, 6.

After 1906 the state land of the original settlers was opened up to private sales, but bannermen elites continued to play a prominent role in Shuangcheng society.[16] During the early Republican (1912–1931) and Manchukuo (1931–1945) eras, many national- and regional-level political elites invested in Shuangcheng land. Table 6 lists eight notable persons who invested extensively in property in Shuangcheng during this time. Five of these eight figures were bannerman descendants, demonstrating some of the effects of the "banner legacy" in Shuangcheng, in which descendants of the original banner settlers continued to be overrepresented in the local elite.[17] Four of them (three bannermen) were also Shuangcheng natives and appear in archival land reform data.[18] Although by 1910 native bannermen comprised only a little over 10 percent of the Shuangcheng population, they continued to make up a large proportion of local elite, especially in the 120 original banner villages of the settlement.[19] Separate banner and civilian administrative offices also existed in the county as late as the end of Manchukuo in 1945.[20] However, perhaps because of sensitivity to possible ethnic considerations, the CCP chose not to explicitly target banner descendants in the course of land reform.[21]

On the eve of land reform the distribution of land in Shuangcheng was exceptionally unequal.[22] Figure 2 compares sample distributions of land before land reform in various regions of China as reported in some recent land reform studies. It is now generally accepted that nationally the distribution of land at this time was less unequal than the CCP claim that landlords and rich peasants, accounting for less than 10 percent of the rural population, controlled 70 to 80 percent of land, while the remaining 90 percent of the rural population controlled only 20 to 30 percent of land.[23] As shown in this figure, sample data from North, Central, and Southeast China do not support CCP claims. Much more exhaustive research on the distribution of land in the early twentieth century has also concluded that it was very rare for landlords and rich peasants to control more than 60 percent of village land.[24] But as the figure also demonstrates, Shuangcheng was one of the exceptions. A survey of four villages near the county seat found that over two-thirds of village households owned less than 3 percent of land. Furthermore, complete county data from Shuangcheng's land expropriation registers, which record the original landholdings of more than six thousand individuals who had their land expropriated during land reform, likewise show that less than 10 percent of all households in the county (including absentee landlords) controlled 75 percent of all county land as late as the summer of 1947.[25] Thus by around 1946, Shuangcheng could be characterized as a society with a relatively high degree of wealth inequality and stark class divisions between a majority of landless farm laborers and a minority of urban absentee landlords. As we will see in the following chapters, however, these conditions did not make land reform any easier.

From 1931 to 1945 Shuangcheng was governed by Manchukuo, a Japanese-sponsored puppet state that established a new network of exploitative rural institutions, which would later play a prominent role

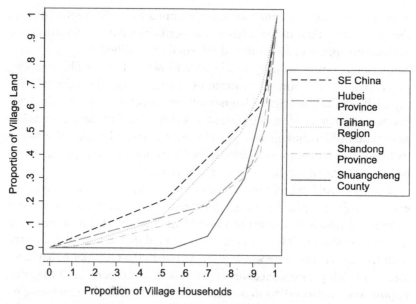

Figure 2. Pre–land reform distribution of land in five regions of China

Sources: SE China includes 235 counties in Zhejiang, Anhui, Fujian, and Sunan, ca. 1950 (Daoxuan Huang, «1920–1940 年代中国东南地区的土地占有——兼谈地主、农民与土地革命,» «历史研究» 第一期 [2005a]: 34–53). Hubei Province includes four districts, pre–land reform (Ronghua Huang, «农村地权研究 1949–1983: 以湖北省新洲县为个案». (上海: 社会科学院出版社, 2006). Taihang Region includes eight villages, in present-day Shanxi, Hebei, and Henan Provinces, pre–land reform (Ping Hao and Yao Zongpeng, «老区土改与乡村社会——以太行革命根据地为中心的考察,» 发表在 «土地改革与中国乡村社会» 学术研讨会, 山西大学, 2013 年8月9–12日). Shandong Province includes eleven villages, 1937 (Youming Wang, «解放区土地改革研究 1941–1948: 以山东莒南县为个案». 上海:社会科学院出版社, 2006). Shuangcheng County includes four villages, 1947 (129-2-3, 51).

Notes: Lorenz curves are derived from aggregate percentages of households and land-holding by class category, as shown in the full table in Matthew Noellert, Byung-ho Lee, and James Lee, "Wealth Distribution and Regime Change in Twentieth-Century China" (Massive open online course [MOOC] lecture by James Lee, A New History for a New China, 1700–2000: New Data and New Methods, Part 1, Coursera, https://www.coursera.org/course/newchinahistory1, released August 12, 2013).

Lorenz curve for Southeast China is based on the percentage of persons, not households, and records only 89 percent of persons and 85 percent of land.

Lorenz curve for Shuangcheng excludes almost 50 percent of village land owned by an unidentified number of absentee landlords.

in the county's land reform struggles. By the 1940s the Manchukuo state had implemented a series of policies giving the state unprecedented control over agricultural production and distribution. In 1938 the government began a grain rationing system (配给), which gradually expanded to include most daily necessities and to outlaw private trade. In 1939 the government established agricultural cooperatives at the county and village levels (兴农合作社), which, together with a grain quota system (出荷) beginning in 1940, took control of the grain market.[26] In addition to these economic controls, the government instituted corvee, or unpaid, labor, which in one county reportedly employed up to half of the adult male labor force.[27] The two main organs responsible for enforcing this new order were the village police and the local Concordia Association (协和会), a state-sponsored political party.[28] As described in numerous land reform reports from Shuangcheng, district heads played a leading role in the administration of these institutions and, consequently, appear as some of the most common targets of land reform violence.[29]

From 1946 to 1948 Shuangcheng played a central role in the CCP's civil war operations in the Northeast. In October 1946 Lin Biao moved the headquarters of the CCP's Northeast Democratic United Army, better known now as the Fourth Field Army, into a former Republican official's courtyard residence in the Shuangcheng County seat, where they would stay for the next two years. Lin Biao reputedly chose Shuangcheng because, in addition to its proximity to Harbin, Shuangcheng's first party secretary (a native bannerman descendant) had been a close friend of his since their days in Yan'an. Beginning in 1946 Shuangcheng occupied a strategic location on the front line between KMT-controlled Changchun and the largest city under CCP control at the time, Harbin. The 250-kilometer stretch of railway connecting these two cities ran through the center of the county. In addition, a branch line running from Harbin to Jilin City cut through the east side of the county. These rail lines were important means of transportation during the war.[30] During this period Shuangcheng was also by far the most populous county of the fourteen counties in Songjiang Province, with a population 2.5 times larger than the average county in the province.[31] Lin Biao's presence and the strategic importance of the county meant that land reform in Shuangcheng would have been closely monitored and more thoroughly carried out than in most other counties. This may be one reason why the county's archival data are so complete, but the practices of land reform they depict are far from what one might expect from a model case.

Overall, on the eve of land reform Shuangcheng was simultaneously more feudal, more colonial, and more commercialized than many other parts of China, but this does not mean it was exceptional. Instead, I see it as a useful case in which the effects of these developments are more salient and easier to analyze than in many other similar counties where political status and semicolonial and commercial exploitation played equally important but less salient roles. As described throughout this book, social developments and state-building efforts leading up to land reform and the process of land reform itself in Shuangcheng County were in many ways similar to those activities in hundreds of other counties. Technological and economic changes, including railways and the commercialization of agriculture, imperialist exploitation culminating in Japanese invasion, and all the social and political effects associated with these developments, affected many areas of China throughout the early twentieth century.[32] Any more detailed comparisons of the similarities and differences, however, will have to wait until similarly systematic analyses are completed for other counties.

The immediate context for understanding land reform in Shuangcheng is the CCP's own administrative framework. Map 3 shows this subcounty framework at the time of land reform, around 1948. This framework comprised a county government, 10 rural district governments, 91 *cun* governments, and 559 *tun* peasant associations (农会, hereafter PAs). Each triangle on the map represents one registered *tun* PA, with the shaded triangles showing the imputed locations of the 91 *cun* government offices in the county. Each district typically contained 9 *cun*, and each *cun* contained on average about six *tun*. Each *tun* represents the location of a PA, the most basic organization of the CCP state, but official statistics from this time, recording as many as 738 village settlements, suggest that some PAs may have administered multiple smaller settlements.[33] Chapter 3 provides a more in-depth discussion of this CCP administration.

Village Society

The CCP's ultimate objective in land reform was to overhaul the political hierarchy of Chinese society from the bottom up by democratizing the village community first.[34] At the time of land reform in Shuangcheng, a typical village community (*tun*) had 50 to 150 households, comprised of a small number of managerial households (10–15%), a slightly larger number of subsistence farmers (15–25%), and a large number of farm laborers and tenants (60–70%) (compare with chapter 1, Table 4). In accordance with CCP concepts of class struggle, the first and last groups comprised the two main village actors of land reform.[35] The first group of managerial households was labeled as landlords and rich peasants and condemned as enemies. The majority of villagers, who also happened to be living on the verge of starvation, were labeled as poor peasants and hired laborers (贫雇农), or simply the masses (群众) or common people (老百姓), and were considered the primary revolutionary allies of the CCP. With the help of CCP leaders who would initially identify a core group of "activists" (积极分子) among the masses, the masses were expected to take power into their own hands, overthrow the landlords, and establish democratic village government bodies called peasant associations (PAs). In practice, however, the enemies targeted in the course of land reform can be more accurately defined as local strongmen, the incumbent group of village powerholders, rather than a class of wealthy landowners. Their power over these communities was sometimes so absolute that they were colloquially called "second emperors" (二皇帝) and had villages named after them. Likewise, the activists tended to be the most disenfranchised and victimized villagers in the community. The following sections explore what some of these actors looked like in Shuangcheng.

Landlords

Landlords comprised a multitiered, heterogeneous social group, not all of whom were directly targeted in land reform.[36] At the top were absentee or urban landlords, individuals who owned large amounts of land but lived in the county seat or larger cities and typically depended more on their investments in urban enterprises than on investments in agricultural land. In the course of land reform, although most of their land was expropriated, their urban wealth was explicitly protected by the CCP and they were able to avoid most of the violence. The next level comprised nonproductive rural landlords, individuals who resided in the countryside, lived off of their rents or engaged in administrative or other nonagricultural occupations. This group was the primary target of land reform policies and local violence and included former village officials, "local bullies," usurers, and other local strongmen par excellence. The last group was productive managerial landlords and rich peasants, individuals who lived off of rents and hired laborers but who were also directly engaged in agricultural management and production. This group was targeted later in land reform with the Outline Land Law and had most of their property expropriated, but as far as villagers judged them to be hardworking, they were typically not subjected to the same retributive violence as their local strongman counterparts.

Urban absentee landlords were often condemned but not personally targeted during land reform. In some parts of Shuangcheng, absentee landlords owned more than half of village land, but they lived in the county seat, or even farther away in regional cities, and used their land as collateral or security for urban enterprises rather than as a primary source of income. The upper stratum of these landlords included the national-level officials in Table 6, while lower stratums included smaller landlords living in the county seat. These urban landlords relied on "secondary landlords" (二地主) residing in the countryside and often knew little about the land they owned. For the sake of the national economy, the May Fourth Directive, Outline Land Law, and later the Agrarian Reform Law all explicitly protected the property of urban industrial and commercial enterprises, these absentee landlords' primary sources of income.[37] In a few cases, villagers traveled to the county seat or even the city of Harbin to drag absentee landlords back to the village to be struggled against, but that process required an introduction letter from the villagers' district government and approval from the municipal government, and the villagers were strictly prohibited from taking any of the landlords' urban property. As one might expect, villagers also usually had a hard time finding these absentee landlords, and many "settling accounts" struggle meetings took place in the absence of the person whose accounts were being settled. Large tracts of land with no owner present made the job of redistributing land simpler, but in such cases the CCP actually found it more difficult to politically mobilize the masses when they were allocated land by the government with no personal enemy to struggle against.

Examples of the lower stratum of these absentee landlords who resided in the county seat are described in a number of cases in which villagers successfully apprehended them in the summer of 1947. One village sent a team of at least seventy villagers into the county seat to apprehend five absentee landlords and their personal valuables. Three out of five had already escaped, but in one landlord's courtyard the villagers uncovered a pot with more than four pounds of official Manchukuo opium. When the village women went to another landlord's house where only the landlord's mother and wife remained, the wife was about to give birth, and the mother tried to bribe one of the villagers. The villager refused the bribe and instead intensified the search for valuables and found underneath the laboring wife a cloth bag containing a gold bar, seven pieces of gold jewelry, and two wristwatches.[38] Based on the villagers' success in the county seat, they also sent two representatives to Harbin to apprehend an even larger "landlord," who owned ironworks in Harbin and Dalian and produced ships and firearms for the Japanese. After reporting to the local authorities, they succeeded in having his factory in Harbin confiscated and handed over to the factory workers, but the landlord was already far away in Dalian, and the villagers returned with only a few personal valuables.[39]

In this book I refer to the primary group of landlords targeted by land reform policies as "local strongmen," because throughout land reform in Shuangcheng these enemies were defined more in terms of their political position than their economic standing, and those who possessed large quantities of land had acquired their wealth through official misconduct and coercion, not feudal or capitalist accumulation. In the words of one CCP Central Committee document on class standards from February 1948:

> Persons who do not legally own large quantities of land, but help landlords collect rent, serve as their stewards, . . . or who use their political power to make a living through embezzlement, extortion, and other means, all of these persons, as long as they meet the other criteria in terms of labor and lifestyle, are to be considered landlords.[40]

Many of the victims of land reform violence who appear in later chapters fit this description more than they fit classic descriptions of large landowners.

The local strongmen who were the primary targets of land reform campaigns comprised a narrow segment of society. For the most part, they were the "local bullies and evil gentry" (土豪劣绅) who gained power and influence in the countryside by taking advantage of a series of government attempts to modernize rural administration that began in the late Qing.[41] They were also explicitly rural. The same central document quoted above exempts from the category of "landlords" individuals whose primary income comes from rents on urban land and housing.[42] More progressive or ambitious rural families in Shuangcheng would have already invested in urban enterprises and moved out of the countryside by the time of land reform, while the majority of rural households were left prey to local strongmen who were content to be "second emperors" over their parochial rural empires. Land reform should be understood as the process through which the CCP and villagers overthrew these local emperors.

In the fall of 1946 one CCP work team targeted three such local strongmen in two neighboring villages. In one village a man known as the "special agent's lackey" (特务腿子) had transformed himself from destitute thug to large managerial landlord in a matter of years during Manchukuo. He began by serving as a Japanese official's underling, made connections with the police, and, with his newfound influence, was able to accumulate over forty hectares of land and build himself a ten-room Western-style villa. He also served as a "secondary landlord" or manager for urban landlords, which enabled him to skim off the top by over-measuring amounts of land and rent. Finally, after the Japanese surrender in 1945, he took the opportunity to sell off some public lands for his own profit.[43]

In the same village, another landlord was condemned for his corruption and oppression during the time he served as district head under Manchukuo. When he collected money or goods from administrative village governments, he was known to always demand more than required and then to keep some for himself. When it was time to allocate the compulsory state grain quota, he gave smaller quotas to his friends and larger quotas to everyone else. Through the Manchukuo rationing system he embezzled various public goods. At least one villager held a grudge against this district head for confiscating his chickens, and another villager accused him of coercive labor conscription.[44]

In the neighboring village there was an infamous administrative village head who before Manchukuo was a fried dough maker (麻花匠). He had a brother who under Manchukuo eventually became head of the Department of Education at the headquarters of the Concordia Association in Jilin Province. The fried dough maker used his brother's influence to become appointed administrative village head, a position he held for more than eight years. After the Japanese surrendered, his brother returned to Shuangcheng and helped organize the county KMT branch and the local underground KMT army, and he continued to serve as administrative village head. Although this village head owned only fifteen hectares of land at the time of land reform, his oppressive leadership made him one of the most notorious strongmen in the area.[45]

Sometimes the abuse ran deeper than just the few years before land reform. Later in the summer of 1947, when a work team was intensifying the struggle in one village, they targeted a large landlord who owned one hundred hectares of land. Everyone in the village said that his family originally owned only several hectares, and his grandfather had accumulated the land through his position as village banner captain (屯达) in the late Qing.[46] Moreover, as director of the village rationing department during Manchukuo, this same landlord embezzled all the best goods available.[47] As I will explore more in chapter 5, hundreds of similar landlords were recorded during Shuangcheng's land reform, but only a few examples describe their rise to power in such detail. Philip Kuhn described such local "headmen" in the Republican period, saying, "In view of local government's rapacity toward the rural inhabitants, landholders without political power were unlikely to hold onto wealth for long."[48] Likewise in Shuangcheng, we find that by the time of land reform the only wealthy landholders left in the countryside were those who held political power. In the eyes of villagers it was their abuse of such power, not the resulting wealth, that was the real crime.

There is not much direct archival evidence of the productive rural landlords targeted for expropriation but not necessarily violent struggle after the Outline Land Law. Documents like the Northeast Bureau's "Letter to the Peasants," however, clearly distinguish between such different types of landlords. This letter first says that "all landlords, no matter large, medium, or small, no matter male or female, no matter resident or absentee, must have all of their land and other property confiscated." But then it goes on to list numerous qualifiers describing certain kinds of landlords and rich peasants who should be struggled against: traitorous, evil tyrant, reactionary, resistant, rumormongering, conniving, and those who carry out sabotage, sow discord, and oppress peasants. In contrast, the letter states that "rich peasants who are honest, hard-working, frugal, and take care of themselves, after they hand over the things that they are required to hand over, can be treated leniently" (see Appendix A). Thus, even at the level of regional policy, there was an important distinction between "class enemies" who should or should not be struggled against.

The Masses

The CCP, like most Chinese leaders before them, saw the majority of rural households as both the givers and receivers of political power.[49] CCP work team reports in Shuangcheng used three different terms when referring to this majority: the "common people," "the masses," or the "poor peasants and hired laborers." In general, work team leaders (the authors of the reports) referred to the majority of rural households as the "common people" when they were apolitical or the object of oppression, and "the masses" when they were acting or expected to be acting as a political force—for example, when they were being mobilized, struggling against a landlord, or developing class consciousness. After the Outline Land Law was instituted, CCP actors employed a more definitive label, the "poor peasants and hired laborers," which implied a specific class of the majority that the CCP expected to be both politically active and their main ally in land reform. Figure 3 illustrates how these three terms for the same group of people changed over the course of land reform in Shuangcheng, based on more than five hundred pages of work team reports. From the fall of 1946 to the summer of 1947, a slight increase in the use of the term "common people" and almost tripling of the use of the term "the masses" reflects both the intensification and politicization of land reform campaigns over these periods. As mentioned above, these land reform campaigns increasingly focused on mass political mobilization, a process that needed the participation of active "masses," not passive "common people."[50] Then after the Outline Land Law, issued in October 1947, we see an explosion of "poor peasants and hired laborers" at the expense of the two former terms. This was, of course, not a new group of actors but a new label with more selective criteria for determining who the CCP could rely on.

The "common people" and "the masses" often coexisted in the same work reports, and sometimes even in the same sentences, making it possible to compare their different roles in the story of land reform. Some early reports from 1946 use the terms interchangeably, perhaps reflecting early work teams' elementary levels of political training, but overall the "common people" are most often seen as the object of landlord oppression. One report from the summer of 1947, titled "How the Masses of Wang Family Shack Overthrew the Landlords," begins by describing how the two biggest landlords in the village oppressed the "common people":

> The common people of the village all view [Mr. Wang] like a mouse views a cat, they are too terrified to even lift up their heads. All the common people call him the "living king of hell." Every single one of the common people, except [the other landlord], is subject to his oppression and exploitation.[51]

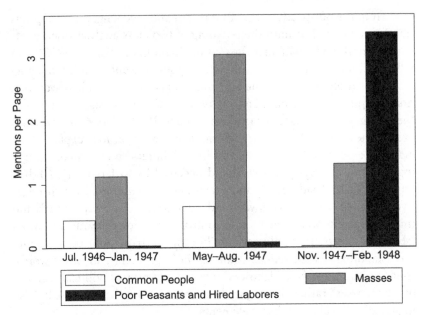

Figure 3. Frequencies per work report page of terms for the rural majority, by work report period, 1946–1948. See Appendix E. Author's calculations based on more than 500 pages of transcribed work reports.

On the following page, however, when the author starts talking about mobilizing villagers to struggle against this landlord, he begins talking about "the masses": "The masses have no [political] awareness, the masses are very apprehensive." He even writes, "A few cadres were assigned to carry out mass mobilization work [in the past], but the *common people* of this village were under the oppression of the 'local emperor,' *the masses* did not dare to struggle against him."[52] Thus, even in a single sentence, we find the same group of people identified in two different ways according to their perceived agency.

The "poor peasants and hired laborers" took the concept of "the masses" as a political force one step further. Formally speaking, the term "poor peasants and hired laborers" applied to a group of people named as one of "the legal executive organs" for implementing the Outline Land Law.[53] The only problem was that when this law was issued, few villagers knew how to define who was a poor peasant or hired laborer. Theoretically speaking, poor peasants and hired laborers were defined by their relationship to the means of production, as semi- or full-rural proletariat. But even from the perspective of CCP cadres in Shuangcheng, this group was not defined as a class until the reissuing of two class analysis documents over a month and a half after the Outline Land Law.[54] For most CCP and village actors in Shuangcheng, therefore, poor peasants and hired laborers were simply defined as the part of the masses that was hardworking, honest, and had experienced adversity. The CCP also designated them as the primary beneficiaries of land reform and the leaders of a new rural order. One local CCP news article from late November 1947 explains how before the term "poor peasants and hired laborers" was coined: "Working comrades always got tricked and deceived by loafers (二流子), bad guys (坏蛋, lit. "bad eggs"), and down-and-out landlords, which negatively affected [land reform] work and led to deviations. Professionals and middle peasants were able to take control over poor peasants and hired laborers."[55] Restricting political mobilization to "true" poor peasants and hired laborers helped reduce some of these problems. In other words, "poor peasants and hired laborers" referred to a refined political segment of "the masses" rather than a purely economic class that admittedly also included politically unreliable elements.[56]

Throughout land reform the CCP treated the majority of rural households like a force of nature, powerful yet difficult to control. As Mao described in 1927, "In a very short time, several hundred million peasants . . . will rise like a fierce wind or tempest, a force so swift and violent that no power, however great, will be able to suppress it."[57] As a political underdog, the CCP wanted to harness this force to their advantage, but they were also careful not to let the masses get out of control. In terms of policy, in the winter following the Outline Land Law, the CCP felt confident enough to give free rein to the masses, but as soon as social order started to deteriorate, the CCP stepped in again. Overall, therefore, despite CCP attempts to mobilize the masses politically, the masses continued to play a fundamentally passive role in land reform, like Mao's hurricane (暴风骤雨), a force that asserts its power but is devoid of human-like agency. In accordance with both Leninist and traditional Chinese concepts of political order, this power of the masses was useless without proper leadership.[58]

Activists

Whenever a CCP work team arrived in a village, one of their first tasks was to identify among the masses a number of individuals capable of agency and leadership. These "activists" were the key to political mobilization of their fellow villagers and also the key by which the CCP was able to open the door to the village community. As such, activists were unofficially endowed with elevated status and typically became the first PA leaders and village cadres. The door thus swung both ways, and villagers were keenly aware that under the CCP, becoming an activist also meant opening the door to their own political advancement. As with many land reform actors, however, the role of activists depended on the presence or absence of a CCP work team. Without a work team there would be no activists. The story of work teams is limited to a few select villages, and likewise the story of activists is illuminating but limited.

In the early stages of land reform in Shuangcheng, work teams were quick to label as activists practically anyone who was willing to help them. Work team leaders were new to the area and had limited resources and often limited time. Their task of political mobilization required that they identify activists before fully understanding the village community and villager backgrounds. As mentioned above, therefore, before the concept of poor peasants and hired laborers, the first people to take advantage of work teams were often loafers, bad guys, down-and-out landlords, professionals, middle peasants, and other opportunists or politically ambitious villagers.[59] The problem with these activists, however, was that as soon as they got into power, they consciously or unconsciously undermined CCP goals of more democratic governance and often acted like the local despots whom they helped dethrone. These new CCP-instated leaders were even referred to as "new local despots," "new overlords," or "the new aristocracy" (新贵) and then had to be purged in later land reform campaigns, beginning as early as the Eliminate Half-Cooked Rice campaign in early 1947.

One work report from the summer of 1947 describes the sad state of land reform village cadres and activists in one village, even after four previous work team visits. In this village, the PA director, the village head, and the village party secretary were all from landlord and rich peasant backgrounds, two of them were opium smokers and womanizers, one was an ex-bandit, and one was an ex-cop fired for extortion.[60] The PA director's son, Rende, had served on a CCP work team in the past and acted as an activist when the new work team arrived in the village in early June 1947. The first night after the work team arrived, Rende called together the masses to stage a struggle session against one of the village landlords. He began by "speaking bitterness" and then forced the masses to speak, but

nobody else said anything, so he told the landlord to confess his wrongdoings, and the landlord yelled out his own complaints. Over the next couple
of days, the work team realized that such struggle sessions were fake and
met with other activists and learned that they all had to report to Rende.
Then at one meeting of activists, after getting Rende's brother-in-law to
leave the meeting, other activists finally told the work team all the bad
things that Rende had done. That same night, the work team called a mass
meeting to struggle against these "bad guys," and Rende confessed to protecting landlords and embezzling six sacks of confiscated goods and one
piece of gold jewelry, further infuriating the masses.[61]

In contrast to these "activists," hardworking and honest poor peasants
were often the last to get involved in politics. In the summer of 1947, in
a village near the one just described, villagers were terrified when they
saw two CCP work team members enter their village; some people ran
away, some went into hiding, and everybody stayed out of sight as best
they could. Seeing it was impossible to get any sense of village conditions,
the two work team members started helping villagers weed their fields.
Through working in the fields, they met one villager who asked them if
the work team was going to beat up people. After explaining to him and
others that the work team was there to serve the people, and after villagers saw the work team helping them in the fields, they gradually began
to open up. The work team eventually identified four such villagers who
"dared to speak" and was able to educate them more about the CCP and
get them to recruit another dozen "property-less and impoverished" villagers to start coming to activist meetings.[62] Thus, even in relatively successful cases, CCP actors defined activists as "property-less and impoverished villagers who dared to speak."

By the winter of 1947, work reports referred to acceptable activists and
village representatives as not just "poor peasants and hired laborers" but
"honest and dependable." In February 1948 District 2 carried out an investigation of all village cadres in the district, and every village elected fifty to
one hundred new representatives. The four criteria villagers used to elect
representatives are as follows:

1. Hardworking and suffering poor peasants and hired laborers.
2. Clean background.
3. Honest work ethic.
4. Resolute in struggle and not ingratiating.[63]

The implication here is that for the first year and a half of land reform, most of the village activists did *not* meet these criteria. Moreover, it is also clear that even during this time, one of the reputed high points of class struggle in the entire Chinese Revolution, formal class definitions played a minor role in village politics.

CCP Cadres

Northeast China is unique in that there was virtually no CCP influence before the Japanese surrender in 1945, but it was also one of the earliest places to complete land reform and is thus considered part of the CCP's "old liberated areas." In practice, what this means is that the CCP carried out land reform in this region with extremely limited time and resources. Shuangcheng was no exception. When the CCP arrived in Shuangcheng in the winter of 1945, only five or six experienced cadres from the old liberated areas in North China were assigned to govern the entire county with a population of roughly four hundred thousand.[64] Most of the county government continued to be staffed by former Manchukuo employees, who cannot be readily considered CCP cadres.[65] Perhaps partially as a result of this initially small core of experienced leaders, the personal characteristics of leadership played a salient role in determining local experiences of land reform.[66] Within this diverse administration, there are three groups of CCP cadres who held prominent roles in the story of land reform: county leaders, district leaders, and work teams.

The majority of county-level cadres in the Shuangcheng CCP government were highly educated urban youth and aspiring revolutionary bureaucrats. According to a register of more than twelve hundred administrative cadres working in Shuangcheng in 1949, 90 percent of county-level cadres were less than thirty years old, and half of them had middle school or higher educations.[67] An earlier register from 1947 also records that only a little over one-third of the seventy-six county-level CCP members came from farming backgrounds, while the other two-thirds were of either student or urban background.[68] During land reform, these young revolutionaries were responsible for leading work teams and setting up subcounty district governments, which involved a combination of military and civil expertise.

The first Shuangcheng County party secretary, Lin Cheng, exemplified a typical CCP county leader in the Northeast at the time of land reform. Lin was a Shuangcheng native and bannerman descendant who left home to attend high school in Tianjin and then universities in Harbin and Beijing. He joined anti-Japanese movements in Tianjin and joined the CCP in Harbin in 1933. After the outbreak of the Sino-Japanese War in 1937, Lin went to work and study in Shanxi. Then after August 1945 he moved with a group of cadres from the Jinsui liberated area to Harbin, where in early 1946 he was appointed party secretary of Shuangcheng.[69] In counties like Shuangcheng where the CCP had virtually no base of support, locals referred to CCP cadres as "guests from inner China" (关里客), and Lin's local family connections sometimes made the difference between life and death. In 1946, shortly after the CCP took control of Shuangcheng and organized a substantial security force, local underground KMT agents sent appointment letters to all the CCP officers, promising to promote them to higher rank if they helped eliminate the "guests from inner China." Fortunately for the dozen or so Shuangcheng cadres, one of the officers was a cousin of Lin who had second thoughts about killing a family member and told Lin about the assassination plot. As a result, Lin and the other cadres were able to avoid the fate of less fortunate cadres in other counties.[70] As much as possible, the CCP took advantage of such local connections in the Northeast and sent experienced CCP leaders back to their hometowns. Especially in the beginning, this social capital was stronger than any political capital the CCP could muster and provided an essential foundation for building the latter.

Below such county-level cadres, district-level cadres represented the highest level of truly grassroot, peasant cadres and were responsible for the actual implementation of land reform policies in the countryside. According to the same 1949 cadre registers mentioned above, in contrast to their county superiors, almost half of district leaders were older than thirty, more than 90 percent were locals, over two-thirds had no more than a few years of primary education, and two-thirds were classified as poor peasants or hired laborers. But this grassroots administration was also one of the ends of land reform, not its means. Beginning in the fall of 1946, members of the Shuangcheng County CCP Committee each led an armed work team into the countryside and established new district governments virtually from scratch. He Fang, one of these county cadres, recounts how he was assigned to the northwest part of the county, given the title of work team leader and district party secretary, and expected to organize a district party committee, district government, district security team, and district work team. Within six months He and his seventy-person armed work team had accomplished all of this, ultimately occupying and replacing the former district government.[71] In other words, while at the county level only the leadership was taken over by a minority of CCP cadres, within the county the CCP completely rebuilt the rural administrative infrastructure. This process is discussed in more detail in chapter 3.

The nature of early district government can be seen in a report from District 8, one of the last districts to be established in Shuangcheng. Before the CCP set up a district government here, a CCP army regiment had occupied the area and organized PAs, elected cadres, and redistributed land in a few villages, primarily for purposes of army recruitment. Later in the spring of 1947, a district government was established and ordered all PAs to redistribute land. Even though this was one of the last districts to be established, one district leader admits that when they arrived in the area, they did not really understand land problems and CCP policies and had no experience in mass mobilization. This leadership was then expected to carry out land reform policies in an area where the PAs were controlled by local strongmen and their lackeys, and when the most visible feature of the CCP was the trainloads of army stretcher crews (担架队) constantly passing through the local train station (transporting wounded soldiers).[72] As late as the winter of 1947, the state of land reform in this district was not very promising.

The best-known agents of land reform are CCP work teams, organized by various levels of government to penetrate directly into the village community and experiment with or investigate CCP policy implementation. However, these ad hoc teams are overrepresented in historical sources, and for a majority of villages they played a limited role in the overall implementation of land reform. The activity of work teams in Shuangcheng is the focus of chapter 4, but here I will briefly introduce the members of these teams. Most of the sources describe the fall/winter of 1946, when land reform work was first getting under way in Shuangcheng. He Fang's militarized work team, mentioned above, was comprised of friends he had made in his previous work at the Shuangcheng academy, local high school, and an earlier rural investigation.[73] In the winter of 1946 another work team working on the east side of the county also had to be fully armed and escorted by a thirty-man guard unit. They spent more time combating bandits and reactionary local elite than implementing land reform policies.[74] A similar team working on the east side of the county in the winter of 1946 consisted of eighteen persons, including one leader who was an experienced cadre from North China, five full-time work team members with less than one year of experience, and twelve temporary members selected from local village cadres and activists. As this team leader lamented, most of these work team members were illiterate and did not understand class struggle or the differences between the CCP and KMT; some could not even name the different social classes. The leader had to explain every single order to them in detail, and none of the other members were capable of working independently.[75] It is no surprise, therefore, to find work team members colluding with local strongmen and sometimes even sabotaging land reform work.[76] These work teams played a crucial role in land reform insofar as they provided the first impression of CCP governance for many villagers, but they visited only a fraction of all the villages in the county, and ultimately the district governments were responsible for enforcing CCP policies in the majority of villages.

Mass Mobilization, Education, and Struggle

Beginning with Mao's *Hunan Investigation* in 1927, the processes of land reform and rural revolution were conceived in terms of mass mobilization (群众运动)—that is, the bottom-up organization of a majority of the population to collectively seize the reins of political power. Mao idealized this process as a spontaneous and inevitable one, and for him the only question was whether to lead, guide, and harness this mass movement or follow in its wake.[77] Successful mass mobilization, however, required both mass uprising and strong leadership; otherwise it would just lead to disorder.[78] Land reform was the realization of such mass mobilization on a national scale and is traditionally understood to be driven by the rural masses' desire for land and dependent on the CCP's ability to provide them with it. On a deeper level, however, land reform's mass mobilization was almost purely political, and its ultimate objective was not just trading land for popular support but mobilizing a majority of the population to be politically active.[79] The basic process of CCP mass mobilization is well known and begins by sending work teams to select villages, identifying activists, identifying enemies, organizing a struggle meeting at which activists lead the village community in collectively denouncing the enemy, and then electing new officers and establishing a PA. Once this process is completed in one village, the district or county government then encourages remaining villages to follow its example.[80] But we need to clearly distinguish between these two different types of mass mobilization. The first type involves a work team encouraging a single village community to become politically active. This is the type that most people think about when they hear the term "mass mobilization." The second type involves a more administrative process of holding meetings at various levels of government, issuing directives, and expecting village cadres to carry out the policy or campaign in their own village. This type is less romantic, but without it there would be no true mass mobilization beyond a select handful of villages. In the following section, I focus on a few particular methods that work teams in Shuangcheng commonly used to mobilize villagers. Chapter 4 explores the more administrative side of mobilization.

Political Education

At the community level, the first step of mass mobilization involved changing villagers' worldviews, educating them, and convincing them that "to rebel was justified."[81] Work teams accomplished this through persuading, reasoning, and discussing with villagers, a process sometimes referred to in work reports as "fermenting" (酝酿).[82] This process of reeducation was a central art of the revolutionary. Mikhail Sholokhov sums it up vividly in his novel about the Russian Revolution, *And Quiet Flows the Don*, in which a Cossack soldier meets a fellow-soldier Bolshevik in the trenches of World War I and falls under his influence:

> Day after day he revealed truths hitherto unknown to Gregor, explaining the real causes of war, and jesting bitterly at the autocratic government. Gregor tried to raise objections, but Garanzha silenced him with simple, murderously simple questions, and he was forced to agree.
> Most terrible of all was that Gregor began to think Garanzha was right, and that he was impotent to oppose him. He realized with horror that the intelligent and bitter Ukrainian was gradually but surely destroying all his former ideas of the Tsar, the country, and his own military duty as a Cossack. Within a month of the Ukrainian's arrival all the system on which Gregor's life had been built up was a smoking ruin. It had already been rotten, eaten up with the canker of the monstrous iniquity of the war, and it needed

only a jolt. That jolt was given, and Gregor's mind awoke. He tossed about seeking a way out, a solution to his predicament, and gladly found it in Garanzha's answers.[83]

China's land reform was largely dependent on the success of this reeducation process. By the late 1940s, however, the CCP did not have the luxury of monthlong personal conversations, as described by Sholokhov, and work teams were expected to "ferment" entire villages in a matter of weeks or even days. As a result, the quality of this fermentation often suffered.

In Shuangcheng one work report from the fall of 1946 talks about this fermentation process in detail, which was also like a process of negotiation between the interests of villagers and the work team. When work team members first started talking to potential activists (honest poor people willing to speak out), some would evasively say, "I am willing to struggle against anyone, but I just don't know what their shortcomings are," or, "Everyone knows that [those two landlords] are bad eggs, but I don't know the details [of their wrongdoings]." Others were more direct but only mentioned personal grudges like "[That landlord] borrowed money from me and never paid me back." Eventually the work team found a handful of relatively reliable activists who were willing to "serve the people" and could act as the work team's key for mobilizing the entire village. The work team then sat down with this core group of activists and made up a list of the crimes and grievances against the two most notorious landlords in the village, as well as a list of the villagers' needs. These two starters— villager grievances and needs—was all the work team needed to "ferment struggle." As activists worked on rallying more villagers, the work team went around to every household, using the landlords' crimes to stimulate the masses, and helped them realize how much the landlords owed them for their past exploitation. Because the grievances against one landlord were so great, fermentation proceeded so quickly that they were ready to hold a struggle meeting on the second day.[84] Here we can see that this fermentation process embodied both natural and artificial components. The work team emphasized the villagers' grievances as the natural starter, but in reality the work team itself functioned as a necessary agent, by convincing villagers that their grievances merited action and that the landlords' behavior was unacceptable. Fermentation was complete when both villagers and work team were convinced that they could get what they wanted— retribution and political support, respectively—by working together. In the fall of 1946, however, the majority of work teams were only concerned with educating activists and village cadres, a focus that was later criticized for undermining more complete mass mobilization.

Work reports from the summer of 1947 increasingly talked about political education for the masses, not just select activists. But as the CCP raised the standards of mobilization to political and ideological levels, in most cases mass education was still deficient. In August 1947 one district leader described how even after six months of intensifying land reform campaigns, even though all the land and household belongings were redistributed to the peasants; PA cadres were all poor peasants and hired laborers; the PA, militia, and other organizations were all established; and production and military service duties were all fulfilled, village governance still lacked proper political awareness. In such a village, a minority of activists and cadres acted without sufficient consensus among the masses or without properly educating the masses about particular policies. Moreover, the masses were eager to redistribute household belongings through economic struggle without differentiating between good and bad people through political struggle. As a result, after the momentary struggle was over, the masses returned to complacency and the cadres replaced the old landlords as a new ruling elite.[85]

In August 1947 one work team leader wrote in his report, "The revolution is obviously a problem of mass education."[86] He went on to describe how in the past, work teams would lecture the masses and then expect them to "speak bitterness," but the masses would just be overwhelmed and fall silent. In other words, there could be no real mass mobilization unless the people themselves understood what they were doing and why they were doing it. This problem of educating the masses reveals both the realities of the village political order in China at this time and the CCP's great ambition in trying to change it. In the existing order, a given village was under the autocratic control of a few powerful men who imposed their own interests over both community and national (state) interests. The CCP proposed a new order in which a village majority would govern themselves democratically and simultaneously merge village interests into national interests.[87] It should not be surprising, therefore, that in the winter of 1947, after over one year of land reform campaigns, some work teams still reported spending nine days in a village doing nothing but "class education" without even mentioning anything about struggling against landlords.[88] In this context it was also understandable that the CCP would need to continually adapt to new local circumstances.

Struggle Meetings

"Struggle" (斗争) was both a means and an end of mass mobilization. In a given village, the work team would first mobilize the masses to struggle against an enemy, and then the struggle itself would help mobilize the masses to organize their own political body, the PA. But what did it mean to "struggle against" someone? At its most basic level, to struggle against someone meant to put them in front of a mass meeting of villagers and publicly denounce and then punish them—that is, hold a struggle meeting. The object of struggle could be just about anyone, but the subject of struggle was always the masses, or at least a group claiming to represent them. Several individuals could be struggled against at the same meeting, and the same individual could be struggled against several times, sometimes even a dozen times, over the course of land reform.[89] The scale of the mass meeting could range from a single village of a hundred people to a stadium in the county seat with tens of thousands of people. Denouncement typically involved reciting a list of crimes or having a number of people in the crowd express their grievances. The punishment typically involved a verbal or written confession, fines, expropriation, confinement, beating, parading through the streets, or death. The struggle meeting was thus like a public performance of justice in which the masses were the judge. This performance was so important that in many cases struggle meetings were held against persons who had already escaped and were therefore not present to actually receive their judgment.[90]

In theory, the concept of struggle was rooted in Marxist economic class struggle, in which property owners and wage laborers inevitably had a conflict of interests. Beyond this theoretical conflict, however, there has been little discussion of how exactly this "struggle" should be accomplished in practice. As mentioned in chapter 1, Mao's 1927 *Hunan Investigation* is one of the earliest examples describing practices of rural political struggle. In 1927 Mao saw these practices as spontaneous actions growing out of the political and cultural context of Chinese rural society, but in Shuangcheng, as recorded in the victim registers, we see that the CCP institutionalized these actions as the official repertoire of land reform "struggle." As is discussed more in chapter 6, however, these "indigenous" practices of struggle like public confessions and humiliations and redistribution of seized property are more suggestive of traditional communal, retributive justice than modern capitalist economic justice or equality.[91] The indigenous origins of these practices in part help explain why village communities seemed to take naturally to struggle meetings, even more naturally than CCP leaders. One report from January 1947 from an area near Shuangcheng wrote that work team cadres need to learn the "peasant style" of holding a struggle meeting. When organizing a struggle meeting, the cadres always wanted to set up a stage with tables and chairs, hang up slogans, appoint chairmen to lead the meeting, and then have accusers come up on stage to speak one by one. The work team finally discovered that these formalities stifled the peasants, so they then tried a new way of struggling without any furniture or formalities. The peasants (masses) immediately crowded around the enemy and let whomever wanted to accuse him speak out. They did not care whether they struggled in a room, in the PA, or in the village school, and sometimes they just walked straight into the enemy's house and struggled against him there.[92]

Ultimately, education and struggle were not the ends of land reform but simply means to politically mobilize a majority of the rural population, in effect merging their interests with the CCP and the nation.[93] For villagers, political mobilization was sometimes best manifested in more immediate terms of public security. In one village, after villagers drove the landlords out of their houses in the summer of 1947 (one of the final acts of the summer campaign), the PA held a meeting to increase surveillance in the village. The village militia increased sentry duty and population registration, and that same night a neighbor overheard a landlord's wife angrily recounting to her husband the names of the people who came into their house and what objects each of them took. The neighbor reported this to the PA, and they prepared to struggle against the landlord for plotting revenge. The next day, the landlord's daughter-in-law died (possibly suicide). In the past, transporting the dead was the obligatory job of a landlord's hired laborer, but now when the landlord tried to find a laborer to help him, the laborer consulted with the masses and they decided he should charge money for the service. In the end the landlord himself carried out the corpse, which was seen by villagers as symbolic of the end of his power and influence in the village.[94] In another village in the summer of 1947, after organizing a people's militia for the masses to protect themselves, a landlord's father-in-law visited the village. The militiamen tied him up and brought him to the PA for a beating and interrogation in order to intimidate him. The father-in-law returned home, and no "bad relatives" dared to visit again.[95] Although a little rough around the edges, work teams used these examples as proof of successful mass political mobilization. The final proof would come in the summer of 1948, when all

PAs in the county completed the equal per capita distribution of land that marked the completion of land reform.

Shuangcheng society on the eve of land reform was a unique product of its own local historical development, while the CCP land reform program was the product of two decades of political experience in various regions of southern and northwest China. The main obstacle to CCP success in land reform in Shuangcheng and other counties was not necessarily the disconnect between Marxist theory and rural Chinese realities, but the disconnect between central administrators and local communities. As seen in the context of Shuangcheng County, one common denominator was local abuses of power that resulted from the fracturing of the social and political order. As personified in the "local bullies and evil gentry," or local strongmen, by the early twentieth century these abusers of power emerged as a pervasive feature of Chinese society and a thorn in the sides of both central and local interests. Likewise, the solution to this problem was to repair the political order, not the economy. This common political problem thus served as an important connecting thread between practices of land reform in very different local communities and between practices of power in Chinese history before, during, and after land reform.

CHAPTER 3

Autonomy and Control

One way to tell the story of land reform in Shuangcheng is in terms of local autonomy and state (central) control. The consensus on modern China is that state control began to deteriorate in the nineteenth century, which meant a loss of control over private appropriation, resulting in the rise of local interests, competition, and general social disintegration.[1] Here I follow Philip Kuhn's definitions of control and autonomy, in which "control" refers to the ability of the state to both "secure its share of society's resources and to insure that its conception of social order is maintained," and "autonomy" means the ability of a village (or other local unit) to "govern certain spheres of its internal affairs according to its own procedures and using its own people."[2] The problem in China was that for most of the past century leading up to land reform, state control and local autonomy were critically out of sync. After millennia of trying to find the perfect balance between autonomy and control, Chinese society had melded them into a single concept, and the power of both state and local administrators was intimately intertwined. However, as Kuhn describes for the early Republican period (1910s–1930s), by this time the control-autonomy relationship was already beyond repair, as enlisting local elite to represent the state and trying to extend bureaucratic controls below the county level drove state and local administrators further away from each other. The CCP's solution in land reform, therefore, was to repair the interdependency between state control and local autonomy. The focus of this chapter is on exploring the political infrastructure that the CCP used to accomplish this reintegration of autonomy and control.

Fundamentally, the concept of "power over property" in China also unites state control and local autonomy insofar as both are practiced through common means of political and personal relationships. In the modern European tradition, in which property forms the basis of power, local elites physically closer to landed property could use this proximity as an independent source of power against a distant state. Likewise in Europe, the feudal state was replaced by a bourgeois state, as landed capital was replaced by urban capital. In the Chinese political tradition, however, personal or social proximity to political elites is a more important source of power. This exercise of power is exemplified in popular stories of the abuse of power by eunuchs and other personal bodyguards of the imperial family and in frequent local rebellions that attack local officials but often claim legitimacy as righteous defenders of the emperor or dynasty.[3] As a result of this common power base, effective local autonomy in China is more dependent on central state control than in the European tradition, and therefore when central control fails, local autonomy also fails in its ability to maintain local order.

The relationship between control and autonomy in China is therefore very different than in the West. In the modern West, state control and local autonomy are independent forces that exist in healthy competition. One consequence of this competition is that in the West an area the size of China (i.e., Europe or the USA) comprises around fifty independent or federated states. In contrast, China's similarly diverse population and geography is largely contained within one single political administrative system, in part because state control and local autonomy are interdependent features of a single political continuum.[4] As implied in the Chinese saying "Do not fear officials, only fear control" (不怕官, 只怕管), state control (officials) was acceptable insofar as it did not interfere in (control) local autonomy. This feature made the CCP's task of state building somewhat easier, because to some degree the norm or ideal in China was to merge state and local interests. Traditionally, the Chinese state accomplished this merger by recruiting or co-opting local leaders, but with the changing nature and functions of the state in the early twentieth century, this strategy was no longer viable.

The CCP relied on land reform to reintegrate state control and local autonomy, a traditional requirement for a strong Chinese state. The process through which this reintegration was accomplished is also characterized by a seemingly contradictory mix of control and autonomy. Here I suggest fitting control and autonomy into a nested hierarchy. In the Chinese political hierarchy, control is exercised between levels, and autonomy is practiced within each level. State control is, in theory, superior to local autonomy but is not explicitly exercised unless local autonomy is ineffective. For example, in Shuangcheng in 1946 the CCP county government ordered all villages to establish a peasant association (PA), but each village was more or less free to define the PA in their own terms, and particular village circumstances determined the nature of a given PA more than the county government's requirements. As one may expect, village elites took control of the situation and set up PAs as they saw fit. This was probably what most of the villagers also expected, because traditionally this was the way village government worked. The problem was that in 1946, the interests of this village elite had become divorced from both the state and the village majority, and neither the state nor the village majority benefited from local elite autonomy. The bottom line, therefore, was that in order to achieve more effective village autonomy, the CCP had to exercise more state control.

The relationship between state control and local autonomy is also a manifestation of the salient tension between state and village, long recognized as a defining feature of Chinese society, past and present. Jean Oi, for example, reduces this tension to a basic conflict over the division of the harvest. Her concept of clientelist relations between CCP state and village under collectivization is also useful for understanding the interaction of autonomy and control.[5] As Oi writes, "The clientelist model assumes considerably more flexibility, subjectivity, and personal sentiment in the exercise of control that may or may not result in effective policy implementation. From the clientelist perspective, authority is routinely exercised through allocating opportunities, goods, and resources over which the elite have monopolistic control and on which the nonelite depend."[6] This flexibility, subjectivity, and diverse range of local implementation is a defining feature of the local autonomy I describe here.[7] The exercise of authority through entitlements to resources is also central to land reform's new social order, as described below.[8] Together, these kinds of interactions between state and village help define social organization more in terms of power than property.

By the early twentieth century, state control had degraded to the point where the central state no longer had a monopoly on violence. In Shuangcheng the first task of the CCP was to protect people and property from roving bandits, local armies, and landlord-controlled vigilante groups. Land reform work and local administration could be carried out only if the CCP had military control of an area. The next step was to set up subcounty administrative systems to provide the organizational support for village PAs. Finally, democratically governed PAs would form the nuclei of a new social order. Success required merging top-down control and bottom-up autonomy, a traditional recipe of Chinese statecraft.[9]

Military Control

Military control of an area, whether it be a county, a district, or just one village, was the most important prerequisite for implementing land reform policies. By May 1948 the CCP Central Committee's first criteria for planning land reform work was that "military strength of enemies has been completely eliminated and the area is not a guerilla zone."[10] At the macro level, land reform mobilization may have played a decisive role in CCP expansion and military victory in the civil war, but military conquest at the micro level, one village and one county at a time, made land reform possible in the first place.[11] In other words, land reform's bottom-up mobilization was dependent on top-down control. How exactly the CCP gained military control of Shuangcheng is beyond the scope of this book, but the sequence of events provides important context for understanding land reform experiences.

The CCP did not gain an effective monopoly on violence in Shuangcheng until the summer of 1947. Moreover, the CCP did not even exist in the county until a CCP army regiment from Shandong occupied the county seat in late November 1945. Before this, when CCP-appointed county officials tried to negotiate with incumbent leaders in Shuangcheng (variously known as former Manchukuo officials and KMT affiliates), they often failed and, even after military occupation, were sometimes rebuffed physically and on occasion violently.[12] Map 4 shows the locations of documented events of counterrevolutionary (anti-CCP) violence during the first year of CCP occupation. For example, shortly after occupying the county seat, the CCP sent out a truck to make contact with a railway station on the east side of the county, but the convoy was attacked in a village along the way and everything, including the truck itself, was lost. Then in December the CCP sent out an eight-person work team, accompanied by ten armed soldiers, to the east side of the county, but as soon as they entered a village they were shot at by local vigilante groups and spent more time in armed skirmishes than political work. One month later, another work team went out to the west side of the county and was taken hostage by a landlord for twelve days before CCP troops could rescue them.[13] In early 1946 only after the CCP won a number of important military victories against some of the larger organized armed forces in the county were they able to send two or three more work teams into the countryside to begin carrying out political work.

The biggest setback to CCP military control in Shuangcheng came in early June 1946, after the CCP lost the second battle of Siping. In the aftermath of this major battle of the civil war, KMT troops advanced to the banks of the Songhua River, within about fifty kilometers of Shuangcheng's southwestern border, and the Shuangcheng CCP government was ordered to evacuate the county.[14] As soon as the CCP left town, county seat residents reportedly hung up Nationalist flags, KMT party and youth group signs, and "Welcome KMT Army" banners.[15] Expecting the KMT army to arrive soon, landlords throughout the county revolted, killing more than twenty CCP cadres and four civilians within one week. As shown in Map 4, twenty-nine out of forty-two documented events of counterrevolutionary violence—at least one in every district—occurred at this time. Because the revolts began when the CCP evacuated on the fifth day of the fifth month of the lunar calendar, a traditional festival day, the event was known locally as the "May Festival Revolt." However, only one day after evacuating, the CCP county government was notified that the KMT would not advance beyond the Songhua River and ordered to return to Shuangcheng. Upon the army's return, the CCP was able to suppress the revolt and carry out a number of summary executions of counterrevolutionaries, including a public execution of nineteen offenders at the county stadium.[16]

Land reform work began in earnest in the fall of 1946 as thousands of cadres throughout Northeast China were sent to the countryside to focus on mass mobilization and implement the May Fourth Directive, but in Shuangcheng these work teams were apparently still confined to those county districts under effective CCP control. The earliest extant work reports come from districts with stationed CCP army regiments, and even they sometimes met violent resistance. On the west side of the county, one of these regiments returned to the county seat in November 1946, leaving a work team to fend for themselves. The work team describes how within two weeks after the army left, bandits had raided five villages, causing widespread panic, and landlords took the opportunity to spread rumors, all but ruining the reputation of the work team. In order to regain the trust of the masses, therefore, the work team decided to mobilize an anti-bandit expedition. After leading a group of forty village militiamen in a victorious battle against a bandit force over one hundred strong, the work team regained their reputation in the area.[17] Few villagers were interested in land reform until they knew the CCP could protect them.

Sometimes the political units of occupying CCP armies were the first to carry out village land reform work, but their objectives could be at

odds with those of later work teams organized by county or district governments. The army regiment stationed on the west side of the county
reported redistributing land and other property in thirty-one villages, but
as soon as they left the area, villagers were left prey to bandits and landlords,
which suggests that the quality of their work was not very high.[18] Similarly,
another regiment stationed in District 8 in the fall of 1946 reported visiting seven villages in eight days.[19] A district leader's report from a year later
describes how this regiment was the first to carry out mass mobilization
in the area, but their main goal was army recruitment. The army work
team set up a PA and elected cadres before redistributing land (and before
understanding village politics); as a result, some "bad guys" were put in
charge of the PA and monopolized power, sabotaging this and subsequent
attempts at land reform in the village.[20] In another nearby village, the army
work team carried out a "peaceful" redistribution of land, in which some
landlords donated pieces of poor land that were redistributed unfairly. The
PA had no members and was led by cadres who were former Manchukuo
cops, opium addicts, and swindlers, who again only caused more problems for future land reform work.[21] With these examples, therefore, we can
see that military control could mark the beginning of land reform work
but definitely not the end of land reform itself.

For every district and village, suppressing bandits and armed resistance was a basic prerequisite for carrying out land reform mobilization,
but even after the mobilization began, another major obstacle was villagers' constant fears of a "change in weather" (变天)—the return of the
KMT. As described in chapter 2, this fear was especially real in a place like
Shuangcheng, located on one of three major fronts in the KMT-CCP civil
war. By the summer of 1947, the CCP had successfully suppressed most
bandits and armed resistance, but given recent events and an ongoing civil
war, many villagers were still weary of throwing in their lots with the CCP,
while many landlords still looked forward to the KMT's return to power.
In District 8, for example, one villager received seven *mu* of land through
redistribution and then decided to rent out five *mu* of it and engage in seasonal labor, because he was afraid that if the KMT returned or landlords
revolted, any effort he spent cultivating extra land would be in vain.[22] An
extreme example comes from a village in District 7, where the landlords
in power were relatives of the KMT mayor of Shenyang (regional capital
of the Northeast) and a former national-level official of Manchukuo. After
three previous work team visits over the past year, in the summer of 1947
a fourth work team found that villagers were still difficult to mobilize and
that PA cadres were corrupt. The work team could only mobilize villag-

ers to struggle against corrupt PA cadres, because everyone was afraid of the landlords' powerful KMT connections. Only after the Shuangcheng County party secretary personally visited the village and pointed out that the real enemy was not the PA cadres but the landlords was the work team able to mobilize villagers to struggle against them.

Villagers' hopes and fears regarding the KMT were not fundamentally changed until the terror of the Mop-Up campaign in the winter of 1947/48. Work reports from after this campaign describe how landlords' attitudes "changed from longing for the KMT to praying on the behalf of the poor peasants and hired laborers for a quick victory in the revolution."[23] The report acknowledges that they prayed for the revolution only in order to avoid being beaten to death by poor peasants and hired laborers, but after nearly eighteen months of land reform work, it may have seemed like such terror was the only way to convince them. In any case, the Mop-Up campaign saw the CCP's condoning of violence and then containing it after it got out of hand, both of which demonstrated their effective monopoly on violence.

Subcounty Administration

The CCP needed military control to come to power, but to stay in power they also needed effective administrative control. In January 1946 one of the CCP county government's earliest extant public notices announced new administrative boundaries to facilitate "penetration of the new government and development of people's rights."[24] This straightforward notice embodied an important principle of the modern nation-state: more rights required more government. Over the next two years of land reform in Shuangcheng, the CCP intensified bureaucratic control from above and organized democratic PAs from below. Combining this political pincer move with the removal of former "autonomous" local leaders made the successful reintegration of local and state interests possible. By 1948 there was more government below the county level, and at least in principle the rural majority had more rights.

Local Government

Subcounty administration, in particular, had been a central focus of Chinese political reforms for at least half a century before land reform.[25] For the previous two thousand years of China's imperial history, the lowest level of the bureaucratic hierarchy was the position of county magistrate. How this magistrate staffed and financed all the administration required to actually run the county was completely up to him, but in general he was dependent on local elites and their established social networks.[26] Beginning in the late Qing, this informal subcounty administration was the subject of theories on "local self-government," which ultimately saw the merging of local and national interests as a prerequisite for a strong nation. In 1902, for example, the prominent political reformer Kang Youwei argued that "by allowing [the masses] self-government and participation in public debate, then the natural workings of enlightened self-interest will bring about vigorous economic development and human improvement."[27] In the traditional system, in other words, by ignoring everyone below the county magistrate, the state effectively denied them these rights. The Qing government officially recognized this need for change through political reforms in the last decade of the dynasty, which included regulations for setting up subcounty administrative units to promote local self-government.

In Shuangcheng modern subcounty administrative control began in 1907 when the county magistrate established a police department and divided the countryside into nine police districts.[28] Throughout the Republican period, such subcounty districts (wards) became the new focal points of local administration throughout China, systematized variously by Yuan Shikai in 1914, Yan Xishan in 1917, and the KMT in 1928 and 1939.[29] Shuangcheng's nine police districts became administrative districts, which continued into Manchukuo (1931–1945). In 1938 one of these districts was redrawn into a neighboring county, and the remaining eight districts were divided into thirty-eight administrative villages (cun, 村).[30] Prasenjit Duara documents a similar evolution in North China, in which cun known as large townships (da xiang, 大乡) were also primarily organized under Japanese occupation as the centralized unit of village government.[31] When the CCP occupied the county in 1945, therefore, there was already a fine structure of subcounty administration in place.

The Manchukuo state's attempts to build subcounty administration in many ways paralleled the CCP's later experience, suggesting that both regimes faced similar problems of autonomy and control. In 1933, shortly after the founding of Manchukuo, the government instituted the baojia system to organize local administration into bao, jia, and pai. The pai was a unit of ten households, the bao was equivalent to the earlier police or administrative district, and the jia was an intermediary unit. After some adjustments, the *bao* was reduced to the size of a large administrative village, and the *jia* was made equivalent to a natural village (*tun*). (In 1935 there was an average of twenty-two *pai* per *jia* and thirteen *jia* per *bao*.) This system also incorporated an obligatory self-defense corps subordinate to the police. Soon after, in 1937, this system was replaced by "street and village administration," which stipulated that the village (*cun*) was a legal entity in charge of managing village public affairs, subordinate to the county, provincial, and national governments. This new village replaced the former smaller *bao*, and a county like Shuangcheng was divided into thirty-eight such village units that effectively acted like small administrative districts. In 1940 this system was replaced again by "neighborhood associations," organizing the countryside into natural villages (*tun*, 屯) and *pai* (排) which were designed as "communal bodies for mutual aid." This new system also stipulated that Concordia Association members were to form the core of these organizations and serve as village and *pai* leaders.[32] Finally, in the 1940s Manchukuo rapidly increased local administrative control through the extraction of economic resources, by mobilizing the concerted power of neighborhood associations, the Concordia Association, and village agricultural cooperatives (兴农合作社). In this final act the Manchukuo government focused on the natural village unit in attempting to integrate political and economic control over the countryside.[33] As mentioned in chapter 1 and further explored in chapter 6, the fact that so many local Manchukuo administrators were targets of villager vengeance bears testament to the intensity of such heightened administrative efforts to govern the Chinese countryside.

Over the course of land reform, the CCP followed a similar process of increasingly fine government penetration. The government notice of January 1946 listed 38 *cun* in 6 districts and announced new names for all of the villages and the creation of a seventh district. Six months later, in June 1946, the CCP divided the county into 11 districts and 91 *cun*. In this division each of the CCP districts corresponded to three Manchukuo *cun*, and each of the original Manchukuo *cun* was split into three smaller CCP *cun*.[34] As shown in Map 3, this was the main administrative system through which land reform was implemented, but in some cases land reform work continued to be organized by the original Manchukuo divisions. In District 2, for example, as late as January 1948 organizational meetings for the Equalize Land campaign were held at three villages in the district, each of which was the location of the original three Manchukuo *cun* offices in the district.[35] Even after the 1948 harvest, District

2 cadres divided the district into three parts for investigation, explicitly stating that they followed the Manchukuo village divisions.[36] Finally, upon completion of land reform in 1948, the county was further divided into 16 districts and 239 *cun*.[37] In other words, in the first two years of CCP governance, the density of district administration doubled, and the density of village administration increased more than sixfold compared to the already well-developed Manchukuo administration. This was perhaps the finest-meshed local administrative system in Shuangcheng's history, and it symbolized a major success of land reform.

One of the objectives of land reform work teams was to create this new system of rural administration. As mentioned in chapter 2, in the fall of 1946 county cadres were given the title of work team leader and district party secretary, and each was sent out into the countryside to organize a district party committee, district government, district security team, and district work team.[38] One extant register of new CCP members recorded in the summer of 1947 can help us understand how this process unfolded. This register records more than ninety-seven new CCP members and their sponsors in at least nine *cun* party branches and two district party branches. Most of these members held positions in district and village administrations, where party membership served as a good guarantee of loyalty. Party membership required an introduction from an existing member, and by analyzing the relationships between sponsors and new members we can see how the CCP penetrated into rural Shuangcheng. As illustrated in Figure 4, two old cadres from North China, Lin Cheng (county party secretary) and He Fang (county committee member), directly or indirectly sponsored eighty-seven out of the ninety-seven party members who joined between January 1946 and July 1947.[39] This represents only one district, but in this way we can imagine how a handful of old cadres from North China could consolidate a handful of fully functioning district administrations through a system of personal sponsorship. While not all administrative cadres were party members, these registers show that the district level and every *cun* in the district had a party branch and that virtually all party members held an administrative position. As He Fang recalls in his memoir, once they established a party branch in a village, the entire village became much more stable.[40] Recruiting local party members was thus one way of directly integrating local and state interests more effectively than simply appointing local administrators.

By the spring of 1947, the CCP in Shuangcheng had set up most district governments in the county. Some districts were established through

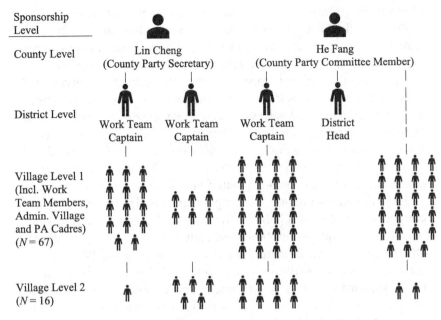

Figure 4. Sponsorship network of 87 new CCP members in Shuangcheng County, January 1946—July 1947. Adapted by the author from information recorded in 129-3-11, 9–21. Each level depicts the direct party sponsor of the level below it.

the efforts of county work teams, as described above, but others appear to have been established more formally, by simply assigning new cadres to the position. In District 8, for example, an occupying army regiment carried out land reform work in a number of villages over the winter of 1946/47, but the CCP did not establish a district government until later in the spring of 1947. The district leader assigned to this district admits that he did not have a clear understanding of CCP policies and had no experience in mass mobilization. This suggests he was not an ideal candidate for the position and was not adequately trained on a county work team, but the arrangement might have been the best the CCP could do at the time. District boundaries were still being hammered out, and the first task of the new district government was to send out an order to all PAs to redistribute land.[41]

Victim registers for all ten rural districts recorded in the summer of 1947 are the most concrete proof that by this time the gears of subcounty CCP administration were in motion. The land expropriation registers are compiled by district in the county archives, and the various individual forms bear the stamps and signatures of a variety of actors, including district governments, district work teams, *cun* governments, and *tun* PAs. Such stamps were not just a feature of bureaucratic paperwork; they also reflect the importance of these units as autonomous actors (even if they were not "official" government-issued stamps). Figure 5 shows examples of six PA and *cun* stamps from these registers, representing units named "Peasant and Worker Federation," "Peasant and Worker Association," "*Tun* Federation," "Peasant Federation," and "*Cun* Administrative Office," respectively. This diversity of organizations again reflects their local autonomy within a fundamentally top-down policy.

From the summer of 1947, district governments played a central role in carrying out land reform policies, from organizing work teams, to holding meetings of village and PA representatives, to authorizing executions. District governments organized district-wide meetings of PA cadres or mass representatives to discuss new policies and disseminate propaganda, often bypassing *cun* officials.[42] A more important sign of the administrative power of district governments, however, was when they served as the ultimate authority in legal matters. When villagers wanted to apprehend landlords in the county seat, they had to get a "stamped" introduction letter from their district government.[43] Furthermore, district governments and work teams directly authorized the killing or punishment of more than 40 percent of the victims recorded in the death and struggle registers (for whom the supervisory authority is known, N = 174).

Even in District 6, which was perhaps the most marginal and least active district in the county in terms of land reform campaigns, the CCP could call on the district government to organize and enlist a district-wide network of civilian stretcher crews to support the war effort. A directive from the county government, dated in late September 1946, and addressed to all district heads, explained:

> Since the establishment of the new regime, it has worked to implement democratic governance and fight for the advancement of peace in the country, to achieve the goal of "land to the tiller," and ensure that the people can live and work to their fullest potential. But the KMT reactionaries have broken agreements and are engaging in large-scale attacks on our armies. In order to prevent these attacks, it is hoped that the districts will dutifully organize civilian stretcher crews according to the following guidelines.[44]

Figure 5. Official stamps of village administrative units, Shuangcheng County, 1947
Sources: 129-3-04, 13; 129-3-05, 5; 129-3-05, 24; 129-3-07, 7; 129-3-10, 38.
Notes: Full text reads as follows (vertically, from left to right):
"District 5 Wanlong *cun* Loushang *tun* Peasant and Worker Federation"
"Shuangcheng County District 6 Handian *cun* Lala *tun* Peasant and Worker Association"
"Shuangcheng County District 6 Zhenghongsi *tun* Federation"
"Shuangcheng County District 8 Youzhi *cun* Fanjia wopu Peasant Federation"
"Shuangcheng County District 11 Zhengde *cun* Administrative Office"

District 6 was the first district to respond to this request and submitted a complete plan one day ahead of the deadline given by the county.[45] This district government divided the entire district into ten stretcher teams of forty persons each and even included a map of the villages to be included in each team. Their response shows a high degree of compliance, which might be unexpected for a district with virtually no prior evidence of land reform mobilization. As we will see in chapters 4 and 5, however, too much local compliance was usually a bad sign, at least in terms of mass political mobilization. Nevertheless, directives like these provide important evidence, and reminders, that alongside mass mobilization campaigns, the CCP was also conducting routine administrative business that often took priority over more "revolutionary" goals.

Within three years of starting land reform, the Shuangcheng CCP government had developed from a handful of veteran cadres to a complex county administration staffed by no less than 1,200 cadres (including more than 280 party members) in charge of a total county population of over 400,000. All of these cadres were individually recorded in the second half of 1949. As reconstructed from this nominal register, at the county level 474 cadres staffed two bureaus (public security and tax revenue), seven departments (finance, agriculture, commerce, civil affairs, education, military, and hygiene), three state-run companies (a department store, a grain company, and a local products store), a court of justice, and a county cooperative. At the district level, 375 cadres staffed 16 district governments, each of which comprised a similar arrangement of departments employing 20 to 30 cadres in each district. And at the cun level, 397 cadres were heads and vice heads of over 200 cun governments. This mature county administration reflects the CCP's two decades of experience in governing soviets and base areas throughout China and no doubt provided a more effective foundation of power than any revolutionary ideology.

Virtually all of the cadres in this CCP county administration were new local recruits, of whom 95 percent began revolutionary work and 98 percent joined the party after the arrival of the CCP in Shuangcheng.[46] Figure 6 presents a timeline of when cadres joined work and the party after November 1945. Over the three years beginning in 1946, we can see that government administration expanded at a relatively constant rate of about 2 or 3 percent per month. The largest expansion occurred in the winter and spring of early 1947, which corresponds to the establishment of district governments mentioned above. Party membership developed more sporadically, and more than 40 percent of cadres joined the CCP in the

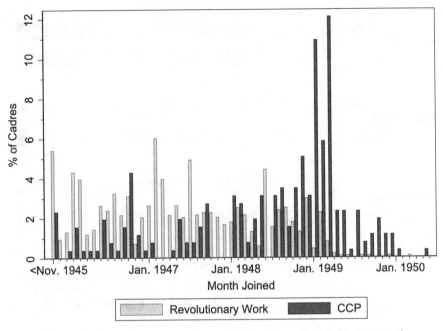

Figure 6. Timeline of cadres joining revolutionary work and the CCP in Shuangcheng County, November 1945 to May 1950. Author's calculations based on 129-1-134 and 129-1-107.

six months spanning the winter of 1948/49. This development was largely the result of CCP policy, in which party recruitment in the county was not made public until August 1948.[47] In earlier periods party recruitment appears to be more closely correlated with land reform campaigns in the fall of 1946, summer of 1947, and early 1948—three periods where we also see the most work team activity.

How did the CCP government in Shuangcheng maintain the loyalty of these new cadres, most of whom hardly knew anything about the CCP before joining them? In official rhetoric, the CCP portrayed themselves as the allies of poor peasants and hired laborers, the rural proletariat. In theory, therefore, persons from these classes were considered naturally loyal to CCP interests and were privileged in the CCP and its administration. In Shuangcheng's county administration, despite some exceptions, lower classes did in fact occupy significant proportions of leadership positions at all levels. The 1949 cadre registers from Shuangcheng record two measures of social status—the class background (成份) and personal background

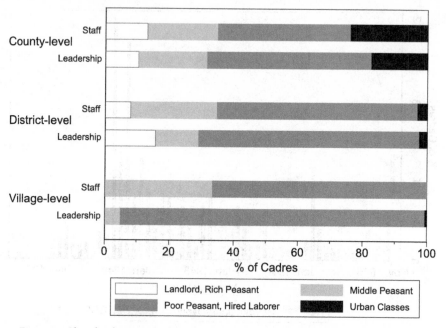

Figure 7. Class background of cadres in the Shuangcheng CCP County government, by level and position, 1949. Author's calculations based on 129-1-134 and 129-1-107.

(出身)—for each individual.[48] The class background refers to the inherited socioeconomic status of the person's family prior to land reform, as categorized into landlords, rich peasants, middle peasants, poor peasants, hired laborers, and other urban classes. Figure 7 illustrates the class backgrounds of county-, district-, and village-level staff and leadership cadres. While there was a decreasing proportion of cadres from poor peasant and hired laborer backgrounds at higher levels of government, within each level these classes occupied the majority of leadership positions. Thus, at the county level, while poor peasants and hired laborers comprised less than half of staff positions, they comprised just over half of leadership positions.

The contrast both between and within administrative levels is even more striking, as shown in Figure 8, when we look at the personal backgrounds of cadres—that is, individual occupation—which can be broadly categorized into farmers, students and intellectuals, and other urban occupations. In terms of actual occupations, as opposed to family class back-

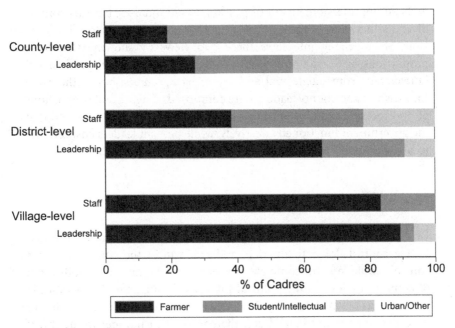

Figure 8. Personal background of cadres in the Shuangcheng CCP County government, by level and position, 1949. Author's calculations based on 129-1-134 and 129-1-107.

ground, about 40 percent of district-level staff and 55 percent of county-level staff were students and intellectuals. However, nearly two-thirds of district leaders and over one-quarter of county leaders were peasant farmers. In other words, the CCP administration in Shuangcheng appears to have had the best of both worlds, employing more professional bureaucrats (which traditionally in China meant students and intellectuals) to staff the district and county levels and then appointing peasant farmers from good class backgrounds to oversee them.

This picture of the composition of CCP county cadres provides a more realistic view of CCP government free of ideological rhetoric. Almost all previous stories of land reform and CCP governance focus on village-level leadership, where the transition from landlord-elite leadership to poor peasant leadership is more straightforward and largely dictated by rural context and policy requirements.[49] Above the village level, however, not much is known about CCP local governance.[50] CCP rhetoric may assert that all CCP officials are poor peasants, which taken to the extreme suggests an unprofessional band of peasant revolutionaries, but this contradicts another view of the CCP as a tightly organized machine. The view from Shuangcheng integrates these two views by showing that large proportions of district and county cadres were (relatively) professional bureaucrats from intellectual and urban backgrounds, but at the same time district and county leaders were comprised of significant proportions of poor peasants and hired laborers. Recruiting bureaucrats ensured that the government functioned effectively, while peasant leaders ensured that local government interests aligned with CCP state interests.

Peasant Associations

Up to now I have focused on the penetration of bureaucratic administrative control down to districts and *cun* within the county, but this control would not be complete without a corresponding mobilization of community-level (*tun*) political interests through the democratically elected peasant associations (PAs). There is no complete, extant list of PA cadres for Shuangcheng, but if there were, their number would dwarf the administrative cadres described above. The household classification registers from the summer of 1948 record 559 PAs in the county, each of which nominally comprised roughly eight elected officers (director and vice director, and commissars of organization, veteran affairs, production, militia, propaganda, and women's associations). The political mobilization of villagers to organize PAs comprised a central focus of land reform work, and in theory the democratic nature of the PAs was to serve as a model for the eventual expansion of representative government to higher levels.[51] In practice, however, PA cadres were under enormous pressure to meet the demands of both their community and the state (i.e., CCP government at the district level and above).

In the spring of 1946, before the May Fourth Directive and before any land reform campaigns began in Shuangcheng, the county CCP government ordered every *tun* to establish a PA. In principle, a PA was a grassroots political organization of the masses (as defined in chapter 2) and for the masses, designed to replace village organizations dominated by local strongmen and to be responsible for all aspects of village governance. In practice, however, the first organically organized PAs (i.e., organized by villagers without CCP work team intervention) in Shuangcheng were virtually all dominated by incumbent local strongmen or their lackeys, and a large part of land reform work involved purging and reorganizing these corrupted PAs. In form, a PA consisted of eight publicly elected officers (cadres) and a membership that included all villagers except expropriated landlords, former Manchukuo collaborators, and other enemy reactionaries. The PA functioned by holding mass meetings to discuss and decide consensually on all village affairs. By the summer of 1947, the organization of an effective PA was seen as the hallmark of a successful land reform campaign, because even if the masses successfully overtook village property, they had no effective power without a PA to organize them and represent their interests.

Several work reports from the fall of 1946 describe the state of organic PA organizations before the arrival of a CCP work team. In one village in District 10, after seeing the directive to establish a PA, the *cun* head, who had served for over eight years during Manchukuo (the former fried dough maker mentioned earlier), consulted with some landlords in the village and called on a few "poor thugs" to lead the PA. They hung up a PA sign, and before the masses knew it, the PA was established. This PA then went about extorting fees from the villagers to purchase weapons, and when a county-wide counterrevolution broke out in June 1946, the PA leaders mutinied and ran off to join a local KMT army. When the CCP army came to restore order, the landlords quickly reorganized a new PA under their control. Shortly after, CCP work teams began carrying out the Anti-Traitor and Settling Accounts campaign, and the PA became a tool for the landlords to deal with any visiting work teams.[52] In another village the PA acted like a landlord's accounting office by confiscating property but then not redistributing it to the masses, in effect managing it for the original owner, even though the original owner had already run off to join a local KMT army.[53] In yet another village, during the 1946 fall harvest the PA officers attended a higher-level government meeting and were ordered to finish harvesting within four days. They returned to the village and then announced that since they only had four days to harvest, everyone had to first finish the landlord's land and deliver the harvest to him. To make things worse, the landlord stood outside his house holding a gun to intimidate villagers, saying, "Look at you poor bastards! Whoever dares cut down my crop will get shot!"[54] Even in relatively good-case scenarios, work teams would complain about the powerlessness of the PAs. In one village, for example, a landlord had slaughtered a poor peasant's pig two years earlier and had yet to compensate him, so the peasant went to the PA to demand justice, but the PA did not dare to act without first asking for an approval letter from a nearby work team.[55]

The message from these early PAs was that the village social and political order was very resilient to outside influences, and it was clear from the beginning that the CCP could not fundamentally change this order by sending out new government directives. By the winter of 1946, CCP work teams had already began purging and reorganizing PAs. Over the course of two months, for example, one work team reorganized twelve village PAs and cleaned out fifty-six "bad elements," which included evil tyrants (恶霸), landlords, lackeys, bandits, cops, and opium and morphine addicts. The work team even organized a "confession training course" for these bad elements, which involved five days and five nights of education through "admonishment and patient conversation," employing the techniques of the Yan'an Rectification movement. Depending on their crimes, some of these bad elements were also paraded through the streets of several villages as a form of public humiliation and collective suppression.[56]

In these early stages of land reform in Shuangcheng, successfully organized PAs mainly functioned like vigilante groups to protect the village. In September 1946 a work team led the residents of one village to hold a public trial and execution of a landlord and his lackey, redistributed their land, and explained to the villagers that now they had to organize a PA and local militia to protect their property. Villagers elected six to eight PA officers, and soon after, the cadres approached the work team to ask for firearms, saying, "[The landlord's cousin] has [organized] over 100 men, and is sure to come back for revenge. If we are not armed everyone will live in terror." The work team decided to give them three rifles, and then the PA held a meeting to organize a spear team and to root out any spies in the village. All non-landlord men between the ages of eighteen and forty-five were enlisted in the village militia. Afterward, in the daytime women performed sentry duty around the village and investigated travelers, and at night men went on sentry duty and instituted travel permits. The PA split into teams to surveil suspicious persons, and everyone had to get permission from the PA in order to leave the village.[57] This was the world that most villagers in North China were living in at this time, and it is no surprise that they were more concerned about safety and survival than revolutionary ideals and class struggle.[58]

By the summer of 1947, PAs had become more sophisticated administrative bodies, and even their shortcomings were described in terms of political efficacy. A work report from August 1947 describes one village's division of political rights into three tiers. Originally, the PA kept two lists, one recording PA membership and one recording the outcasts (landlords, etc.). Now, after redistributing the household belongings of the landlords, the PA split the village into three groups, as recorded in a red, a yellow, and a white list. The red list recorded regular PA members, who had the rights to speak, vote, veto, and be elected at PA meetings. This group included individuals with "clean class backgrounds, poor peasants and hired laborers, workers, poor merchants, clean middle peasants, poor people who have corrected past small mistakes, and loafers who have pass[ed] the investigation and approval of the masses." The yellow list recorded alternate PA members, who had the right to speak but not make a decision and the right to vote but not to veto or be elected. This group included rehabilitating loafers, minor lackeys, and repentant bandits and KMT affiliates. Finally, the white list recorded the outcasts, who had no rights and were barred from PA meetings. This group included expropriated landlords, former Manchukuo and KMT collaborators, and other enemy reactionaries.[59]

One more important feature of these PAs was that membership was typically confined to adult males, while females had their own women's associations and youth had their own youth groups. One of the PA cadre positions was for a woman who acted as the head of the women's association. The women's association was officially a part of the PA, but it was also often treated as separate. In the village mentioned above, men, women, and youth split into separate groups to determine which men, women, and youth, respectively, should belong to which of the three name lists. The women decided that if a household's male head was not in the red list, then a woman of the household could not be in it either, because there still existed "feudal gender relations."[60] In terms of decision making, it is not clear whether or not women had an equal say. In theory they did, but in practice men were in charge of men's affairs and women in charge of women's affairs. For example, during struggle meetings it was common for men to struggle against the men of a household while women simultaneously struggled against the women.[61]

The job of a PA cadre, who had to fulfill both state and village demands, was not easy.[62] One district leader found that the masses' and PA cadres' mutual fear of each other was affecting village administration. The PA was responsible for assigning government work duties, which at this time of civil war included the requisition of labor and grain in kind, military service, and stretcher duty (担架), as well as local duties like serving as village sentries. Villagers were afraid that PA cadres would assign them a heavier workload and that if they resisted the cadres would label them a counter-revolutionary. At the same time, the cadres were afraid that the masses would struggle against them or report them to their superiors. Cadres complained that "village affairs are tough; it's difficult for one person to follow a hundred opinions," and "you have to take care of one hundred affairs, but if you screw up just once you are out of luck." As an example of the latter, "because of one small misunderstanding" the masses in one village had made the cadre in charge of agricultural production wear a dog hide and crawl up and down three village streets.[63]

Democratic decision making also placed an enormous burden on PA cadres. In most cases the cadres just made decisions among themselves, despite sometimes being accused of holding "secret meetings." Even if the cadres wanted to discuss with the masses and reach a consensus, they often did not know how to do it effectively. In one village, for example, a PA meeting to discuss the new summer land reform campaign proceeded as follows:

> CADRE: What do the landlords eat now? What do they wear now?
> MASSES: The landlords eat and wear stuff better than us.
> CADRE: Is our *fanshen* (翻身) complete or not?
> MASSES: It's not complete!
> CADRE: If it's not complete, what should we do?
> MASSES: We still have to struggle![64]

These three exchanges thus amounted to a democratic decision to begin another round of struggle sessions. Despite such shortcomings, however, it is clear that by the summer of 1947 some PAs in Shuangcheng had made enormous progress, from a landlord's lackey hanging up a PA sign to lecturing PA cadres on democratic decision making.

However, many PA and administrative village cadres were so busy with administrative work that they had no time to farm their own land. In the fall of 1947 one *cun* head in District 6 wanted to resign because, he said, after redistributing land all the common people were richer, but cadres like him had become poorer. He could not even afford his own clothes and was looked down on when he had to ask his family to give him some. Similarly, in one village in District 6, all the PA cadres were reportedly busy transporting and distributing relief grain for seventy days straight in the summer of 1947. Because of the famine that year, the cadres had to travel to the county seat to get relief grain, bring it back to the village, assess who needed it or not, and distribute it to them. It was a two-day journey to the county seat and back, and then it took five days to assess villager needs and distribute the grain each time. Altogether they made ten such trips to the county seat, which kept all seven PA cadres busy all summer. As a result, the PA head, in order to not burden the villagers, hired a laborer to work his land, which cost him over forty thousand *yuan* for the summer and put him into debt.[65] In such a high-demand job, it is no wonder that many cadres, like their former landlord counterparts, were desperate for some personal gain.

When work teams began experimenting with the Outline Land Law in Shuangcheng in the winter of 1947, one of the first things they did after arriving in a village was to dissolve the existing PA leadership and organize a new "poor peasant and hired laborers" assembly to take control of village governance. After the summer of 1947, although some PAs may have been functioning effectively, it appears as if the majority continued to be dysfunctional, lying on a spectrum somewhere between landlord control and corrupted cadres. Equally as important, however, was Article 5 of the Outline Land Law, which stipulated that "village peasant meetings and their elected committees" should be the legal executive organs for carrying out land reform. In theory, former PA cadres could continue to serve but only after passing an investigation by an assembly of poor peasants and hired laborers and demonstrating that they had clean backgrounds and could truly serve the interests of "poor people."[66] Ultimately, the goal of these new land reform measures was to reorganize PAs based on a purely organic, bottom-up process of communal decision making.[67]

The motivation for this reorganization was that despite all the accomplishments of land reform up to the fall of 1947, the majority of villagers were still not politically active and did not fully exercise their political rights. In the majority of villages, PA cadres had won their positions through direct work team influence or other nondemocratic means, and as a result, village governance continued to serve the interests of a privileged minority, just as it did before the formation of the CCP government. Some villages had functional PAs, however, and were not enthusiastic about the new policy. In one village in December 1947, after announcing the dissolution of PA leadership, villagers said, "If good cadres are not fit to serve, we would be even worse," and of course the laid-off cadres were even more despondent. In this village the work team reported that the masses supported six out of seven incumbent cadres and five out of six activists, and everyone needed extra guidance to understand the point of this new campaign.[68] But even this case demonstrates the success of the CCP, since the implication is that the village already had an effective PA, and the problem was no longer consolidating administrative control but perfecting it.

The New Social Order

The final measure of CCP state control was the party's ability to cooperate with local PAs to institute a new social order. At the community level, the CCP placed poor peasants and rural and urban manual laborers at the top of this new order and landlords and rich peasants at the bottom, effecting a complete reversal of the preexisting social order. In Shuangcheng there is little evidence that villagers invested in this new order until early 1948, when they began classifying every single household according to official class standards. Before this, work reports suggest that most villagers dealt with the CCP state and land reform policies in a typically perfunctory way.

More important, however, was that the CCP did not announce official class standards until the winter of 1947/48, eighteen months into land reform, and even then the standards were distributed for internal reference, not as explicit policy.[69] Moreover, these standards were not new but reissued from two class-analysis documents originally published in 1933 in the Jiangxi Soviet. If the CCP had already laid out the standards of rural class struggle more than a decade earlier, why did they wait until the end of land reform in 1948 to implement them? This delay seems puzzling, considering that classification lay at the heart of all land reform policies and essentially determined the fate of every household in the new political order. Yang Kuisong suggests that this delay may have been an intentional strategy designed to allow peasants to take matters into their own hands without stifling them with official regulations.[70] This sounds reasonable, especially considering that there was a precedent from the early 1930s in the Jiangxi Soviet's land revolution. In this early regional attempt at land reform, the CCP implemented similar policies of land expropriation and redistribution based on class categories first, only to announce the actual classification standards later.[71] One way to understand this logic is that the ability to dictate social categories was an end, not the means, to power. Thus, for most of land reform in Shuangcheng, the CCP tried gradually introducing class theories through land reform struggle, but they did not force the issue until they had built up sufficient control.

In the summer of 1947, for example, the victim registers record both class and crime of the individuals, implying that class itself was not the primary justification for punishment. Furthermore, as mentioned in chapter 1, instructions on these registers also explicitly stated that persons should be recorded "regardless of their class status" and that the struggle registers were to record "non-landlords" only. As late as January 1948, village representatives at a district mass meeting were found to have "bad class backgrounds" and sent home.[72] During the Mop-Up campaign in the same month, some landlords and rich peasants could still be found driving the sleds of poor peasant and hired laborer mop-up teams, a practice that was soon condemned under official class policies.[73]

The Mop-Up campaign in January 1948 marked the turning point in class struggle in Shuangcheng. On the one hand, the CCP promoted the campaign as the climax of class struggle, in which poor peasants and hired laborers would unite as a class across village boundaries and mutually overthrow all the landlords and rich peasants. On the other hand, since the campaign focused on expropriating hidden wealth, villagers took the opportunity to plunder neighboring villages, which resulted in the strengthening of community solidarity to protect village property and ran counter to concepts of larger class solidarity. Rather than losing control, however, the CCP took this opportunity to institute a new order on their own terms, finally making classification a central focus of land reform. Insofar as the Mop-Up campaign was the most violent part of land reform in Shuangcheng, it appears as if the CCP waited for the old order to fall apart completely before setting up a new one.

The primary objective of the Classification campaign in early 1948 was to draw class lines and institute a new social order. Several reports describe how this campaign naturally grew out of the discovery of class enemies participating in mop-up teams. In one instance in District 11, a mop-up team went to mop up a neighboring village at night. No one could recognize anyone else in the dark, but after "mopping up" a dozen or so households, one of the team members yelled at a dog, and his voice was immediately recognized by one of the villagers, who called out, "Is that your village's grandson of Mr. Zhang? How could an expropriated rich peasant be able to go out mopping up other villages?" As a result, the mop-up team returned home, tied up the imposter, and had the youth group give him a beating before calling a mass meeting to discuss classification.[74] Sometimes this campaign resulted in several rounds of classification. Since one's class would automatically determine one's property entitlements, villagers were more concerned about classification than anything else. In addition to rereleasing the two 1933 documents on class analysis in November 1947, in January 1948 Ren Bishi gave a speech in the Jinsui liberated area in which he criticized previous subjective attempts at classification and emphasized concrete measures based on the proportion of household income derived from capital or labor exploitation.[75] This speech was then widely disseminated throughout the liberated areas, including the Northeast. At least in Shuangcheng, however, in practice, class categories were also highly localized and more complicated than the official guidelines suggest.

Villagers in Shuangcheng appear to have taken the classification process very seriously, because their final class labels are much more complicated than the official guidelines. This can be seen in the household classification registers, which record the final class status of every one of the more than eighty thousand households (over seventy thousand rural) in the county. The CCP documents from the winter of 1947/48 present a straightforward class structure comprised of eight rural classes: landlords, bankrupt landlords, rich peasants, tenant rich peasants, rich middle peasants, middle peasants, poor peasants, and hired laborers.[76] Northeast Bureau guidelines published in December 1947 also mention three grades of landlords (large, middle, and small) and small rich peasants but only explicitly define the latter.[77] In comparison, Shuangcheng's classification registers from the summer of 1948 record nine types of landlords, seven types of rich peasants, five types of middle peasants, two types of poor peasants, and hired laborers, for a total of twenty-four distinct rural classes. As shown in Table 7, more than thirteen thousand households in Shuangcheng were classified as "unofficial" classes, including more than two-thirds of landlords. Such a highly stratified class structure seems more like a lesson in social hierarchy than in class struggle.

Surprisingly, this final classification was also more complicated than earlier attempts prior to the release of official guidelines. The victim registers from the summer of 1947 record over seven thousand observations of class labels defined before official CCP definitions were released. These registers record almost as many different class labels as the later classification registers described above but in much smaller proportions. Table 8 illustrates how local class labels recorded in the victim registers were simpler than those recorded in the 1948 classification registers. The classification registers record nearly twice the proportion of unofficially classed landlords, eight times the proportion of unofficially classed rich peasants, and over ten times the proportion of unofficially classed middle peasants.

Table 7. Class Categories Recorded in Shuangcheng's Classification Registers, 1948

Class Category	Qualifier	Defined in Official CCP Documents (1933/1948)	Recorded in Shuangcheng's Classification Registers (1948) (# of Households)
Landlord		X	1,562
	Large		511
	Middle		788
	Small		1,842
	Bankrupt	X	41
	Rich Peasant		34
Managerial Landlord			497
	Large		8
	Middle		23
	Small		10
Rich Peasant		X	3,963
	Large		11
	Middle		21
	Small		215
	Tenant	X	1,778
	New		21
Middle Peasant		X	8,674
	Rich	X	521
	Small		45
	Tenant		2,715
	New		4
Poor Peasant		X	13,747
	Tenant		6,625
Hired Laborer		X	30,551
Total			74,207

Source: Author's calculations based on classification registers.

This complicated social hierarchy stood in opposition to the CCP's stated objective of drawing clear and simple boundaries between the enemies and allies of struggle. Ideally, there were supposed to be only three camps in this revolutionary struggle—enemies, friends, and allies, with the latter two comprising up to 90 percent of the rural population. The actual class hierarchy devised by villagers, however, blurred such clear divisions of social groups.

There were such fine lines between these categories that sometimes

Table 8. Comparison of Class Categories Recorded in Shuangcheng's Victim and Classification Registers, 1947–1948

Class Category	% Category Recorded in	
	Victim Registers (1947)	Classification Registers (1948)
Landlord	77.6	29.6
Other Landlord	22.4	70.4
Total	100.0	100.0
N	4,108	5,282
Rich Peasant	95.4	65.6
Other Rich Peasant	4.6	34.4
Total	100.0	100.0
N	1,023	6,043
Middle Peasant	97.2	72.5
Other Middle Peasant	2.8	27.5
Total	100.0	100.0
N	649	11,959

Sources: Author's calculations based on linked victim and classification registers.

the labor of one elderly man in the household could mean the difference between classification as a small rich peasant or a middle peasant (which meant the difference between enemy and friend). One village report from February 1948 describes seven households that were previously misclassi-fied. One of the households was classified as a small tenant rich peasant because they cultivated thirteen hectares of rented land in 1944, and their old man, who was still capable of delivering food, was not counted as part of household labor. They were struggled against as a result, but now count-ing the old man's labor and the rent they paid for the land, the household was to be reclassified as tenant middle peasant. Three of the other house-holds also had similar stories.[78]

There were also nearly two thousand persons who appear in both the victim and classification registers, making it possible to do a direct com-parison of changes in their class labels. Of these individuals who can be linked across registers, almost half of them stayed within the same major class category, one out of three were classed higher, and one out of five were classed lower in the 1948 classification registers compared to the 1947 victim registers. Table 9 breaks down these changes by category. Here we can see that landlords were the most stable category; 70 percent of land-lords were already identified as such by the summer of 1947. At the same time, however, more than one out of four landlords in 1947 were not land-

Table 9. Individual Changes in Class Category in Shuangcheng's Victim and Classification Registers, 1947–1948

Class Category in 1947	% Class Category in 1948			Total %	N
	Lower	Same	Higher		
Landlord	27.9	72.1	--	100.0	831
Rich Peasant	9.5	35.2	55.3	100.0	463
Middle Peasant	3.7	18.9	77.4	100.0	381
Poor Peasant	46.1	32.8	21.1	100.0	232
All	20.5	47.8	31.7	100.0	1,933

Sources: Author's calculations based on linked victim and classification registers.

lords by official CCP standards but were reclassified as rich and middle peasants in 1948. Other than landlords, class definitions seem to have been very haphazard in 1947. Nearly two out of three rich peasants and poor peasants, and more than five out of six middle peasants, were reclassified in 1948. Considering that these individuals were recorded in the victim registers in 1947 and therefore already considered enemies, the fact that the majority of rich and middle peasants were classed higher in 1948 more likely suggests that they successfully "underclassed" themselves in 1947, rather than being "overclassed" in 1948.

Furthermore, the new social hierarchy did not just stop at class status—many villages held daylong meetings to individually rank every household, and even every person, from the poorest to the richest.[79] The 1948 classification registers list every household in rank order in addition to their class status, because this ranking often determined the actual order of land allocation. A number of reports describe how in many villages, mass meetings were held to openly discuss and rank households within each class according to criteria such as character and moral standing. At first each household put forward a single representative to be ranked in front of a mass meeting, but then it was discovered that even within households there could be good and bad people. In one household, for example, the household head did not have a particularly good character, and his wife had helped hide the wife of a bandit, so when it came time for them to be ranked, they always put forward the head's hardworking younger brother as the household representative.[80] As a result, villagers ultimately demanded that ranking be based on an overall evaluation of every household member.

In District 10 another village, which served as a model for the entire district, also found that class labels and even household rankings were not enough and ended up individually ranking all men and women in the village. A report on how this process developed describes how during the height of the Mop-Up campaign several households were reevaluated upward—for example, from middle peasant to rich peasant—before being reevaluated back down again. As in the previous example, villagers quickly became dissatisfied with the household ranking, because they all recognized that even within a single household there were good and bad people. The villagers' solution, decided upon in a mass meeting, was to rank men and women individually. They also decided on the following criteria for ranking within the poor peasant and hired laborer classes:

1. Hardworking or lazy
2. Frugal or wasteful
3. Personal character
4. Household wealth

Using this new method, there were many cases in which a husband's and wife's ranks substantially differed. For example, in one family the husband was a hardworking hired laborer and was ranked seventh among all village men, but his wife had "poor morals" (品行不好) and came from a landlord family, so she was ranked much lower among village women. In another family, the husband had poor morals and was ranked seventy-first, but his honest and hardworking wife was ranked ninth.[81]

The ranking of class enemies (i.e., "expropriated households") in this village was seen as a completely separate affair, which was undertaken only to keep them from starving to death after all their belongings had been expropriated. After the Mop-Up campaign, the poor peasants and hired laborers saw that members of the expropriated households were going around begging for food and did not even have enough clothing to wear. So the poor peasants and hired laborers called another mass meeting and decided that it was better to distribute some supplies to them than to have them going around begging for food from everyone. The poor peasants and hired laborers then gathered up the expropriated households and told them to rank themselves in order to determine who gets what. The criteria for ranking the expropriated households were as follows:

1. Who exploited more people?
2. Who oppressed others?

3. Who was counterrevolutionary?
4. Who employed more lackeys?

Through this process, they found that even the small landlords and rich peasants hated the "bad" landlords and rich peasants and ranked them last. One of these bad landlords was notoriously oppressive in the village, and his brother was the director of the county agricultural cooperative under Manchukuo, while one of the bad rich peasants was a bandit who stole draft animals, raped a villager's daughter, and was in cahoots with the Manchukuo police. As a result, in the process of ranking many of these enemies were struggled against again.[82]

One consequence of finely classifying and ranking the entire community was that it could cause divisive quarreling among enemies. Since landlords and rich peasants were also entitled to a fair share of land, they also had to be ranked to determine who would get which plot of village land. In one village, for example, two managerial landlords quarreled about who should be ranked first. One said, "We are both managerial landlords, but I engaged in less exploitation, so I should be in front of you," but the other replied, "How could we be the same? During Manchukuo you were in cahoots with the police, didn't work, and oppressed poor peasants and hired laborers."[83] In terms of class struggle, driving wedges between enemies could be beneficial, but at the same time, as implied in the previous example, it also could have made some people wonder why some small landlords and rich peasants were lumped together with the "bad guys."

In any event, the immediate purpose of ranking every household was to fairly determine the order in which to allocate village land. Because every plot of land was not created equal, in order for the redistribution to be fair, every household had to be ranked so that the poorest household could get the nearest and most fertile plot of land while the richest or most notorious household got the farthest and most unproductive plot. One report describes how once all the land had been evaluated and households ranked, the actual allocation could take place: "Because most commoners were illiterate, a map [of all village land] was hung up on the wall . . . and [each plot of land] was marked by grade . . . then according to class, rank, and household size, [each household] chose which plot of land they wanted."[84] Although there is no record of the location of plots, the classification registers record the quality of allocated land and demonstrate that indeed throughout the entire county, village land was carefully allocated according to quality.[85]

The Classification campaign and its resulting household classification registers demonstrate the creation of a new social hierarchy that was a synthesis of local and state interests but did not really resemble either. The CCP wanted to create a class hierarchy in which to wage class struggle, but villagers in Shuangcheng wanted to get in an orderly line to collect their fair share of land. The result was a social hierarchy that went beyond class categories to rank each household and even each individual in order to determine their fair share of land. Given previous campaigns in which social boundaries were drawn more roughly and villagers felt that property was distributed less fairly, it seemed like the only way to achieve fairness was to define every household's entitlement individually. Thus, although villagers embraced the CCP's class labels, they used them for their own purposes of defining status entitlements rather than organizing a class-based social revolution. But in this regard the desire to use political categories to determine a hierarchy of entitlements was shared by both village and state.[86]

The goal of both state control and local autonomy was guaranteeing this fair, but technically unequal, social order. Social order was characterized by a fair distribution of village resources according to a combination of household need and merit. State control, from military to social categories, was necessary to build a stable social and political hierarchy, and this hierarchy was necessary for maintaining a social order in which villagers had the power to fairly determine who got what. In the past the deterioration of control and autonomy was manifested by the unfair distribution of resources, in which villagers who needed food did not receive it and unmerited officials monopolized village resources. Both this collective past and individual histories determined the new social order, in which it was only fair that previously wronged villagers be privileged and previously unfair behaviors be punished. Such an order was dictated by local autonomy and made possible by state control.

CHAPTER 4

Between State and Village: The Work Team

Much of our knowledge of land reform comes from the perspective of CCP work teams. These teams were regularly dispatched by higher-level administrators to implement and investigate land reform policies in selected villages and can be considered the eyes and ears of CCP policy makers. As a result, CCP work teams have left us the greatest volume of firsthand accounts of land reform mobilization campaigns, and their narratives continue to dominate our understanding of how villagers experienced this revolution. William Hinton was a member of one work team that visited a village toward the end of land reform, and his classic 1966 account, *Fanshen,* is in many ways an expanded English version of a typical work report from the final stage of land reform in 1948.[1] More recent studies of land reform also overwhelmingly rely on work team reports.[2] Despite their importance, however, these sources have received relatively little critical evaluation. Who were the work teams, where did they go, what was their job, and who read their reports? The formal answer to these questions is that work teams were higher-level state agents who were sent to select test sites to carry out mass mobilization and then report back to their superiors about their successes and shortcomings. But these questions are seldom answered for specific contexts and in relation to the content of specific reports, despite the fact that many competing claims about land reform can be traced to the selection of work team reports describing different campaigns or phases of the movement. This chapter is therefore dedicated to the world of land reform work teams in Shuangcheng.

In Shuangcheng work teams could vary from one or two cadres dispatched to investigate a village to hundred-person survey teams. These work teams were almost always temporary units organized to fulfill a specific task over the course of a few days to a few months. Work team leaders were typically CCP administrators at the district level or higher, and work team members could comprise a mix of logistical support and cadres in training. After the work team's mission was complete, the team would dissolve and many of the members would return to either their regular administrative positions or home to become the next generation of village leaders.[3]

The temporary nature of work teams was partially dictated by conceptions of the policy process and the role of the state. Work teams were one part of a larger policy process—they represented neither the beginning nor the end of land reform. Land reform in Shuangcheng was a two-year-long process, as outlined in the first section of chapter 1 (see Figure 1). But no single work team operated for the entire two years. Nevertheless, many land reform narratives are based on single work team reports describing a complete mobilization process from contacting activists and fermenting revolution to overthrowing local strongmen. In reality this process occurred over and over again, and the final results often had little relation to earlier work team experiences. A typical work team report describes only one campaign, in one village, and it is rare to be able to link multiple reports to a single work team or to link multiple campaigns to a single village. We can see this in Shuangcheng, for example, where reports from the same policy campaign in different districts could sound very similar, but reports on different policy campaigns in the same village may sound completely different.[4]

There are two basic interpretations of the role of the work team in CCP policy making. One is the role of experimenter, as first implied in Charles P. Cell's work and as I describe here. Another role, as emphasized by Li Lifeng, Chen Yaohuang, and others, is that the work team is a tool that the central state uses to directly penetrate into local society.[5] The first role implies a cooperative relationship between state and village, work team and local cadres, while the second role implies a competitive relationship between the two. Theoretically, as described by Cell and others, work teams embodied the "perception" stage of Mao's mass line politics, in which administrators would gather experience and understanding of real-world practices to apply toward policy making or theory formulation. In this part of the political system, characterized as "emphasizing direct contact between leader and led, stressing mass participation and mobilization over hierarchical control and bureaucratic management," the work team played a key role.[6] Evidence from Shuangcheng supports this view of the work team more than as a tool for direct state control. At the same time, however, I emphasize the policy-making side of this process, recognizing that work teams and their mass line politics were also subject to a fair share of "hierarchical control and bureaucratic management."[7]

In practice, in the overall policy process the work team's role was to inform policy, while policy enforcement continued to operate through a more conventional administrative or bureaucratic hierarchy. From the perspective of the state, the work team was a participant-observer that CCP bureaucrats relied on to gather source material for effective, practical policy formulation. From the perspective of villagers, the work team was a powerful state agent, and without direct work team involvement there is little evidence that village mass mobilization was effective. But the team's role as experimenter came first, and when they had gathered the necessary source material, they typically left the village to return to its status quo. By comparison, the more important source of effective CCP control continued to be the administrative hierarchy described in chapter 3. The bulk of land reform was accomplished through government directives and leadership meetings, not work team–led mobilization.

In essence, Shuangcheng's administrative records are what make it possible to flesh out the process of land reform beyond the work team. The victim and classification registers are the product of the general mobilization or implementation of policies throughout the entire county, and they give substance to the organizational work of directives and leadership meetings that is mentioned only in passing in work reports. One main argument of this chapter, therefore, is that the role of work teams cannot be fully understood without taking into account the larger context of policy making in which they operated.

State and Village Perspectives

Shortly after the May Festival Revolt in June 1946, which left dozens of CCP cadres dead and led to the violent suppression of reactionaries throughout the county (see chapter 3), the Shuangcheng County committee asked He Fang to organize a group of students and teachers and conduct a rural survey in preparation for land reform work. He Fang was part of the first cohort of CCP cadres to reach Harbin after the end of World War II. In June 1946 he was a county-level cadre in charge of education and had just finished reorganizing Shuangcheng's middle-high school, where he also taught politics and literature to both teachers and students. During the revolt a large cache of firearms had been stolen from the school's storage room, and a number of politically suspect students and teachers were in hiding. Nevertheless, He selected more than one hundred reliable stu-

dents and teachers to form a temporary rural survey team and set out for
one administrative village about fifteen kilometers east of the county seat.
After over a month of surveying in July and August, He wrote a report
titled "A Survey of Shuangcheng County's Yongle Village," which was published in the book *Northeast Rural Investigations* by the Northeast Bureau's
propaganda department in March 1947.[8]

He's published report contains an overview of rural economic relations,
designed to introduce CCP officials from North China to the unfamiliar
conditions of the Northeast countryside. The report contains four sections: "Land ownership and class relations," "Tenancy issues," "Hired labor
issues," and "Draft animal issues." Overall, He describes a rural economy
characterized by extremely unequal distributions of land and draft animals, high rates of tenancy, and a population dominated by property-less
hired farm laborers. Compared to North China, CCP officials would have
been surprised to find such a revolutionary situation as He describes in his
report. He focuses almost exclusively on relations of production, setting
the stage for an inevitable rural class struggle.

But this is just one side of the story of Yongle village. Shuangcheng's
county archives contain five draft reports describing two other versions
of He's experiences in this village. The first document, titled "The Great
Transformation: A Survey of Yongle Village," is comprised of two parts.
The first part is a more detailed version of the published report, in which
He references Lenin's analysis of rural class relations in Russia to con-
firm his Marxist framing of the rural economy. The second part describes
the "great transformation" that took place after the "masses' struggle
to *fanshen*," in which the proportion of landless households in the village dropped from more than 75 percent to less than 3 percent. In this
part, however, He describes the enemies targeted for struggle as "loyal
collaborators during the period of Japanese imperialist occupation" and
categorizes them into four different types: Manchukuo high officials,
Manchukuo traitorous special agents and merchants, local bullies, and
Manchukuo village officials and runners. He then goes on to describe how
his team confiscated more than 900 hectares of land from these enemies
and distributed it to at least 350 landless households, and how the peasants also established their own political organization and militia to protect
their new property.[9] Here there is already a clear disconnect between the
economic analysis of the first part and the identities of the enemies in the
second part. The enemies targeted for confiscation were not the largest
landlords but former traitors and collaborators who used their political

positions to oppress villagers. In this version of the story, however, one can still assume that these enemies were former traitors because they were wealthy landowners.

Four other fragmented work reports tell yet another version of this village story, focusing on mass political mobilization and struggle.[10] These reports provide a more detailed narrative of events in the village from the spring of 1946 to He's work team activity in July and August 1946. Here we learn that in the spring, the county government ordered all villages to reduce rent, equalize land, and establish peasant associations (PAs). Tenant rich peasants benefited the most from these policies, while nothing changed for most villagers. In one of Yongle's natural villages, village 4, the Manchukuo administrative village head, Z, organized a PA with the help of other landlord households, including the "evil tyrant" H, and in village 5 peasants tried to settle accounts with a resident landlord but failed to mobilize. In June 1946, during the May Festival Revolt, H contacted a local underground KMT army and forced a CCP cadre to step down, while the other village 4 PA members ran off to join the local KMT army. When the CCP returned to the area, H fled to the county seat, the restored CCP cadre ordered the confiscation of all of H's property, and local landlords scrambled to set up a new PA. Before He's work team arrived, this new PA warned the masses not to tell the work team anything.

He's team arrived in village 4 on July 22, 1946. By this time, Z and H had already fled the village, and villagers tried to avoid the work team as much as possible. After two days of investigation, He's team found some villagers who were willing to talk to them. Even though He and his team knew some of these people were "loafers out for revenge," they decided to organize a struggle meeting against Z (in absentia) and invite villagers from all six *tun* of Yongle *cun*. Nearly five hundred people attended the meeting, but the villagers who were prepared in advance to accuse Z did not show up, and in the course of the meeting more grievances were voiced against H (also in absentia). Villagers also called out four more enemies to struggle against: a Manchukuo village clerk turned KMT bandit, another evil tyrant, a Manchukuo district head, and a former Manchukuo division head serving as the new CCP village head. At the end of the meeting, everyone called for redistributing Z's property. The meeting chairmen declared it a free-for-all, and five hundred people swarmed into his abandoned house, and "everything disappeared in a blink of the eye."

The next day, He's work team organized another struggle meeting against the four newly identified enemies. More than five hundred people attended this second meeting, at which they settled accounts with the Manchukuo district head and village clerk (in absentia; both had already escaped), paraded the evil tyrant around the village in a tall dunce cap, and executed the former Manchukuo division head. This division head, who is recorded as a middle peasant in the death registers, was condemned to death for committing murder, raping more than ten women, extracting excessive grain quotas during Manchukuo, and continuing to practice graft and corruption as current village head. At this meeting they also confiscated over three hundred hectares of land.

After this second meeting, a hired laborer from village 5 approached the work team and asked them to organize a struggle meeting against M, a local strongman in his village. The next day He sent a few members to investigate, but when they arrived in village 5 they found that M's house was empty and his entire family was gone. Later they learned that another former district head, B, had also fled the night before they arrived. After a few days of investigation in village 5, the work team organized a third struggle meeting at which more than twenty people condemned M and B (in absentia) and decided to tear down M's Western-style villa. The next day they called the entire village to redistribute M's household belongings, again by declaring a free-for-all. They also confiscated over 140 hectares of land from M and two other absentee landlords whose crimes were exposed at the meeting.

Through these struggles, He describes how they were able to educate some reliable activists about class struggle and the importance of organizing a PA to take over village affairs. After organizing their own PAs in early August, villages 4 and 5 each organized their own struggle meetings against absentee landlords. First village 4 went to the county seat and brought back a few absentee landlords to the village to struggle against them and also approved the confiscation of land from more distant absentees, in total confiscating another 270 hectares of land. Shortly after, the village 5 PA organized another struggle meeting of their own against three absentee landlords and one resident managerial landlord who was in cahoots with the police during Manchukuo, spread evil throughout the community, and had tried to bribe the work team and undermine the masses. They also carted in the landlords from the county seat, made them all parade around the village, and confiscated a total of more than 400 hectares of land. But when this land was redistributed, after a few days those villagers who did not receive any land got jealous and asked the work team if they could confiscate some more. Finally, the work team organized Yongle's sixth struggle meeting, at which they confiscated over 500 hectares of land and redistributed it to 84 percent of households in village 5.

In this version of the story we can see that He's investigation of class and property relations played a small role. The prominent enemies in these struggles are all described as taking advantage of their political position to unfairly accumulate wealth, a common theme repeated throughout this book. Z, M, and B are some of the local strongmen introduced in chapter 1 who rose to prominence through collaborating with the Japanese, embezzling public goods, and intimidating villagers. In addition, besides the absentee landlords, whose crimes are not listed, five out of six of the other enemies targeted for struggle are identified as Manchukuo officials or in cahoots with them. As for their landholding, the land expropriation registers record that Z, B, and H owned only between 16 and 22 hectares of land, while the largest known landholding of the persons mentioned was 72.5 hectares.[11] Moreover, the one enemy condemned to death for violent crimes is recorded as a middle peasant in the death registers.

These various versions of He's experience in Yongle village demonstrate how information was translated up and down the CCP's ideological hierarchy. At the village level, if left untouched, incumbent local strongmen continued to control village affairs and comply with government orders. The work team's job in the village, therefore, was to identify these local strongmen and then motivate villagers to overthrow them and collectively take control of village affairs. He's report on "The Great Transformation" spoke to the CCP state's belief that redistributing land was the primary benchmark for measuring such political change. Finally, in He's published report, this political process was further distilled into purely economic relations of production. This hierarchy of meaning can be summarized as follows:

1. Economics of class struggle (CCP state [above county level])
2. Redistribute land as proof of political mobilization (county-level work teams)
3. Overthrow corrupt local strongmen and institute collective democratic governance (village-level PAs)

For all the CCP officials with more than a decade's experience in rural revolution and who understood the relations between these three levels, He's published report was tantamount to a secret code that conveyed all the politics and violence of the draft reports hidden behind numbers of landholding and landless households, rural rents and incomes. The work team was the primary medium through which this translation from politics into economics took place, but rarely does the historian get to see beyond the translated output of the finalized work report.

What's more, the story of Yongle village does not stop with the six struggle meetings described in the draft reports. A few months later in November 1946, a Songjiang provincial leader wrote a letter addressed to other provincial leaders and the Shuangcheng County party secretary describing some failures of the mass movement in this part of Shuangcheng.[12] Apparently around this time the Northeast Bureau also sent a representative to investigate conditions in rural Shuangcheng, and one of the places he visited was Yongle village. The letter describes how the PA cadres were now all of good class backgrounds, but because the evil tyrant H was still hiding out in a nearby village, the cadres told the investigator that "as long as [H] is still here, if the KMT comes all we can do is run away!" This was clear evidence that even after all the struggles described above the masses were still not in full control of village affairs. The investigator also found that few villagers had actually received any of the confiscated property. Most of it was taken over by the PA, and the most valuable of it was handed over to the county government. As a result, the PA cadres hoarded it for themselves, and the masses did not really get any land, clothing, or other goods. In fact, He's work reports also hint at this issue, because they mention confiscation more than redistribution. Although one report describes in detail the agreed-on method of redistribution, it does not say how it was actually carried out.

This provincial-level letter thus brings our story of Yongle village back full circle. He's work team spent great effort in identifying village enemies, organizing struggle meetings, confiscating property, and organizing PAs in accord with the prevailing May Fourth Directive. But the provincial letter concluded that this had been a lost battle, because the PA was still afraid of the local strongmen and villagers had not received the "fruits of struggle" (斗争果实). The tone of this letter set the stage for the beginning of the next regional campaign to "eliminate half-cooked rice," and a regional directive was issued the very next day. He's work team, and his published report, had served their functions, supplying the regional government with the information it needed to move forward in the complex and difficult process of land reform. The parts of this process can be fully understood only in relation to the whole. Otherwise the narrative will become biased toward either a state or village perspective—the state being focused on issues of class struggle, and the village being focused on issues of community justice.

The Policy Process—"From Point to Plane"

At the level of policy making, work teams played a dialectical role in adapting central policies to local circumstances and communicating local circumstances back to central leaders to improve policy. This policy-making process was standard procedure under the CCP, practiced in the Jiangxi Soviet in the 1930s through the Cultural Revolution in the 1970s, and is the subject of several other studies. In brief, the process operated as follows:

1. Central leaders hold a meeting of local leaders and devise a new policy.
2. Local leaders organize work teams to experiment with implementing the new policy.
3. Work teams report to local leaders on their experiences and, based on these reports, local leaders devise a strategy for general implementation at the local level.
4. In the process of general implementation, as new issues arise, local leaders identify common issues and summarize them in reports to central leaders, and the process repeats from step 1.[13]

Local leaders and work teams colloquially referred to steps 2 and 3 as moving "from point to plane" (从点到面). The points referred to single villages that served as sites for work team policy experimentation, and the plane was the remainder of the vast countryside beyond direct administration. In effect, this policy process reflected the realities of governing an agrarian society in which as much as 90 percent of the population lived in semi-autarkic communities scattered over a vast area. Direct administration of every village was unsustainable, and using key point villages to provide role models for other villages to follow was more efficient.

Beginning at the top, central policy makers emphasized local feedback in the policy process. Mao's *Hunan Investigation* is a classic example in which he investigated five counties in the span of one month by calling meetings of experienced peasants and movement leaders in villages and county seats.[14] The reports of these local leaders thus provide the main source material for what became one of the most influential manifestos of rural revolution. The May Fourth Directive is also framed in terms of a response to local experiences, declaring, "According to reports by comrades who have recently come to Yan'an from various places, mass movements have been unfolding on a broad scale in the Liberated Areas in Shanxi, Hebei, Shandong and central China. . . . Under such circumstances, our Party cannot do without its own resolute policy" (Appendix A). And finally, the Outline Land Law was the product of a two-month-long national conference at which "comrades from the various liberated areas [gave] reports and shared their experiences of land reform, raised suggestions for how to precede with the reform, and engaged in repeated discussions."[15] This process was thus replicated at every level, from the village up to the central government.

Central policies, like the May Fourth Directive or Outline Land Law, are only four to five pages long and are more like general guidelines than strict laws. The fact that local practices under the May Fourth Directive could range from "peaceful" land reform to torturing wealthy households for their hidden belongings, and, under the Outline Land Law, could range from the Mop-Up campaign to systematic classification and equal reallocation of all village property, shows just how open to interpretation these central policies could be. Similar to work team reports, central policy documents can be considered only one part of the overall policy process.

From the beginning, the implementation of land reform policies in Shuangcheng followed a strategy of "breaking through one point" (突破一点) of the rural landscape in order to set a precedent for the rest of the area. One early work report from October 1946 describes how villagers were not motivated to struggle against "reactionary landlords" until the work team successfully carried out the first struggle. The work team leader, apparently from China proper, noted that work was difficult in the Northeast because the people there had never experienced intense struggle before. The work team therefore had to show the people that struggle was possible in the first place, and then only after the struggle could land be redistributed and the masses organized. Thus the work team found that holding a struggle meeting or executing a "reactionary landlord" in one village was an effective way to mobilize surrounding villages as well.[16] In his memoir He Fang also mentions this strategy of starting from one point and then spreading out to the surrounding area. His description, however, implies that safety, or military control, was also an important issue. His work team, a fully armed team of more than seventy men, first occupied one village (chosen because it was the home village of one of his bodyguards) in an area he describes as "especially out of control, with bandit activity everywhere and villages governed by vigilante groups."[17] In both cases, however, all village eyes were on the work team, and their success depended on whether or not they could set a good example.

But even in these key points it is easy to overexaggerate the power of the work team. Another work report from the fall of 1946 in District 9 reveals how difficult it could be to "break through" one point. This work team split up to redistribute property in five *tun*, and after three days the team members all came back and reported to the work team captain that the villages were all in good shape, with no problems. The captain, not believing them, sent them back to keep investigating, and after another two days they all discovered problems. The captain also went to one of the villages where the PA had held on to all of the property they confiscated. The captain told them that they had to completely distribute it to the masses, and after a two-day meeting the PA said it was all distributed, and the masses said they all received it. But then the captain asked who was allocated the house in which they were holding the meeting, and no one responded. Then he asked who got the next house over, and again no response. He asked who got the horses in the courtyard, and still no response. Since this was clearly a case of fake redistribution, the captain immediately redistributed the houses and horses, but of course one can imagine what may have happened when the captain and the work team left the area shortly after.[18]

The largest part of the policy process, general mobilization, operated through government directives and leadership meetings. Unfortunately, these are also some of the most ephemeral parts in terms of historical evidence, but Shuangcheng's records contain many clues. Reports from District 2 provide a detailed description of the broader process of going "from point to plane" following the announcement of the Outline Land Law. From November to the end of December 1947, the county carried out policy experiments in villages in Districts 3, 4, and 7. Then in early January, the county government held a meeting of district leaders to discuss the results of these experiments. After returning from this meeting, the District 2 government held three mass meetings of more than fifteen hundred PA representatives at three key *cun* in the district, where they explained the objectives of the policy. After the district leader's speech, representatives from each *tun* split into small groups to discuss how to implement the policy in their village, and from then on each village was basically free to carry out the policy as they saw fit.[19] This process, in other words, involved moving from experiments to general implementation, which depended on issuing directives and holding meetings at each administrative level in succession.[20]

The degree of administrative control achieved through land reform can also be seen in a series of directives communicating from the regional down to the *cun* governments in District 2 following the compilation of the classification registers: On May 10, 1948, the general office of the Northeast CCP Political Council sent out a directive asking provinces to report by May 20 on numbers of rural persons, households, land parcels, and amounts of land, in order to determine how many land deeds were needed. On May 15 the Songjiang provincial government forwarded the directive to county governments, asking them to report back. Two days later, Shuangcheng's county head forwarded the directive to all the district heads in the county, asking them to report back by May 28. On May 22 the District 2 government forwarded the county directive to *cun* heads, asking them to cooperate with PAs to compile the necessary numbers, determine how many deeds they need, and report back by May 25. On May 27 the District 2 head wrote that about half of *cun* have yet to report back, and requested them to report to the district that same night. On May 28 the county head sent out another memo to district heads saying that the deadline is today, but he has not received any reports yet. That same day, the District 2 head submitted his report with the required numbers.[21] The regional government appears to have been a little optimistic in thinking that they could get new statistics on hundreds of thousands of households and millions of land parcels within ten days, and by late May only two out of ten districts in Shuangcheng had even completed recording their classification registers. Nevertheless, this chain of directives demonstrates that the regional government could get in touch with thousands of village cadres within about two weeks' time, a much greater feat than temporarily mobilizing a single struggle meeting in a single village.

Patterns of Land Reform Activity

Shuangcheng's data provides one of the first opportunities to describe the actual outcomes of such policy processes for an entire county. Until now, understandings of land reform have been based almost entirely on policy documents (including work team reports) or anecdotal evidence from select villages. In both cases the narrative's power depends on the assumption that either the policy was applied evenly throughout China (or at least the region in question) or that the single anecdote was typical of most experiences. The problem, however, is that most China scholars also recognize that neither of these assumptions holds true in general for China, even at the regional level. Policies are designed to operate within specific social and geographic boundaries and be adapted to local circumstances, and virtually every village experience is unique enough to be unrepresentative of the next village.

This section explores one very basic but until now virtually unstudied dimension of land reform: the spatial dimension. In part because of the fragmented and selective nature of previously studied sources, it has been impossible to reconstruct geographic descriptions of land reform experiences and analyze developments over time and space. As mentioned in chapter 1, this spatial dimension exists in some form only at the level of entire regions of the country, like between North and South China, old and new liberated areas. Shuangcheng's data, in contrast, make it possible to map out at community-level resolution the virtually complete spatial development of land reform from the first work team experiments to the final redistribution of land for an entire county. The series of maps that follows presents the first ever spatial analysis of land reform events in China, and as such, the methods I use are equally primitive. My analysis involves simply locating places mentioned in work team reports and events recorded in the victim registers, displaying them on maps of the county at different points in time, and then looking for visual patterns and correlations.[22] As the following pages demonstrate, however, this method suffices for making some important new discoveries about how land reform was implemented.

In particular, work reports identify the "points" of work team activity in the county, and the victim registers and later district statistics describe events in the "plane." We can split up work reports into the six local subcampaign stages outlined in chapter 1 and split up events into the two main policy periods of the May Fourth Directive and Outline Land Law (compare with Figure 1). Work report data includes the locations of all villages mentioned in the more than seventy extant work reports in Shuangcheng's county archives (see Appendix E). In many cases the work team may not have actually visited the village mentioned but just heard a rumor or gathered some information about it. These data also include retrospective work team activity—that is, when a later report mentions that another work team had already visited the village. These data should therefore significantly overestimate the actual extent of work team activity. Event data includes events that occurred in the points of work team activity, in addition to the rest of the county for which there is no evidence of work team activity.

The victim registers recorded in the summer of 1947 allow for a more detailed look at the points and plane of the May Fourth Directive period, the first year of land reform in the county. Map 5 illustrates the extent of work team activity during this period, divided into three campaign stages: "Anti-Traitor and Settling Accounts" in fall 1946 (red), "Eliminating Half-Cooked Rice" in spring 1947 (yellow), and "Cutting Down and Digging Up" in summer 1947 (blue). Each marker indicates a *cun* mentioned in a work report. The color of the marker indicates the stage of the work report, and the size of the marker represents the number of *tun* mentioned in the report. For the first year of land reform the CCP did not have a monopoly over violence in Shuangcheng, and early work team activity could be carried out only in certain parts of the county under CCP control (see chapter 3). The red and yellow markers on the map show how land reform work began on the east and west margins of the county, where it was closely associated with CCP military movements. The activity in Districts 8 and 9 is centered on railway stations located in those two districts.[23] Reports likewise mention the stationing of CCP troops in District 5, and records of extensive conscription of civilian support in District 6 in the fall of 1946 also suggest a substantial military presence there.[24] The political divisions of these army units were often the first agents to carry out mass mobilization work, which involved confiscating and redistributing property, in many of the villages marked in red and yellow on the map. This map thus reflects a similar analysis of early CCP activity by Roy Hofheinz Jr., who also concluded that "the expansion of communist forces in any area during any period was likely to be better correlated with communist presence in the vicinity than with any other social phenomenon."[25]

Another feature of work team activity illustrated by this map is that there was often little overlap between campaigns. In the first year of land reform, work teams had visited every district in the county and thirty-nine out of ninety-one *cun*. However, only nine *cun* (10 percent) are mentioned in more than one campaign. Many of these cases are based on retrospective information from later work teams, and no extant reports exist to conduct more detailed comparisons. The two villages in District 8 that appear to have reports from all three campaigns, for example, in reality have extant reports only from the summer of 1947 that mention earlier work team visits. Simply put, this extensive rather than intensive pattern shows that the work team's priority was not helping village communities but fulfilling campaign objectives. Because each campaign was implemented by a new work team and because local circumstances were always in flux, it was probably easier to carry out policy experiments in a new village each time. This may have been effective for policy testing, but for many villages briefly sojourning work teams only reinforced perceptions of state power as distant and spasmodic.

To some extent we can see work teams branching out over time. Activity in the fall of 1946 was concentrated in the narrow corridor between the county seat and southern Harbin, where much of the CCP provincial and regional government was located. In the spring of 1947 there was some limited expansion between Districts 5 and 8, but this appears to be temporary. The summer of 1947 then saw greater expansion into Districts 2, 3, 10, and 11, filling in much of the eastern half of the county. But again, this pattern was more a function of the expansion of CCP control within the county than of progress in mass mobilization. Each new campaign stage highlighted the shortcomings of the previous campaign, but work teams seldom returned to the same villages to correct those shortcomings. Instead, they simply moved on to new village test sites.

From the perspective of the state (i.e., CCP officials at the county level and up), land reform was a continuous process of increasing mobilization, but from the perspective of any given village, there was no unified land reform experience. This also helps to explain why there was little relation between perceived campaign outcomes over time. As described in chapter 5, the final allocation of land in the summer of 1948 that marks the completion of land reform was carried out virtually independent of any previous campaigns. In a way, all of the previous campaigns and work report experiments were simply the means to developing this final policy, not to gradually guide villagers down the road to political and economic emancipation. This is in contrast to each work report and larger official narrative of land reform, in which the process is portrayed as gradually educating, organizing, and mobilizing peasants to take control of village affairs. This gradual process is a myth of the state perspective, as exemplified in Hinton's *Fanshen* and criticized in Edward Friedman and his colleagues' *Chinese Village, Socialist State.*[26] The more complete spatial picture of work team activity in Shuangcheng challenges this mobilization myth that forms the premise of this debate.

The key to integrating these state and village perspectives lies in the "plane" of land reform practices. Shuangcheng's victim registers allow us to map out the distributions of events of land expropriation and violence during the first year of land reform in the county. Together with the map of work team activity, we can furthermore explore the relationships between the points and planes. Map 6 adds the percentage of *cun* land expropriated by the summer of 1947 to our work team activity map. Broadly speaking, the areas with more work team activity in the northeast corner of the county expropriated more than half of all *cun* land, while *cun* in the more remote southwest part of the county expropriated less than half of their land. However, there is no clear linear relationship here. Villages with the most work team activity did not always expropriate the most land, and vice versa. The more impressive part of this picture is that all ninety-one *cun* in the county carried out land expropriation to some extent (the least amount still being several hundred hectares). Even if in the first year most of this expropriation existed on paper only, village PAs still recorded detailed records for thousands of individual landowners.

But by the winter of 1946, CCP officials had already made it clear that such land expropriation was useless if the process did not involve the mobilization and participation of a majority of villagers. Over the first year of land reform in Shuangcheng, this mobilization was manifested in struggle meetings and the public humiliation of local strongmen. Campaigns increasingly expanded the scope of such "struggles," beginning with the most notorious large landlords but eventually including corrupt PA cadres who began abusing their power almost as soon as they took office. Map 7 shows proportions of struggles per one hundred households in the first year of land reform. Here we can see a very different picture of land reform. Struggles are highly concentrated in pockets of work team activity in parts of District 9 and 10, and to a lesser extent in parts of Districts 4, 8, and 11. The unshaded *cun* do not record any events of struggle, and the majority of villages record less than two struggles per one hundred households. This map suggests that political mobilization was highly dependent on the efforts of work teams, but it also reflects the fact that the May Fourth Directive was intentionally cautious about encouraging open conflict. Work teams experimented with it, but in general officials did not openly promote it until the summer of 1947.

There was also not a clear relationship between deaths and the other land reform events just described. As illustrated in Map 8, the few areas of the county responsible for the most deaths do not stand out in terms of land expropriation or other struggles. Although CCP land reform is perhaps best known for using violence to expropriate land and other property, this map suggests that this understanding is based on highly selective information from exceptional cases. This violence is examined in greater detail in the following chapters, but one pattern to point out here is that killings appear to occur more frequently *in between* areas of work team activity. The black spot on the map, where more than twice as many deaths occurred as in the second most violent village, is not mentioned in any extant work reports throughout the entire two years of land reform. This pattern suggests that killing was a consequence not of CCP control but a lack of it. As we will see in chapter 6, the deaths in this spot and District 5 were directly related to the suppression of violent counterrevolutionaries, not land reform mobilization.

Overall, the first year of land reform in Shuangcheng was marked by compliance to CCP policy more than revolutionary support and spontaneous mobilization. CCP control restricted work team activity to certain parts of the county. Mass political mobilization occurred where work teams organized it, but most villages simply complied with CCP directives by demonstrating that they had expropriated land from landlords. Reflecting on this earlier period from the summer of 1947, one work report from District 8 describes how before spring 1947, the work team scrambled to sort out land rights for spring planting, to recruit soldiers in a few villages, and, later, to work on mobilizing bandits to confess their wrongdoings. The work team was coercive and bureaucratic, and the masses passively depended on the work team and received property according to government policy. Only a few exceptional villages were "half-cooked," and the other 99 percent were in chaos.[27] This local response set the stage for the Outline Land Law, a policy aimed at redistributing property in theory but in practice focused more on political mobilization.

Under the Outline Land Law, the focus of work team activity within the county shifted slightly to the south and west. Map 9 illustrates the distribution of work team activity over the three local campaigns of the Outline Land Law: "Equalize Land" in fall 1947 (orange), "Mop-Up" in winter 1947/48 (green), and "Classification" in spring 1948 (purple). As shown on this map, initial work team experiments in the fall of 1947 were concentrated in Districts 3, 4, 8 and 11.[28] However, later activity did not significantly expand beyond these parts of the county. Reports from the winter of 1947/48 primarily document mop-up team activity, which as shown by the green markers on the map remained concentrated in the central-eastern parts of the county, where the CCP presumably had more control. Otherwise, again in this period we can see the spatial disconnects between campaigns, where only three *cun* have evidence from all three local campaigns. All three of these *cun*, moreover, had little or no work team activity before the Outline Land Law (compare with Map 5).

Combining Maps 5 and 9 gives an impressive picture of work team activity covering most of the county, but at the same time it reveals how fragmentary work team experiences were. Although covering 80 percent of *cun* (72/91), work team reports actually only mention just over one third (208/559) of all *tun*, or PAs, in the county. As noted above, moreover, these maps illustrate all of the villages that are simply named in work reports;

extensive, several-page descriptive accounts of land reform experiences exist for only one or two villages per district. Finally, virtually all of the detailed accounts that do exist for those few villages describe only one out of six local land reform campaigns. For the historian, therefore, such work team reports can really be used only to provide anecdotes of particular events in particular villages and should not be considered reliable sources for understanding land reform as a whole, even for a single village.

Evidence on general implementation under the Outline Land Law demonstrates a less "natural" development of land reform over time, suggesting that events continued to be correlated to CCP control more than any intrinsic socioeconomic or other local factors.[29] Extant data for this second year of land reform are limited to district-level statistics recorded in March 1948, but they are still useful for comparing general patterns of land expropriation and violence. Map 10 shows the percentage of land expropriated under the Outline Land Law, which follows an almost identical pattern as we saw in Map 6 for the May Fourth Directive. If there was any continuity over time, we would expect an inverse pattern, in which areas where most of the land had already been expropriated would have less expropriation later, and vice versa. Instead, the pattern more closely reflects work team activity or CCP control rather than the expansion of land reform practices throughout the county. The fact that the northeast side of the county repeatedly expropriated over half of their land also supports claims that the expropriation recorded in the first year was not "real" but either expropriated on paper only or expropriated and then returned later. The details of this redistribution are further addressed in chapter 5.

As will be discussed in the following chapters, the nature of violence under the Outline Land Law was somewhat different than it was under the May Fourth Directive, and this difference was also expressed spatially. Whereas in the first year of land reform, struggle meetings were closely related to work team activity and deaths were inversely related, in the second year struggles and deaths were more closely related to each other and less related to work team activity. Maps 11 and 12 illustrate the distribution of beatings and deaths per one hundred households under the Outline Land Law.[30] As described in work reports, deaths in this period were often the result of beating and interrogating people to turn over their hidden property, which partly explains the closer relationship between beatings and deaths in these maps as compared to the first year, in which struggles were more about public humiliation and deaths were more about counter-revolutionary violence. In terms of work team or mop-up team activity, however, it is interesting to compare Districts 10 and 11. These two neighboring districts had comparatively active mop-up campaigns, but District 10 had exponentially more violence. In fact, District 10 in the winter of 1947/48 represents roughly one-fifth of all recorded deaths for the entire two-year period of land reform in Shuangcheng. The only explanation I have been able to find so far has nothing to do with land reform policies or socioeconomic context but extreme famine conditions produced through a combination of natural disaster and CCP state grain extraction in the 1947 season (see chapter 5). One commonality between overzealous grain extraction and radical violence under the Outline Land Law could be the personality of the district leadership, but the nature of violence during the mop-up campaign/famine seems to have been related more to village desperation than to zealous mass mobilization.

The two-year picture of land reform that emerges from this series of maps is a process in which both work team activity and general policy implementation were influenced by CCP control more than anything else. The northeastern half of the county was consistently more active, while the southwestern half had consistently less work team activity and land reform events like expropriation and violence. Multiple perspectives need to be reconciled here. The events or outcomes of general implementation represent the perspective of all the PAs in the county. PAs in the northeastern half of the county were consistently more responsive to policy directives, partly as a result of more intensive CCP and work team activity in the area. PAs in the southwestern half of the county, in contrast, were less responsive and also saw less work team activity. It is unclear how such areas without a significant and prolonged work team presence experienced land reform, but all sources suggest that it was not very spontaneous or "revolutionary." In this respect, what characterized the completion of land reform was not carrying out a complete series of incremental campaigns in every single village in the county but to some extent striking a balance between formal compliance and effective mobilization.

From the perspective of the CCP state, land reform comprised a composite image of mobilization over time and space in which the experience of one campaign in one village could be replicated ad infinitum at multiple levels. In this view a work team experimentally implements a central policy in one village by educating, organizing, and mobilizing villagers; the results of the experiment are reported back; and the policy is adjusted accordingly. At the central level, this cycle was repeated twice over the course of two years, and at the local level this process was repeated three times within each larger central policy cycle. In this composite image, each campaign was an improvement over the last, in a gradual progression toward the ultimate

goal of politically mobilizing a majority of villagers and equally redistributing all village land. As shown in this chapter, however, the results of policy
experiments came from different villages each time, and in reality not a
single village experienced the entire series of campaigns.

The work team acted as the mediator between state and village perspectives by creating the fragments of village experiences that the state
could then use to piece together its composite image of a revolutionary
movement. Moving on to different villages each time was probably also a
strategy for expanding land reform over space, but the maps in this chapter also demonstrate that this expansion remained limited even from a
county perspective. In reality perhaps it would be more accurate to say that
the CCP was using the entire countryside like a giant sandbox in which
to experiment with different policies. The series of policy campaigns was
designed to help the state figure out the most effective policy, not to help
villagers gradually mobilize, or *fanshen*. In this process the work team also
functioned as a flexible and effective means of training cadres, both old
and new. As such, the work team played a dual role as both policy labora-
tory and training grounds.

The basic pattern of policy implementation described here can be
found in CCP campaigns spanning much of the twentieth century, but
why such a diverse array of campaigns always follows a similar pattern
is still not well understood. Charles Cell explains it as the CCP's quest to
resolve contradictions in society, in which "campaigns are aimed at resolv-
ing these contradictions, and their resolution produces further contradictions needing to be resolved."[31] This perspective may help explain cyclical
campaign patterns and why, for example, the process of land reform in
a place like Shuangcheng was similar to the process of the Jiangxi Soviet's land revolution. Even if the CCP knew exactly what they were doing,
they still had to let the process take its course, because new environments
would yield new results at each step. But insofar as with each campaign
work teams focused the eyes of the state on a new village, they could not
avoid introducing new contradictions and seeing the village through the
lens of previous campaigns, even though those campaigns may not have
affected their newly selected village. This discontinuity between state and
village experiences continued to be a decisive weak point in CCP land
reform and state building in general. In many respects, however, such dis-
continuities also created a useful gray area in which otherwise contradictory local and central interests (e.g., communal political norms and class
struggle narratives) could coexist.

Maps

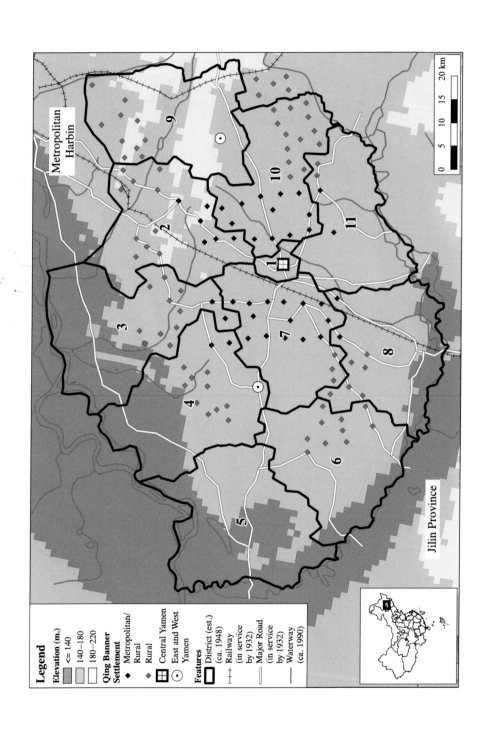

Legend

Elevation (m.)
- <= 140
- 140–180
- 180–220

Qing Banner Settlement
- ◆ Metropolitan/Rural
- ◆ Rural
- ⊞ Central Yamen
- ⊙ East and West Yamen

Features
- ▢ District (est.) (ca. 1948)
- ┼┼ Railway (in service by 1932)
- — Major Road (in service by 1932)
- — Waterway (ca. 1990)

Metropolitan Harbin

Jilin Province

0 5 10 15 20 km

Map 2. Topographical map of Shuangcheng with 120 original village settlements

Sources: Map produced using QGIS 3.8.1. Subcounty administrative boundaries adapted by the author from village addresses recorded in Shuangcheng's classification registers. Original district boundaries and village locations drawn in ArcMap 10 by Deng Ying at The Hong Kong University of Science and Technology using a scanned image of Harbin Transportation Department, "Shuangcheng City Highway and Transportation Map" (n.d.) provided to the author by Ren Yuxue. Village locations and administrative boundaries further georeferenced and revised by the author using Google TerraMetrics map data (2017). Railway and river data from ESRI and Defense Mapping Agency, "Digital Chart of the World Files, China," 1990, reprocessed and distributed by Penn State University, 1997, and released by CHGIS, Version 4. Cambridge: Harvard Yenching Institute and Fudan Center for Historical Geography, Jan. 2007. Road data drawn by the author using georeferenced images from *Manshu 1:200,000 Zu* (Tokyo: Rikuchi Sokuryobu, 1933). made available by Stanford University Library at https://stanford.maps.arcgis.com/apps/SimpleViewer/index.html?appid=c1e874ab-8bec4d6fa5b2e743a77d8ca9. Accessed July 30, 2019. Elevation data from CHGIS, 2015, "CHGIS V5 DEM (Digital Elevation Model)," https://doi.org/10.7910/DVN/E1FHML, Harvard Dataverse, V8.

Notes: The roads shown existed as major roads as early as ca. 1933. Railways running through the county were completed in 1903 (Chinese Eastern Railway, running by the county seat) and 1932 (branch line from Harbin to Jilin City on eastern edge of county) (SCXZ, 66). The major rivers encircling the county also existed ca. 1948, but some of the smaller waterways running into the county may be canals and reservoirs constructed after 1949.

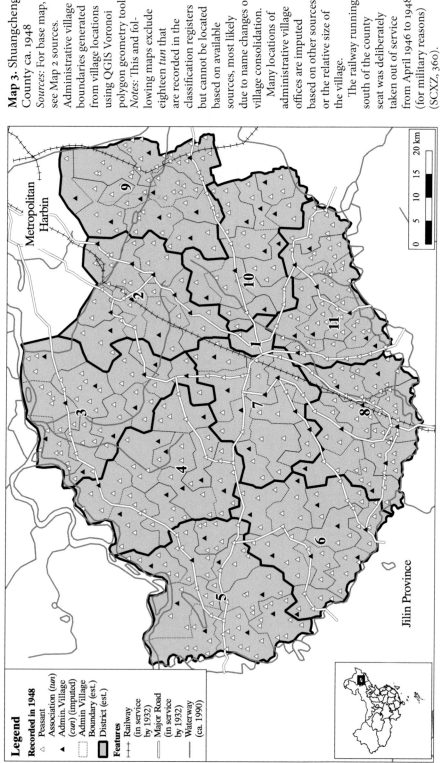

Map 3. Shuangcheng County ca. 1948

Sources: For base map, see Map 2 sources. Administrative village boundaries generated from village locations using QGIS Voronoi polygon geometry tool.

Notes: This and following maps exclude eighteen *tun* that are recorded in the classification registers but cannot be located based on available sources, most likely due to name changes or village consolidation.

Many locations of administrative village offices are imputed based on other sources or the relative size of the village.

The railway running south of the county seat was deliberately taken out of service from April 1946 to 1948 (for military reasons) (SCXZ, 360).

Metropolitan Harbin

Jilin Province

Legend

Recorded in 1948

△ Peasant Association (*tun*)

▲ Admin. Village (*cun*) (imputed)

⬚ Admin Village Boundary (est.)

▬ District (est.)

Features

┼┼ Railway (in service by 1932)

━ Major Road (in service by 1932)

━ Waterway (ca. 1990)

0 5 10 15 20 km

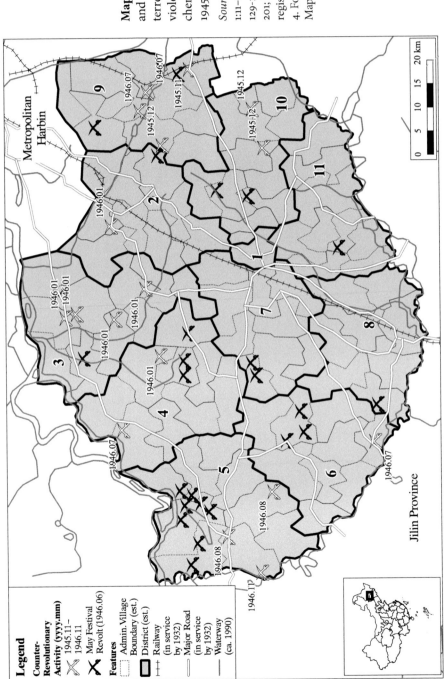

Map 4. Locations and dates of counterterrevolutionary violence in Shuangcheng County, 1945–1946

Sources: SCWZ, 1:11–19; 129-1-3, 11, 43; 129-1-16, 131, 175–76, 201; linked victim registers; SCJZSGS, 4. For base map, see Map 2 sources.

Legend

Counter-Revolutionary Activity (yyyy.mm)

✗ 1945.11– 1946.11

✗ May Festival Revolt (1946.06)

Features

Admin. Village Boundary (est.)

District (est.)

╬ Railway (in service by 1932)

Major Road (in service by 1932)

Waterway (ca. 1990)

Metropolitan Harbin

Jilin Province

0 5 10 15 20 km

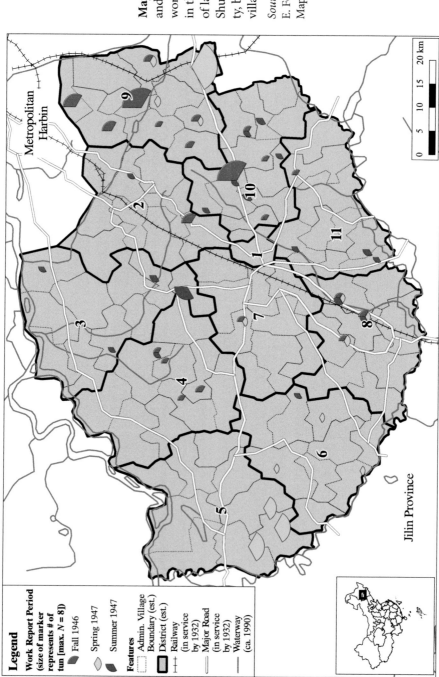

Map 5. Locations and frequency of work team activity in the first year of land reform in Shuangcheng County, by administrative village, 1946–1947.

Sources: See Appendix E. For base map, see Map 2 sources.

Metropolitan Harbin

Jilin Province

Legend

Work Report Period
(size of marker represents # of tun [max. *N* = 8])

◆ Fall 1946
◆ Spring 1947
◆ Summer 1947

Features

Admin. Village Boundary (est.)

District (est.)

┼┼┼ Railway (in service by 1932)

Major Road (in service by 1932)

Waterway (ca. 1990)

0   5   10   15   20 km

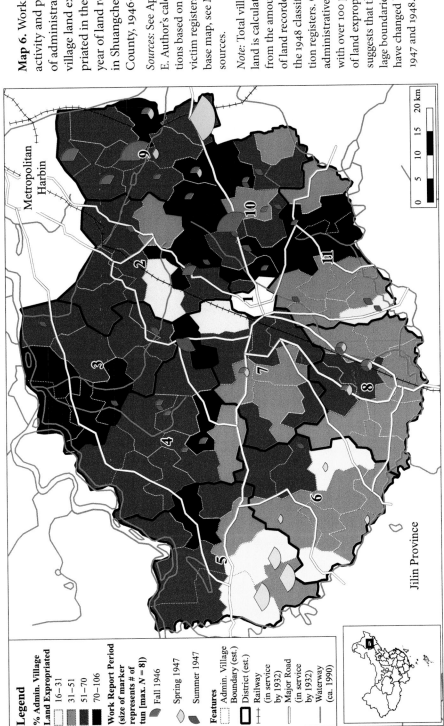

Map 6. Work team activity and percent of administrative village land expropriated in the first year of land reform in Shuangcheng County, 1946–1947

Sources: See Appendix E. Author's calculations based on linked victim registers. For base map, see Map 2 sources.

Note: Total village land is calculated from the amount of land recorded in the 1948 classification registers. One administrative village with over 100 percent of land expropriated suggests that the village boundaries may have changed between 1947 and 1948.

Metropolitan Harbin

Jilin Province

Legend

% Admin. Village Land Expropriated

- 16–31
- 31–51
- 51–70
- 70–106

Work Report Period
(size of marker represents # of tun [max. *N* = 8])

- Fall 1946
- Spring 1947
- Summer 1947

Features

- Admin. Village Boundary (est.)
- District (est.)
- Railway (in service by 1932)
- Major Road (in service by 1932)
- Waterway (ca. 1990)

0   5   10   15   20 km

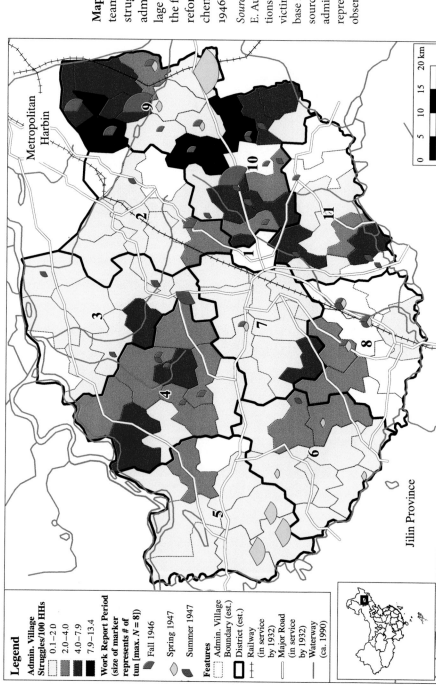

Map 7. Work team activity and struggles per 100 administrative villages households in the first year of land reform in Shuangcheng County, 1946–1947

Sources: See Appendix E. Author's calculations based on linked victim registers. For base map, see Map 2 sources. Unshaded administrative villages represent missing observations.

Metropolitan Harbin

Jilin Province

Legend

Admin. Village Struggles/100 HHs

- [ ] 0.1–2.0
- 2.0–4.0
- 4.0–7.9
- 7.9–13.4

Work Report Period (size of marker represents # of tun [max. N = 8])

- Fall 1946
- Spring 1947
- Summer 1947

Features

- [ ] Admin. Village Boundary (est.)
- [ ] District (est.)
- Railway (in service by 1932)
- Major Road (in service by 1932)
- Waterway (ca. 1990)

0   5   10   15   20 km

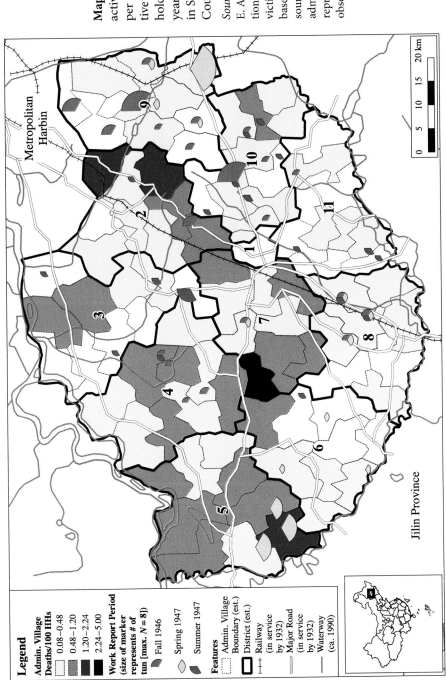

Map 8. Work team activity and deaths per 100 administrative village households in the first year of land reform in Shuangcheng County, 1946–1947

Sources: See Appendix E. Author's calculations based on linked victim registers. For base map, see Map 2 sources. Unshaded administrative villages represent missing observations.

Legend

Admin. Village Deaths/100 HHs

- 0.08–0.48
- 0.48–1.20
- 1.20–2.24
- 2.24–5.00

Work Report Period (size of marker represents # of tun [max. N = 8])

- Fall 1946
- Spring 1947
- Summer 1947

Features

- Admin. Village Boundary (est.)
- District (est.)
- Railway (in service by 1932)
- Major Road (in service by 1932)
- Waterway (ca. 1990)

Metropolitan Harbin

Jilin Province

0   5   10   15   20 km

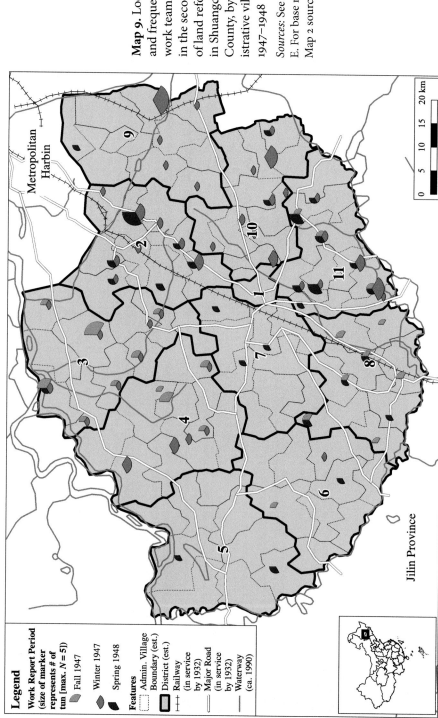

Map 9. Locations and frequency of work team activity in the second year of land reform in Shuangcheng County, by administrative village, 1947–1948

Sources: See Appendix E. For base map, see Map 2 sources.

Legend

Work Report Period
(size of marker represents # of tun [max. *N* = 5])

- Fall 1947
- Winter 1947
- Spring 1948

Features

- Admin. Village Boundary (est.)
- District (est.)
- Railway (in service by 1932)
- Major Road (in service by 1932)
- Waterway (ca. 1990)

Metropolitan Harbin

Jilin Province

0 5 10 15 20 km

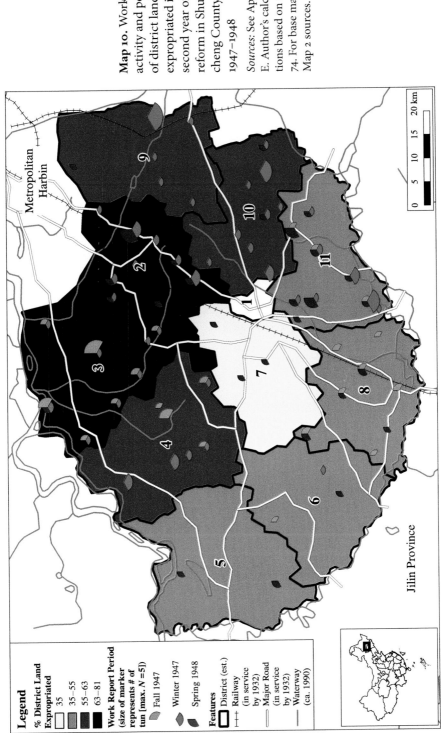

Map 10. Work team activity and percent of district land expropriated in the second year of land reform in Shuangcheng County, 1947–1948

Sources: See Appendix E. Author's calculations based on 129-174. For base map, see Map 2 sources.

Metropolitan Harbin

Jilin Province

Legend

% District Land Expropriated

35
35–55
55–63
63–81

Work Report Period (size of marker represents # of tun [max. *N* =5])

Fall 1947
Winter 1947
Spring 1948

Features

District (est.)

Railway (in service by 1932)

Major Road (in service by 1932)

Waterway (ca. 1990)

0 5 10 15 20 km

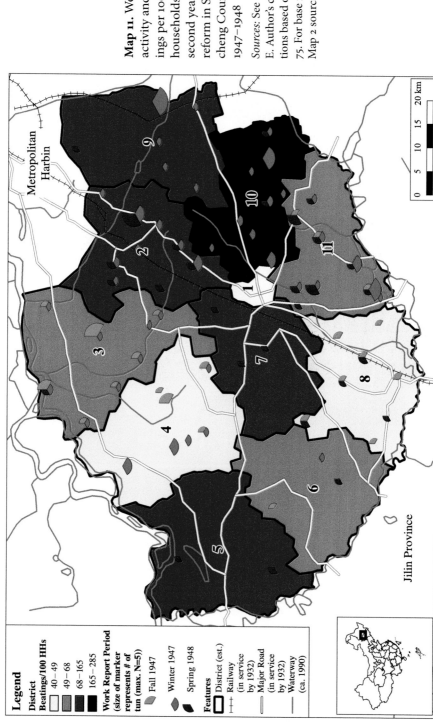

Map 11. Work team activity and beatings per 100 district households in the second year of land reform in Shuang-cheng County, 1947–1948

Sources: See Appendix E. Author's calculations based on 129-1-75. For base map, see Map 2 sources.

Legend

District

Beatings/100 HHs

- 40–49
- 49–68
- 68–165
- 165–285

Work Report Period
(size of marker represents # of tun (max. N=5)

- Fall 1947
- Winter 1947
- Spring 1948

Features

- District (est.)
- Railway (in service by 1932)
- Major Road (in service by 1932)
- Waterway (ca. 1990)

Metropolitan Harbin

Jilin Province

0 5 10 15 20 km

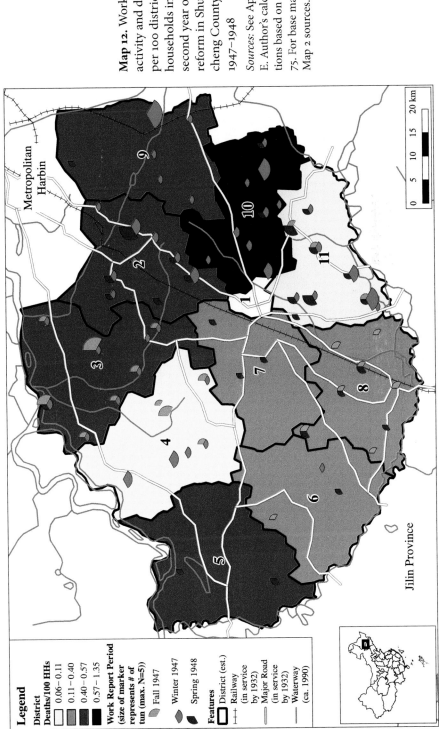

Map 12. Work team activity and deaths per 100 district households in the second year of land reform in Shuang-cheng County, 1947–1948

Sources: See Appendix E. Author's calculations based on 129-175. For base map, see Map 2 sources.

Legend

District
Deaths/100 HHs
- 0.06 – 0.11
- 0.11 – 0.40
- 0.40 – 0.57
- 0.57 – 1.35

Work Report Period
(size of marker represents # of tun (max. N=5))
- Fall 1947
- Winter 1947
- Spring 1948

Features
- District (est.)
- Railway (in service by 1932)
- Major Road (in service by 1932)
- Waterway (ca. 1990)

Metropolitan Harbin

Jilin Province

0 5 10 15 20 km

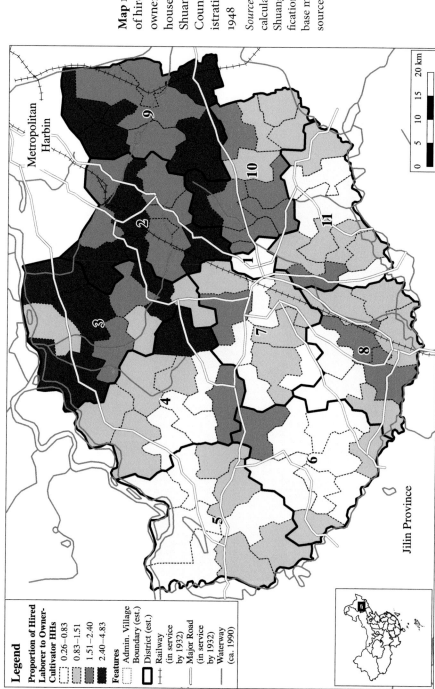

Map 13. Proportion of hired laborer to owner-cultivator households in Shuangcheng County, by administrative village, 1948

Sources: Author's calculations based on Shuangcheng classification registers. For base map, see Map 2 sources.

Legend

Proportion of Hired Laborer to Owner-Cultivator HHs
- 0.26–0.83
- 0.83–1.51
- 1.51–2.40
- 2.40–4.83

Features
- Admin. Village Boundary (est.)
- District (est.)
- Railway (in service by 1932)
- Major Road (in service by 1932)
- Waterway (ca. 1990)

Metropolitan Harbin

Jilin Province

0 5 10 15 20 km

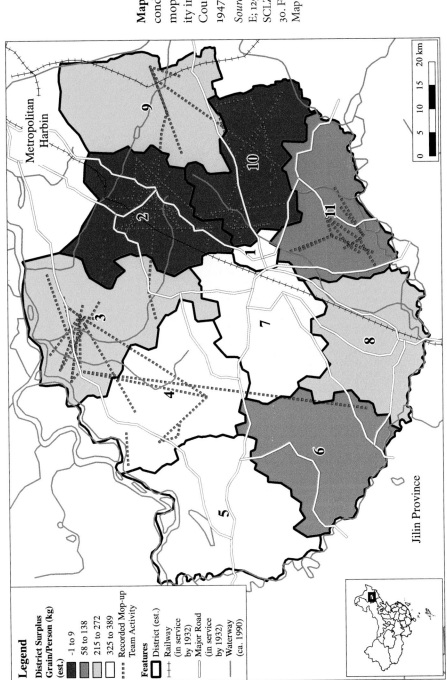

Map 14. Famine conditions and mop-up team activity in Shuangcheng County, winter 1947/48

Sources: See Appendix E; 129-1-31, 22–27; SCLZ, 84–99; 129-2-30. For base map, see Map 2 sources.

Legend

District Surplus Grain/Person (kg) (est.)

- -1 to 9
- 58 to 138
- 215 to 272
- 325 to 389
- Recorded Mop-up Team Activity

Features

- District (est.)
- Railway (in service by 1932)
- Major Road (in service by 1932)
- Waterway (ca. 1990)

Metropolitan Harbin

Jilin Province

0 5 10 15 20 km

CHAPTER 5

Property and Violence

Competing claims to the legitimacy of the use of violence to supplant or support different property arrangements are often an integral part of political regime change, especially in Chinese history. The story in this chapter focuses on the extent to which competing claims over property in Shuangcheng led to violence. Violence is an extreme expression of power, ultimately manifested as control over life or death. The basic implication of violent conflict over property is that property is an important source of power that its owner will not willingly or readily give up. This chapter challenges this idea of the essential relationship between property and power by first demonstrating that the violence of land reform was not directly related to conflicts over property ownership—landed property in particular. This chapter examines the entire process of the redistribution of property in Shuangcheng, from preexisting economic conditions to the completion of land reform, in order to show how and why the violence of land reform involved conflicts between villages and between village and state actors, not between property owners and the propertyless. Then in chapter 6, I focus on practices of violence to show how conflicts over political status and entitlements led to more violence than conflicts over property. Combining these two chapters, I argue that violence followed lines of political conflict, rather than economic conflict, because such political relationships were a more important source of power in Chinese society.[1]

In this chapter I begin with a brief introduction to the nature of Shuangcheng's rural economy and relations of production on the eve of land reform. Local CCP investigations and more systematic data suggest that Shuangcheng's economy was significantly commercialized and characterized by relatively capitalistic relations of agricultural production. Considering that the Northeast in the 1940s was one of the most industrialized and globalized macroregions of China, rivaled only by Jiangnan, the nature of Shuangcheng's rural economy should come as no surprise.[2]

In this respect Shuangcheng also appears to support Jeffrey M. Paige's "land and wages" theory of agrarian revolution, but as I show in practice there is little evidence in Shuangcheng of Paige's rural class conflict.[3] In the end, the implications of this chapter are more in line with relational theories of property rights, in which social relations, not legal or private rights, play a definitive role in property relations.[4]

An analysis of thousands of instances of expropriation and violence in Shuangcheng's five hundred-some *tun* demonstrates that in the first year of land reform most expropriation of land did not involve interpersonal violence, and most violence did not involve property. On the contrary, local strongmen preempted CCP policies by voluntarily donating land, and peasants were reluctant to attack landowners. Many previous land reform narratives describe similar practices and interpret them as either justifying violent revolution or challenging theories of class struggle.[5] More systematic evidence from Shuangcheng makes it possible to draw broader conclusions about the nature of rural Chinese society. "Peaceful" land redistribution was more than just a "landlord trick"; it reflected the nature of social and political relationships between the state, local leaders, villagers, and agricultural production. Compliance was the primary weapon local leaders used in dealing with the state (i.e., county officials), and they complied with land reform policies more to maintain their political position vis-à-vis the state than to evade economic loss. In contrast to Prasenjit Duara, who defines power as the ability to obtain compliance, here I suggest that in the context of Chinese society compliance was regularly used to undermine power rather than to reinforce it.[6]

An analysis of less systematic data from the winter of 1947/48 reveals a surge of violence related to the expropriation of household belongings, carried out in the context of wartime state extraction and widespread famine. This violence resulted from conflicts over non-landed property, and these conflicts were between the state and the village and between neighboring villages, not between competing social classes, rich and poor, within a given village community. Conditions may have been so dire that even after confiscating all village wealth, many villages still did not have enough to survive and were forced to raid other villages, but even so there is more evidence of village solidarity than class solidarity.[7]

Finally, the egalitarian per capita redistribution of land in the summer of 1948 that marked the completion of land reform in Shuangcheng was surprisingly systematic and uniform. In light of the initial "peaceful" and passive redistribution of land, one may wonder why the CCP didn't just begin with this egalitarian redistribution in the first place. Here again this process betrays the fact that the essential goal of land reform was a redistribution of political power. Redistributing land, at least on paper, was easy. The hard part was making a majority of villagers actively participate in the process. In this process, education and political mobilization were more important than coercion and material incentives. Retributive struggle and material incentives were used as catalysts in a two-year fermentation of "the consciousness of the masses," and the completion of land reform was defined by villagers' personal investment in redistribution more than the actual results of redistribution.

These findings challenge prevailing understandings of land reform, all of which focus on violent conflict in the name of landed property. In Chinese society, political status was the primary determinant of property entitlement, both before and after the revolution. Property holding was a function of state-defined status, an entitlement, not a source of political power or a right.[8] Violent conflict occurred in the name of political status. Initially, when the CCP's own political status was suspect, entitlement to redistributed property was defined simply by one's participation in a CCP land reform campaign—for example, by helping a work team struggle against a local strongman. By the summer of 1948, however, as a result of the CCP's consolidation of power in the region, the CCP was able to define their own status hierarchy and formal classification itself became the primary means of defining property entitlements in the new society.[9]

As such, land reform experiences in Shuangcheng provide strong evidence that the fault lines of social tension did not run between socioeconomic groups but between levels in a political hierarchy.[10] In the context of China, state confiscation and redistribution of wealth was not so revolutionary, because in many ways the distribution of wealth was one of the traditional, expected roles of the state.[11] What was most revolutionary about the CCP's land reform was its confiscation and redistribution of the political status of local strongmen, which in theory involved not only a transfer to different leaders but also the restructuring of grassroots power from local autocrats to a representative or self-governing system. For the Chinese state as a whole, the logic had little to do with the economic structure of society. The early twentieth-century modern ideal of representative government, combined with the bottom-up hierarchical structure of Chinese society defined by family and village units, dictated that representative politics had to begin at the bottom, if they were to begin at all. In comparison, the top-down *political* reforms of the late Qing and Nationalist governments and the bottom-up *economic* reforms of the Nationalist agrarian programs were misguided.

The success of the CCP depended on their ability to concentrate all social pressure on local strongmen, that political class who occupied the lowest level of power.[12] Over the course of land reform in Shuangcheng, the CCP no doubt had many shortcomings, including the heavy extraction of resources for military support, mishandling of natural disasters, and the ineptitude and corruption of many newly appointed CCP village leaders and cadres. But rather than leading to society's mass rejection of the CCP system as a whole, the integration of this political system within society made it possible to blame the immediate power holders in local society instead of the state itself (because the state was not a separate entity divorced from society). In other words, the Chinese state's characteristic integration of state and society did not imply less conflict but only that political conflicts were more social in nature.

Rural Economy

Even more so than English translations suggest, the language of CCP land reform overwhelmingly focused on land. The May Fourth Directive's original title is "Directive on the Land Question," Hinton's "Draft Agrarian Law" is literally the "Outline Land Law," and what is commonly called the 1950 Agrarian Reform Law of the PRC is literally the "Land Reform Law."[13] The central slogan of agrarian reform in China from the time of Sun Yat-sen was "Land to the Tiller!" At the time of land reform in China, tillers, or those who labored on the land, comprised about 90 percent of the rural population and about three-quarters of the entire population. In the context of China's traditional agrarian political economy, land symbolized the foundation of the Chinese state itself. Land reform could therefore be interpreted as both a general call for widespread social equality and a fundamental revitalization of the nation.

Shuangcheng's rural economy was distinct from the North and South China macroregions, the two major focuses of previous land reform studies. Since there is already general consensus about these regional economies, I only briefly outline them here. On the eve of land reform in China, land was more equally distributed than in most agrarian societies, past or present.[14] In the North China plain's dryland agriculture, as exemplified by Hebei Province, owner-cultivators or middle peasants comprised the vast majority of villagers, tenancy and wage labor were relatively limited, and landholding was relatively equal.[15] South China's rice agriculture, in contrast, was characterized by large proportions of absentee landlords and tenants, active and complex tenancy and wage labor relations, and higher inequality of landholding.[16] Shuangcheng was characterized by highly commercialized, large-scale dryland agriculture, with high proportions of absentee landlords and wage laborers, high inequality, but relatively low tenancy.[17] It took some time for CCP cadres from North China to understand this rural economy. For example, when the CCP implemented rent reduction policies in Shuangcheng in the spring of 1946, tenant rich peasants were the unintended beneficiaries, while the majority of the population, landless laborers, saw little benefit.[18]

As outlined in chapter 1, traditional narratives of China's land reform are split into two periods, before and after 1949/50, with the earlier period portrayed as more violent and the later period as more formalized. These two periods also correspond to a North-South divide, which thus leads to either conceptions of violent land reform in a countryside where the entire premise of the reform (land inequality) was misguided (in the North), or formal land reform in a countryside where the reform could accomplish a fair redistribution relatively painlessly through a transfer of rights from absentee landlords to their tenants (in the South).[19] Shuangcheng, and Northeast China in general, presents a third model of early, violent land reform in a countryside where, at least in principle, such reforms could be accomplished through a simple transfer of rights.

But simply measuring land ownership and its distribution among the population does not tell us very much about different households' actual economic relations to land. The economic investigation mentioned in chapter 4 provides details on the pre–land reform incomes of lower-class households in a village located about fifteen kilometers from the Shuangcheng County seat. In this village, just over one-quarter of villagers owned any land at all. Another half rented land, while the last quarter relied almost entirely on rural wage labor. Overall, land was the primary source of income for just under half of village households. Figure 9 shows the composition of household incomes for the nearly three-quarters of households in the village who were classified as landless (N = 301). There is no similar information on landed households, but here I assume that they all primarily depended on income from land. At least at the aggregate level, this figure demonstrates a close correlation between a household's class status and primary source of income on the eve of land reform.

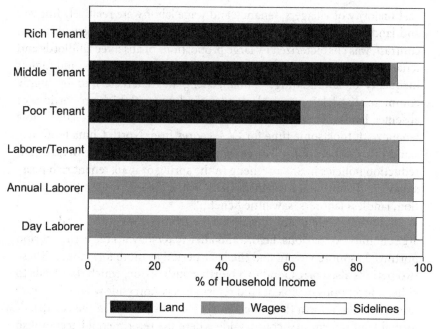

Figure 9. Composition of household incomes of landless households in one administrative village, Shuangcheng County, 1946. Author's calculations based on 129-2-3, 54–59.

Further details on the expenditures of these landless households suggest that on the eve of land reform in Shuangcheng, tenancy was not a viable way to earn a living. As shown in Table 10, after subtracting living costs, farm inputs, rent, and taxes from their gross annual income, only rich tenants and hired laborers had something left over at the end of the season. Middle and poor tenants were a dying breed, and soon enough most of them would have to move either up or down this ranking in order to survive. This table is thus economic evidence that in Shuangcheng a reform of land tenure was necessary to prevent rural society from polarizing into a few large managerial farms hiring masses of wage laborers.[20] Economically, it is also clear that the easiest way to save tenants was to remove rent from their list of production costs. As shown in Figure 10, rents accounted for some 60 percent of middle and poor tenant production costs. For both of these groups, rent meant the difference between deficit and surplus.

On the other side of the equation was the rentier class of landlords,

Table 10. Mean Annual Household Surplus of Landless Households in One Administrative Village, Shuangcheng County, 1946

Class	Mean Annual Household Surplus (kg of millet)
Rich Tenant	775.9
Middle Tenant	−42.0
Poor Tenant	−232.7
Laborer/Tenant	273.2
Annual Laborer	16.0
Day Laborer	304.0

Source: Author's calculations based on 129-2-3, 54–59.

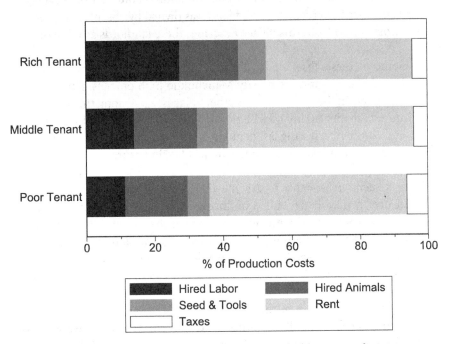

Figure 10. Mean production costs of landless households in one administrative village, Shuangcheng County, 1946. Author's calculations based on 129-2-3, 57–59. Rents are not recorded for laborer/tenants.

although it is unclear how dependent they actually were on income from land rent. For example, a large absentee landlord in one village in District 3 is recorded in the expropriation registers as owning nearly one hundred hectares of land before expropriation, placing him in the top 1 percent of landowners in the village. Based on this fact alone, one could assume that a majority of the man's income came from renting out this land. However, a work report from this village mentions that the man also owned two ironworks factories in Harbin and Dalian, two of the most industrialized cities in China at the time, producing ships and arms for the Japanese.[21] In light of these enterprises, one could safely assume that his landhold-ings were far from his main source of income. Unfortunately, there is not enough systematic information to determine the incomes of most land-lord households in Shuangcheng, one-third of whom were recorded in the expropriation registers as absentee landlords.[22] Although few absentees would have been such large industrialists, most of them probably did not directly rely on their landholdings as their primary source of income.[23]

In the particular village under consideration, about half of all village land and over 85 percent of rented land was owned by absentee landlords. The work report from this village describes these landlords as follows:

> Some of these absentee landlords live in China Proper or South Manchuria . . . and are mostly Manchukuo high officials. Another group live in the county seat or other villages. . . . Among this group are merchants (many of whom managed distribution and traitor-ous commerce during Manchukuo), others who worked for the Japanese in the past, and some who just live in leisure.[24]

Here it seems reasonable to assume that only the last group, who "live in leisure," primarily depended on income from land rent, while the rest were more similar to the previous example of the industrialist from Dis-trict 3. In addition, there were twenty-five resident landlord households in the village, but altogether they owned less than one-fifth of village land (about four hundred hectares) and rented out less than half this amount. This means that many of these households were managerial landlords who oversaw the cultivation of their own land and that overall less than half of the income from landlord-owned land came from rents. If we were to strictly focus on land tenure problems, therefore, in this village there would be about a dozen rentier households and over sixty tenant households with an annual deficit, in total no more than one-fifth of all village households.

Nevertheless, the premise of CCP land reform was that the three-quarters of landless households in the village wanted to possess their own land. For half of these households who were hired wage laborers, however, it is not clear that they were either willing or able to manage their own farm. The reality was that under the circumstances, making a profit from land was not easy, and it was also not easy to convince many villagers otherwise. At the same time, hired laborers were indeed heavily exploited, and after working all year round they had little to show for it at the end of the year. In principle, therefore, they would probably be content with better wages. Given the nature of Shuangcheng's rural economy at the time, however, the only thing the CCP had to offer them was land.

This reevaluation of rural classes based on their relations to land suggests that Shuangcheng's rural economy was already undergoing profound changes. In theory, land reform was designed for a rural economy in which a small rentier class possessed a majority of land and lived off rents, while the majority of peasants labored on the land in exchange for bare subsistence. However, the timing of land reform was perhaps more important. In reality, if landlords overwhelmingly lived off rents and peasants overwhelmingly lived off rented land, then a land reform would be difficult to carry out.[25] By the eve of land reform in Shuangcheng, however, a significant proportion of landlords used their land to invest in urban enterprises, and a majority of villagers gave up land altogether and labored for wages. Not only tenants but rentiers too were a dying breed, which made it possible for the CCP to succeed in land reform and take the lion's share of the credit before it was too late.[26]

A simple spatial analysis further illustrates how Shuangcheng was in the midst of a transformation in land relations on the eve of land reform. Map 13 shows the proportions of hired laborer to owner-cultivator households (small rich, middle, and poor peasants) recorded in the 1948 classification registers. As demonstrated above, these classifications fit closely to actual economic conditions on the eve of land reform. Hired laborers made a living from wages in cash or kind and were no longer directly dependent on land. Small rich, middle, and poor peasants, in contrast, depended primarily on owning and cultivating their own land. The key feature of Map 13 is that metropolitan Harbin, the capital of Heilongjiang Province, is located in the upper right-hand corner. *Cun* closer to this metropolis could have over four times as many hired laborer as owner-cultivator households, while *cun* farther away had up to four times as many owner-cultivator as hired laborer households. Here we can see that Harbin's market, which was semicolonial and highly export-oriented under Manchukuo, penetrated halfway into the county and created a large population of landless agricultural wage laborers.[27] Moreover, looking more closely within the county, *cun* near train stations—located in the middle of District 2, the southeastern corner of District 9, and the middle of District 8—also had relatively higher proportions of hired laborer households. Within this context of commercialized, not "feudal," agriculture, the CCP occupied Shuangcheng and began to carry out the expropriation and reallocation of farmland.

Comparing this map with the maps described in chapter 4, there also appears to be a correlation between land reform events and the proportion of hired laborers. As shown in chapter 4, the northeast side of the county saw more expropriation and violence, especially after the Outline Land Law. In terms of expropriation, it is likely that the higher concentrations of landholding and absentee landlordism on the northeast side of the county made it easier to expropriate higher proportions of land. As we will see below, this often had little relation to violence. Based on work team reports and counterrevolutionary activity in this part of the county, it is also not clear that the CCP revolution naturally flourished because of the high proportion of hired laborers in the area. In the end it appears as if the proximity to Harbin played a larger role in determining both rural socioeconomic structure and CCP control in this part of the county.

The "Peaceful Redistribution of Land"

In the fall of 1946 when land reform experiments were just beginning in Shuangcheng, one CCP county work team reported from District 9 that "peaceful land redistribution is very serious and exists in all the villages. More villages carry out peaceful land redistribution than those that redistribute land through struggle."[28] Throughout the first year of land reform in Shuangcheng, the CCP was faced with the problem of peaceful redistribution more often than landlord resistance. In other words, local strongmen's first reactions to government directives were compliance. The problem for the CCP county government, however, was that this outward compliance was used to mask intra-village noncompliance and is proof that the new government was still incapable of controlling what happened in village communities. As we already saw in chapter 4, the iterative and cyclical nature of CCP policies was in part a strategy for overcoming the impotence of direct policy implementation.

In Northeast China, freshly liberated from fourteen years of Japanese colonialism, this gradual process began almost immediately with the expropriation and redistribution of former Manchukuo government and Japanese colonial land. The earliest extant CCP county government notice in the Shuangcheng County archives, dated December 5, 1945, announces that all land seized by the Manchukuo government for Japanese colonization was to be returned to its original owner. Completely devoid of any revolutionary language, and even using the term "original landlord" (原地主), this notice appears as if it could have been issued by the KMT, not a revolutionary CCP government.[29] Three months later, on March 4, 1946, the Songjiang provincial working committee (the province to which Shuangcheng then belonged) promulgated a document titled "The Chinese Communist Songjiang Provincial Working Committee's Preliminary Methods for Handling Enemy Property," which called for the equal redistribution of Manchukuo government and Japanese colonial land to landless and land-poor peasants. This document references "Mr. Sun Yatsen's principle of 'Land to the Tiller'" but also explicitly states that "no change should be made to any privately owned land."[30] Two weeks later, on March 20, 1946, the CCP Northeast Regional Bureau issued a directive titled "Chinese Communist Central Northeast Bureau Directive on Handling Japanese Manchukuo Land." In addition to ramped up revolutionary language throughout the directive, the first article states, "The property and land rights of the people should be protected. Other than enemy land and the land of Japanese nationals and large traitors, no other persons are allowed to be illegally infringed on."[31]

Thus, even before the May Fourth Directive, we can already find gradually intensifying and contradictory policies of land expropriation and redistribution. Of course, seizing the abandoned land of a defeated enemy regime was minimally controversial. The Shuangcheng County notice simply returns it to its original owner. Three months later, however, the provincial document claims that this land should be equally redistributed to landless and land-poor peasants, and the regional directive expands the scope of expropriation to include the "land of Japanese nationals and large traitors." There are virtually no extant sources describing the effects of these policies in Shuangcheng, but in theory, if the first policy were carried out and enemy land returned to its original owners, then the second policy would necessarily involve expropriating these owners in order to redistribute the land to peasants. On top of this, the third policy then allowed for the further expropriation of some private individual land, albeit most "Japanese nationals and large traitors" would have abandoned their land and fled by then. Nevertheless, these policies no doubt reflected the changing political position of the CCP in the region more than the realities of how enemy land was being dealt with. As far as I know, there was not a significant amount of such enemy land in Shuangcheng, and early land reform work reports in the fall of 1946 treat villages as if nothing had changed over the past year.[32]

Actual records of land expropriation and redistribution in Shuangcheng come from the expropriation registers, compiled in the summer of 1947, and the classification registers, compiled in the summer of 1948. Together, these two sources document the distribution of land on the eve of land reform, at the end of the May Fourth Directive phase, and at the completion of land reform, as shown in Figure 11. This figure highlights the main features of Shuangcheng's land reform experience. First, land was very unequally distributed on the eve of land reform around 1946: the top 10 percent of households possessed 75 percent of farmland in the county, and the bottom 50 percent of households possessed virtually no land. Second, under the May Fourth Directive, more than half of all farmland in the county was expropriated by the summer of 1947. There are no direct records of how this land was redistributed, but qualitative evidence suggests that it was redistributed "unfairly." The dotted line represents the estimated redistribution of land in the summer of 1947 if poor peasants and hired laborers received only half of their equal per capita share. Third, in the summer of 1948 all farmland in the county was redistributed on a highly equal per capita basis according to the Outline Land Law. In theory, if this redistribution was carried out on top of the previous one (the dotted line) then the change from 1947 to 1948 was much less dramatic than that from 1946 to 1947, but from the maps in chapter 4 we know that much of the same land was redistributed multiple times.

The May Fourth Directive, which guided the first half of CCP land reform from May 1946 to October 1947, was a transitional policy between rent reduction measures in effect since 1942 and the complete redistribution of all land under the Outline Land Law.[33] This policy was cautious and began by claiming that in the course of mild agrarian reform policies in recent years, peasants tended to spontaneously move toward the direct expropriation and redistribution of village land. This policy overwhelmingly focused on classifying people and prescribing how they should be treated in the course of these changing land relations. Of the first nine articles outlining different categories of people, eight stress restraint and

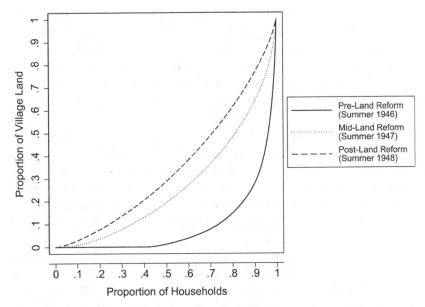

Figure 11. Household Distribution of Land in Shuangcheng County, 1946–1948. Author's calculations based on linked expropriation registers and classification registers.

1. Pre–land reform distribution: The landholding of households not recorded in the 1947 expropriation registers is estimated based on their class status as recorded in the 1948 classification registers and local standards of landholding (hired laborers have 0 land, poor peasants have 2 *mu* per person, middle peasants have 5 *mu* per person, and rich peasants have 8 *mu* per person).

2. Mid–land reform distribution: The land received by households not recorded in the 1947 expropriation registers is estimated based on the total amount of land expropriated divided by the number of persons registered as poor peasants or hired laborers in the 1948 classification registers. Each poor peasant or hired laborer household is then allocated half of their arithmetically equal per capita share of expropriated land (this assumes that the redistribution was not egalitarian).

3. Post–land reform distribution is based on complete landholding of every registered household in the classification registers, excluding public lands (approx. 3 percent of registered county land).

some form of concession.[34] Regarding the "various solutions to the land problem" developed by the masses, the eleventh article lists:

1. Confiscate and redistribute the land of major Han traitors.
2. After rent reduction, landlords voluntarily sell off their land, and their tenants are given priority in purchasing this land.

3. Because tenancy rights are guaranteed after rent reduction, landlords voluntarily give their tenants 70 to 80 percent of the land and retain 20 to 30 percent to cultivate themselves.
4. In the course of settling accounts of rent, interest, land seizures, labor obligations, and other irrational exploitation, landlords sell their land to peasants in order to clear their debts.[35]

Only the first point here involves direct expropriation, and it is limited to the most despised group of people in postwar China—Japanese collaborators. The second and third points are logical continuations of earlier rent reduction policies. The fourth point implies a style of settling accounts that went beyond financial accounts and often involved moral retributive justice (i.e., settling scores), although here the policy still suggests some degree of economic compensation.

As mentioned in chapter 1, in Shuangcheng and other parts of the Northeast rent reduction policies played a minor role and the Anti-Traitor and Settling Accounts campaign only began after the May Fourth Directive, which created an environment quite different from that described in the directive. For starters, agrarian reform in Shuangcheng included just the first and fourth types of expropriation mentioned here. The expropriation registers provide the most systematic data of land expropriation and redistribution under the May Fourth Directive ever studied. In these registers recording over six thousand individual instances of expropriation and accompanying work reports, there is no evidence of landlord compensation. In practice, moreover, the fourth type of expropriation was treated more like landlords using their land to compensate peasants in kind.

Despite the lack of compensation, hundreds of landlords in Shuangcheng voluntarily donated their land for redistribution. As shown in Table 11, in more than two-thirds of cases in *cun* with non-missing observations of violence, land expropriation was carried out without recourse to interpersonal violence. Over seven hundred of these cases record that the landowner either donated his land or was innocent or absent (i.e., there was no explicit crime or justification for expropriation).[36] Why would so many landlords give up their land, and why was it so easy for the CCP to take land without a fight? There are two plausible reasons for this counterintuitive finding. One, it was not worth it. In the most industrialized region of China, agricultural land was not the only or even the best way to make a living, so if the government wanted land, they could have it (of course this implies some degree of political coercion, too). CCP work reports

Table 11. Most Violent Outcomes of Individuals Targeted for Land
Expropriation in Shuangcheng County, 1946–1947

Most Violent Outcome	Individuals	%	Cum. %
Killing	30	0.8	0.8
Public Humiliation	1,089	27.9	28.7
Escape	153	3.9	32.6
Expropriation	2,628	67.4	100.0
Total	3,900	100.0	

Source: Author's calculations based on linked victim registers.
Note: Restricted to 59 administrative villages with at least one observation of violent expropriation.

from the summer of 1947 further substantiate this claim by the hyperbole
that for many landlords, expropriating only their land was like "removing
one hair from among nine oxen" (九牛去一毛)—their other property was
much more valuable.[37]

A second reason that the CCP could so easily appropriate land is that
landlords manipulated CCP policies for their own benefit by preemptively
handing out some scraps of land to villagers to temporarily satisfy them
and undermine the political goals of land reform. This method gave landlords the upper hand in village politics and preempted any ideas of struggling against them. It is also the reason why the work report from District
9 considered peaceful land redistribution a "serious" problem. In other
words, this strategy was an act of passive resistance that was so common
in village-state relations in rural China.[38]

In reality, both of these reasons operated simultaneously depending on
the type of landlord targeted. Most absentee landlords would have been
expropriated nonviolently, and as described later in chapter 6, even in
cases of recorded struggle meetings many victims were in absentia. While
these landlords may not have directly donated their land, they did not
actively resist expropriation, either. Moreover, as we saw earlier, absentee landlords could own up to half of all village land, which meant that
a majority of village land could be "peacefully" expropriated. The landlords who did attempt to donate their land to undermine the land reform
were most likely resident landlords, and although the CCP emphasized
the power of these "feudal" landlords, they were often in the minority in
Shuangcheng.

Not only landlords, but as late as the Equalize Land campaign in the fall of 1947, many work teams and village cadres also directed "peaceful" redistributions. One report from District 2 describes how in November 1947, when district work teams were experimenting with the Outline Land Law in test villages in Districts 2 and 3, the leadership still thought in terms of peaceful redistribution and was worried primarily about how to fairly or rationally distribute land. It was only after the county work team finished up their experiment in late December and all the work teams were retrained that they learned the new policy was about politically mobilizing poor peasants and hired laborers to overthrow feudalism, not just redistributing land.[39] After reading the overwhelmingly economic text of the Outline Land Law, it seems hard to blame these work teams for focusing on land. But as we also saw in chapter 3, one reason that local cadres continued to simply redistribute land without mobilizing villagers to do it themselves is because it was much easier to make decisions among themselves than to manage mass meetings and negotiate "hundreds of opinions" from often confused and untrained peasants.

In any case these findings demonstrate a salient disconnect between expropriation and violence in Shuangcheng's land reform, as illustrated in an example from one village in District 9. Of the thirty-one landlord and rich peasant households recorded in this village's land expropriation registers, twelve were struggled against, thirteen were absentee landlords who had their "accounts settled," and six "voluntarily" donated their land.[40] The absentee landlords and volunteers, over 60 percent of cases, have no crime recorded, while only six of the individuals struggled against were charged with "exploiting poor people."[41] Furthermore, looking at the escape registers, four of the persons struggled against had escaped to Harbin or elsewhere before September 1946, almost one year before the land expropriation register was recorded.[42] The two records of execution for this village, which took place at a work team–supervised people's court, were of a former police officer and a bandit and had no relation to land expropriation.[43] In other words, only one-fifth of expropriated landowners were charged with class exploitation, only about one-quarter of them were actually present to be struggled against, and none were executed.

Statistically speaking, there was also little correlation between landholding and violent outcomes. As illustrated in Figure 12, in nearly six thousand instances of expropriation, individuals who were killed, publicly humiliated, or who fled did not necessarily possess more land. In this figure the shaded boxes represent the twenty-fifth to seventy-fifth percentiles of household landholding in each outcome category. The line in each box

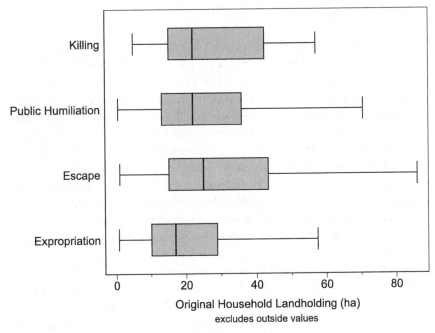

Figure 12. Original household landholding by violent outcome category, Shuangcheng County, 1946–1947. Author's calculations based on linked expropriation registers.

marks the median landholding, and the whiskers extending beyond the boxes mark the lower and upper adjacent values. Median landholding of individuals killed was only a few hectares more than individuals who were "peacefully" expropriated. Why they were subject to greater violence is the subject of chapter 6, but this is clear evidence that violence was not significantly proportional to landholding.

These practices challenge common assumptions about how CCP policies led to unnecessary violence by forcibly expropriating landowners. Instead of assuming the importance of private property and how both landowners' and poor peasants' desires for land would lead them into violent conflict, in Shuangcheng, at least for the first year of the movement, land was expropriated relatively peacefully, and most violence was unrelated to expropriation. In reality the discourse of land reform betrays the CCP state's own preoccupation with land, not necessarily individual interests.

Violent Struggle

The landlord compliance and peasant apathy of "peaceful" land reform signaled that this reform was not a simple matter of economic restructuring but a political battle over village governance. Village leaders were content to comply with whoever was in charge higher up as long as they could maintain their political position in village affairs, and most peasants saw little incentive to get involved in the risky world of politics. In terms of property, however, while land was tied up in the political battle between state and village leaders, household belongings became a focus of community violence that the CCP tried to harness for more effective political support. Confiscating household belongings—that is, movable property beyond the major means of agricultural production—became a prominent part of land reform mobilization in the summer of 1947 and continued through the Mop-Up campaign in January 1948. The Outline Land Law identified more types of property to confiscate than were included in the May Fourth Directive, which dealt almost exclusively with land (see Appendix A), but this central policy does little justice to the widespread practices of property expropriation that took place at the local level in Shuangcheng and elsewhere.

Between the fall of 1946 and the summer of 1947, there was a clear evolution in the types of property that CCP work teams and administrators recorded. One of the earliest work reports from the fall of 1946 records the following "fruits of struggle and settling accounts" confiscated from seven villages and one railway town in District 9:

Land—184+ ha [hectares],
Housing—306 rooms,
Horses—28,
Carts—3,
Grain—4,000+ kg,
[Commercial] Goods—worth 400,000 *yuan,*
Cash and Shares—49,000 *yuan,*
And other accessory items.[44]

As one might expect, over half of the housing and all of the commercial goods and cash were from the railway town. Land, horses, carts, and grain thus comprised the focus of rural wealth confiscation (despite the fact that the May Fourth Directive only mentions land). In comparison, by the summer of 1947, district statistics on the "fruits of struggle" record the following types of property from throughout the county: land, housing, carts, horses, oxen, mules, donkeys, pigs, sheep, grain, cash, gold and silver, clothing, blankets, cloth, cotton, furniture, crocks and jars, lumber, trees, handguns, rifles, and ammunition. As described in work reports from dozens of villages, villagers were most proactive in the confiscation of grain, cash, gold and silver, clothing and blankets, and guns. With the exception of grain, none of these are typical types of agricultural wealth.

At least one report from the summer of 1947 mentions three types of rural property that correspond to the progression of expropriation policies over time.[45] Land stood alone as a special type of immovable, productive property and remained the central focus of all land reform policies. The second type was movable, productive property (浮产), which included housing, livestock, carts and other farm implements, and seed grain. Although housing was effectively immovable, it was not as permanent, and also not as important in the production process, as land.[46] As seen in the example above, this type of movable property was also targeted for expropriation from early on, at least in practice if not in writing. The third type of property was household belongings (家底 or 底产), comprised of foodstuffs, cash, gold and silver, clothing, blankets, cloth, cotton, furniture, crocks and jars, lumber, trees, handguns, rifles, and ammunition. These household belongings were not targeted until the summer of 1947.[47] In Shuangcheng everything besides land was typically referred to as "movable goods" (浮物), although this term only first appears in the summer of 1947.

It is interesting to note that this distinction between landed and movable property is echoed in Marxist conceptions of the evolution of private property. Marx wrote in part 1 of *The German Ideology*:

> In the case of the ancient peoples, since several tribes live together in one town, the tribal property appears as State property, and the right of the individual to it as mere "possession" which, however, like tribal property as a whole, is confined to landed property only. Real private property began with the ancients, as with modern nations, with movable property. In the case of the nations which grew out of the Middle Ages, tribal property evolved through various stages . . . to modern capital . . . i.e. pure private property, which has cast off all semblance of a communal institution and has shut out the State from any influence on the development of property.[48]

In this framework, conflicts over the possession of land occurred between local strongmen and the state, not between individual households. Movable property, however, existed more like "real private property," and therefore conflicts over this type of property were more likely to play out between individuals within the community and be characterized by interpersonal violence. Land reform itself is proof that the Chinese state has not been "shut out" from influence over property. The equal allocation of land that marked the completion of land reform further demonstrated how in China redistributing landed property was more an administrative procedure than a revolutionary movement.

The policy of cleaning out all landlord wealth began early in the summer of 1947 with the Cut Down and Dig Up campaign. It was during this campaign that work teams discovered villagers were more easily mobilized to struggle for the household belongings mentioned above. One village report from District 8 describes how after two attempts of "peaceful" land expropriation, the struggle for household belongings in the summer of 1947 was more successful in politically mobilizing villagers.[49] Both villages were visited twice by different work teams, once in the fall of 1946 and once in the spring of 1947 before spring planting. In one village the land was "peacefully" divided up according to government policy, and a peasant association was organized under the leadership of a local landlord. The land expropriation register for this village also records that twenty out of twenty-five individuals donated their land. When a district work team visited the village again in June 1947 to carry out a new campaign of intensified struggle, the villagers fled at the sight of the team and later asked if they were going to beat up anyone. In order to motivate villagers to struggle, the work team confiscated some of a landlord's household belongings and distributed them to the people. After giving the people some "material benefits," the work team was able to organize multiple struggle meetings at which villagers accused landlords, made them parade around several villages wearing a tall hat and confessing their misdeeds, and strung them up and whipped them until they confessed to where they were hiding their valuables.[50]

Expropriating household belongings was always more violent than expropriating land. One report from the summer of 1947 in District 10 lists the following methods for extracting movable property: "beating, whipping, deceiving, accusing, crushing, intimidating, women's association beats landlord women, exploiting family conflicts, extorting, causing physical discomfort, and using a branding iron."[51] One interviewee's most vivid memory of land reform in Shuangcheng includes an episode in which villagers dug a large hole near the center of the village and corralled all the village landlords in it before going to confiscate their valuables.[52] One logical reason for this violence is that it was much easier for local strongmen to hide grain, clothing, and other valuables than to hide land. But perhaps another reason was that such household belongings were more symbolic of the evils of private accumulation and corruption. Any poor villager would be enraged to discover a cellar full of rotting grain after experiencing years of half starvation.

The Outline Land Law, formulated at a two-month national CCP land conference from July to September 1947, was more a result than a cause of such land reform developments in Shuangcheng and elsewhere. Many of the policy directions of the new law, for example, were already apparent in one provincial leader's report in late June at a meeting of county party secretaries in Songjiang Province. Some of the main themes of this report include "boldly releasing" the masses to let them take matters into their own hands, recommending leaders study Mao's 1927 *Hunan Investigation* and not be afraid of radicalism, upholding the "mass line," and laying out more detailed guidelines on the entitlements and disentitlements of specific classes.[53] The themes of mass politics are formalized in Article 15 of the Outline Land Law and the "Chinese Communist Party Northeast Central Bureau's Letter to the Peasants" (see Appendix A). I focus here on the guidelines regarding expropriation.

The more specific guidelines of expropriation are summarized in Article 8 of the Outline Land Law and further elaborated in item 6 of the "Northeast Liberated Area Supplementary Methods for Implementing the Outline Land Law" (see Appendix A), which states:

> Article 8 of the Outline, pertaining to the expropriation of rich peasants' excess property, refers to foodstuffs and housing in excess of the typical rich peasant household, after taking into account seed stock. For draft animals and farm implements, those in excess of the village average are to be expropriated. Household belongings and other property are to be handed over in their entirety and then one share allocated back [to the rich peasant household]. Regarding small rich peasants (primary family members all engage in labor, and only exploit between one half and one laborer), grain, housing, draft animals and farm implements are to be handled according to the above method, but household belongings and other property are not to be touched.

According to this guideline, regular rich peasants could keep their fair share of food, housing, draft animals, and farm implements but had to turn over all of their household belongings. (As also mentioned in Article 8, landlords had to turn over all of their property, without exception, and then be reallocated a fair share.) This curious arrangement to some degree reflects land reform's conflicting goals of increasing agricultural production while also carrying out a political revolution. Rich peasants were entitled to some of their movable means of production, but the expropriation of their household belongings also made them prime targets of the violent struggles over these belongings in the second half of 1947.

The transition to the Outline Land Law is typically identified as a radical turn in CCP land reform policy. As early as the summer of 1947, local CCP leaders employed a quote from Mao's 1927 *Hunan Investigation* to explain this process: "to right a wrong one must overcorrect it; otherwise it cannot be made right."[54] In the beginning this logic was used to encourage more radical land reform policies in response to the shortcomings of the more moderate May Fourth Directive. Likewise, beginning as early as January 1948, consequent excessive and uncontrolled violence was condemned, but the CCP solution continued to follow the same logic: now that land reform practices had become "overcorrected," it was time to make things right again (i.e., the beginning of the Rectification campaign). Previous interpretations for this radical turn in CCP land reform policy identify two main factors: the progress of the land reform and the progress of the civil war.[55] As we saw in previous chapters, as early as November 1946 CCP leaders in the Northeast were already disappointed with the progress of land reform, and throughout the year of 1947 policies were increasingly aimed at political mobilization.[56] The Outline Land Law was the officially sanctioned culmination of this trend. At the same time, however, late 1947 has also been identified as the turning point in the civil war, when the CCP began to take the offensive in the Northeast theater of the war.[57] The Outline Land Law can also, therefore, be seen as a parallel turning point for the land reform movement.[58] However, such understandings neglect the fact that for most of their history, CCP policies regularly followed a similar cyclical trajectory of accommodation, radicalism, and rectification, regardless of the historical circumstances (see chapter 4).

In early January 1948, rumors spread through Shuangcheng of thousand-man "mop-up" teams driving hundreds of horse-drawn sleighs across the snow-covered countryside, feasting and looting wherever they went. Village granaries were attacked, and some peasants started to stockpile anything of value or slaughter their animals and gorge themselves before someone else could. Amid this chaos, a mop-up team from District 3 arrived in a village in District 9, carrying rifles. The village had a few sleighs set up awaiting orders, and some additional local security forces from a neighboring village were there to help them guard their granary. Villagers were marching in the streets, beating drums and shouldering long, red-tasseled spears. The mop-up team, which had come to unite with the poor peasants and hired laborers in the village and help them overthrow feudalism, decided to play it safe and wait until the next day to try to meet with the villagers. The next day the team members held a mass meeting at which some villagers said the village had already overthrown feudalism. When one team member asked if the villagers needed any help, the reply was, no thanks. According to local policy, a village was technically not allowed to refuse the help of an outside mop-up team, but given the circumstances, the team did not want to cause trouble, so they canceled their visit.[59] Other mop-up teams were not so kind. A few days earlier when a different team visited the village, a woman came out to greet them. As soon as she told them that a small landlord in the village did not have anything left, the team's women forced her to the ground, beat her, and called her a lackey.[60]

In Shuangcheng and elsewhere, January 1948 was the climax of terror and violence during land reform, but there exist two very different interpretations of this period. All of the county's land reform archives describe this period as the Mop-Up campaign, the final blow of the Outline Land Law, in which poor peasants and hired laborers broke down village boundaries to unite together in overthrowing the landlord class and their feudal power once and for all. It was turbulent and violent because, just as Mao had said two decades earlier, "a revolution is not a dinner party."[61] Mop-up teams went from village to village, squeezing every last piece of clothing and kernel of grain from class enemies and forcing them to bow before the power of the masses. Land reform would not be considered complete without this revolutionary display of power.

At the same time, however, Shuangcheng was experiencing one of the worst famines in its history. Continuous rain for over two months in the summer of 1947 had flooded more than one-quarter of all farmland and reduced the annual harvest in nearly three-quarters of villages in the county. The total harvest was only half of a normal year, not even enough to feed the county's own population. On top of this natural disaster, grain quotas to support the CCP war effort took much of the remaining harvest.

By November 1947 the county government was already working to alleviate grain shortages in the county. By the summer of 1948, nearly eight hundred people had died of starvation, more than all the victims of land reform violence combined.[62] In this context, the violence and looting of the Mop-Up campaign appear more like a desperate struggle for survival.

Combining data from various archival sources illustrates a close correlation between famine conditions and Mop-Up violence, as shown in Map 14.[63] This map illustrates the amount of surplus grain left over in the fall of 1947 for each district, after poor harvests and state levies. The overlaid blue dotted lines represent mop-up team activity and trace the routes of mop-up teams traveling between villages, as mentioned in over two dozen work reports describing this campaign in the county. In Shuangcheng at this time, the average annual consumption of coarse grain per person was about 320 kilograms. It is important to note that in addition to the rural population, there were also roughly forty thousand draft animals in the county, needing an additional 300 kilograms of grain per head per year.[64] As shown in Map 14, therefore, only three out of ten rural districts had enough surplus grain to survive the year, but only if they let all their animals starve. As discussed in more detail in chapter 6, Districts 10 and 2 experienced the most violent Mop-Up campaigns, and Map 14 provides the clearest explanation of why: the complete lack of grain in both districts in the winter of 1947 meant that the only way to get food was to literally fight for it.[65]

Nevertheless, the more than two dozen work reports mentioning at least 80 *tun* involved in the Mop-Up campaign describe mop-up team activity in triumphal terms of finally accomplishing the total overthrow of feudalism (i.e., nonproductive land ownership). As one county leader concluded in February 1948, "In the previous '[Eliminate] Half-Cooked Rice' and 'Cut Down and Dig Up' campaigns, landlords hardly changed one bit. This time after one torrential Mop-Up campaign, landlord men act like morphine addicts, and landlord women act like rabbits, wandering around the streets with their heads down."[66] CCP work teams and villagers alike were amazed when visiting mop-up teams uncovered hidden caches of salt, pork, grain, clothing, and other valuables from landlords whom fellow villagers believed were already completely expropriated. One report from District 10 describes how a mop-up team discovered clothing, grain, and pork hidden inside chimneys, unused cooking stoves, and piles of sorghum stalks.[67] In another village in District 11, a landlord hid an entire cart under a pile of manure, a bagful of clothes in a haystack, and jewelry and silver and gold bullion in a pot buried under a pig trough.[68]

However, the Mop-Up campaign's emphasis on poor peasants and hired laborers breaking through village boundaries to unite as a single class in the struggle against class enemies also revealed just how resilient these boundaries could be. One of the professed benefits of allowing outside mop-up teams to struggle against landlords in other villages was the ability of outsiders to "cast away all considerations of face" (撕破脸皮) in struggling and searching for hidden property.[69] The problem, however, was that in practice this idea often backfired, and the threat of mop-up teams carting off village property led both landlords and poor peasants in a single village to unite in opposition to outsiders. In the previous example from District 11, for instance, a mop-up team struggled against the landlord and beat him to a pulp, but he still did not tell them about his hidden belongings. He waited until after the team left to confess it to his own village's poor peasants and hired laborers, because, as he admitted, "The people I exploited were our own villagers. If I let outsiders take away the stuff, as soon as they left my own villagers would kill me."[70] For a similar fear of village property leaving the village, sometimes even village cadres would help shelter landlords whenever a mop-up team came to the village.[71] Such village solidarity was especially necessary in times of hardship, because as all villagers were well aware, "distant water cannot put out a fire close at hand" (远水不救近火).

Recorded reasons for attacking lower-class villagers during the Mop Up campaign also reflected village, not class, solidarity. In tallying up the violence of this campaign, districts were required to explain why middle and poor peasants were victimized. The following is a list of the various reasons given:

- Misclassification (classification not clear, classified as rich peasant; classification overestimated; classified as landlord)
- Bandits, "running dogs" for landlords, sheltering landlords, some were bad eggs
- Some served as Manchukuo police and district heads, Manchukuo officials and staff
- KMT [member] jumped into a well and committed suicide for fear of being struggled
- (Moral) character correction
- Assist landlords in hiding things, Han traitors, peasant association corruption
- One poor peasant was beaten to death for sheltering a local bully and embezzling fruits of struggle[72]

In six out of seven districts that recorded reasons, middle and poor peasants were caught assisting, sheltering, or serving as lackeys for landlords. Many of these reasons resonate with those recorded in the 1947 victim registers, suggesting that such intra-village collaboration was a salient feature of rural society that could persist through at least two years of land reform mobilization.

Paradoxically, the Mop-Up campaign was championed as the violent climax of a revolutionary rural class struggle but in reality it was the climax of a power struggle between village and state. County-wide famine was partially a result of the CCP state's expropriation of grain from the countryside, which was accomplished through the CCP's superior political entitlement. Villagers responded to this political exploitation with communal solidarity, a proven strategy for troubled times.[73] But this alienation of central and local interests was counterproductive to the CCP's state-building goals, and the Mop-Up campaign was called off within a month. No matter how strongly work team reports emphasized the rhetoric of class struggle, there is clearly no place in this story for an economic struggle between rich and poor. Instead, this story of the political relations between state and village foreshadows many of the power struggles that were to come in the following decades of the PRC.[74]

Equal Allocations and Unequal Entitlements

The Outline Land Law was unequivocal in its abolition of landlord property rights and the completely equal per capita allocation of all village land. However, as discussed in the last section of chapter 3, the focus of this process was not on measuring and calculating village land devoid of community politics but on politically classifying villagers to determine their entitlements according to the new law. Again, similar to the work reports in chapter 4, the Outline Land Law itself emphasized the economic logistics of equal land distribution, while local documents increasingly emphasized the political logistics of classification and categorical entitlements. In other words, the actual redistribution of land in Shuangcheng was an almost completely social process.

One of the central features of this new law was that PAs comprised of poor peasants and hired laborers were responsible for its implementation, which required a significant amount of ideological training. One effective way of reeducating peasants to understand the new land system was through a calculus of labor exploitation. This calculus was called "settling detailed accounts," in contrast to the earlier and more subjective practice of "settling accounts" with local strongmen. Villagers, for the sake of survival, were already very adept at these calculations. In one village in District 8, for example, villagers calculated how much a landlord had exploited an annual laborer (sharecropper) over the past four years:

1. One laborer's annual salary is 2,400 kg of grain, over 4 years is 9,600 kg of grain.
2. Each year one annual laborer can work 6 hectares of land, which over 4 years is 24 hectares. Each hectare can produce 1,000 kg of grain, which over 4 years produces a total of 24,000 kg of grain.
3. Over 4 years, each hectare of land requires hiring an ox team for 160 kg of grain, which for 24 hectares is 3,840 kg of grain. Over 4 years, one annual laborer needs 800 kg of food and cooking fuel worth 1,000 kg of grain, for a total of 5,640 kg of grain spent on production costs.
4. If the laborer worked on his own 24 hectares of land, over 4 years he could earn 24,000 kg of grain. Subtract the laborer's salary worth 9,600 kg, then subtract 5,640 kg worth of production costs, and he would have 8,760 kg of grain left over.
5. This 24 hectares of land can also produce about 24,000 bunches of stalks (for cooking fuel), worth a total of 4,800 kg of grain. Add this to his leftover grain, and the laborer would have earned 13,560 kg of grain. This is therefore the total amount of grain that the landlord exploited from his labor.[75]

Simply put, the harvest was split exactly two to one between landlord and sharecropper. The total value of grain plus stalks was 28,800 kilograms of grain, and the sharecropper received 9,600 kilograms of it. The landlord, however, also paid the production costs, plus land taxes and fees (not mentioned in the above calculations), which would have left him with little more than the sharecropper. But the point is that the landlord received more profit out of the land while contributing no labor toward it. As long as villagers subscribed to this labor theory of value, this calculus was very effective in demystifying their poverty.[76] According to this work report, until such detailed settling of accounts, the masses did not understand what property was supposed to be expropriated, or why, and knew only that the landlords who bullied and oppressed the people were bad. Through this process, villagers learned that the institution of landlordism itself was bad.

The Equalize Land campaign began in the winter of 1947 but it was not completed until the recording of the classification registers the following summer in 1948. Once again, despite being called the Equalize Land campaign, local reports from November and December 1947 overwhelmingly focused on the political issues of educating and organizing the associations of poor peasants and hired laborers that the Outline Land Law specified as the new "legal executive organs for the reform of the agrarian system" (Article 5).[77] The state of village PAs at this time can be seen in a description of a district-wide meeting of poor peasant and hired laborer representatives from forty-three natural villages in late December 1947 in District 3. For this meeting the district government ordered that every village elect ten to twenty representatives who met the following qualifications:

1. Laborer, hardworking, experienced hardship, and has not done anything bad
2. Unrelated to any landlords in the village
3. Resolute in struggle, disregards personal feelings (人情)
4. Young and promising, dares to take initiative and get things done
5. Not assigned by a village cadre, must be elected [by the village]
6. Resident in the village for at least five years[78]

The gap between the language of these qualifications and that of the Outline Land Law should be obvious. The job of work teams was to figure out how to translate the law into local terms like these. Except for the occupational reference in the first part of the first qualification, for example, none of these criteria are related to class labels or exploitation. Nevertheless, when all the representatives were assembled at the district office, work team members split up to talk to each village's representatives and ended up sending back some who did not meet the above criteria, including the entire delegations of two villages.

The "Chinese Communist Party Northeast Central Bureau's Letter to the Peasants" was the regional government's attempt to translate the Outline Land Law into more local terms (see Appendix A). This document, issued on December 1, 1947, was addressed to "peasant brothers and sisters," written like a speech to be read aloud at a village mass meeting, and indeed was typically announced alongside the Outline Land Law whenever a work team visited a new village.[79] The letter outlines a plan for equally allocating land in which landlords and rich peasants are attacked, democratic PAs are organized to take control of village governance (away from both enemies and corrupt cadres), class divisions are drawn, and property is allocated according to individual entitlements. I discussed much of the political and organizational work of this process in previous chapters; here I focus on the logistics of property allocation.

Every individual in the county was allocated an equal share of farmland, but not all farmland is created equal. In determining entitlements to land shares, inequalities in the quality and location of land were mapped onto the new status hierarchy. A detailed example of the allocation of land in one representative village in District 2 in February 1948 clearly illustrates the inequalities involved in "equalizing land." The first step was evaluating all the land in the village. In order to accomplish this, villagers at a mass meeting elected more than thirty veteran farmers (no one under forty years old) to determine the grade of every parcel of land. They divided all the land into three grades based on measures of firmness, soil quality, water retention, and productivity, and determined that each person in the village could be allocated 0.66 hectares of land. The next step was calculating population. After trying to figure out how many people were in each household, villagers decided to simply use groups, in which households with five people or less would receive one parcel of land, and households with six people or more would receive two parcels.[80] Then, because most villagers were illiterate, the final preparatory step was hanging up a big village land map on the meeting-room wall and circling each parcel on the map with a different color to illustrate its grade.[81]

Once everything was ready, the allocation process involved the entire village lining up and choosing parcels of land one household at a time. The order of selection was determined by class, rank (within class), and household size, from first to last: hired laborers, singleton households, poor tenants, poor peasants, middle tenants, middle peasants, and, finally, "struggled households" (i.e., rich peasants and landlords). Singleton households were also given extra land to compensate for their extreme demographic poverty. As discussed in the last section of chapter 3, within each of these class categories households were further ranked according to moral standing in the community. Table 12 shows how a well-ordered property hierarchy was formed through the combination of land grade (productivity)

Table 12. Standards for the Allocation of Land in One Natural Village, Shuangcheng County, 1948

Class	Household Size	# of Parcels	Grade	Productivity/ ha (kg)	Location
Hired Laborer	5 or less	1	1	1,000	near
	6 or more	2	1	1,000	near-far
Poor Peasant	5 or less	1	1	1,000	middle
	6 or more	2	1–2	933	middle-near
Middle Peasant	5 or less	1	2	800	near
	6 or more	2	1–2	866	far-middle
Landlord/Rich	5 or less	1	3	600	n/a
Peasant	6 or more	2	3	600	n/a

Sources: 129-1-68, 97; Estimated productivity from three grades of land recorded in 7-1-10-2 (Sept. 1946).

and location (distance from village). This hierarchy mirrored a new social order based on a combination of past exploitation and moral character, integrating Marxist ideology with Confucian governance.

Nevertheless, during the winter of 1947/48 experiences of this process of reallocation still had some kinks to be worked out. In the above village, for example, there was a significant amount of unwanted first- and second-grade land left over (close to sixty hectares) after everyone had chosen their new land. Some households were afraid of not having enough labor power to farm their share of land, and some households chose second-grade land close to the village over first-grade land farther away.[82] Moreover, in the cases of this and a few other villages that experimented with equalizing land in the winter, the data recorded in work reports differs significantly from what is recorded in the classification registers for these same villages six months later in the summer of 1948. This was a learning process, and few villages could get it right—that is, they were unable to equally reallocate all village land in a fair way that could satisfy a majority of villagers—on their first try.

Unlike the haphazard mobilization of earlier campaigns and the chaos of the Mop-Up campaign, the final act of equalizing land in the summer of 1948 was highly coordinated in its methods and implementation. For starters, the recording of the classification registers was organized by district, suggesting that most of the process was directed by county-level administrators. Figure 13 plots the recorded date of registration for 512 PAs over time, sorted by district. In this figure each circle represents one PA, and the

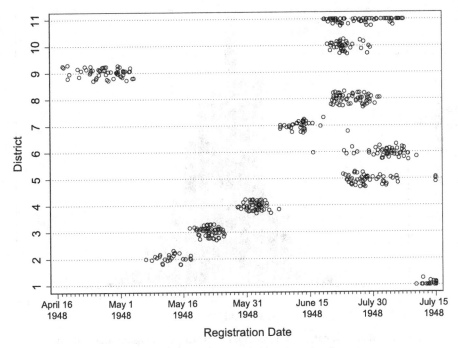

Figure 13. Timeline of classification register recording, by district, Shuangcheng County, 1948. Author's calculations based on classification registers.

Note: One circle represents one *tun* peasant association or urban equivalent unit (in the case of District 1). $N = 512$ (excludes 84 units with no recorded date).

PAs are grouped together on the y-axis by district and along the x-axis by registration date. Thus, beginning in the second half of April 1948, all the PAs in District 9 was registered in about two weeks. After a short break, from early May to mid-June, all the PAs in Districts 2, 3, 4, and 7 were registered one week at a time. Then, beginning in the second half of June, PAs in the remaining five districts in the south and southwest parts of the county were registered in about three weeks. Despite a lack of direct reports on the process of register recording, this timeline suggests a standard CCP policy process as outlined in chapter 3. District 9, one of the earliest and most consolidated areas of CCP control, served as the experimental site of registration in the county. Following this experiment, we can assume that county administrators and work teams held a series of meetings to debrief their experiences before moving forward. Districts 2, 3, 4, and 7 were also experi-

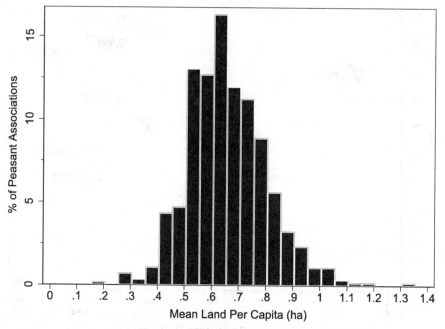

Figure 14. Mean allocated land per capita within each peasant association, Shuangcheng County, 1948. Author's calculations based on classification registers.

mental sites for the Equalize Land campaign over the previous winter, so it makes sense that they would also be given priority in the concluding act of the Outline Land Law. Finally, after the county administrators coordinated registration in half of the county, the other half was opened up to general implementation, in which district administrators were in charge of registering their own districts, and the process then proceeded simultaneously across multiple districts. In other words, while every PA determined their own method of allocation through communal discussion and ranking, the overarching registration process was highly centralized.

An analysis of the classification registers shows that practically all PAs in the county carried out a process of allocation similar to the example above. Figure 14 illustrates the actual mean allocated land per capita for 559 PAs, in which we can see a highly normal distribution of about 0.6 hectares per person. This distribution reflects the uniformity of policy implementation within the county, but it could also be seen to reflect a uniform development of the village communities themselves, demon-

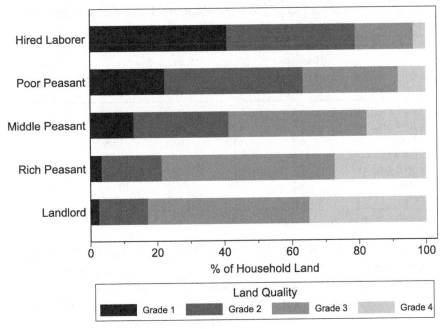

Figure 15. Quality of allocated land by class, Shuangcheng County, 1948. Author's calculations based on classification registers.

strating that they all had similar ratios between population and land. Figure 15 shows how for the county as a whole, within the equal allocation of land there was intentional inequality in the quality of land that each class was entitled to receive. Over 40 percent of all the land allocated to hired laborer households was first grade, while over 80 percent of all the land allocated to landlords and rich peasants was third grade or worse. Again, this was legitimized in revolutionary terms as privileging the exploited and punishing the exploiters.

PAs also appear to have used unequal allocations of land to alleviate the enduring demographic inequality between classes. As in most agrarian societies, in rural China household wealth was interrelated with household size—the more resources a household had, the more people they could support; and the more labor a household had, the more wealth they could accumulate. Table 13 shows how this inequality was mitigated through the allocation of land in Shuangcheng. On average, a rich peasant household had at least two more persons than a hired laborer household,

Table 13. Summary of Household Size and Landholding at the Completion of Land Reform in Shuangcheng County, 1948

Class Category	Mean Household Size (persons)	Mean Household Land (ha)	Mean Land per Capita (ha)	Households %	% of Households Singleton
Landlord	6.2	3.53	0.59	6.7	1.8
Rich Peasant	6.9	4.15	0.61	8.2	0.8
Middle Peasant	6.3	3.87	0.64	15.9	1.5
Poor Peasant	5.1	3.13	0.65	27.3	5.3
Hired Laborer	4.5	2.78	0.69	41.9	10.6
Total	5.2	3.21	0.66	100.0	6.3
N				70,507	4,459

Source: Author's calculations based on classification registers.

which meant they would receive at least two more shares of land than the hired laborer.[83] As seen above, this inequality was partly alleviated by allocating the rich peasant lower-quality land. Table 13 also shows how, on average, landlords and rich peasants were allocated quantitatively less land per capita. This difference was almost wholly the effect of the privileged entitlements of singleton households. As mentioned above, singleton households were given entitlements to extra land, because they were either bachelors that were regarded as so poor that they could not even afford to get married or widows who needed extra land to offset their lack of labor. Thus, regardless of class, singleton households received on average more than one hectare of land each, nearly twice the average per capita.

These results of land reform thus demonstrate a multidimensional hierarchy of "fair" entitlements tailored to the realities of rural life. Land was measured in terms of quantity, quality, and location, and household entitlements were defined in terms of past exploitation (class), demographics (household size), and moral character. At the top of the hierarchy, honest, exploited singletons were entitled to more, better, and nearby land. At the bottom, large, profiteering landlords were entitled to less, worse, and distant land. Taking into account livestock and all the other property that was presumably redistributed together with land would have required an even more sophisticated calculus of "fairness."[84] The key to everything, however, was a common understanding of what was fair or just. For the CCP, the Marxist labor theory of value dictated that it was only fair for laborers to have possession over the product of their labor. For villagers, community morals dictated that it was only fair for everyone to have an equal right to subsistence. But for both villagers and the CCP, justice could be achieved only through retribution and repayment for past injustices. In this respect, the opposite of inequality was not equality but an inverted inequality in which "the last shall be first, and the first last."[85]

In this chapter we have seen a land reform in which land was expropriated without violence, violent struggles over basic necessities broke out when the state left villagers with little other option, and in the end everyone got their fair share of agricultural wealth. One common theme throughout this process is the overarching power of the state. Village leaders complied with whatever the state asked of them in order to maintain their local political advantage, the state was able to effectively extract grain even when there was nothing left to eat, and then the state still had the power to completely reallocate all rural wealth. At the same time, however, this state power was tempered by village communities that proved imperviable to state mobilization, stood united in the struggle for survival, and determined their own standards for reallocation. In the end the village majority was politically mobilized through increased interactions and negotiations with the state, not through a class struggle for property. As we will see in the next chapter, the fact that land reform violence targeted state agents more than anyone else provides even stronger evidence that village mobilization was organized along political, not socioeconomic, lines.

CHAPTER 6

Violence and Power

China's land reform was more than just the redistribution of land. It was violent insofar as its main objective was the redistribution of political power, and in early twentieth-century rural China power was often exercised through brute force. As early as 1927 Mao himself made it clear that China's rural revolution was first and foremost a political struggle. In his *Hunan Investigation*, Mao wrote, "[If the political struggle] was not successful, then all economic struggles, such as reducing rents and interest and the struggles for capital and land, etc., would have no chance of success."[1] The political struggles Mao described in 1927 likewise appear prominently in Shuangcheng's land reform, such as parading victims around the village in a dunce cap, confinement, escape or "banishment," and execution.[2] The CCP would later envision these political struggles as lower-class peasants struggling against the landlord class. In Shuangcheng, however, most recorded violence targeted corrupt local officials, a political category that cut across such class lines.

The CCP in Shuangcheng separately recorded three types of outcomes associated with the political struggles of land reform: escape, public humiliation or violent struggle, and killing. The number of deaths caused by land reform, is commonly used as the sole measure for understanding such authoritarian policies, perhaps because it is the simplest: if lots of people died, then the policy is bad; if no one died, then it is good. However, this chapter shows that the first two types of outcomes were not only far more common than killings but also more revealing of the nature of land reform experiences. Table 14 summarizes the most violent outcomes recorded for more than twenty-five hundred individuals recorded in Shuangcheng's victim registers.[3] Killings are broken down into the first three outcomes—executed, beaten to death, and other deaths; and public humiliations are broken down into outcomes four through seven—parading, struggle meeting, public confession, and confinement/imprisonment. Half of the

Table 14. Most Violent Land Reform Outcomes in Shuangcheng
County, 1945–1947

Most Violent Outcome	Individuals	%	Cum. %
1. Executed	127	4.9	4.9
2. Beaten to Death	116	4.5	9.4
3. Suicide/Other Death	30	1.2	10.6
4. Parade/Dunce Cap	344	13.3	23.9
5. Struggle Meeting	1,190	46.0	69.9
6. Public Confession	112	4.3	74.2
7. Confinement	34	1.3	75.5
8. Escape	633	24.5	100.0
Total	2,586	100.0	

Source: Author's calculations based on linked victim registers.

Note: This table excludes more than 4,500 individuals for whom the only recorded outcome is expropriation, i.e., have no record of violence, and who were the subject of the previous chapter.

observations in this table come from the expropriation registers, which record only whether or not the person was "struggled against," which I include under struggle meetings. Many of these struggle meetings also may have involved punishments like parading and public confessions, or in some cases they may have even been held in the absence of the victim, but the expropriation registers do not provide more detail.[4]

Two common characteristics that all of these outcomes record are the class status of the victim and the crime of the victim or reason for punishing them. Analyzing each of these characteristics presents a very different picture of violence. Figure 16 shows the class composition of the victims of each of the three types of violence recorded in Shuangcheng. In accord with official narratives of land reform as class struggle, the majority of victims (about 60 percent overall) were identified as landlords and rich peasants.[5] At the same time, however, middle and poor peasants (including hired laborers) comprised between one in four and one in three persons killed or publicly humiliated. This seems like a lot for a social group that was supposed to be among the friends and allies of the revolution, but we will explore these victims in more detail in the following sections.

In revolutionary terms, being a landlord or rich peasant was in itself a crime, but the fact that these registers also record a separate crime or reason for each individual victim makes it possible to go beyond such rhetoric. In other words, Figure 16 supports the official class struggle narrative insofar as one defines landlords and rich peasants

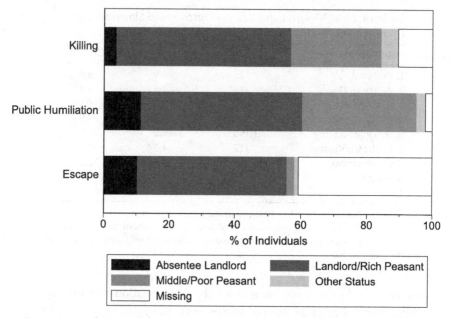

Figure 16. Violent outcomes by class status of victims, Shuangcheng County, 1945–1947. Author's calculations based on linked victim registers.

as persons guilty of the economic exploitation of land and labor.[6] The problem, however, is that only one-quarter of all recorded reasons for violence are related to such class exploitation. Figure 17 breaks down the three major outcomes by the recorded reasons for violence. Compared to Figure 16, this figure presents a completely opposite picture of violence. In Figure 16, 60 percent of victims were landlords and rich peasants, but in Figure 17 60 to almost 90 percent of these same victims were punished for political reasons.[7] Of course this comparison reflects the fact that these local elite consolidated their power through both economic and political means, but the Marxist assumption has always been that land formed the foundation of this power. In contrast, the recorded reasons for violence demonstrate that from the perspective of villagers, and often CCP work teams too, power (and wealth) came from political position, not land.

Practically all of the initial targets of struggle mentioned in work reports are also described in similar terms of political power. Several of these strongmen were introduced in chapter 2, but here I would like to reempha-

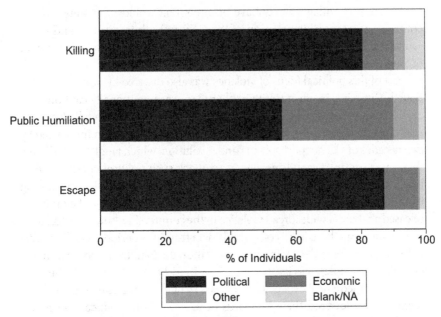

Figure 17. Violent outcomes by crime of victims, Shuangcheng County, 1945–1947. Author's calculations based on linked victim registers.

size how these persons were targeted not only because they held political positions of power or served under former regimes but also because they abused their power for personal gain. One of the most notorious strongmen in the work report analyzed in chapter 4, for example, served as a village agent of the Japanese and is described as using his position to seize seventy hectares of land, build a ten-room Western-style house for himself, and eat polished rice and fine noodles even during the height of coercive resource extraction in Manchukuo. Villagers despised this behavior so much that after the man escaped, they decided to tear down his villa instead of using it for their own housing.[8] Such behavior was in effect a moral failing, which required rectification through public displays of humiliation. Even though the man had already escaped, villagers still held a struggle meeting to condemn his behavior. One implication of such displays, therefore, is that villagers did not necessarily object to the political hierarchy; on the contrary, they objected to the abuse or breakdown of this hierarchy. Seen from a hierarchical perspective, in other words, villagers understood the abuse of power by local strongmen as a lack of moral-political control from above.

In this context, villagers may have been content to have the state enforce control, but a central innovation of the CCP, in both traditional and modern terms, was to mobilize villagers to participate in this enforcement through public displays of violence.[9]

Part of this political focus of violence was also dictated by policy. The May Fourth Directive, in effect until October 1947, was intentionally cautious and explicitly targeted "evil" landlords and traitors, not necessarily all class enemies.[10] At the same time, however, this policy was just as much influenced by two decades of CCP experience in rural revolution, which taught CCP leaders that it was easier to mobilize villagers to attack such political enemies rather than class enemies. In contrast, the Outline Land Law, in effect beginning in October 1947, targeted all relatively large landowners. This policy initially released a terror of widespread violence in the countryside, but, unfortunately, in Shuangcheng there is no comparable data from this period recording individual reasons for violence. In one respect the data do not exist because in this period, in principle, class itself was a crime. In reality, however, while the CCP raised their theoretical expectations of class struggle, villagers in Shuangcheng seem to have lowered their standards of violence from political and moral rectification to inter-village feuding over household belongings, as described in chapter 5. The resulting violence was in effect a consequence of attempting to fit the square head of class struggle over property in the round hole of a society organized around political power. Thus, many villagers paradoxically understood the increased emphasis on property as debasing violence. In the end, however, everything still boiled down to a struggle for political advantage or access to political entitlements.

Another salient manifestation of the politics of land reform violence was the struggle against the "new aristocracy," those CCP-supported village leaders who began abusing their newfound power as soon as they were elected and were likewise condemned in the same fashion as the former local strongmen they originally helped overthrow. As seen with the fried-dough-maker-cum-administrative-village-head mentioned in chapter 2, villagers often regarded power abusers from humble backgrounds with even more disdain than those from privileged backgrounds. The CCP was also quick to condemn the moral character of corrupt village cadres, but it was more difficult to convince villagers that there was a qualitative difference between these leaders and former local strongmen. For most villagers, power abusers were all the same, and perhaps they were right—the endemic tensions in this political hierarchy would continue to plague the modern Chinese state.[11]

The following sections explore the three types of violence of Shuangcheng's land reform in greater detail. Escapes foreground village violence, because only those persons who chose not to flee could be subjected to more violent punishments. Struggle meetings and their related forms of violence should then be seen in terms of public performances of humiliation, retribution, and moral rectification.[12] Abusing power, not class exploitation, was the central social problem in rural China. As a result, both old village leaders identified as landlords and rich peasants and new village cadres from poor peasant backgrounds who unfairly used their political position to accumulate personal wealth were targeted for struggle. In struggle meetings, this bad behavior was exposed, condemned, and punished as if the balance of power could be restored, and moral-political norms reinforced, through "an eye for an eye" retribution, such as smacking a landlord who once smacked you. Even the economic act of "settling accounts," in which villagers calculated how much income and grain a landlord had extracted from a worker or tenant over the years and then demanded its reimbursement, was expressed in similar terms of retribution.[13] Finally, for those local strongmen whose crimes could not be undone and who were unrepentant, death was seen as a just sentence. In most cases, however, villagers saw death as a last resort. Altogether about half of recorded killings were formal executions of violent counterrevolutionaries who not even the CCP bothered to identify as class enemies. Overall, land reform violence was shaped by village power struggles, not state coercion. In rural China power was often exercised through political entitlement, not property ownership. It makes sense, therefore, that land reform was practiced through political struggle rather than political reform being practiced through the redistribution of property.

Escape

Village strongmen who knew a CCP work team was planning to come to their village had two choices: to stay or to leave. Because word travels faster than horse cart, most villagers knew in advance when a work team was headed to their village. Strongmen also already heard rumors about work teams organizing villagers in other places to publicly denounce local elites, confiscate their property, and maybe even physically harm them. Under the circumstances, therefore, it is surprising that anyone chose to stay. The fact that many did choose to stay and tough it out suggests that these strongmen had confidence in their local power or, perhaps ironically, were misled by CCP rhetoric of economic exploitation and did not realize the degree to which they and their positions of power were at risk in land reform. But many local strongmen also chose to leave, maybe to temporarily stay with a relative in a neighboring village, or to move to their other house in the county town, or even to rent a place in a provincial or regional city. In the process these semi-urban strongmen fully urbanized, focused on their urban enterprises, and, at least for the moment, escaped many of the negative consequences of land reform. As the old saying goes, "Of all the strategies [of warfare], escape is the best" (三十六计, 走为上计).

Like many policies in China, land reform was not all-encompassing but limited to a specific sector of society—the rural community. This meant that evading land reform violence could be as easy as making a trip to the nearest town. This simple fact is overlooked in practically all narratives that portray land reform as an all-consuming revolutionary movement. As Steven Levine writes, "That the self-same evil landlord could become magically transformed into a legitimate merchant or entrepreneur by merely passing through the city gates was an incomprehensible subtlety of Marxist class analysis."[14] Records of escapes provide concrete evidence for demystifying these features of both land reform and Chinese politics in general. In most narratives of land reform, escape plays a minor role, often portrayed as a landlord's futile attempt to escape his fate. In contrast, escape played an important role in land reform in hundreds of villages in Shuangcheng. Shuangcheng's escape registers record nearly six hundred individuals who fled between 1945 and the summer of 1947, and even as late as the Mop-Up campaign in early 1948 many work reports likewise describe enemies fleeing before they could be struggled against. Altogether, therefore, in this period there were more than twice as many records of escapes than of killings.

Shuangcheng's escape registers make it possible to recreate the political-spatial landscape in which land reform took place. When people escaped, where they escaped to, and why they escaped all followed clear patterns. These patterns were already identified by Mao in his 1927 Hunan Investigation, in which he described escape as "banishment" and considered those who escaped to be "the most notorious criminals among the gentry," who were forced to run away to avoid being punished for their crimes.[15] In this conception of escape, however, the factor pushing such criminals to run away is their imminent punishment as a result of rural mobilization

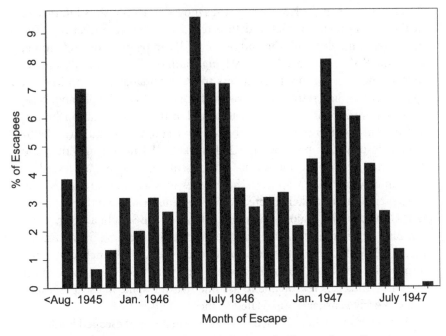

Figure 18. Timeline of recorded escapes by month, Shuangcheng County, 1945–1947. Author's calculations based on linked victim registers (*N* = 596). *Note:* Escapes in August 1945 represent all escapes dated before the end of World War II in August 1945.

and revolution. Therefore, we would expect that during land reform in Shuangcheng, for example, escapes should increase in a given area during land reform campaigns and work team activity.[16] In contrast to this hypothesis, at least for the first half of land reform in Shuangcheng, the opposite was true. Figure 18 shows that in reality, escapes peaked during impending war and invasion, not during land reform activity.

This timeline makes it clear that "banishment" was a misnomer: politically empowered peasant associations (PAs) were not driving away criminals; these people were leaving the countryside to seek basic safety and security, most likely because they simply had the means to do so. Moreover, major land reform mobilization often occurred *after* many of these people had already left. The first spike in escapes happened around the end of World War II, when the surrender of Japan led to the flight of large numbers of Japanese collaborators and other former officials. The subsequent two spikes in escapes in this figure coincided with regional events of the civil war, when the KMT army twice moved to within sixty kilometers of the Shuangcheng border and threatened to advance on Harbin. The first spike coincided with the end of the CCP campaign to defend Siping, when the KMT recaptured the city lying south of Changchun, Jilin Province, about three hundred kilometers south of Shuangcheng, on May 18, 1946.[17] As Lin Biao retreated across the Songhua River, the Shuangcheng County government was ordered to abandon the county seat on June 3, and the railway running south of the county seat to Changchun was deliberately destroyed to prevent the KMT advance.[18] This was also the time of the May Festival Revolt and its subsequent suppression, as described in chapter 3 (see also Map 4).[19] The escapes in May, June, and early July were therefore most likely related to these events. The second spike similarly coincides with major military activity along the Songhua River, when Lin Biao began a series of attacks south of the river, lasting from January through March 1947.[20] At the end of January, the KMT launched a counteroffensive and once again announced they were planning to march on Harbin.[21] Thus it is reasonable to assume that the spike in escapes, especially in early February, was related to these events.[22]

In 1927 Mao further claimed that the destinations of escaped landlords closely corresponded to their political rank within the local elite, with the first rank fleeing to national capitals, the second rank fleeing to regional capitals, the third rank fleeing to provincial capitals, the fourth rank fleeing to the county seat, and the fifth rank staying in the village to surrender to the local PA.[23] Shuangcheng's escape registers closely reflect this hierarchy, in which the regional capitals were Changchun and Shenyang, and the provincial capital was Harbin.[24] Figure 19 breaks down the destinations of escapees by their political position, as identified in their reasons for escape. Here we can see that over half of the former county-level or higher officials under Manchukuo who escaped fled to a regional capital. In contrast, no former subcounty officials fled beyond the provincial capital. Although the status of other escapees is more difficult to ascertain, traitors and reactionaries, who tended to be relatively "notorious" local elites, were also much more likely to flee the county: over 90 percent of escapees labeled as traitors fled the county.[25] This clear spatial hierarchy illustrates another dimension of how political power relations shaped individual social and economic outcomes.

Movements within this spatial hierarchy suggest that to some degree, land reform brought social/spatial mobility to enemies and allies alike. More notorious or higher-ranked elites had more cause to flee farther

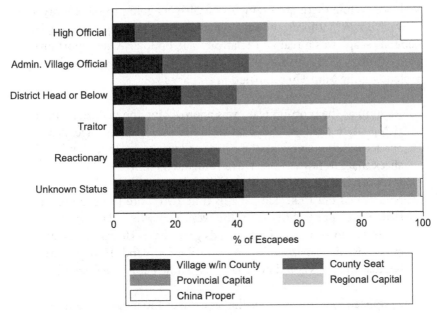

Figure 19. Escape destinations by position/status of escapee, Shuangcheng County, 1945–1947. Author's calculations based on linked victim registers (*N*s of reasons for escape = 14, 25, 50, 29, 32, and 116, respectively).
Note: Under Manchukuo administration, the district was a smaller unit below the administrative village, and administrative villages were the equivalent of townships in other parts of China proper.

away in order to find safety, but they also fled farther up the spatial hierarchy because their previous positions provided them with the means to do so. A high official would have had the opportunity to make connections in larger cities and amass the social and economic capital required to live in such a metropolis, while subcounty officials likewise had the opportunity to make connections only at the provincial level at best. One unintended consequence of the CCP's rural revolution, therefore, was the upward mobility of county elites into regional cities and subcounty elites into provincial cities.

At the same time, nearly half of escapees with a known destination did not leave the county and often fled just temporarily to escape a particular campaign or work team. Of course, there was a selection bias, because those who fled farther were less likely to be located, but these local escapees demonstrate that one did not have to go very far to escape land reform violence. While there are examples of villagers going to the county seat to track down landlords and take them back to the village to struggle, in general escape was a real and relatively safe option.[26] One report gives a detailed description of how a rich peasant was able to escape from the violence of the Mop-Up campaign in January 1948:

> As soon as the mop-up team was approaching the village, [Han, a rich peasant,] ran away to a small house west of the village. It was about one kilometer from the village and was a very lonely and cold shack that saw few visitors. He ran and hid there. When the mop-up team reached the village they saw that all of the landlords ran away, and fanned out to search. At this time two more [mop-up team] sleds were approaching from the west, and when Han saw them he started to run, and the two sleds gave chase. He ran faster, and cut across the horizontal furrows of the farmland. Han got away because the sleds could not travel perpendicular to the furrows.[27]

One implication of this story is that as soon as the mop-up teams left the village, all of their enemies could have just as easily returned home. In other cases, villagers were well aware of where escapees were but could be indifferent, afraid, or even protect them.[28] Furthermore, linking individuals in the escape registers to the classification registers recording the final allocation of land shows that nearly one-fifth of "escaped" individuals reappear in the classification registers and were allocated land in their home village at the completion of land reform in 1948. While it is possible that these persons were not physically residing in the village at the time, their successful allocation of land forces us to take escape seriously as an effective strategy of self-preservation.

But the relative ease of escape overlooks the potentially more important public spectacle of local strongmen fleeing for their lives. For villagers and work teams who described such events of escape, the point was not to show how easy it was to escape government policies. Escaping symbolized weakness. In the past it was the vulnerable and destitute villagers who often had to flee their homes in the face of coercive officials and ravaging armies. Even in earlier land reform campaigns, local strongmen still sat at home and orchestrated struggles to dupe visiting work teams. In this context the sight of a strongman fleeing in the face of a band of poor peasants was the visual display of a reversal of power relations, and this is exactly why work teams documented them, as proof of a job well done. One work report from District 3 summarizing the Mop-Up campaign describes "the complete overthrow of feudal power" in these terms:

> Whenever a mop-up team arrived in a village, all the landlords would run for their lives, as if they trembled in fear at the mere mention [of the mop-up]. Some would be eating dinner when they heard that a mop-up team was coming, and would disappear with their dinner still on the table. With this it can be shown that their feudal power has collapsed.[29]

Before this campaign, the CCP and villagers had already struggled against many landlords and confiscated all their property, but only such terror could convince people that these former powerholders had been truly humbled.

The option of escape, which could be as simple as going off to hide for a day or two, likewise raises questions about those strongmen who were physically caught and struggled against. Why did they stay, even after they had heard rumors about land reform and after a work team was stationed in their own village?[30] Presumably these strongmen were either unusually obstinate or simply did not have the means to leave their homes. In either case, their families may have been running things in the village for several generations, and they were not prepared for a modern state to come push them out of their sinecure. The strongmen who were left to be struggled against represented the low-hanging fruit on the Chinese political tree. Focusing on low-hanging fruit meant that many other strongmen, including "the most notorious criminals," could easily avoid persecution. However, this strategy also ensured that the CCP could reap the most fruit with the least amount of effort. In other words, what this meant in practice is that land reform violence targeted a political category of people, not an economic or class category. Most local strongmen had their land confiscated, but only those few strongmen who tried to physically hold on to power in the rural community were subjected to violent struggle.

Looking at the recorded crimes of escapees over time further demonstrates that more prominent enemies tended to escape earlier. Figure 20 looks at the reasons for escape by land reform campaign period. Here we can see that nearly half of all individuals who escaped for political reasons, which included many former officials and counterrevolutionaries, escaped before the start of the first land reform campaign in the county, in July 1946. By the beginning of the more intense Cut Down and Dig Up

Figure 20. Time of escape by reasons for escape in Shuangcheng County, 1945–1947. Author's calculations based on linked victim registers (Ns of reasons for escape = 314, 148, 62, and 60, respectively). Excludes twelve observations of missing or other reasons.

campaign in the summer of 1947, over 90 percent of political escapees, who accounted for 60 percent of all recorded escapees, had already fled. In contrast, more than half of individuals escaping for economic reasons did not move before 1947. The fact that these escape registers were all recorded in the summer of 1947 also precludes changing standards or shifting campaign rhetoric over time. We can therefore conclude that the bigger the enemy (of land reform, the CCP, or the people), the earlier they left and the farther they fled. The effect of these patterns of escape was that as the number of potential enemies decreased, the intensity of land reform campaigns increased. Or from a different point of view, as more prominent and powerful enemies escaped, those who remained in the countryside would become all the more vulnerable.

One example provides a better idea of landlord decision making at this time. One village that was the subject of the work report in chapter 4 held two struggle meetings nearly one month apart against six landlords.

The first two landlords, who were the targets of the first struggle meeting, had already escaped before the work team arrived in the village. This struggle meeting consisted of villagers publicly condemning the landlords and deciding how to redistribute whatever property they had left in the village. The second struggle meeting was held against three absentee landlords, whom villagers brought back from the county seat, and one resident managerial landlord, F, who was still in the village. After the first struggle meeting, the work report records, F was already apprehensive and sent his son out of the village (to be safe). Later, F was talking with another resident landlord, G, who said that this time he was even more afraid and decided to kowtow before the work team and ask them to redistribute his land. G tried to donate his land to the PA, but he did not offer enough to satisfy them. Over the next few days, F decided to try to bribe the work team and bribed a couple of loafers to infiltrate the masses, but they were caught and chased off, which led to F being struggled against.[31] Since this story takes place during the first land reform campaign in the county in the fall of 1946, it is important to note that not all landlords were targeted.[32] The classification registers for this village, which record the entire population in the summer of 1948, record ten small landlord and fourteen regular landlord households. The six landlords mentioned in this story thus comprised no more than one-quarter of village landlords. That being said, F was known to be in cahoots with the police during Manchukuo, which would have made him a potential target as a traitor. Nevertheless, one implication of this story is that if F had not tried to get the upper hand, he might not have been targeted. F and G are two examples of how staying in the village was unsuccessful. But even for those landlords who do not appear in this work report, the expropriation registers for this village record that by the summer of 1947, thirty-one landlords had been struggled against. This suggests that, at least in this village, staying at home was not the best choice in the long run.

This examination of the people who fled during land reform in Shuangcheng provides a more nuanced understanding of the spatial contexts in which land reform experiences took place. First, the "most notorious criminals" usually made clean getaways. There were spikes in escapes *before* the CCP arrived in the county in the fall of 1945; *before* the first land reform campaign, in the fall of 1946; and *before* the intensification of land reform in the summer of 1947. While these people might have fled in anticipation of these developments, evidence suggests it is more likely that they were escaping from the more immediate ravages of civil war, which also tended to precede land reform work. Second, as a result of the first finding, this spatial divide created a win-win situation for both the CCP and their enemies. Although fleeing one's home might not be a desirable option, under the circumstances, land reform policies—not to mention civil war—in effect pushed people of means out of the countryside and up China's spatial hierarchy. In the broader historical context of industrialization, this invariably meant increased opportunities in the long run. For the CCP, the flight of local elites also meant an increasingly isolated and vulnerable countryside and thus an easier task of land reform. Third, and finally, land reform policies explicitly took advantage of this fractured spatial hierarchy, which left the rural community, occupying the lowest rung of the hierarchy, ripe for the picking.

Public Humiliation

As we now know from looking at escapes, stories of land reform took place exclusively in rural communities where any remaining local strongmen were politically vulnerable and at the mercy of their fellow villagers. In this section we will see that the violence that played out in these contexts likewise continued to be organized around power, not property. In a classic land reform narrative, this section might be called something like "the struggle for land," but hundreds of instances of violent struggle in Shuangcheng make it clear that the ultimate goal was not land but stripping offenders of their social and political influence in the community through performances of public humiliation.

As introduced in chapter 1, the main event of CCP land reform was the act of "struggle," in which villagers rallied together to publicly accuse a "struggle target" and then humiliate him or her through confession, beating, or parading them around the village. Such violence is often interpreted in terms of either legitimate Marxist class struggle or illegitimate state coercion.[33] In Marxist terms, only wealthy villagers should be targeted. In non-Marxist terms, property should be redistributed through economic and legal means, and violent persecution is unnecessary. The identities of victims, reasons for struggle, and methods of struggle recorded in Shuangcheng challenge both of these interpretations and suggest a new framework in which struggle was used to reinforce moral norms and hierarchies of political power.[34] The premise for virtually every struggle recorded in both Shuangcheng's victim registers and work reports was that the victim had used their political position (as village head, for example) to unfairly accumulate resources for personal gain instead of to carry out their perceived duty of fairly distributing resources within the community. That these victims included both former officials who served under Manchukuo (in the case of Northeast China) and new officials serving under the CCP further suggests that such abuse of power was systemic enough to bridge the revolutionary divide and not simply a function of property ownership. Struggle by means of public humiliation thus aimed to undermine a victim's political position in the community, condemn abuses of power, and either implicitly or explicitly promote proper political norms like consensual decision making.[35] In these respects, land reform violence revitalized the structure of power in rural China more than it revolutionized it.

A detailed example of one village's struggle will give a better sense of what this structure of power looked like. In the summer of 1947 a new work team was sent to a village in District 8 to carry out the latest land reform campaign (Cut Down and Dig Up). This was the fourth time a work team had visited the village, which already had a well-established PA. On the same day the work team arrived, the PA head's son organized a struggle meeting against a resident landlord, W, but villager participation was low. The next day, while working out in the fields, the work team met seven activists and organized a meeting that same night to encourage them to "speak bitterness," or voice their grievances against local strongmen. In following with campaign objectives, the work team encouraged the masses to confiscate the landlord's household belongings. One woman said that during Manchukuo when she went to pick up loose grains in W's field after the harvest, he accused her of stealing his grain and beat her. Another reserved peasant got up and said that in 1942, when W was serving as district head, he farmed some land and W requisitioned a pig from him. He did not have a pig or the money to substitute for one, and as a result W had the local police come and rough him up. He sold all of his grain and cooking fuel but still did not have enough money, so he was forced to sell his two daughters too. This meeting gradually expanded to include grievances against another resident landlord, and finally some activists encouraged the group to struggle against W. By the end of the night, the activists tied up and beat W and the cousin of another landlord, the women's group beat up W's wife, and the youth group beat up the W's son.[36]

As a typical episode of land reform violence, this might be the end of the story: the work team organized a handful of activists to lead the masses, condemn and beat up a landlord family, and confiscate some of their belongings. But the next day the work team announced that these struggles were all fake: some activists had acted unilaterally without the support of the masses, some "bad guys" continued to inform the landlords of what was going on, the masses were reluctant to act, and some of the beatings were even staged. The work team met with some of the activists again and discovered that the PA head's son had served on a CCP work team in the past and since then had used his political capital to take control of village affairs. This man, named Rende, was in cahoots with the resident landlords and embezzled confiscated goods; all the other village cadres and activists were afraid of him. The work team then asked the activists if they would rather struggle against the landlords or these bad cadres, and everyone said the bad cadres. They rang the village bell to call a mass meeting and this time brought Rende and four other PA cadres before the crowd. Men, women, and children all started beating them at once, hitting them with shoes and spitting in their faces, and then they made them publicly confess their wrongdoings. Rende confessed to protecting the landlords, receiving bribes, and embezzling a confiscated piece of gold jewelry. When everyone heard this, they started beating the cadres again and yelling about how they had teamed up with the landlords to oppress them, calling them the "new aristocracy." After the beating was over, the villagers locked the cadres up, and the work team reported that this was the most successful struggle meeting yet. The activists all agreed that Rende should be executed, because, in their words, "if you don't kill a tiger it will come back to hurt you" (打虎不死反要伤人), but the work team insisted that they should struggle against the landlords first, before killing anyone, and they made plans to parade these five bad cadres around the village and then struggle against the landlords.[37]

The next day the five corrupt village cadres were made to wear dog hides and tall dunce caps and paraded up and down two village streets while everyone shouted slogans. Then the cadres wrote out formal letters of confession and were released to guarantors. That afternoon, crowds from four neighboring villages came to hold a struggle meeting against W. After talking about all the oppression they suffered under him, W and his wife were brought out, and the struggle naturally split into two groups, with the men criticizing and beating W and the women accusing and beating W's wife. Even women carrying small children participated in the beating, and children who couldn't reach made the victims kneel down to get beaten. Rende also started complaining and crying and stole one of the activists' leather belts and beat him back, but then they ripped off his shirt and tied his shoulders up with rope to beat him. W was also beaten all over his entire body, and after he passed out they took him back to be locked up. The women beat up W's wife even worse. The villagers wanted to finish all the struggling at one time, so they also dragged in an escaped landlord's younger brother and gave him a beating, but not as heavy, because his crimes weren't as bad as his brother's. When they were finished, they locked up the landlords again to prepare for smaller struggles and the confiscation of their belongings.[38]

A few days later, after reorganizing the village PA, the work team asked the masses if the landlords still had any belongings left, and the masses decided to find out by stringing up W and whipping him until he confessed to his hidden belongings. While this was going on, some people noticed that a landlord from a neighboring village was standing in the back of the crowd, so they caught and tied up him and his wife, and he confessed to keeping five sacksful of W's clothing. Upon hearing that the landlord's belongings had been spread around to other households, the masses flew into a rage. They also strung up the cousin of an escaped landlord and demanded he turn over his pistol and other possessions. The cousin was lashed until he couldn't bear it anymore and gradually confessed to hiding one, two, and then three sacksful of goods. This evasion only made the villagers angrier, and they started lashing him harder the more he confessed. They began cursing him and gang-whipping him until he passed out and stopped breathing. Some people said he was playing dead and threw water on his face, but he still did not wake up. With this some villagers got scared, and the activists went to the work team for help before the man was finally revived. The women were also very successful in this struggle and wrested five pounds of jewelry from the landlord's women.[39]

In this story, in one village within the span of one week, we can catch a glimpse of the entire spectrum of land reform violence in Shuangcheng. At first villagers were unmotivated and the struggles were staged to impress the sojourning work team. Most villages were like this in the early stages of land reform in the county. Then the work team discovered that the village PA was corrupt and obstructed the mobilization of the majority. Again, this was one of the central problems in land reform work throughout 1947. Finally, violence was used to extract hidden personal belongings after the work team learned that such immediate material incentives proved effective in mobilizing villagers to attack local strongmen. In the winter of 1947 this last violence was seen as the most successful, because it not only mobilized villagers but also could be conceived in terms of a struggle over property.

In all of this violence, however, there is little evidence to support a class struggle narrative. Villagers condemned both W and the escaped landlord for bullying, extortion, and other strongman tactics, and everyone else who was beaten and humiliated were lower-class accomplices. The line was thus drawn between proper and improper exercise of power, which meant that anyone who assumed a position of leadership was at risk. The result was that many villagers had learned to avoid politics to reduce their risk of getting in trouble, while both former wealthy leaders and new poor leaders were equally likely to become targets of struggle. The first "real" public display of violence in the village therefore involved the parade and confession of poor village CCP cadres. This seems like a strange way to win over villagers to the CCP cause, but the more obvious effect was to demonstrate that the CCP was not going to tolerate any abuse of power, even within their own ranks. This type of justice was something that villagers could buy into.

Established social relations also conditioned which people were most vulnerable. Previously both W and the other landlord fled the village, but the villagers were only able to capture and bring back W. The landlord who escaped was described as more notorious, but he was also the senior head of the major family lineage in the village. W was an "independent household," which likely meant his family was not one of the original settlers of the village. In other words, W bore the brunt of violence because he was more socially vulnerable, not necessarily more deserving.[40] The man who was almost beaten to death was a cross-cousin of the escaped landlord, making him likewise more distant and vulnerable in kinship terms. These relations made violence more arbitrary (i.e., less related to the absolute gravity of crimes), but they also reflected a more fluid society in which it was often possible to evade punishment because certain social categories were never absolute. In other words, social and political connections could be more important than actual practices of oppression and exploitation in determining who was victimized. Many villagers might prefer this more subjective approach, just in case they were ever targeted.

Shuangcheng's victim registers indeed record that one out of three victims of public humiliation were middle and poor peasants (see Figure 16).

Table 15. Top Ten Crimes/Reasons for Public Humiliation of Middle and Poor Peasants in Shuangcheng County, ca. 1947

Highest Crime	Individuals	%	Cum. %
Graft and embezzlement	102	17.4	17.4
Running dog/lackey	72	12.3	29.7
Moral misconduct	50	8.6	38.3
Sabotage the revolution	42	7.2	45.5
Criminal behavior	39	6.7	52.1
Political oppression	35	6.0	58.1
Other exploitation	33	5.6	63.8
Manchukuo subcounty official	30	5.1	68.9
Violent counterrevolution	25	4.3	73.2
Extortion and appropriation	24	4.1	77.3
Total	452	77.3	

Source: Author's calculations based on linked victim registers. Excludes 22.7% of middle and poor peasant victims humiliated for other reasons.

As summarized in Table 15, the top ten crimes, which accounted for the reasons for humiliating more than three-quarters of these peasants, were virtually all related to their political position. Graft and embezzlement typically involved CCP village cadres keeping confiscated property for themselves. "Running dog" was a name euphemistically applied to typically poor peasants who served as the agents or lackeys of local strongmen or former officials. Moral misconduct included many peasants identified as "loafers" and "bad guys." As may be expected, the only economic crime to make it into the top ten is "other exploitation," and even in many of these cases involving lower-class peasants, it appears as if "exploitation" referred to village cadres using their political position to exploit villagers.[41]

Overall, 206 victims were explicitly identified as CCP village cadres, and the vast majority of them were punished by parading or public confessions. These observations come from a total of 50 *cun* and at least 150 *tun*. For four of these *cun*, the only recorded victims of struggle were all former cadres. Over one-quarter of all *tun* and half of all *cun* in the county, therefore, had at least one corrupt cadre.[42] By comparison, Huang Daoxuan's study of cadre rectification during this period cites a Taihang region (southeastern Shanxi) survey from late 1946, in which more than half of the 248 county and district cadres were reported to have "made mistakes."[43] But it is not clear how many of them, if any, were punished as a result. Li Lifeng furthermore presents data from two districts of a county in eastern Hebei in November 1947 that characterize three-quarters of local leaders as "vagrants, lackeys, or sympathetic to landlords and rich peasants," terms that all appear frequently in Shuangcheng's registers as well.[44] Compared to these findings, Shuangcheng's struggle registers paint a relatively more positive picture of local leadership, but again this discrepancy could simply be an effect of the selective nature of Huang's and Li's data, which come from work team reports aimed at identifying such corruption as a major goal of those campaign periods.[45] Previous studies have pointed out that the first activists and CCP supporters in an area were often from marginal social groups, or "lumpenproletariat," which inevitably led to local leadership problems for the CCP.[46] But it is also clear that such problems of official corruption outlived this first generation of CCP leaders.

The position of "running dog" (走狗, 狗腿, 腿子) is so ubiquitous that it constitutes its own crime category and deserves more attention. As highlighted in the earlier example, village enmity toward "running dogs" or lackeys of local strongmen could be even greater than enmity toward the strongmen themselves. Again there are two ways to understand this phenomenon. One explanation is that it is easier to attack such lower-class lackeys because they are more vulnerable and less powerful than the strongmen above them. In several villages, villagers were much more reluctant to attack local strongmen with relatives in high places or who were known leaders of local bandit groups capable of taking revenge on the village. In the fall of 1946 in one village in District 10, for example, a notorious local landlord and his lackey were put on public trial together (i.e., a struggle meeting in which plaintiffs voice their grievances and sentence the accused) and sentenced to public execution. The night before the execution, however, the landlord's wife and children went around to all the households in the village crying and begging for mercy. The next day, the lackey was executed after confessing all of his crimes, but after the landlord read out his confession, villagers decided to spare him and simply confiscate his property. The wife's plea no doubt softened the hearts of many villagers, but the work report also mentions that this landlord's cousin, who had escaped earlier that year, was the known leader of a local bandit group at least one hundred strong and was sure to get revenge on the village if anything happened to his cousin.[47] Here again we see that political connections were a crucial determinant of violence.[48]

Another explanation is that, morally speaking, the wealth and position of local strongmen made them somewhat more justified in exercising power than lower-class lackeys, not to mention that in practice the lackeys were responsible for actually carrying out the "dirty work" of their masters.

Table 16. Top Ten Crimes/Reasons for Public Humiliation of Landlords and Rich Peasants in Shuangcheng County, ca. 1947

Highest Crime	Individuals	%	Cum. %
Other exploitation	348	34.4	34.4
Manchukuo subcounty official	90	8.9	43.3
Political oppression	82	8.1	51.4
Traitor	62	6.1	57.5
Land exploitation	62	6.1	63.6
Class status	57	5.6	69.3
Manchukuo clerk/accountant	37	3.7	72.9
Manchukuo police	30	3.0	75.9
Other collaboration	29	2.9	78.8
Manchukuo high official	23	2.3	81.0
Total	820	81.0	

Source: Author's calculations based on linked victim registers. Excludes 19% of landlord and rich peasant victims humiliated for other reasons.

Abuses and oppression aside, several work reports mention that peasants believed that the determinants of who got wealth and power were out of their control and that some families were destined to be rich and powerful while others were destined to be poor and destitute. In explaining why it was so difficult to mobilize villagers to redistribute land, a CCP leader in District 8 declares the number one reason as being the "traditional moral belief" that people were "poor because they had poor fate, and rich because they had rich fate" (穷是命穷, 富是命富).[49] In such a worldview, lackeys could be seen as doubly illegitimate for trying to exercise power in the first place and then abusing it. Taking this concept a step further, in a world where local strongmen were often seen as "local emperors," their lackeys can also be compared to corrupt ministers or lower-level officials. Throughout Chinese history, such intermediate officials have often been the target of social discontent and blamed by both leaders and subjects as the main cause of social disorder and state decline. Insofar as intra-village politics formed a microcosm of state politics, here too political middlemen often bore the brunt of popular indignation.

The other two out of three victims of public humiliation were identified as landlords and rich peasants. Table 16 shows that these victims were targeted for very different reasons. In line with official land reform narratives, economic exploitation (the first, fifth, and sixth top crimes in the table) comprises the main reason for targeting landlords and rich peasants, and this reason accounts for just under half of all upper-class victims.

But an equal number of upper-class victims were targeted because of their political position or abuse of power, as illustrated by the other seven out of ten top crimes. Six of these crimes, moreover, explicitly identified victims as former Manchukuo officials or other traitors, and as described in many work reports, this also implied official misconduct. Political oppression was similar and directly refers to strongman tactics such as extortion, beating, bullying, and, in a few cases, burying people alive. Overall, therefore, two-thirds of lower-class victims and half of upper-class victims were humiliated or punished for abusing power. To some extent, the only difference between these two types of victims was whether they had previously served in office and had more time to accumulate wealth or only recently came to power under the CCP and were still relatively poor.

Former Manchukuo officials were particularly prominent targets because of their double-whammy illegitimate use of power. Their identity as agents of the Japanese-backed Manchukuo state automatically defined their exercise of power as illegitimate and at odds with local (Chinese) community interests. On top of this, many of these local strongmen also explicitly abused their power by embezzling public resources. Many of the urban and rural landlords described in work reports and introduced in chapter 2 are characterized in this way. In a power-based world, one could even argue that the confiscation of these victims' wealth was also interpreted in political terms as villagers reclaiming their political entitlement to a fair distribution of resources. These strongmen did not use their ownership of the means of production to accumulate more capital through exploitation but instead used their political positions to interfere in the state- or community-organized distribution of resources.[50] One of the most detailed examples of this behavior in Shuangcheng comes from a description of an early struggle meeting in the fall of 1946 on the eastern border of the county. This meeting was attended by over one thousand villagers, and the report lists out the following fourteen of the more than forty grievances voiced against the accused "landlord":

1. He was head of the administrative village Concordia Association, and director of the agricultural cooperative and the distribution office [during Manchukuo]. He practiced corruption, and once seized a villager's residential land. When he served as district head he extracted conscript labor at will and used the police to intimidate people.
2. New immigrants that moved into the village in 1941 paid their

village dues but received nothing from the distribution office because he embezzled all the money.

3. Every time workers were conscripted [for government labor], his brother's name was on the list but his brother never served.

4. He gave all of the good cloth from the distribution office to his relatives and friends and people who bought him opium, and when one villager tried to get some good cloth the landlord called the police to detain him, and intimidated him, saying, "every person who doesn't dress properly and freezes to death is one less person [to worry about]."

5. The previous year every one of the 10,725 persons in the administrative village was supposed to be allocated 6 catties of salt, but they only received 1.3 catties each, and were not refunded their money, either.

6. In 1944 he withheld 3 out of every 10 yards of cloth allocated to the tax-paying households, saying it was for the dependent (non-tax-paying) households, but then he just kept it for himself.

7. The previous year every household in the administrative village was supposed to be allocated 1 blanket, which cost 1.6 *yuan* each, but he did not distribute a single one.

8. The previous year he was supposed to distribute 10 *yuan* of seed to every household. He collected the money but then did not distribute any seed or refund any money.

9. In 1941 every household was supposed to be allocated boxes of matches, but no one ever received them.

10. In 1943 every conscripted worker was taxed 80 *yuan* and hauled in eight carts [worth of goods], but nothing was ever distributed to the people.

11. In 1944 the village received a military [recruitment] award of 30,000 *yuan*, but the people never received a cent of it.

12. In 1943 some brand name silk cloth was distributed to village governments, but he only handed out poor quality cloth to villagers, and some households did not get any cloth at all.

13. He collected 6.6 *yuan* per hectare of land (for all 11,000 hectares in the administrative village) to build a police station in the central village, but then the station never got built and the money was never refunded.

14. After the end of the Sino-Japanese War he held on to some

cloth distributed by the county government, and then during the disorder of the post-war period he hid the cloth in his attic and said that the common people stole it.[51]

It should be clear that this list comes from a world in which power brings wealth and not vice versa. Unfortunately for the villagers, however, this landlord had escaped long before this meeting took place, thus making this another example of a struggle meeting in which the accused was absent. It is unclear if this landlord was ever brought to justice, but presumably whatever belongings he left in the village were redistributed among the villagers.

The fact that struggle meetings with as many as one thousand participants could be held in the absence of the accused suggests that violently punishing enemies was not the only goal of struggle. Of the roughly one thousand individual records of struggle in Shuangcheng's expropriation registers, other recorded information suggests that more than two hundred of the victims were not present.[52] If the goal of CCP land reform was to persecute landlords or local strongmen, what was the point of struggling against someone in absentia? The practice of such symbolic struggle meetings suggests that the objective was not simply to persecute enemies and redistribute their property but to reinforce an ideal moral order in which abuses of power could and should be openly condemned.[53] Indeed, if a landlord had already fled the village, there would be no need for a struggle meeting, since the villagers could just redistribute his abandoned property. For the CCP, however, the symbolic struggle meeting accomplished the larger goal of politically mobilizing a majority of the population to govern themselves instead of being governed by others. As highlighted throughout this book, the ultimate goal of land reform in Shuangcheng was to motivate villagers to establish some form of democratic self-government as the prerequisite for a fairer distribution of resources. Even when a struggle object had already fled, therefore, the struggle meeting served to empower and organize villagers who otherwise would have passively received property handed out according to another new government policy.[54]

After the Outline Land Law was implemented, public displays of violence not only increased but also fundamentally changed in nature from humiliation and moral rectification to outright robbery. Thousands of villagers were beaten up and intimidated for not handing over their household belongings. At first the CCP justified this violence in terms of class struggle, insofar as it involved poor peasants attacking the (relatively) wealthy and confiscating their property. With the Mop-Up campaign in January 1948, however, this struggle clearly devolved into inter-village robbery. The details of this violence were explored in chapter 5, but the way in which the CCP mitigated this winter of terror was once again through a form of social-moral rectification and ordering of the village community. This was the Classification campaign, which was less punitive and more focused on creating a new social order, as described in chapter 3. Together, violent public humiliation and relatively peaceful social ranking followed a similar logic of reinforcing a certain set of moral and political norms and entitlements, which remained surprisingly similar across old and new regimes in rural China.

Killing

Most criticism of CCP land reform begins from the premise that violating private property rights is illegitimate, while the only counterargument is an ideological one asserting that it is legitimate to punish people who for decades had indirectly harmed others through class exploitation. Moreover, after this revolutionary counterargument went out of style in the 1980s, the only option for official CCP narratives has been to downplay the role of violence in land reform and other campaigns. Critics have also easily found plenty of evidence of fatal violence in China's revolution to challenge this latter claim, but at least for land reform, these debates are based on aggregate reported or calculated death statistics and typically assume that the victims were all identified as class enemies (landlords and rich peasants) and targeted because of their class label. In this section, however, I will demonstrate that the evidence on killings in Shuangcheng County makes it possible to fundamentally redefine the terms of the debate over revolutionary violence in rural China. As with the violence explored above, killings followed political fault lines and had little relation to property or class struggle.

Shuangcheng's victim registers record 266 deaths over a span of two years for a county with a rural population of more than 370,000 people. In addition, district-level aggregate statistics after the Mop-Up campaign record 300 deaths over a span of about four months ending in March 1948. Of these, over 50 deaths recorded in the victim registers occurred during the Mop-Up campaign and are therefore likely to be double counted.

None of the extant work reports contain any evidence of widespread killings in the county beyond this potential total of roughly 500 deaths. This total averages out to about 15 deaths per 10,000 rural inhabitants, or 6 deaths per *cun*. As such, Shuangcheng County provides more than five hundred counterexamples to more violent land reform narratives like Frank Dikötter's, in which in some villages more than 70 people, or 10 percent of the village population, died, and in a single county much smaller than Shuangcheng, more than 2,000 people died.[55] The situation in Shuangcheng is perhaps more comparable to Hinton's account, in which he writes, "At least a dozen people were beaten to death by angry crowds. . . . But the reader should keep in mind that not many villages in China followed such a tortuous path to liberation or experienced so much pain on the way."[56] Likewise in the 91 *cun* in Shuangcheng, there are more examples of moderate to low violence than excessive violence. More important, however, for Shuangcheng, the story does not end here with extreme examples and aggregate estimates. For most of the 266 killings recorded in the victim registers, we also know where, why, and how these deaths occurred as well as the characteristics of the killers and the killed.

Mass killings or executions (of more than five persons) were rare and occurred no more than a dozen times over the two-year course of land reform in all of Shuangcheng. For half of the ninety-one *cun* in the county, fewer than 5 total deaths are recorded. Figure 21 illustrates the distribution of killings in sixty-five *cun* with extant, non-missing records of deaths. Here we can see that only four *cun* record more than ten deaths. The top three most violent villages provide useful examples of the types of mass killings that could take place during land reform.

The village in District 7 with the highest total death count experienced multiple episodes of violence over the course of land reform. First, after the May Festival Revolt in the summer of 1946, a militarized CCP work team was met with gunfire while passing through the village, and a local landlord tried to seize their weapons, but otherwise there were no casualties at the time.[57] Later, in February 1947, an Eighth Route Army unit passing through the village was again attacked. This time CCP army headquarters summarily shot ten of the offenders. One year later, in early 1948, this same village also hosted the most violent mass rectification meeting in the county. At this meeting a dozen people were beaten to death, some of whom appear to be directly related to the earlier counterrevolutionary attacks.[58] Half of the victims were identified as lower-class peasants, and none of the recorded reasons for killing were related to economic class

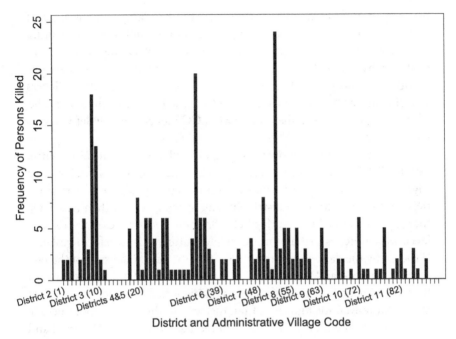

Figure 21. Distribution of reported killings by administrative village in Shuangcheng County, 1946–1948. Author's calculations based on linked victim registers (*N* = 266). Twenty-six administrative villages have missing records.

exploitation. One feature of this violence should be immediately apparent: it has little relation to landowning or class struggle and instead stems from an armed conflict between civil war opponents. The third most violent village, located in District 2, was also the site of a public mass execution at which eight reactionary bandits were decapitated and thus exhibited similar features.

In the second most violent village, located in District 5, fourteen out of seventeen deaths were a result of beatings by mop-up teams from other villages during the Mop-Up campaign in January 1948. These deaths were most likely not the result of a single organized mass killing, therefore, but related to the more random violence of inter-village struggles for food. Almost all of these victims were identified as landlords and rich peasants, but the only recorded reason for killing them relates that they were beaten to death for not handing over their hidden belongings. As discussed in chapter 5, it is also hard to define this violence in terms of class struggle, because as in this example, during the Mop-Up campaign the lines of violence were drawn between village communities, not intra-community socioeconomic classes. Unfortunately, there is not enough evidence to explain why this village in particular was so violent, but the one work report from this period that mentions this village suggests that villagers saw violence as the only effective way to extract hidden belongings, and after trying to convince them otherwise, CCP leaders finally let villagers have their way.[59]

The victim registers allow us to pinpoint village locations of violence, but the district-level statistics recorded after the Mop-Up campaign tell a slightly different story of killings within the county. Figure 22 compares these two sources for each district in Shuangcheng. Other than District 5, there appears to be little overlap between these two sources at the district level, which means that a more complete picture of land reform violence is shown by the dark grey bars representing the combined sum of the two sources. In general, Districts 7, 5, and 2 continue to stand out as some of the most violent districts in the county, as identified in the victim registers above. Moreover, for four out of ten districts in the county, more people were killed in the four months after implementation of the Outline Land Law than in the more than twelve months of land reform that preceded it. Unlike in the victim registers, however, here Districts 3 and especially 10 experienced extraordinary violence during the Mop-Up campaign. According to work reports, these two districts had some of the most active mop-ups in the county, but so did District 11, with the lowest frequency of killings. District 10 also records the highest numbers of beatings and confinements during the Mop-Up campaign (more than eight thousand!), and indeed, a major proportion of all land reform violence in the county was concentrated in District 10 in the winter of 1947/48. The only way to break down killings within this district, comprised of ten *cun* and nearly forty *tun*, is to infer from contemporary work reports, which mention one dozen mop-up team visits involving over twenty *tun* in nine *cun*. If we assume that all of the more than eighty reported deaths occurred during this activity, this would average out to about seven deaths per mop-up team visit and ten deaths per *cun*. This was indeed a time of terror in District 10, but the evidence suggests that even within this extreme example there were villages that remained relatively unaffected.

Returning to the nature of land reform killings, two distinct modes of killing recorded in Shuangcheng's victim registers challenge the assumption that this violence was motivated by some form of class struggle over

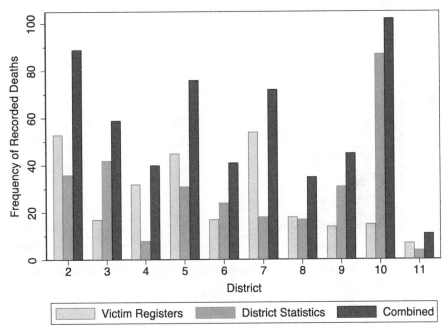

Figure 22. Comparison of Death Records in Shuangcheng County, 1946–1948. Author's calculations based on linked victim registers and 129-1-75.

property. In the first mode the CCP state organized the formal execution (by gun, sword, or spear) of lower-class peasants identified as bandits and counterrevolutionaries. Figure 23 illustrates how nearly two-thirds of persons executed were middle and poor peasants and that about half of these executions were carried out by CCP agents (i.e., work teams, district governments, and military units). Figure 24 illustrates how 80 percent of middle and poor peasants were killed for their political affiliation as enemies of the CCP. These killings may make sense in the context of civil war, but they also obviously complicate our land reform story. On the one hand, we might expect some lower-class peasants to be killed but not by the CCP. On the other hand, we might expect that two-thirds of killings involved political enemies of the CCP but not that so many lower-class peasants would be hostile toward a party that claimed to be fighting for their class interests. A better explanation requires a new understanding of the CCP and land reform. In land reform the CCP targeted a political group, not a socioeconomic group of rural inhabitants. This political group included

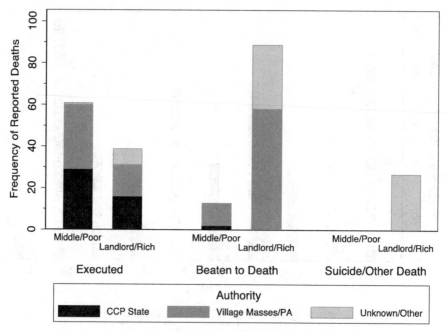

Figure 23. Persons killed by authority, class, and method in Shuangcheng County, 1946–1948. Author's calculations based on linked victim registers.

anyone who was complicit in the preexisting social and political disorder as perceived by either villagers or the CCP. In this context any wealth possessed by these enemies was a symptom of their political affiliation, not the cause.

One village in District 8 was rumored to be so violent during land reform that later in 1949 the county CCP government imprisoned several village activists for killing too many landlords.[60] However, a work report from the summer of 1947 describing this same village recounts how villagers beat up at least a dozen landlords at one struggle meeting, but the only two persons killed (at that time) were a gun-toting old lady and a bandit, both of whom were known for their bullying more than their wealth.[61] These are two representative examples of formal executions approved by the CCP state although not necessarily carried out by CCP agents. The first victim, Ms. Wang, was already in custody at the county police station, but at this time during the 1947 summer campaign, villagers requested that she be brought back to the village to be struggled against and expropriated.

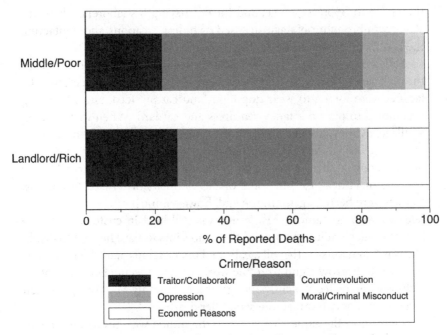

Figure 24. Crimes/Reasons for killings, by class of victims, Shuangcheng County, 1946–1948. Author's calculations based on linked victim registers. Excludes seventeen observations of blank or N/A reasons.

She owned only 1.2 hectares of land and some other personal belongings, but, more important, she also possessed two pistols, one semiautomatic and one Mauser military pistol. One pistol had already been confiscated by the county police, and the main objective of struggling against her was to make her confess to the location of the second pistol. After stringing her up to a tree and beating her for two days, she confessed that the pistol, along with four bullets, was buried three feet below the floor of the inner room of her house. Some villagers went to her house in the county seat and dug down five feet without finding anything, so they returned to the village and without a word continued to beat her. One night she escaped and the next day was found hiding in a cornfield; she was brought back to the village, strung up, and beaten unconscious. Village activists decided to hold a struggle meeting the next day to struggle against Ms. Wang and twenty other enemies. Fifteen of these people, including two lackeys, were beaten until they could barely move. The worst of these victims was condemned for having a well and not letting other villagers use it, for using the police to oppress people, and for not paying his laborers. Then Ms. Wang was brought on stage, accused of hiding weapons and contacting the KMT, and beaten senseless by the women's association.[62]

Following this meeting, the villagers decided to parade the victims through several villages. They were all made to wear tall dunce caps, the lackeys were forced to wear dog hides and eat pig feed, and Ms. Wang was forced to put on a fancy red dress and eat lard. When they entered a village, as they crawled through the streets, every hundred paces they were forced to confess their wrongdoings or receive a beating, and some literally crawled their knees down to the bone. Then they returned to the struggle meeting stage but some of the victims still refused to confess, so they were beaten again. In the end, however, most of the victims were released with guarantors. Ms. Wang was still held in custody, and only later the village militia petitioned their superiors to have her put to death. She was taken outside the village, beaten unconscious, and then the militia asked to borrow a gun from the work team to execute her.[63] The other victims were treated violently enough as it is, but only Ms. Wang was seen as a serious enough threat to warrant her death.

Later on in the same village, when the militia was discussing how to control reactionaries, they heard a fight outside and went out to find two brothers beating up their uncle. The militia tried to mediate but could not stop them. They found out that the two brothers were living in a house without paying rent, and one of the brothers was an ex-Manchukuo soldier who tried to extort money from his uncle and other villagers. The militia decided that these "bad eggs" needed to be struggled against, so they brought them on stage to confess their wrongdoings to the village. But when they did not fully fess up, the militia flew into a rage and whipped them with willow switches. The two brothers were released after confessing to how they oppressed and extorted villagers, but the militia continued to struggle against a third brother (identified as the ringleader) and within an hour had beaten him unconscious. He was revived with cold water and carried off to an empty room, and after recuperating he was beaten several more times until the villagers requested that he be put to death. This brother was accused of being a bandit, and as accountant of the village storehouse he had extorted money, grain, and feed from more than forty-five villagers. After getting approval from the county government, villagers dragged him outside the village, tied him to the leg of a horse, and sent the horse running.[64] These stories appear unrelated to the later imprisonment of village activists but demonstrate that, at least into the summer of 1947, killings targeted violent political enemies more than class enemies.

In the second mode of killing, local strongmen were beaten to death by village mobs for abuses of power. This mode more closely resembles the classic struggle meeting that has come to define land reform violence, in which a peasant mob publicly condemns a landlord and beats him to death in an emotional frenzy.[65] The village community serves as the judge, jury, and executioner, and the condemned victim is identified as a landlord or rich peasant. In most cases a CCP work team or other state agent is also involved in organizing the struggle meeting. In principle, in these meetings what makes the difference between public humiliation, as described in the previous section, and death is the seriousness of the victim's crimes. In practice, as we have already seen, violence was shaped by socio*political* relations. Despite evidence to the contrary, however, most stories of land reform continue to interpret the legitimacy of this violence in terms of socio*economic* relations. That is, either it is illegitimate to kill someone just for their land, or it is illegitimate to kill someone who is not a class enemy. The former view is critical of violent land reform, and the latter view is critical of the contradictions between CCP policies and Chinese realities.[66] While this latter view reflects the current mainstream understanding of land reform, it still falls short of actually explaining these contradictions.

The ideological lens of class struggle has so colored our view of land reform that even though many of the most sympathetic narratives suggest that violence followed sociopolitical fault lines, they still continue to interpret land reform through a Marxist framework of class struggle and property ownership. From early revolutionary propaganda like *The White Haired Girl* (1950) and Zhou Libo's *The Hurricane* (1948) to documentary accounts like Hinton's *Fanshen* (1966), many landlords and other victims are explicitly targeted for their abuses of power, oppression, and political affiliations. In *The White Haired Girl* film's final climactic struggle meeting, the landlord is publically condemned for driving a village girl's father to suicide, then kidnapping and raping the girl, and ultimately driving her to live in exile in the wilderness for three years. The film ends with the landlord and his lackey being sentenced to death as retribution for these crimes. In this case there is little attempt to even make the connection between the victim's class status and his crimes and punishment, but it is nevertheless taken for granted that his wealth is the ultimate source of his wrongdoings. This logical leap from abuses of power to landowning is an ideological assumption. In contrast, Shuangcheng's victim registers directly record that three-quarters of landlord and rich peasant deaths were justified in terms of political affiliation and abuse of power (i.e., oppression) (see Figure 24).[67] This systematic evidence forces us to see even the most classic propaganda in a radically new light.

In Shuangcheng, however, other than the victim registers there is surprisingly little qualitative evidence of local strongmen being beaten to death by angry mobs. Most of the killings described in work team reports were formal executions of lower-class enemies like the two examples above.[68] Otherwise evidence suggests that beating to death persons identified as landlords and rich peasants occurred most frequently during the Mop-Up campaign, when outside mop-up teams inadvertently beat to death wealthy villagers who refused to confess to their real or assumed hidden belongings. The more than one-quarter of landlords and rich peasants who were killed because of their class exploitation virtually all come from Mop-Up-related deaths. As in the second most violent village described above, in many of these cases the only recorded reason for killing is that they were beaten to death for not handing over their hidden belongings. I therefore categorize these deaths in terms of class exploitation only by inferring from campaign rhetoric and the class labels of victims that they were targeted as class enemies more than anything else.[69] As demonstrated in chapter 5, however, it could be just as plausible to argue that these victims died as a result of the chaos of the famine at that time.

A Post-Mop-Up work report from District 10, the most violent district in the county, also attempts to explain the violence during this campaign in terms of poor leadership and inter-village differences, not economics:

For the district as a whole, there were a little too many people killed. Some people who should not have been beaten to death were beaten to death, and some people who should not have been driven to suicide were driven to suicide. This must be considered a deviation. The cause of this mainly stems from the fact that when the campaign began, the thought of leaders was not clear enough, and the stance of the poor peasants and hired laborers was not secure, which together led to some leftist deviation. At the time it could already be seen that beatings were common, and that there was the danger of physically exterminating landlords. When a mop-up team went to mop up another village, their beatings and tortures were sometimes divorced from the [intentions of the] local masses, and precisely as a result of this some women were driven to suicide, and some people died after being beaten for not handing over their hidden belongings. At the time, leaders did not have the courage and resolve to correct these kinds of occurrences, primarily because they were afraid that such hidden belongings could not be thoroughly expropriated, and feudalism could not be completely wiped out, without physical violence. Although this was a little leftist, at the time they were only concerned with wiping out feudalism.[70]

After one year of trying to implement land reform policies with little real effect, some local leaders felt the only way to make village strongmen conform was through brute force. Moreover, in the context of rural China, after decades of war and disorder villagers learned that brute force was perhaps the only effective means of exercising power over scarce resources. In following our new sociopolitical understanding of violence, however, another important determinant of violence at this time was that the mop-up teams were outsiders in the villages they visited, often with few social connections to their victims. As we have seen throughout this chapter, victims with fewer sociopolitical connections in a given context were often treated more harshly.

Finally, the incidence of suicide also deserves mention. As shown in Figure 23, virtually all recorded suicides were identified as landlords and rich peasants, and nearly one out of five recorded landlord and rich peasant deaths were the result of suicide or other reasons.[71] Suicides are particularly important because in the context of rural China, it is not the person who kills themselves who is at fault, but the other who is perceived to have driven the person to suicide. In other words, killing oneself is equivalent to making one's antagonist a murderer. People are seen to be driven to suicide as a result of a specific person or offense, not because of some personal or abstract social problem. In this respect, in the context of land reform, suicides can be used as a measure of the coercive force of particular local or state agents, and these agents were thus especially concerned about suicides, because suicide deaths were in effect a symbol of poor leadership, as implied in the above excerpt from District 10. It appears that most suicides recorded in the victim registers occurred during the Mop-Up campaign, which we have already identified as the most violent period of land reform. One episode from a village in District 9 describes how a mop-up team drove one middle peasant woman to suicide. When a mop-up team from two districts over came to the village, some of them stayed in a middle peasant's household. As soon as they settled in, they assigned their host a class label and threatened to beat him to death if he was not honest about all of his belongings. The hostess heard this, got scared, and hanged herself. In the morning the villagers accused the mop-up team of driving the woman to suicide, then strung up and beat a few of the team members and released them only after district officials intervened.[72] This is another example of how this winter of terror came to symbolize the failure of class struggle in the context of rural China, but fortunately for the CCP, this was an exception rather than a rule of land reform practices.

The idea that land reform was not really a class struggle and that many victims were not really class enemies is not necessarily new.[73] What is new in this chapter is that the violence of land reform was not just arbitrary authoritarianism or mob rule, but reflected deeper mechanisms and relationships between Chinese state and society This state was a product of the local contexts of rural China more than of Marxist-Leninist ideologies. The foundation of this state was a world organized by relations to power, in which the distribution of resources was shaped by political status (relations to the state) more than property rights (relations to economic production). In rural China under the CCP, local cadres continued to have exclusive authority over resource distribution, but the goal of mass mobilization was to make these cadres more accountable than former local leaders. Insofar as violence can be seen as the exercise of raw, physical power, the state used it to reinforce moral-political norms of official conduct and villagers used it to take justice into their own hands.[74] This logic, more than class struggle or state coercion, is what shaped land reform violence in Shuangcheng.

CHAPTER 7

Toward a Modern China

The research for this book began with thousands of individual experiences of CCP land reform, and it took me several more years to fully understand the implications of these experiences within the context of larger historical and global developments. I use these larger contexts and implications only to bookend my empirical findings, not predetermine them. Historically, similar expressions of power over property at both central and local levels—in the sense of state persecution of political opponents and the expropriation and redistribution of their wealth, as well as in the sense of local moral-political power being more important than personal wealth—have been common in China since the second century BCE. Globally, in the twentieth century there was general consensus that agrarian reform was the basic solution to world poverty and economic development. CCP land reform embodied the convergence of these two developments on the lives of roughly one-third of the developing world's rural population around 1950, and, as such, it deserves a more nuanced treatment than "Communist takeover" or authoritarian regime motifs.[1]

A well-known Chinese historical example of power over property comes from the late second century BCE, when Emperor Wu of the Han dynasty (206 BCE–220 CE) implemented a wealth tax to increase state revenue and to limit the accumulation of wealth by large merchants and landowners. Merchant wealth was taxed at a rate of 6 percent, landowners taxed at 3 percent, and certain possessions like carriages and boats were also taxed. Those who tried to evade the tax were to have their property confiscated, and any person who reported such evasion was to be rewarded with half of the property. A few years later, an official was specially appointed to (re)investigate evaders of this tax, and his investigation resulted in the direct confiscation of "property valued in the hundreds of millions [of cash], tens of millions of slaves, thousands of hectares of land from every big county and hundreds of hectares of land from every small county, and similar amounts of housing, and as a result many large merchants were bankrupted."[2]

Writing in the 1950s, the Chinese historian He Changqun described this campaign as a Marxist economic struggle between the state and local elites over the control of land. However, the details of the story more closely resemble the dynamics of power over property that we have seen in Shuangcheng. He not only explains that the "rich merchants, large lineages, and powerful landlords" of the early Han dynasty were none other than the political elite of the previous regime but also documents how Emperor Wu allied with the "middle and lower classes" to attack these political competitors. The rapid expansion of the bureaucracy in the process of this attack, which is documented as increasing by over one hundred thousand persons in less than a decade, is likewise understood as the consolidation of a new political elite.[3] Even though He appears to have been deeply influenced by recent events in his own country in the 1950s, he draws a clear line between the "centralized autocratic feudalism" of Imperial China and the political system of the PRC.[4]

Emperor Wu's large-scale confiscation of wealth helped establish what He calls the nationalization of land, in which government "ownership" was the essential precondition for the regular appropriation and redistribution of land by Chinese states for most of the following millennium until the late Tang dynasty (618–907 CE).[5] Here again He asserts that the power of the Imperial Chinese state derived from its control of land—in effect, that property is the basis of political power. In practice, however, as just described, Emperor Wu initially used his political power to confiscate the property of his political opponents and consolidate a new political elite based on their relationships to the state, not their wealth.

While the Imperial Chinese state developed political supremacy over property, at the village level local leaders called *sanlao* (三老) were selected based on their ability to maintain order through moral example and persuasion, thus reinforcing a system of local political legitimacy not originating in personal wealth or landholding. One of the earliest records of the appointment of these village officials describes how in 205 BCE, immediately after Han armies gained control of an area in North China, they awarded civilians official titles, forgave two years of rent and taxes to the people for helping supply the army, gave soldiers one year leave, and appointed one person in each village who was "aged over 50, had experience, and could lead the masses to be good" to serve as *sanlao*.[6] In other words, after gaining military control of an area, the first thing Han leaders did to consolidate political control was to carry out economic relief and grassroots political reform based on restoring a moral order.

Although steeped in myth, the *sanlao* embodied an early ideal of local governance through moral example that continued to be developed in the village covenant system (乡约) from the Northern Song dynasty (960–1127). As Philip Kuhn describes it, this system was originally designed as a voluntary, autonomous association under the supervision of a locally selected leader that fulfilled many basic community functions such as public welfare, local defense, and "the rectification of village life through group criticism sessions."[7] Kuhn suggests that this originally local initiative (created in Lantian County, Shaanxi Province) was later appropriated and bureaucratized by the Ming and Qing states. In the early twentieth century, however, Liang Shuming revived the original idea of a more autonomous village association. Guy Alitto writes, "Liang's [village covenant] would be formed both by bureaucratic fiat and by moral suasion and local initiative. Through 'positive, activist' organization of enthusiastic mass participation, it would 'build up the power of the peasantry' so essential to the rest of Liang's program."[8] Liang's concept of a modern village covenant system provides a key link between traditional Chinese social and political organization and the political mobilization and PAs of CCP land reform.

Both the early Han dynasty and the early PRC share a similar historical context of massive political consolidation, and in both cases the practice of power and legitimacy are very different than in the European tradition. These few historical comparisons should suffice to show that CCP land reform does not just represent the domination of one party or one modern ideology over Chinese society but in fact demonstrates the resilience of deep-seated Chinese political traditions and their continuing ability to shape historical developments.[9] The large volume of grassroots records describing practices of land reform in Shuangcheng makes it possible to bring the resilience of such local experiences to life. Practices of CCP land reform were shaped by local social interests and were arguably successful only insofar as they fulfilled these interests. Likewise, even central CCP land reform policies were ultimately shaped by two decades of experimentation in rural China more than by communist ideology, no matter how much they were framed in terms of class struggle and equality.

In 1950 nearly two-thirds of the world's population lived in extreme poverty, and world income inequality reached its highest point in known history.[10] For the 60 percent of the world's population at this time who made their living from agriculture, the United Nations identified unequal relations of land tenure and labor as the primary causes of their poverty.[11] Agrarian reform was a top priority for most if not all of the governments struggling to industrialize their countries in the twentieth century.[12] One common solution was to remove or neutralize a whole class of people who could profit from rising land rents without producing anything of social value. In China the CCP labeled these people "feudal landlords," in which "feudal" meant they were unproductive. The goal of agrarian reforms around the world, therefore, was to drive economic (industrial) growth by "setting free the rural productive forces."[13] China's Communist Revolution must be understood within this global context as one of the largest consequences of this world inequality as well as one of the largest factors ultimately contributing to the gradual alleviation of extreme poverty after 1950.[14]

Agrarian reform had been a top priority among reformers within China since the early twentieth century. Beginning in 1905, Sun Yat-sen founded the Revolutionary Alliance Society and claimed "equalizing land rights" to be one of their four fundamental objectives.[15] Later reformulated as a call for "land to the tillers," by the 1920s the communist faction within the KMT became this policy's biggest, but not only, supporter. After the KMT-CCP split in 1927, both parties began to carry out land reforms. The KMT Legislative Yuan passed a land law in 1930 that aimed to limit land rents, but the law was never thoroughly implemented, and later the KMT focused more of their efforts on increasing agricultural productivity to alleviate rural problems.[16] Other regional governments also implemented similar agrarian reforms, like Yan Xishan's "Village land ownership" program beginning in 1935 in Shanxi and rent reduction programs in Sichuan.[17]

Twentieth-century agrarian reforms were formulated in a global historical context of fundamental economic transformations of labor and land that began in the nineteenth century. In the early 1860s, two of the largest systems of unfree rural labor—American slavery and Russian serfdom—came to an end. Although typically understood in terms of a moral triumph, the global coincidence of the end of unfree labor was the outcome of an emerging global consensus that continued economic growth required a free labor market.[18] Together with this global transformation of labor relations came an equally fundamental transformation of land and capital relations. In the last quarter of the nineteenth century, Henry George, an influential American journalist, argued that the contradiction between America's simultaneous prosperity and social misery following in the wake of industrial capitalism was due to the private monopolization of revenue from rising land values, values that derived from the advancing enterprise of society as a whole and not from direct individual efforts. The only way to solve the contradiction, therefore, was to return this new land revenue to society as a whole—for example, by creating a national land tax.[19] Around the same time, reformers in Germany began calling for land nationalization, a more radical solution to a similar problem of increasingly unjust land rents.[20] In 1899 Vladimir Lenin and Karl Kautsky each produced studies describing the effects of similar economic developments on the agricultural systems of Russia and Germany, respectively.[21] In both countries they observed a distinct process of "differentiation," "disintegration," or "proletarianization" of the peasantry taking place in proportion to the commercialization of agriculture.[22] It was in this work that Lenin first identified three rural class categories—poor, middle, and well-to-do (rich)—that would come to play a definitive role in both the Russian and Chinese Communist Revolutions.[23] Echoing the liberal reformers mentioned above, Kautsky described how under the capitalist system the functions of justice, protection, and military that used to be the responsibility of feudal lords had been taken over by the state. This meant that these feudal landowners became "completely superfluous," served no social function, and simply collected rents that accrued to them purely as a consequence of private property in land.[24]

Insofar as the nineteenth century was defined by a labor revolution, the twentieth century was defined by a land revolution. By the early twentieth century, dozens of countries had already implemented policies to eliminate or equalize the private ownership of land. Furthermore, multiple and often contradictory policies were enacted within the same country. In Russia, for example, first from 1905 to 1911 the Stolypin reforms encouraged private ownership and free transactions of land rights, but then in 1917 the new land decree of the Bolsheviks stated that "the right of private property in land is to be abolished for all time."[25] In Mexico, after the 1910 revolution, land reform laws were developed over the next two to three decades, which resulted in the annulment of an 1856 law outlawing collective ownership of land, the breakup of large hacienda farms, and the increase of landowners from 3 to 50 percent of the rural population.[26] Similar processes took place in countries like Japan, where in 1868 the Meiji government established new institutions of private land ownership, which were then overturned when post-1945 reform laws were passed that required the government to buy up land from large landowners and resell it to their tenants.[27] In this context, the CCP's preoccupation with agrarian reform does not seem out of place.

After World War II, agrarian reform emerged as an ideological front in the Cold War. The Soviet Union and the PRC aimed to solve the problem of rural inequality and poverty by reorganizing labor and social relations. In response, the United States–led agrarian reform programs in Taiwan, Japan, and South Korea aimed to solve the problem by reorganizing capital and wage relations. Both of these approaches developed in response to the same basic problem; both also sought to rationalize tenancy relations and achieve economies of scale. They shared a common goal of increasing agricultural production to alleviate poverty and fuel industrialization.[28] As such, the primary difference between these two approaches was their political or ideological means of implementation.[29]

In principle the communist model of agrarian reform was relatively more political and the capitalist model relatively more economic. What this means is that the communist model was realized by reorganizing relations between groups of people and between the state and the village, and the capitalist model was realized by reorganizing relations between prices and goods and between labor and capital. Historically, the communist model was more violent and often involved personal attacks on owners and the direct confiscation of their property. The capitalist model involved little to no interpersonal violence, but similar effects of social dislocation—for example, structural constraints that forced farmers to purchase certain goods or change their ways of life—are often overlooked.[30]

In the twentieth century, agrarian reforms were also closely tied to social and political revolution. The two most dramatic and influential social revolutions of the last century occurred in the two largest agrarian empires in the world—Russia and China. In many smaller agrarian countries as well, agrarian reform was often synonymous with social and political revolution, simply because their national politics and economies were so dependent on agriculture. Classic theorists like Barrington Moore Jr. were quick to point out that the shapes of these modern social revolutions were largely determined by the social and historical contexts in which they occurred. The relative strengths of the peasantry, the bourgeoisie, and the aristocracy are all determined by long-term, complicated, and interdependent processes of social development.[31] In other words, to understand these changes we need to look beyond the immediate domination of new political regimes.

One of the underlying themes of this book is the relationships between global economic processes and local social processes that are central to such conceptions of social revolution.[32] The hegemony of economic processes like the spread of capitalism and communism, both of which broadly define societies in terms of relations to property, makes it difficult to conceptualize and interpret local social experiences in any other terms. In this context it takes tens of thousands of individual observations and hundreds of thousands of words from Shuangcheng's county archives—the data used in this book—to even begin to crack the surface of global narratives and conceive of an alternative world defined in terms of local social and political relationships. One lesson from this exploration of local social processes is that global narratives represent only one particular perspective (i.e., a top-down, state perspective), and there is no inherent reason why this perspective should have priority over other perspectives.

A deeper understanding of the local contexts and practices of land reform likewise brings global processes into clearer focus. Many of the experiences that we have seen in the first two years of CCP governance in Shuangcheng continued to shape PRC politics for the next seventy years. One important conclusion, for example, is that land reform must be understood as a selective policy that targeted only a small segment of society: rural strongmen. In principle the CCP effectively replaced these strongmen with a more loyal cadre of village representatives, but this was just a first step toward an overhaul of the entire sociopolitical system. At a higher level, as we have seen throughout this book, experiences in Shuangcheng's land reform can pose new questions and approaches for studying the relationships between politics and economics, state and society, tradition and revolution.

A New Land Reform Narrative

A basic question that remains to be answered is, How did the CCP revolution alter the basic organization of rural Chinese society? The fact that today we accept the teleology of "Socialism with Chinese characteristics" is proof that we still do not have a good answer to this question.[33] China today is not exactly capitalist or communist/socialist, and to make matters more complicated, before the revolution it was not feudal either.[34]

The answer offered by this book is that the CCP was successful insofar as it reintegrated rural Chinese society, from local communities up through the central state, into a single, unified hierarchy. This organization may resemble Imperial China more than any modern capitalist or communist models and is distinguished by the primacy of power, or political relations, in its maintenance and functioning.[35] Balazs' description of the Chinese imperial state as "a hierarchical, authoritarian state, paternalistic yet tyrannical; a tentacular welfare state; a totalitarian Moloch of a state," in general holds true.[36] The PRC still uses differential (political) entitlements to resources as a primary tool for maintaining social order and organizing production.[37] But one of the keys for understanding this social structure is to recognize the autonomy enjoyed within each level of the "totalitarian" social-political hierarchy. The durability of the social structure is what makes such autonomy possible, and social functioning in turn depends on mechanisms of both control and autonomy. In other words, the "totalitarian" nature of the Chinese state needs to be understood as an expression and extension of local autonomy, or what could be understood as "local totalitarianism" in the sense that local organizations have some degree of absolute control over their own internal affairs.[38] Partly as a result of this arrangement, maintaining and repairing this unified structure itself has become a basic goal of Chinese social organization.

One main finding of this book is that land reform achieved the revitalization of a traditional, ideal social hierarchy.[39] The population living in scattered village communities looked to the state to enforce order and guarantee subsistence, and the state looked to the villages to support its claims to legitimacy.[40] Actors on both sides of this divide operated within an all-encompassing, integrated hierarchy of power from the central government to the village. Over the course of the first half of the twentieth century this hierarchy was extended and strengthened below the county level, but villages continued to be far removed from the state and, for better or worse, were allowed to take care of themselves as long as they responded to sporadic state demands.[41] Beginning with CCP land reform, representatives at all levels were replaced by party members and other allies and increasingly disciplined, but as we saw in Shuangcheng, this did not significantly alleviate basic systemic failures like the abuse of power and localism.[42]

A new understanding of land reform must begin before the arrival of the CCP in Shuangcheng. Northeast China is special in this regard because prior to land reform the Manchukuo state had spent more than a decade imposing government control over rural society. Subcounty village governments and associations, market control through rural cooperatives and distribution offices, and social control through institutions like the

Concordia Association made the Northeast countryside more administratively sophisticated than perhaps anywhere else in China in the 1940s.[43] The fact that in Republican China and the PRC many of these institutions were imitated or replicated—with peasant associations, agricultural and supply and marketing cooperatives, and village party branches—suggests that such institutions were considered widely effective. In many ways there was more similarity than difference between the pre- and post-CCP countryside in the Northeast.[44] But an essential difference is that in the case of Manchukuo, it was a Japanese colonial regime, and the rural controls were designed to benefit the colonizers at the expense of the colonized.

Despite all the sophistication of Manchukuo's rural administration, not to mention the relative peace enjoyed by the region in comparison with the occupied areas in North China during the Second Sino-Japanese War, land reform data from Shuangcheng paint a picture of a countryside plagued by corruption, predatory village officials, and widespread misery. In these respects Shuangcheng appears similar to many other parts of Republican China.[45] During land reform, new village officials were entrusted with total control over production and distribution but a lack of corresponding oversight and accountability made it easy for these officials to continue to appropriate resources for themselves. Local strongmen, old and new, play a leading role in stories of land reform because their private accumulation came at the expense of both the state and the village.

Above all, experiences of land reform make it clear that the distribution of land in China continued to be a function of political entitlements, not private property rights. As Philip Kuhn writes, "In view of local government's rapacity toward the rural inhabitants, landholders without political power were unlikely to hold onto wealth for long."[46] In this context the honest and hardworking rich peasant lived a transient existence; he could choose to either invest in urban enterprises and eventually move out of the village, stay in the village and serve as an official, or eventually lose his hard-earned savings to his own vices or his fellow villagers' avarice. No matter how powerful the rhetoric of class struggle, in rural China individual and family economic standing was a function of political standing. Most poor peasants were poor because they had no political rights and were victimized by corrupt local officials, and most landlords were rich because they had served as a local official or cultivated political influence at some point and used their power to appropriate theoretically "public" wealth.[47]

The CCP's solution in land reform was to define and enforce new entitlements to land by appealing to traditional moral principles of need and effort. Throughout the revolution the CCP's emphasis on the economics of class struggle masked the fact that they were also appealing to local social norms. Land reform in this sense restored a moral order to village communities by distributing power to "hardworking" persons and distributing property according to need. Even the moral-political principle of guaranteeing fair subsistence and opportunity for all was not necessarily new.[48] The only question was whether the CCP and its cadres could be truer to this principle than the previous regime(s).[49]

The CCP promoted the democratic governance of village affairs as the primary means to enforce these new entitlements.[50] In this regard the challenges of political mobilization, mass participation, and accountable leadership throughout the two years of land reform in Shuangcheng were all manifestations of the struggle to establish new institutions capable of balancing "the forces of cleavage and consensus" in rural communities.[51] After decades of political and social disorder, many leaders believed that the only way to ensure justice was to give everyone a chance to speak, seek broad consensus on every policy decision, and make village leaders accountable to the will of the majority of the village.[52] In other words, one of the CCP's solutions, a common one elsewhere in the twentieth century, was to expand its base of popular support by including previously disenfranchised populations like the poor and other marginal social groups. But as one village PA head in Shuangcheng put it, "It's difficult for one person to follow a hundred opinions."[53] As described in chapter 3, this new village democracy made the position of village leader even more demanding and even less rewarding than ever before, thus creating new tensions between accountability and corruption.

The completion of land reform in a village was measured by the equal per capita redistribution of all village land, but in the context of rural China this directly reflected an equal redistribution of village power. There were three basic stages of redistribution in Shuangcheng's land reform. First, incumbent village leaders feigned compliance with CCP policies and nominally redistributed village land. Next, newly elected village cadres oversaw the redistribution of confiscated land, but they too either embezzled too much of it or redistributed it unfairly (and undemocratically) among villagers. In the final stage, poor peasant and hired laborer assemblies directly oversaw the redistribution of land, ensuring that the majority of the village agreed on how redistribution was to be carried out and who received what land. In each stage the distribution of land mirrored the distribution of decision-making power.

One way to understand this practice of power over property is by viewing land as a public good. The CCP claimed ultimate jurisdiction over land, and they legitimated this claim by using the land to provide for the general welfare of the people. At the village level, access to land and patterns of distribution change from year to year.[54] Through the uncertainties of everyday life and individual or household differences, natural and unnatural imbalances in initially fair distributions of land and other village resources were bound to develop. Managing the distribution of such resources is one of the primary functions of the state in Chinese society, and it does so through hierarchies of political entitlement. Perhaps one of the best examples of this management comes from the history of Shuangcheng itself.[55]

From this perspective, other episodes in twentieth-century Chinese history come into clearer focus. The transition from land reform to collectivization, for example, does not appear as contradictory if we interpret it in terms of political relations instead of property rights. Land reform gave individual peasant households full ownership over agricultural land (所有权), but this was understood to exist within the sphere of the state.[56] As mentioned in chapter 1, for example, in rural areas surrounding large cities in North China, land was directly nationalized during land reform. Even in areas like Shuangcheng, where households were nominally given full ownership, beginning as early as the spring of 1947, seasonal state-organized production drives to encourage villagers to farm their land were constant reminders that they dide not have the complete right to freely dispose of their property.[57] Collectivization was simply a process of organizing more-efficient agricultural production, which involved a compromise between the needs of individual households and the state.[58]

Narratives of the series of policy campaigns that comprised the complete CCP land reform movement are narratives from the perspective of the state. Most previous narratives of land reform rely on this state perspective to fill the gaps in their village case studies. Hinton's *Fanshen*, for example, does not provide any firsthand accounts of village events between the fall of 1946 and the spring of 1948, when he arrived in the village. Instead, he constructs a seamless chronological narrative using descriptions of official campaign objectives as if they represented real experiences.[59] Friedman and his colleagues likewise do not describe any village events between the fall of 1946 and the fall of 1947 and rely on regional and other aggregate statistics to fill in their narrative.[60] Other influential accounts, like Ding Ling's fictional *The Sun Shines on the Sanggan River*, describe only a single work team's one-month sojourn at the very beginning of land reform in the summer of 1946.[61] As we saw in chapter 4, during land reform the CCP very selectively pursued and described their goals of mass mobilization in the countryside. For the historian or social scientist to understand land reform on a deeper level, these state perspectives are not enough.

In addition to the state perspective, the preceding chapters describe the diverse experiences of land reform from the perspective of villagers, which ultimately suggests that the whole idea of a coherent and integrated series of campaigns over the course of two years is itself a myth. What did the entire land reform look like from the village perspective? Villager memories, work reports, and administrative registers all contain pieces of the puzzle, but scattered among more than five hundred PAs over twenty-four months, virtually no single village has extant records of their entire experience. Given Shuangcheng's relatively complete records, this suggests that the vast majority of villages had fragmented experiences of the "ideal" land reform movement, and they were largely left to their own devices to achieve the state-required redistribution of land.

For the hypothetical "typical" village in Shuangcheng, land reform began with rumors and government directives.[62] We know, for example, that in the spring of 1946, before the May Fourth Directive, every village in the county was ordered to establish a PA. We can also be pretty sure that at this time not a single village in the county knew what a PA, in CCP terms, was supposed to be or do. But many villagers had almost certainly heard about the CCP and may or may not have regarded them as serious contenders for state power. As late as January 1948, many outlying or remote villages in the county still knew about land reform only by hearsay.[63]

For most of the villages in the county, land reform also concluded with rumors and government directives. More than seventy work team reports mention working in just over two hundred PAs during the course of two years, and even in the majority of these two hundred PAs direct work team implementation was cursory at best. In villages without intensive work team involvement, village cadres, and maybe even former strongmen, continued to dominate village affairs. Classic land reform narratives have also alluded to this reality of rural governance. Hinton writes that for the final stage of land reform work in Lucheng County:

> In the 11 "basic villages" all of this work was to be carried out as
> rapidly as possible by the work teams. On the other hand, in the re-
> maining villages in the county, the so-called "production villages,"

only the correction of past errors was to be handled right away, and this by a short cut. Instead of classifying the whole village according to the latest standards, only those families who had been attacked were to be classified.[64]

In Hinton's county, therefore, it was explicit policy that only eleven villages were to be subject to this closing rectification campaign. He goes on to write that the rest of the villages would be rectified later in the slack winter months, but at least in his book this process is also largely hypothetical.[65]

At the same time, while the CCP state was busy with its own organization and policy making, villagers were also busy with their own preparations for life under a new government. Former elites at all levels who had accumulated political, social, and economic resources under previous regimes and whose futures in the countryside looked bleak simply moved to the nearest city. On the other side of the village social divide, many previously impoverished villagers seized the opportunity to become the next generation of local political elite. Unfortunately for some of these new village cadres, however, they quickly learned that it might not be as lucrative a position as it used to be. As for everyone else, they most likely tried to avoid the risks of politics.

A large part of the success of land reform stemmed from its focus on a highly select group of rural strongmen. Rural elite who invested in urban enterprises were for the most part protected, and hardworking farmers who had accumulated some property were also protected by CCP policy. Although expropriation eventually expanded to include all large landowners by the end of land reform, related violence remained overwhelming focused on local strongmen who were regarded as immoral power abusers. As a result, the amount of violence varied greatly across villages as well as over time. For example, one elderly villager in contemporary Shuangcheng whom I interviewed recalled that land reform in his village was not very violent, because all of the landlords and rich peasants escaped, leaving their land, housing, and valuables behind. This situation allowed rich peasants from a neighboring village to simply move in (and in the process escape from their home village as well). The availability of abandoned property also made redistribution straightforward.[66] Overall, the greatest sources of violence in Shuangcheng were the civil war and famine, not mass mobilization campaigns.

Most land reform violence was retributive in nature and based on village politics, not state coercion.[67] Village officials, past and present, who had embezzled public goods were expropriated and humiliated in front of the community to reinforce a village moral order in which personal gain was subordinated to general public welfare. Most victims were physically punished in proportion to the amount of physical suffering they had caused others in the past. However, personal relations could make it possible to avoid severe persecution, while a lack of personal relations could increase vulnerability.

The end of land reform was marked by mass village meetings consensually assigning class labels to define what villagers considered to be fair entitlements to property. But from the beginning it was clear that such ideal governance was not very sustainable, even at the village level. Classification meetings could last several days and impact agricultural production, village consensus was elusive, and village cadres were overworked and underpaid. In this respect as well, land reform was only a temporary solution or a first step.

Land Reform and the PRC

These experiences of land reform contain the seeds for understanding the following thirty years of PRC history and beyond. Already by the late 1940s, the CCP had developed organizational strategies that they could apply in very different contexts. The direct reissuing of land reform policy documents from the Jiangxi Soviet in 1933 across vast areas of North China in 1947/48 is perhaps one of the clearest examples of this common strategy. In 1950, moreover, these same classification standards (with minor revisions) were applied to the entire country. But this expansion from an area of several million to several hundred million was more than just the result of efficient administration. The CCP's success also reflected certain characteristics shared throughout rural China. Although each village had its own unique social dynamics, they all had similar relations with the state and were tied into a political hierarchy that set similar boundary conditions for the development of each individual community. At the same time, the often very nebulous language of CCP policies was conditioned by the diverse range of social contexts to which they spoke.

One of the characteristic features of Chinese public policy is the use of highly focused campaigns that are often personally motivated, target specific social groups, and last for only a limited time. The policies of land reform are good examples. Land reform policies targeted a select group of rural strongmen and landowners, which made it both effective for the CCP and possible for targeted persons to evade the policy by changing their social identity. The shifting focus of policy campaigns over time meant that targeted persons could sometimes even return to their previous lives once a campaign was over. Such policies are the product of a very different political and legal context than in the European tradition. Fundamentally, these policies characterize a state that exercises its power selectively and spasmodically.[68] This kind of exercise of power is in part determined by the scale of the Chinese polity. The Chinese state has spent much of the past two millennia governing one-quarter of the world's population, and it would be prohibitively inefficient to try to centrally govern such a large society as closely and uniformly as a European city-state.[69]

The flexibility of these policies thus characterizes both their strength and weakness. In terms of strength, the policy is sufficiently vague to apply to a diverse range of contexts, while at the same time targeting a specific social group. The targeted group typically exists in general but can be conceived or defined in different ways in different communities.[70] Targeting a specific group also isolates it from the larger society, facilitating less disruptive policy implementation. Without this kind of divide-and-conquer strategy, the state would be incapable of managing such a large polity. In other words, in land reform and beyond, the CCP has governed by concentrating its power on small segments of the population for short periods of time, a strategy that may be more similar to historical China than the modern West.[71]

In terms of weakness, these flexible policies can lead to never-ending series of political cat-and-mouse games. Charles Cell and others have described this feature of mobilization campaigns in terms of shifting objectives over time, or what Sebastian Heilmann and Elizabeth Perry describe as "guerrilla policy style." As just mentioned, targeting specific social identities makes it relatively easy to evade the policy by manipulating either the terms of the policy or individual identities. In land reform, for example, the targeting of rural strongmen and landowners made it possible for large numbers of such persons to evade the policy by simply moving out of the countryside. Rural landowners could also move between villages to evade policies as they were implemented over time in different areas. In places like Shuangcheng, therefore, the Campaign to Suppress Counterrevolutionaries that began in 1950 was intended to eliminate enemies who had evaded land reform.[72]

The series of PRC campaigns from land reform to the Cultural Revolution can be characterized in terms of gradually targeting increasingly higher levels of sociopolitical elites. The Campaign to Suppress Counter-revolutionaries (1950–1953) followed closely on the heels of land reform and targeted urban instead of rural local strongmen. As mentioned in the discussion of escapes in chapter 6, many of the most "notorious" CCP enemies were able to flee to cities and avoid persecution during land reform. Shuangcheng's escape registers in part reflect the CCP's awareness of this problem, but during the Civil War they still tread carefully in urban areas. After 1949, however, as counterrevolutionary incidents continued in many parts of the country, Peng Zhen, leader of CCP legal work, argued in a May 1950 report that in correcting mistakes of "wanton beating and killing" (likely a reference to pre-1949 land reforms), CCP policy had overcorrected and become too lenient, giving counterrevolutionaries too much room for evasion.[73] The Campaign to Suppress Counterrevolutionaries thus began in response to one of the major weaknesses of land reform policies.[74]

Soon after, in 1951 and 1952 the Three-Anti and Five-Anti campaigns targeted urban bureaucrats, merchants, and industrialists. The three "antis" referred to corruption, waste, and bureaucratism, and the five antis referred to bribery, embezzlement, tax evasion, fraud, and theft of state economic information. In this book we have seen how many of these practices were already targeted in the countryside during land reform. These campaigns continued this struggle in the cities by targeting urban enemies and mobilizing urban workers to criticize and struggle against their bosses in mass meetings. Rather than seeing these campaigns as a reversal of policies to protect urban enterprises and property during land reform, therefore, they are instead consistent in terms of a targeted political strategy that aimed at only one group at a time in order to maximize effectiveness.

Next, in 1957 the Hundred Flowers and Anti-Rightist movements targeted political elites and intellectuals, the next groups up the political hierarchy. As in both previous and future campaigns, this movement targeted "bureaucratism, sectarianism, and subjectivism" within the CCP. In land reform terms, this basically meant undemocratic and selfish leadership. Mao called on intellectuals to criticize CCP leaders in this regard, but in this case the mobilization attempt appears to have backfired. Instead, intellectuals were purged as rightists and sent to labor camps, imprisoned, or exiled to the countryside. Previous narratives tend to rationalize this movement as an intentional strategy to expose reactionary intellectuals, but in light of the CCP's history of self-criticism and rectification, the initial campaign to criticize CCP leaders is more straightforward.[75]

Then, after the failure of the Great Leap Forward, the CCP returned to its roots by targeting rural cadres, whom they considered to have become a new class of local strongmen. In the mid-1960s the Four Cleanups, as part of the Socialist Education movement, again shared many common features with the struggle against corrupt village cadres during land reform. This movement grew out of the Great Leap Forward, the aftermath of which gave rise to "corruption, sabotage, and spontaneous capitalism in the Chinese countryside."[76] The Four Cleanups originally referred to cleaning up account books, storehouses, finances, and work points and later expanded to politics, economic, organization, and ideology. Between 1963 and 1966 the Four Cleanups campaign gradually expanded from the investigation of rural cadre corruption (labeled "capitalist tendencies") to a complete reclassification of the entire countryside, which has even been called a second land reform. Cadres were struggled against, expropriated, or relieved of their duties, village government was handed over to poor and lower-middle peasant assemblies, and it seemed as if the whole revolution was starting over again from scratch.[77]

But with the Four Cleanups this campaign process was radically accelerated and rolled over into the Great Proletarian Cultural Revolution, which targeted "local strongmen" within party headquarters itself. This movement was in many ways an expansion of the purging of "capitalist tendencies" that began during the Four Cleanups, but it went one step further and aimed to totally destroy and rebuild the entire party-state system itself. Andrew Walder, in trying to define the Cultural Revolution, writes, "Mao appears not to have had a clear plan in mind at the outset, and he was repeatedly forced to improvise and change course. . . . The struggles that he set in motion repeatedly moved in directions that he had not anticipated, forcing him to react and reconsider."[78] During the Cultural Revolution the usual strategy of targeted policies was pushed to its breaking point.

One way to interpret this history of the early PRC, therefore, is not as a series of contradictory and haphazard campaigns but as a concerted program of targeted policies to discipline and overhaul increasingly higher levels of the political hierarchy.[79] We have seen in Shuangcheng how the very same problems of rural/local discipline and governance that have plagued the PRC up to the present day appeared just months after land reform began in 1946. Former village leaders were persecuted for appropriating public goods and oppressing villagers, and then the village CCP cadres who replaced them proceeded to do the same thing. The following three decades would further demonstrate that this problem was endemic. Dealing with these issues of hierarchy and accountability shaped the development of China more than issues of market regulation and economic growth, precisely because the premise in China is that the political hierarchy determines the allocation of resources.

Political power continued to dominate in Deng Xiaoping's reform era (1978–1990s). Typically championed as a qualitative break from Maoist politics and a turn toward economic market reforms, Deng's "Reform and Opening Up" progressed gradually under close state supervision and the "Four Cardinal Principles" later incorporated into the 1982 PRC Constitution.[80] One of the primary tools of the reform was the Special Economic Zone, a prime example of a targeted policy in which market reforms were restricted to a select number of port cities. The lasting spatial inequalities created by radically uneven investments and entitlements of the state in select cities and provinces is well known today. Market reforms thus represent the latest in a series of state policies that operate through differential entitlements to resources.[81]

One paradox of twentieth-century China's rural revolution is that it has created its opposite: an urban industrial society. While we tend to equate global historical development with the Western European experience in which basic industrialization and urbanization were completed over a century ago, in reality China and much of the rest of the world were predominantly rural until the twenty-first century. This means that today the fate of a post-agrarian world has yet to be determined.[82] Is the political economy of power over property described in this book ultimately just a product of an agrarian society, or can it also function effectively in industrial or other forms of social organization? Perhaps this is a central question that China, and the world, will have to come to terms with in the twenty-first century.

Appendixes

Appendix A

English Translations of Land Reform Policy Documents

Directive on the Land Question

May 4, 1946

According to reports by comrades who have recently come to Yan'an from various places, mass movements have been unfolding on a broad scale in the Liberated Areas in Shanxi, Hebei, Shandong and central China. In combating Han traitors, settling accounts [with landlords] and reducing rent and interest, the people have seized land directly from the landlords, thus realizing the principle of "land to the tiller." Their enthusiasm is at a high pitch. Where the mass movement has been thorough, the land problem is being or has basically been solved. In some places the movement has progressed to the point where the principle of "equal distribution of land" has been put into effect, with everybody (even the landlords) getting three *mu* of land.

On the other hand, some of the Han traitors, evil gentry, despots and landlords who have fled to the towns or cities are heaping abuse on the mass movement in the Liberated Areas, and some middle-of-the-roaders have reservations about it. Even within our Party a few people think that the movement is going too far.

Under such circumstances, our Party cannot do without its own resolute policy, and it cannot but support the masses in their direct implementation of land reform. We must give them planned guidance in the light of the scale and extent of the development of the mass movement in the various Liberated Areas, so that the reform can be completed as quickly as possible.

In the face of the large-scale mass movement, the Party committees of all localities should not be afraid of a general change in land relations in the Liberated Areas. Nor should they fear the peasants' acquisition of a considerable amount of land and the landlords' forfeiture of it, the abolition of feudal exploitation in the rural areas, the abuse and slander of landlords or the temporary dissatisfaction or vacillation on the part of the middle-of-the-roaders. Rather, they should firmly support all the peasants' reasonable demands and just actions and endorse the transfers of land which have occurred and those which are now taking place. We should repudiate abuse by Han traitors, evil gentry and landlords, give explanations and remove the doubts in the minds of middle-of-the-roaders and educate the comrades within the Party who hold incorrect views.

The Party committees of all localities should understand clearly that solution of the land problem in the Liberated Areas is the basic historical task confronting our Party and the key link in all our present work. With maximum determination and effort, they must boldly arouse the masses and lead them in accomplishing this historic task. They should correctly guide the current mass movement in accordance with the following principles:

(1) Our Party should firmly support the demands of the masses as they realize the principle of "land to the tiller" by taking land from the landlords, as they combat Han traitors, settle accounts [with the landlords], reduce rent and interest, and get the landlords to return the overcharged portion of rent and interest.

(2) We should resolutely use every means to draw the middle peasants into the movement and see that they benefit by it. It is impermissible to confiscate their land. As for those middle peasants who have been dispossessed of land, we should try to return it to them or compensate them for the loss. Throughout the movement, we should try to gain the genuine sympathy of all the middle peasants, including the well-to-do ones, and make them feel satisfied.

(3) Generally speaking, the land of the rich peasants shall not be confiscated. If, in the course of land reform and related struggles, the confiscation of some of their land cannot be avoided due to the demands of the masses, we should see to it that the rich peasants are not subjected to overly heavy blows. They should be treated differently from the landlords. With rich peasants, emphasis should be on reducing rents and they

should be allowed to keep that part of the land which they till themselves. If the rich peasants are hit too hard, the middle peasants will waver, and production in the Liberated Areas will be adversely affected.

(4) As for the gentry and landlords whose family members include anti-Japanese servicemen and cadres, and the enlightened gentry and other people in the Liberated Areas or the Kuomintang (KMT) areas who co-operated with us during the anti-Japanese war and do not oppose the Communist Party, we should treat them prudently, give them due consideration and, as a rule, adopt methods of arbitration or mediation in dealing with them. One the one hand, we should persuade them not to turn down the reasonable demands of the masses but to adopt an enlightened attitude of their own accord. On the other hand, we should educate the peasants so that they will give these people a bit more land and help them save face in consideration of their service in the War of Resistance Against Japan, or of the service of their family members as anti-Japanese servicemen or cadres.

(5) Proper consideration should be given to the livelihood of the middle and small landlords. They should be treated differently from the big landlords, evil gentry and local despots. Disputes between them and the peasants should most often be solved through arbitration or mediation.

(6) Attention should be concentrated on waging resolute struggles against Han traitors, evil gentry and local despots, so as to isolate them completely and make them hand over their land. We should, however, leave them a certain amount of land from which to make a living. We should adopt the policy of winning over and disintegrating the ranks of those middle and poor peasants and others from poor families who were used as stooges by Han traitors, evil gentry and local despots, and we should work on them so that they will make a clean breast of their crimes and mend their ways. We should not take away their land. When they have confessed and mended their ways, they should receive the benefits due to them.

(7) With the exception of those owned by Han traitors who are found guilty of heinous crimes, the shops, workshops, factories and mines of the rich peasants and landlords should

not be confiscated, but protected, so that the development of industry and commerce will not be impeded. The methods used in solving the land problem and combating the feudal landlord class in the rural areas should not be applied in dealing with the industrial and commercial bourgeoisie. There is a difference in principle in our attitude towards these two classes. In some places, the mistake is made of applying the method of settling accounts with feudal landlords in rural areas to the owners of factories and shops. An immediate halt to this practice must be called for, or the consequences will be disastrous.

(8) We should accede to the people's demands for the execution of those Han traitors and public enemies who have committed heinous crimes by sentencing them to death after trial by the courts. Apart from this, however, we should generally enforce a policy of leniency and refrain from executing people or beating them to death, and we should refrain from making too many arrests, so as not to isolate ourselves by playing into the hands of the reactionaries. To combat Han traitors and settle accounts [with the landlords] is essential, but the number involved should not be too large, or else the masses will become panicky and the reactionaries will have a pretext for attacking us.

(9) We must do our utmost to win over all intellectuals who can be united with, and we should give them the chance to study and work. As for the enlightened gentry, the non-Party personages and the liberal bourgeoisie in the cities, so long as they are in favor of our democratic program, we should continue to co-operate with each and every one of them, bar none, no matter how many shortcomings they may have or how skeptical or discontent they may be with the current land reform. This will help to consolidate the united front against feudal dictatorship and for peace and democracy. As for the landlords and others who have run away, they should be allowed to return home, and they should be provided with the opportunity to earn a living. Even if some of them return with the intention of making trouble in the Liberated Areas, it will be to our advantage to let them stay and have them placed under the supervision of the masses. This would reduce the anti-popular forces in the cities.

(10)   In places where the masses have not yet been aroused to solve the land problem, we should set about it right away and see to it that the problem is completely or at least largely settled by the end of this year, not dragged on into the next. In the struggle, it is imperative to stick to the mass line, conduct the fullest possible discussions and get the masses really mobilized so that they will pitch in and settle the land problem themselves. Any approach that contravenes the mass line, such as commandism, monopolization of affairs and bestowing favors on the masses, is forbidden.

(11)   The masses have come up with various solutions to the land problem. For example:

   a. Confiscating and distributing the land of major Han traitors;

   b. Giving priority to the tenant-peasants in the purchase of the land which landlords are willing to sell after rent reduction;

   c. Guaranteeing the tenant-peasants the right to rent land after rent reduction with the result that the landlords give the tenant-peasants 70 to 80 percent of their land while retaining the remainder to till themselves; and

   d. Allowing the landlords to sell their lands to compensate the peasants in the course of settling accounts on such issues as rent and interest, seizure of property, shifting of financial burdens and other forms of irrational exploitation.

   The peasants have obtained land by the above means and most have also obtained ownership deeds prepared by the landlords. Thus, the land problem has, in the main, been solved by methods quite different from those adopted during the first civil war period (1927–1937). These methods, which have put the peasants in a legal and tenable position, can be applied in various places in the light of local situations.

(12)   The fruits of the movement should be distributed equitably and rationally among the poverty-stricken family members of martyrs, anti-Japanese soldiers, cadres and their families, and peasants with little or no land. Having obtained a share of land on a fair and rational basis and having their ownership of the land fixed, the peasants will gain in enthusiasm for production and so will work diligently, practice economy and become rich and prosperous. This will help to expand produc-

tion in the Liberated Areas. The inviolability of the property of those who have, after the solution of the land problem, prospered and become rich through hard work, thrift and good management should be safeguarded. It is not advisable to drag out the settling of accounts and the waging of struggle, for this will only dampen the peasants' enthusiasm for production. As for idlers and sluggards, we should educate them and encourage them to engage in production so as to improve their livelihood.

(13) Both during the movement and after the solution of the land problem, attention should be paid to the consolidation and expansion of the peasant associations and the militia, the expansion of the Party organization, the training and promotion of cadres, the reorganization of governments at district and township levels and the education of the masses for both the struggle in defense of their land and the democratic governments and the struggle for the democratization of the country.

(14) Generally speaking, in outlying areas where our political power is not yet consolidated and which are thus vulnerable to enemy harassment, no action should be taken to arouse the masses to demand land. Even in our efforts there to reduce rent and interest, we must be prudent and must not act in the same way as we are doing in the central areas, in order to avoid sustaining damage in the confrontation between revolution and counter-revolution. Of course, it is quite another matter in areas where conditions permit such actions.

(15) Party committees in various localities should go all out to launch and lead the mass movement in the Liberated Areas and solve the land problem resolutely in accordance with the principles outlined above. So long as we adhere to these principles, keep over 90 percent of the rural population on the side of our Party (farm laborers, poor peasants, middle peasants, handicraftsmen and other impoverished people make up about 92 percent of the rural population, and landlord and rich peasants about 8 percent) and maintain a broad anti-feudal united front, we will not make adventurist mistakes. Solving the land problem in the Liberated Areas with a population of over 100 million will help substantially to consolidate these areas and promote the nationwide movement towards

democratization. If, however, we fail to guide the movement correctly according to those principles, if we encroach on the land of the middle peasants or deal the rich peasants overly severe blows and if we fail to give due consideration to those who are entitled to it, there will be a split among the people in the rural areas. As a result, we shall not have more than 90 percent of the rural population on our side, the poor peasants, farm laborers and our Party will be isolated, the landlords and the reactionaries in the cities will become stronger and the mass movement for land reform will run up against enormous obstacles. Certainly this would be very disadvantageous to the masses. Therefore, we should convince the masses and cadres that adherence to these principles is for the good of the people.

(16) It is therefore essential to hold meetings of cadres in each area to analyze experience and discuss the directives of the Central Committee, to have these directives distributed and explained among all Party cadres, to draw up plans for carrying out the directives in the light of the condition prevailing in each area and to assemble a large number of cadres for short-term training before sending them to newly liberated areas to carry out the directives. At the same time, it is necessary to make appropriate explanations to non-Party personages. We must ask them to support the demand of the peasants, pointing out to them that the solution to the land problem is the just demand of over 90 percent of people, it is in accordance with Dr. Sun Yat-sen's principles and the resolution of the Political Consultative Conference and what is more, it considers the interests of people of all walks of life including the rich peasants and the landlords. Meanwhile, the cadres in various places, especially those at the district and township levels, should be educated to give play to their spirit of serving the people, a spirit characteristic of Communist Party members, and to refrain from securing undue benefits by taking advantage of their leading position. Otherwise, the masses will feel incensed and turn against the cadres. In cases where such things have already occurred, we should persuade the cadres to act justly when dealing with people, so as to avoid alienating themselves from the masses.

(17) In the past few years, various localities have correctly implemented the decision on land policy made by the Central
Committee in 1942 and have launched large-scale mass
movements, rendering support to the anti-Japanese war. Now,
as the movement to settle accounts and reduce rents spreads
and deepens, we have to make a major change in our land
policy in keeping with the demands of the people. This does
not mean, however, changing everything, for we are not aban-
doning the policy of rent reduction altogether.

(18) With regard to the "Right" and "Left" deviations manifested
within the Party concerning the land question, all localities
should correct them in accordance with this directive by conducting education with great warmth and sincerity. This will
help us to lead the masses in the struggle to accomplish the
land reform and consolidate the Liberated Areas.

Source: Adapted from Liu Shaoqi, *Selected Works of Liu Shaoqi* (Beijing:
Foreign Language Press, 1984), vol. 1, 372–78; «关于土地问题的指示» in
Liu Shaoqi, «刘少奇选集», vol. 1, 377–83.

(End)

*Resolution on the Chinese Communist Party Central Committee's
Promulgation of China's Outline Land Law*

October 10, 1947

China's land system is extremely irrational. Speaking of general conditions, landlords and rich peasants who make up less than ten percent of
the rural population hold approximately 70 to 80 percent of the land, cru-
elly exploiting the peasantry. Farm laborers, poor peasants, middle peasants, and other people, however, who make up over 90 percent of the rural
population hold a total of approximately only 20 to 30 percent of the land,
toiling throughout the whole year, knowing neither warmth nor full stom-
ach. These grave conditions are the root cause of our nation's subjection to
imperialism, oppression, poverty, and backwardness, and the basic obstacles to our country's democratization, industrialization, independence,
unity, strength and prosperity.

In order to change these conditions, it is necessary, on the basis of the demands of the peasantry, to wipe out the land system of feudal and semi-feudal exploitation, and realize the system of "land to the tillers." For 20 years, and especially in the last two years, under the leadership of the Chinese Communist Party, Chinese peasants have obtained enormous achievements and rich experiences in carrying out land reform. In September of this year, the Chinese Communist Party convened a nationwide land conference, and at the conference did detailed research into conditions of the Chinese land system and experiences of the land reform, and enacted the Outline Land Law to serve as a proposal to the democratic governments of all areas, peasants' meetings, peasants' congresses and their committees. The Central Committee of the Chinese Communist Party is in complete accord with the Outline Land Law, and is furthermore publishing it. It is hoped that the democratic governments of all areas, peasants' meetings, peasants' congresses, and their committees will discuss and adopt this proposal, and furthermore will work out concrete methods appropriate to local conditions, to unfold and thoroughly carry through a nationwide land reform movement, completing the basic task of the Chinese revolution.

China's Outline Land Law

(Passed by the Chinese Communist Party National Land Conference on September 13, 1947)

Article 1: The land system of feudal and semi-feudal exploitation is abolished. The land system of "land to the tillers" is to be realized.

Article 2: Landownership rights of all landlords are abolished.

Article 3: Landownership rights of all ancestral shrines, temples, monasteries, schools, institutions and organizations are abolished.

Article 4: All debts incurred in the countryside prior to the reform of the land system are cancelled.

Article 5: The legal executive organs for the reform of the agrarian system shall be the village peasants' meetings, and the committees elected by them; the assemblies of the Poor Peasants' League and organized landless and land-poor peasants of villages, and the committees elected by it; district, county, provincial and other levels of peasants' congresses, and committees elected by them.

Article 6: Except as provided in Article 9 Section B, all land of landlords in the villages, and all public land, shall be taken over by the
village peasants' associations, and together with all other village
land, in accordance with the total population of the village, ir-
respective of male or female, young or old, shall be unifiedly and
equally distributed. With regard to the quantity of land, surplus
shall be taken to relieve dearth, and with regard to the quality of
land, fertile land shall be taken to supplement infertile, so that
all the village people shall obtain land equally; and it shall be the
individual property of each person.

Article 7: The unit for the distribution of the land shall be the township (*xiang*) or administrative village (*cun*) equivalent to township.
But district or county peasants' associations may make certain
necessary adjustments between various townships, or equivalent
administrative villages. In areas where the district is extensive and
the population sparse, and for the purpose of convenient cultivation, comparatively small units below the level of the township
may be taken as units for the distribution of the land.

Article 8: Village peasants' associations shall take over the landlords'
animals, agricultural implements, houses, grain and other properties, and shall further expropriate the surplus animals, agricultural
implements, houses, grain and other properties of rich peasants;
and these shall be distributed to peasants lacking in these properties, and to other poor people, and furthermore an equal portion
shall be distributed to the landlords. The property distributed to
each person shall be his personal property, thus enabling all the
village people to obtain proper materials for production and for
life.

Article 9: Methods for dealing with certain special lands and properties, provided as follows:

Section A: Woods and hills, irrigation and waterworks, land in
reeds, orchards, pools, waste land and other distributable land
shall be divided in accordance with the ordinary standards for
land.

Section B: Great forests, great hydraulic engineering works, large
mines, large pasture land, large waste lands and lakes shall be
administered by the government.

Section C: Famous sites and historic spots shall be securely protected. Special libraries, antiques, works of art, and so forth,

which are of historic or academic value, and which have been taken over shall be inventoried and turned over to the high government of the area.

Section D: Ammunition, arms, and those large quantities of money, valuables, and grain left over after satisfying the needs of the peasants shall be inventoried and turned over to the high government of the area for settlement.

Article 10: Methods for dealing with certain special questions in the distribution of the land, provided as follows:

Section A: Poor peasants with only one or two persons in the family may be given land equivalent to that of two or three people by the village peasants' meetings, in consideration of prevailing conditions.

Section B: Rural laborers, individual professionals, and their families, in general, shall be given land equivalent to that of peasants; but if their profession is sufficient for constant maintenance of all or most of their living expenses, they shall not be given land, or shall be given a partial portion of land, as determined by the village peasants' meetings and their committees in consideration of prevailing conditions.

Section C: For all personnel of the People's Liberation Army, democratic governments, all people's organizations, whose home is in the countryside, they and their families shall be given land and properties equivalent to that of peasants.

Section D: Landlords and their families shall be given land and properties equivalent to that of peasants.

Section E: For KMT army officers and soldiers, KMT government officials and personnel, KMT party members and other enemy personnel, whose homes are in rural areas, their families shall be given land and properties equivalent to that of the peasants.

Section F: For all Han traitors, collaborators, and civil war criminals, they themselves shall not be given land or properties. If their families live in the countryside, have not taken part in criminal activities, and are willing to cultivate the land themselves, they shall be given land and properties equivalent to that of the peasants.

Article 11: The government shall issue deeds to the ownership of the land given to the people, and moreover recognize their right to free management, buying and selling, and under specially de-

termined conditions to rent out the land. All land deeds and all
notes on debts from prior to the reform of the land system shall be
turned in and shall be null and void.

Article 12: The property and legal operations of industrial and commercial elements shall be protected from encroachment.

Article 13: For the sake of making the land reform thorough and
complete, people's courts shall be established to try and punish
those who resist or violate the provisions of this law. The people's
courts shall be organized from personnel elected by peasants'
meetings or peasants' congresses and from personnel appointed by
the government.

Article 14: During the period of the reform of the land system, for the
sake of maintaining the order of the land reform and protecting
the wealth of the people, the village peasants' meetings or their
committees shall appoint personnel, by definite procedure to take
necessary steps for carrying out the responsibilities of taking over,
recording, liquidating and holding all transferred lands and properties, to guard against damage, waste, corruption and destruction. The peasants' associations shall forbid anyone from, for the
sake of interrupting equitable distribution, deliberately butchering
animals, felling trees, destroying agricultural implements, irrigation and waterworks, buildings and construction works, or crops
or other materials; and the acts of thieving, seizing, secretly giving
away to others, concealing, burying, dispersing, or selling their
goods. Violators shall be tried and punished by the people's courts.

Article 15: For the sake of guaranteeing that all measures of land
reform shall be in accord with the will and interests of the overwhelming majority of the people, the government shall take
the responsibility for securing earnest democratic rights for the
people; securing full rights for the peasants and their representatives at all meetings freely to criticize and impeach all cadres of all
kinds and levels; and full rights at all appropriate meetings freely
to remove and change and to elect all cadres of the government
and peasants' organizations. Anyone who infringes on the above
democratic rights and powers of the people shall be punished by
the people's courts.

Article 16: In places where the land has already been equally distributed before the promulgation of this law, and provided that
the peasants do not demand redistribution, the land need not be
redistributed.

Source: Adapted from Hinton, *Fanshen*, Appendix A, 615–18; «中国共产党中央委员会关于公布中国土地法大纲的决议» in ZZWX, vol. 16, 546–50.

(End)

Northeast Liberated Area Supplementary Methods for Implementing the Outline Land Law

December 1, 1947

1. Article 3 of China's Outline Land Law (hereafter "Outline"), pertaining to the abolition of ownership rights in land, refers to land [owned] prior to the implementation of Land Reform. Land that was acquired through Land Reform is exempt.

2. Article 4 of the Outline, pertaining to the annulment of village debts, refers to debts between peasants and landlords or rich peasants incurred prior to November 1947. Debts between poor peasants, hired laborers, and middle peasants should be resolved by the peasants themselves. Moreover, unsettled commercial debts incurred after July 1946 in the countryside and between city and countryside are exempt.

3. Supplement to Article 6 of the Outline: when equally redistributing land, each locality must assess the land and equally redistribute it in a standardized way. The method for redistribution can be either completely breaking up all [previous landholdings] and starting from scratch, or taking from the plenty and giving to the needy, taking from the fertile and giving to the barren, to be chosen based on local conditions and by the opinion of a majority of peasants. In cases of completely breaking up all previous landholdings, middle peasants typically choose voluntarily [whether to break up their land or not].

4. Wasteland cleared in 1947 should belong to the person who cleared it and is exempt from equal redistribution. Previously abandoned land that has been cleared should be included in equal redistribution if it belongs to landlords or rich peasants. If it belongs to hired laborers, poor peasants, or middle peasants, then it should be exempted.

5. For urban manufacturers and merchants who are willing to invest in clearing wasteland and engaging in agriculture, the government will provide them with incentives. For cleared wasteland, the government will only collect 5 percent of the agricultural tax in the first year, 10 percent in the second year, and then from the third year on will collect according to the [standard] grain quota. However, the land is to be nationalized. The government guarantees that the property of agricultural operations will not be infringed upon.

6. Article 8 of the Outline, pertaining to the expropriation of rich peasants' excess property, refers to foodstuffs and housing in excess of the typical rich peasant household, after taking into account seed stock. For draft animals and farm implements, those in excess of the village average are to be expropriated. Household belongings and other property are to be handed over in their entirety and then one share allocated back [to the rich peasant household]. Regarding small rich peasants (primary family members all engage in labor, and only exploit between one half and one laborer), grain, housing, draft animals and farm implements are to be handled according to the above method, but household belongings and other property are not to be touched.

7. Supplement to Article 9, section 1 of the Outline: forests, silkworm farms, waterworks, orchards, marshland, prairie land, wasteland, etc. can be equally redistributed if feasible and agreed upon by the peasants in a given locality, but if equal redistribution is not conducive to management, a method of joint management can be adopted.

   Supplement to section 2 [of Article 9]: mining land that has already begun mining or is ready to be mined is not to be redistributed. Mining land that has already been discovered but for the moment will not be mined can be redistributed to peasants for cultivation, and then re-appropriated when it is time to mine it. [In this case] the local government is to arrange other land for the peasants and compensate them for any production losses.

8. Thirty to fifty meters on each side measured from the center of railways is to be relegated as railway land and is not to be redistributed.

9. Supplement to Article 10, section 2 of the Outline: railway
    line workers and their families whose salaries are not enough
    to support themselves can be redistributed some land, to be
    decided upon through a discussion by the local peasant as-
    sociation.

    Supplement to section 3 [of Article 10]: regarding soldiers
    who joined the army before November 1947 and have already
    received land, in cases where landholdings are completely
    broken up for equal redistribution, they are not allowed to
    be given less land in terms of both amount or quality than
    what they already received. Land allocated to lackeys who
    joined the army is to be held in custody and rented out by the
    peasant association. Martyrs who sacrificed themselves in war
    or for the revolution should still receive a share of land and
    [other] property equal to [that of] other peasants, as support
    for their surviving family. The land of soldiers preparing to be
    honorably discharged or retired from service is to be held by
    the county government and not redistributed.

10. After the equal redistribution of land, district and adminis-
    trative village governments and peasant associations are not
    allowed to keep [any] public land. In villages with schools,
    three to five hectares of school land can be kept. Land kept
    by local army or government units before November 1947
    is to be returned to the local poor peasant and hired laborer
    assembly or peasant association for redistribution. If there is
    excess land after fulfilling the needs of the peasants, then the
    local army or government units can keep a part of this land
    for production. If there is no excess land, then the local army
    or government units should clear their own wasteland.

11. Supplement to Article 11 of the Outline: the format of land
    deeds is to be standardized by the Northeast Administrative
    Committee, printed by provincial governments, and then sent
    to county governments, who are responsible for filling out
    and issuing them.

12. Supplement to Article 13 of the Outline: district and adminis-
    trative village levels [of government] should organize people's
    courts. The detailed rules and regulations for the organization
    and governance [of these courts] will be issued by the North-
    east Administrative Committee.

Regarding the final authority in cases of the death penalty, in basic liberated areas, the county government and above can authorize [the execution of] offenders who are the struggle objects of the masses (i.e., evil tyrants, traitors, landlords, rich peasants, cops, bandits, etc.). The provincial government or above must authorize [the execution of] offenders who are cadres or involved in political cases (i.e., underground armies, state special agents, etc.). In newly recovered areas, work teams equivalent to the county level can authorize [the execution of] offenders who are the struggle objects of the masses. One level above such work teams can authorize [the execution of] offenders who are cadres or involved in political cases.

13. Within the borders of the Northeast liberated area, ethnic minorities should be redistributed land the same as Han people and enjoy [the same] ownership rights.

14. These methods have been announced and implemented by the Northeast Administrative Committee. The Northeast Administrative Committee has the [sole] right to interpret and amend them.

December 1, 1947

Source: Translated by the author from «东北解放区实行土地法大纲补充办法», in 东北日报社编，«平分土地文献». 东北书店，1948 年1月，29–32.

(End)

Chinese Communist Party Northeast Central Bureau's Letter to the Peasants

December 1, 1947

Peasant brothers and sisters:

On October 10, the Central Committee of the Chinese Communist Party announced "China's Outline Land Law," calling on us to completely eliminate feudalism and completely redistribute land equally. [This law] calls on us to unite together to take action and take control of government. The emancipation («翻身») of us farmers depends on ourselves.

Laborers are the creators of all wealth in society, and peasants are the creators of all wealth in the countryside. Peasants are the ones who cleared all land for cultivation. But under the old, feudal system in Chinese society, laborers did not get enough to eat, and peasants did not have any land. Landlords idled away but ate their fill every day and possessed large tracts of land. This kind of land system is irrational and must be eliminated. It is only proper that the peasants should get land and its fruits. This is land and wealth returning to its rightful owners.

After liberation on August 15, [1945], the Communist Party and the Eighth Route Army have helped emancipate us by suppressing bandits, settling accounts, redistributing land, cooking half-cooked [areas], and digging up wealth. [We] have gotten land, housing, oxen and horses, farm implements and other property, ensuring our livelihoods and a foundation for the development of production. But the attack on feudalism is still not complete, and land is still distributed irrationally. This time feudalism must be completely eliminated and land completely and equally redistributed. The method for equally redistributing land will be implemented according to the Outline Land Law and the Northeast Government Council's Supplementary Guidelines.

Overthrow Landlords, Eliminate Feudalism

Completely overthrow landlords and completely eliminate the foundation of their feudal economy. All landlords, no matter large, medium, or small, no matter male or female, no matter resident or absentee, must have all of their land and other property confiscated and turned over to the entire body of the peasantry and the peasant association for redistribution. In the past landlords kept too much land; it must be taken. Their household belongings were not dug up; they must be dug up.

Completely overthrow landlord power . All traitorous, evil tyrant, and reactionary landlords can be handled as everyone («大伙») sees fit. Resistant, rumormongering, and conniving landlords can be struggled against as everyone sees fit.

Reveal landlord tricks. All landlords who have infiltrated the communist party, the liberation army, the democratic government, public schools, factories, and shops, commercial railways and all public units, and have used these public units for protection to carry out sabotage, sow discord, or to oppress peasants can be apprehended and struggled against as everyone sees fit. Landlords who have infiltrated work teams, peasant associations, people's militias, and security forces must be cleaned out. All public servants who cover up, protect, or hide landlords must also be struggled against.

Cut off the social relations of landlords. All lackeys who are in contact with landlords and all poor and suffering persons who hide landlords' goods must be convinced to confess and feel remorse.

Stop landlord activities, monitor landlord movements, and prevent landlord retaliations.

In a word, [we] must make landlords bow their heads and submit.

The feudal exploitation of rich peasants must also be stopped. Rich peasants must also hand over their excess grain, housing, draft animals, farm implements, and other property, for redistribution by the peasant association. Traitorous, evil tyrant, and reactionary rich peasants can be handled as everyone sees fit. Resistant, rumormongering, and wily rich peasants can be struggled against as everyone sees fit.

Peasants can organize people's courts to prosecute traitorous, evil tyrant, and reactionary landlords and rich peasants, and all persons who destroy property and sabotage the equal redistribution of land.

Regarding rich peasants who are honest, hardworking, frugal, and know their place, after they hand over the things that they are required to hand over, they can be treated leniently.

Equalize Land, Establish the Roots of Prosperity

This time the redistribution of land must be completely equal. The objective of the completely equal distribution of land is (1) to completely eliminate feudalism and (2) to establish the roots of prosperity and facilitate the development of production. In the past land was distributed irrationally. Landlords and rich peasants kept too much land, there was lots of unreported ("black") land, some [households] were allocated a lot of land and some were allocated a little, some [households] were allocated good land and some were allocated bad, and some [households] were allocated fragmented plots of land difficult to cultivate. This time the redistribution of land must include a land assessment and a unified, equal redistribution. The method for redistribution can be chosen from: either completely break up all [previous landholdings] and start from scratch, or take from the plenty and give to the needy, take from the fertile and give to the lean. The entire body of the peasantry in any given locality can decide. In cases of completely breaking up all previous landholdings, middle peasants can voluntarily choose [whether to break up their land or not]. Landlords and rich peasants are not to keep any land, but hand it all over and demonstrate submission, before being allocated a share equal to that of the peasants. In the course of equally redistributing land, and with the consent of the peasants, every household must, as much as possible, be allocated adjacent parcels of land, in order to facilitate the development of production.

In half-cooked areas and in areas where landlord wealth has not been dug up, [peasants] should continue to dig up landlord wealth and distribute it to peasants, for the purpose of purchasing horses and ensuring their livelihoods. All of the confiscated property must be handled by specially elected representatives; there must not be any waste, destruction, theft, or corruption.

Land is the lifeline of peasants. This time the redistribution of land cannot be treated apathetically. Everyone must discuss [how to do it], [to ensure that] the redistribution is fair and rational.

Poor Peasants and Hired Laborers Take Control («作主»), Unite with Middle Peasants

Poor peasants and hired laborers represent the vast majority of the rural population; they experience the most hardship and are the most exploited, and are most in need of emancipation. Poor peasants and hired laborers are the most resolved in struggling against traitors, evil tyrants, reactionary landlords, and feudal power. Poor peasants and hired laborers are the main forces of Land Reform, and all power belongs to them. The entire body of poor peasants and hired laborers [must] take control, take action, and unite with middle peasants to completely eliminate feudalism and completely and equally redistribute land. Poor peasant and hired laborer assemblies and congresses should first be held at the administrative village and district levels to discuss the equal redistribution of land. Then middle peasants should be invited to participate in a general peasant assembly to discuss and carry out the equal redistribution of land.

In order to prevent the isolation of poor peasants and hired laborers in one administrative village or one district, the poor peasants and hired laborers of an entire district, an entire county, an entire province, and an entire liberated area must rise up together and equally redistribute the land.

Draw Class Divisions, Recognize Enemies and Friends

Before redistributing land, class divisions must be clearly drawn. Hold class comparison meetings, draw class lines, define class labels, compare living [standards], compare household property, investigate landlords, and investigate bad origins («坏根»). Speak bitterness, dispel confusion, settle detailed accounts, uncover the roots of poverty and establish the roots of prosperity. Investigate peasant association members and cadres, militiamen and self-defense teams. Draw class divisions, recognize enemies and friends, raise awareness, and unite in struggle.

Govern Fairly and Justly, Encourage Democracy

Have the poor peasant and hired laborer assemblies elect committees for the redistribution of land and fruits [of struggle]. [These assemblies] must select [representatives who are] longtime workers, poor peasants and hired laborers, upright and proactive, and fair and just. If anyone has embezzled fruits [of struggle], or has not governed fairly and justly, then everyone does not need that person. Those who have embezzled fruits [of struggle] in the past must also be taken to justice.

In governing, peasant associations should encourage democracy. A single person cannot make decisions; everyone must have a say before making a decision. Everyone must discuss and come to agreement and be opposed to leaders monopolizing control («包办») and being coercive («压力派»).

If in the past there were peasant association, government, or work team cadres who governed unfairly or undemocratically, everyone can criticize, investigate, and replace them.

Get Organized, Peasants Take Charge («当家»)

If everyone is not of one mind, then they will be powerless. If everyone gets organized and embraces the collective group, then they will be powerful. In the process of redistributing land, peasants must be well-organized; everyone should join the peasant association and elect good people to govern. The people's militia and self-defense team must also be well-organized and clean out bad elements. District and administrative village governments must also be reformed. In a word, [we] want peasants to take charge and govern [themselves].

After overthrowing landlords and equally redistributing land, everyone should get organized, work hard, ensure their livelihoods, and diligently develop production.

Support the Front Lines, Work toward Victory

Peasants: The Northeast Liberation Army is fighting on the front lines with Chiang's army, precisely in order to protect our equal redistribution of land. [We] emancipated peasants must put forward all of our strength to support the front lines, send [them] troops, grain, stretcher teams, civilian support, and horse carts. The power of emancipated peasants can not only overthrow landlords but is also able to overthrow Chiang Kai-shek. Only by overthrowing Chiang Kai-shek can our victory, and our land, be secured.

> Overthrow landlords, equally redistribute land!
> Overthrow Chiang Kai-shek, victory in the revolution!
> Long live the liberation of the peasants!
> Long live the Chinese Communist Party!
> Long live Chairman Mao!

Chinese Communist Party Northeast Central Bureau

December 1, 1947

Source: Translated by the author from 《中国共产党东北中央局告农民书》, in 东北日报社编, 《平分土地文献》. 东北书店, 1948 年1月, 21-27.

(End)

Appendix B

Class Categories

Shuangcheng's classification registers from the summer of 1948 provide the most complete picture of a single county's prerevolutionary social structure since Mao's 1930 *Xunwu Investigation*.[1] As summarized in Table 17, these registers record more than eighty-two thousand urban and rural households, the entire county population, assigned to thirty-six unique social class categories. These categories were assigned based on the socioeconomic status of each household on the eve of land reform (ca. 1946). For purposes of analysis throughout this book, I aggregate these class categories at two levels according to the official CCP standards at that time. Level 1 represents the actual categories as recorded in the classification registers. Level 2 represents the primary categories recorded in official CCP policy documents. Level 3 represents aggregate categories used to broadly distinguish between the friends and enemies of land reform and the revolution in general.

The CCP did not disseminate official classification standards until late November 1947 and did not publicly release them until late May 1948, after peasant associations in Shuangcheng had already begun compiling their classification registers. The classification registers are therefore also the first reliable record of class categories, despite the purported centrality of class in all previous land reform policies and the common recording of classes in the 1947 victim registers and numerous work reports. As discussed in the last section of chapter 3, the official classification standards used throughout land reform in Shuangcheng and elsewhere from 1948 until 1953 were a slightly modified version of standards first developed in the early 1930s Land Revolution of the Jiangxi Soviet.[2] A full analysis of these standards deserves its own monograph, but for our purposes here the main criteria for determining the class of a rural household involved calculating what proportion of household income was derived from the exploitation of land or labor and whether the household had to sell out

Table 17. Class Categories of Households in Shuangcheng County, Summer 1948

Level 3	Households	%	Level 2	Households	%	Level 1	Households	Persons
Landlord/Rich Peasant	11,325	13.7	Landlord	5,282	6.4	Landlord (Generic)	1,562	9,764
						Large	511	3,464
						Middle	788	4,979
						Small	1,842	9,820
						Managerial (Generic)	497	3,376
						Large Managerial	8	76
						Middle Managerial	23	242
						Small Managerial	10	61
						Bankrupt	41	195
			Rich Peasant	6,043	7.3	Rich Peasant (Generic)	3,963	25,684
						Large	11	127
						Middle	21	170
						Small	215	1,438
						Tenant	1,778	13,383
						New	21	204
						Landlord/Rich Peasant	34	226
Middle and Poor Peasants	62,882	76.2	Middle Peasant	11,959	14.5	Middle Peasant (Generic)	8,674	51,578
						Rich	521	3,533
						Small	45	231
						Tenant	2,715	19,647
						New	4	19
			Poor Peasant	20,372	24.7	Poor Peasant (Generic)	13,747	69,268
						Tenant	6,625	33,978
			Hired Laborer	30,551	37.0	Tenant	30,551	135,573

Urban Classes	7,372	8.9	Bourgeoisie	348	0.4	Capitalist	6	39
						Merchant	31	165
						Petty Bourgeoisie	311	1,670
			Semi-Proletariat	1,527	1.9	Handicraftsman	421	2,095
						Artisan	381	1,697
						Shop Clerk	406	1,627
						Peddler	220	1,038
						Self-Employed	99	459
			Proletariat	5,497	6.7	Technician	38	194
						Industrial Worker	175	670
						Transport Worker	57	294
						Urban Poor	5,227	22,640
Other Status	118	0.1		118	0.1		118	509
Missing/Blank	817	1.0		817	1.0		817	3,626
Total	82,514	100.0		82,514	100.0		82,514	423,759

Source: Author's calculations based on classification registers.

part of its labor or possessed adequate capital for self-employment. There was also the issue of determining the length of time in which to evaluate these criteria, which could range from three family generations to just the three years before 1947.

Before these official standards, one of the earliest extant work reports in Shuangcheng mentions using Lenin's criteria for classification.[3] According to the report, these criteria consisted of three factors: ownership of the means of production, primary source of income, and the share of the product captured in the process of redistribution.[4] The report's descriptions of the different classes are thus very similar to the CCP's 1933 standards.

However, many of the rural classes recorded in Shuangcheng's classification registers do not appear in any extant official CCP documents. In particular, the primary categories of landlord, rich peasant, and middle peasant (level 2) are broken down into large, medium, and small, which suggests that households were further classed according to size, in terms of either population or property holding, or perhaps also according to scale of exploitation. The original property of most households is unknown, but there is a close correlation between these level 1 categories and mean persons per household. On average, large landlord and rich peasant and rich middle-peasant households did indeed have more persons per household than their middle and small counterparts. Rich, middle, and poor peasants were also further divided into owners and tenants, categories that can be found in some of the earliest work reports in Shuangcheng, too.[5] In chapter 3 I suggest that these subcategories reflect a "bottom-up" classification process in which peasant associations devised a universally "fair" classification scheme that a majority of villagers could agree on. In many ways, these complicated class categories reflected the complex inequalities of different pieces of land. For many villagers, the question of classification was not who were their friends or enemies but who would get to choose the village's prize parcel of land first.

In contrast, CCP leaders were more concerned with the big picture of just how much of the population they could count on for political support. In October 1947 the "Resolution on the Chinese Communist Party Central Committee's Promulgation of China's Outline Land Law" (see Appendix A) claimed that landlords and rich peasants comprise less than 10 percent of rural households and implied that the goal of the Outline Land Law was to benefit the other 90 percent. After a couple months of experimenting with this new law, in January 1948 Ren Bishi, a CCP Politburo commissar, cautioned against classifying too many people as enemies (landlords and rich peasants) in a pivotal speech titled "Some Problems during Land Reform." Echoing the "Resolution," Ren estimated that "under the old regime, landlords typically comprised about 3 percent of rural households, and rich peasants comprised another 5 percent, for a total of 8 percent of rural households and 10 percent of the rural population. In the old CCP liberated areas [of North China], moreover, many landlords and old rich peasants have already changed, and there they should comprise less than 8 percent of rural households." But in a report from northwest Shanxi Province, Ren heard that an administrative village there had classed more than 20 percent of households as landlords or rich peasants. Ren condemned such overclassification as a threat to the entire revolution, equivalent to "aiding the enemy and isolating oneself."[6] Shuangcheng experienced similar problems in the winter of 1947/48, but the classification registers record the more "objective" class categories determined following the correction of overclassification in the Classification campaign.

These class categories defined household rights and entitlements in the new CCP state. Politically, middle peasant or lower class status was a basic requirement in order to become a village-level leader and was favored at higher levels as well (as illustrated in chapter 3, Figure 7). As implied in Article 5 of the Outline Land Law, moreover, poor peasants and hired laborers were entitled to act as the new representatives in village government. Landlords and sometimes rich peasants, in contrast, were denied participation in peasant association meetings and decisions. But the focus in land reform was also on property entitlements. Table 18 summarizes the different property entitlements for each rural class category at the completion of land reform in Shuangcheng. Each village could choose on their own whether to completely break up all previous landholdings and reallocate from scratch or to just make adjustments to existing landholdings by leveling out above-average and below-average household holdings.

An analysis of the urban classes recorded in the classification registers is beyond the scope of this book. Since land reform policies were applied only to the rural population, urban class categories were not covered in policy documents. The categories I use here are adapted from actual categories recorded in the classification registers, the 1933 document's section on nonagricultural "poor people," and Mao's *Analysis of All the Classes in Chinese Society* (1925).

Table 18. Property Entitlements by Rural Class Category in Shuangcheng County, Summer 1948

Rural Class Category		Land	Animals	Farm implements	Housing	Grain	Household belongings, etc.
Landlord	Right to keep	None					
	Entitled for allocation	1 inferior share per capita					
Rich Peasant	Right to keep	All	Village average		Rich peasant average		None
	Entitled for allocation	1 inferior share per capita	None				1 inferior share per capita
Small Rich Peasant	Right to keep	All	Village average		Rich peasant average		All
	Entitled for allocation	1 inferior share per capita	None				
Middle Peasant	Right to keep	All					
	Entitled for allocation	1 average share per capita					
Poor Peasant Hired Laborer	Right to keep	All					
	Entitled for allocation	1 superior share per capita					

Sources: Adapted by the author from information described in Appendix A, "China's Outline Land Law," "Northeast Liberated Area Supplementary Methods for Implementing the Outline Land Law," "Chinese Communist Party Northeast Central Bureau's Letter to the Peasants"; Chapter 5.

Appendix C

Crime Categories

The crimes or reasons for struggle recorded in Shuangcheng's victim registers are extraordinarily diverse. While the classification registers group over eighty thousand households into thirty-six unique categories, the victim registers record hundreds of unique crimes for more than seven thousand individuals. Furthermore, in many cases multiple crimes are recorded for a single individual. As introduced in chapter 1, these data were recorded at the village level by work teams and peasant associations and intimately document some of the direct motivations behind thousands of recorded events of land reform and interpersonal violence. The categorization of these crimes is crucial for the argument of this book. To some extent, how one categorizes these crimes determines what kind of argument can be made. In this appendix, therefore, I lay out as much as possible all the decisions I made in developing the categorization scheme summarized in Table 19.[1]

The original four sets of archival registers, recording events of land expropriation, escape, death, and struggle, were first transcribed in their entirety by a dedicated team of coders from the Lee-Campbell Research Group. The data was entered into Excel spreadsheets and reproduced as much as possible the original format of the archives. After realizing that these four sets were not necessarily mutually exclusive, the same coders then went back and manually linked individuals across registers based on first and last name and address and confirmed by other common characteristics like class. This linking process resulted in more than four hundred individuals who could be linked across registers. In the raw data there were also many cases of the same individual being recorded multiple times within the same register set. This occurs, for example, when a single landlord owned land in multiple villages, and each village separately recorded the expropriation of each plot of land, recording him as the owner each time. (In this respect the unit of recording in the land

Table 19. Crime Categories of Land Reform Victims in Shuangcheng County, Summer 1947

Level 3	Persons	%	Level 2	Persons	%	Level 1	Persons	%	Raw Text Examples
Political	3,024	41.7	Traitor/collaborator	1,625	22.4	Manchukuo high official	130	1.8	伪军官;伪县长;伪股长;伪满大臣;伪官僚
						Manchukuo sub-county official	422	5.8	伪区长;伪屯长;伪村长;伪区长迫削劳人;伪区长压迫劳人
						Manchukuo clerk/accountant	205	2.8	伪职员;伪村职员;伪协和会长;伪事务员;村配给所主任
						Manchukuo police	164	2.3	伪警察;伪警尉;伪警佐;伪满警察汉奸;伪满当警察剥削任屯买地
						Commercial collaboration	64	0.9	奸商;奸商利徒;奸商劣绅;奸商恶霸;奸商剥削劳人
						Other collaboration	189	2.6	伪满汉奸;伪律师;伪排长;伪校长;伪特务
						Traitor	451	6.2	汉奸;汉奸地主;地主汉奸;汉奸剥削;汉奸恶霸
			Counter-revolution	616	8.5	Violent counter-revolution	257	3.5	反动派;反动打八路军;反动地主;胡匪联络反动派;有子弹
						KMT/bandit	118	1.6	土匪;中央胡子;国民党;特务;通匪
						Sabotage the revolution	99	1.4	小看穷人;开小会;扰乱会场;挑拨离间;逃兵
						Resist expropriation	46	0.6	给地主藏物品;将东西管上了;有物不现;藏黑地;隐瞒私枪
						Running dog/lackey	96	1.3	狗腿子;走狗;地主狗腿;压迫劳人地主狗腿;警察狗腿

Major category		Subgroup		Category	Count	%	Chinese descriptors
Oppression	783 / 10.8			Physical maltreatment	21	0.3	打公骂婆; 虐待工人; 农会主任打人放枪; 好打群众; 打打活的
				Extortion and appropriation	84	1.2	勒脖子; 霸占土地; 勒索民财; 逼索租粮; 独裁及侵占公有粮食
				Graft and embezzlement	130	1.8	贪污; 独裁; 偷取公有衣服; 受贿; 私卖农会粮
				Political oppression	383	5.3	压迫; 剥削及压迫; 剥削老百姓; 势力封建; 连络警察
				Local bully	165	2.3	恶霸; 劣绅; 土豪; 大地主; 恶霸地主
Economic	3,073 / 42.4	Economic reasons	3,073 / 42.4	Profiteering	99	1.4	高租剥削劳人; 重租; 图财慕利; 交租子年斗; 剥削佃户年年涨租
				Land exploitation	371	5.1	地主剥削; 剥削佃户; 剥削地广; 专门吃租; 外地主剥削
				Labor exploitation	37	0.5	剥削雇工; 工作剥削; 剥削劳力; 剥削工资; 剥削打活的
				Other exploitation	2,147	29.6	剥削劳人; 剥削; 因剥削; 租粮剥削; 粮栈剥削
				Class status	182	2.5	地主; 地主老财; 富农; 大财阀; 资本家地主
				Absentee	237	3.3	外地主; 城内地主; 在哈尔滨住户; 外屯户; 里城客
Other	733 / 10.1	Moral/criminal misconduct	154 / 2.1	Criminal behavior	80	1.1	吸大烟; 小偷; 贩卖鸦片; 奸淫; 赌博
				Moral misconduct	74	1.0	坏蛋; 二流子; 思想不良; 人格不正; 兵痞子

Table 19—Continued

Level 3	Persons	%	Level 2	Persons	%	Level 1	Persons	%	Raw Text Examples
			Innocent/voluntary	579	8.0	Voluntary	361	5.0	自动; 自愿; 开明; 自动分出; 送产
						Lack of labor	154	2.1	无力耕种; 劳力少不能耕种; 不守业; 地多人少不能耕种; 耕种不了
						Innocent	64	0.9	无; 无罪恶
Blank/NA	416	5.7	Blank/NA	416	5.7		416	5.7	
Total	7,246	100.0	Total	7,246	100.0		7,246	100.0	

Source: Author's calculations based on linked victim registers.

expropriation registers is plots of land, not individuals.) Because these registers were compiled at multiple levels, with each administrative level sometimes producing copies of the original records, duplicate records also occur as a result of multiple extant copies of the same register pages. The raw data transcriptions include all of these records, and there was no selection or interpretation involved at the data entry stage.

This data construction process resulted in a data set containing multiple observations of individuals with multiple crimes and event outcomes (outcomes are explained in Appendix D). Originally, I used unique crimes as the unit of analysis and tabulated results based on the number of crime observations, not individuals, but this unit was too abstract and difficult to understand in terms of individual experience.[2] Here, I develop a ranking system in which each unique individual is assigned a single, highest-ranking crime. This is based on all the recorded crimes across all registers for each individual, for which I assume that their highest-ranking crime is the most important reason for being targeted.[3] Compared to my original analysis, the results are largely consistent and therefore provide a second level of support for my broader conclusions.

Ranking the crimes in this way requires interpretation. My interpretation is based on local experiences of land reform, violence, and social conditions as described in over two hundred thousand Chinese characters of work reports from 1946 to 1949 in Shuangcheng County. This is supplemented by other regional reports and official CCP documents and policies, and other land reform narratives also largely agree with this ranking. The level 1 crime categories in Table 19 are listed in rank order, with one exception. In the actual processing of crime categories, I rank moral and criminal misconduct above economic crimes, because in reality villagers despised opium smokers, gamblers, and "bad eggs" more than they despised "class enemies" proper.

But perhaps the best way to explain this ranking scheme is with some examples. For simplicity, I will use the rank of level 2 categories as follows:

1. Traitor/collaborator
2. Counterrevolution
3. Oppression
4. Moral/criminal misconduct
5. Economic reasons
6. Innocent/voluntary

One individual in the data set records the following five crimes: "1) seized residential land, 2) did not pay his workers, 3) Relied on the authority of the police sergeant to bully people, 4) sold grain at high prices, 5) held back wages." The respective ranks of these five crimes are 3, 5, 3, 5, 5. This individual's highest crime is therefore categorized as 3, oppression. In this case one might argue that quantitatively he is charged with more economic crimes and should be categorized as 5. The implicit argument in this ranking scheme, however, is that his oppression is more fundamental than his economic crimes, in terms of both logical causation and from the perspective of villagers. From the perspective of villagers his economic crimes were understood as a function of political power (e.g., ties to the police), not economic exploitation based on his ownership of capital. But this is an extreme case—over 80 percent of individuals in the data set record only one crime.

This ranking scheme is primarily based on the perspective of villagers involved in internecine struggle, not the perspective of the CCP organizing class struggle. Of course, from the official CCP perspective, economic reasons should be ranked first, which might tip the analytic balance in favor of economic reasons, but even so there would still be thousands of political reasons. In fact, as I have shown throughout this book, there is also plenty of evidence that, unofficially, CCP agents highlighted and targeted collaborators, counterrevolutionaries, and strongman ("feudal") oppression more often than strictly class enemies. In other words, the ranking scheme I use is based in local practices, not official discourse.

In this respect, the definition of "exploitation" requires further investigation, because it is the most frequently recorded crime. The Chinese term, boxue (剥削), typically translated as "exploitation," was adopted by the CCP to describe exploitation in the economic or Marxist sense of taking advantage of unequal ownership of the means of production. The 1933 documents outlining the CCP's official standards of classification define a "landlord" as anyone whose main source of income is derived from the exploitation of peasants through land rent or usury. A "rich peasant," by comparison, is anyone who relies on the exploitation of labor, land, or usury for more than 15 percent of their annual income for more than two years. These standards thus distinguish between two forms of exploitation—land or liquid capital, and labor—and define "exploitation of land" as the collection of rent, and "exploitation of labor" as claiming the surplus value of hired laborers. Before Marx, however, "exploitation" (剥削) in both English and Chinese had a broader meaning as simply taking advantage of others for personal benefit, often by relying on inequalities in status or power. In this more general sense, "exploitation" could be synonymous with "oppression," in which a local strongman uses his political position to take advantage of villagers.

When the only crime recorded for an individual is the single word "exploitation," that makes it difficult to define and categorize. In order to *underestimate* political crimes, therefore, I categorize all instances of unspecified exploitation and exploitation involving economic relations—for example, "exploit poor people," "landlord exploitation," etc.—as economic reasons (a total of over 2,100 observations). However, when exploitation is explicitly mentioned in relation to political or social oppression—for example, "oppression and exploitation," "exploit the masses/common people"—I categorize the crime as political oppression (a total of only 383 observations). In practice, however, there is extensive evidence that much of the unspecified exploitation also referred to political oppression. For example, one large landlord in District 8 is recorded in the land expropriation registers as "exploiting poor people," but a CCP work report from the summer of 1947 describes him as follows:

[W] was a university graduate. During Manchukuo he coerced the common people and took money to go study abroad in Japan. . . . His brother served as a district head and police captain during Manchukuo, and he used his brother's name to mercilessly exploit and abuse the common people. When the people cultivate land they have to work for him first, and are not allowed to work outside [the village]. . . . He is in charge, and none of the public funds are spent. He holds power over the village; he curses whenever he opens his mouth, and beats people whenever he lifts a hand.[4]

Strictly speaking, even most work reports do not talk about exploitation in "Marxist" terms until at least the fall of 1947, after most of the victim registers were compiled.

The twenty-eight level 1 categories in Table 19 were formed out of the prevailing themes found in the raw data. If one type of crime had enough observations, I assigned it its own category. Former Manchukuo officials, for example, could simply be a single category, but the detail and frequency of these crimes make it possible to separate them into more specific official positions. Other categories are based on official standards. Labor exploitation, for example, has only thirty-seven observations, but

I leave it as a category because of its traditional importance in CCP class policy. The category of "other exploitation" is the most problematic, as mentioned above. Ideally it could be broken down into smaller subcategories, but the vagueness of the crimes defies any more detailed categorization. The raw text examples give a sense of some of the most commonly recorded crimes in each category. Levels 2 and 3 further aggregate these categories for the purposes of analysis in this book.

Appendix D

Outcome Categories

As described in chapter 1, Shuangcheng's victim registers comprise four sets of nominal lists, each designed to record the main outcomes of land reform—expropriation, escape, struggle, and death. For outcomes, therefore, I retain these basic categories as the level 2 categories of analysis, as shown in Table 20. Actual recorded methods of punishment in the registers also make it possible to disaggregate these categories into more detailed level 1 categories. The level 1 categories in the table, although originally based on the prevailing themes in the raw data, are also surprisingly similar to the nine types of political struggle originally described in Mao's 1927 *Hunan Investigation*.[1] During land reform in Shuangcheng, however, deaths were recorded in greater detail. In addition to formal executions, the registers also distinguish persons who were beaten to death, committed suicide, or otherwise died an unnatural death—for example, freezing to death outside in the Manchurian winter while hiding from a mop-up team.

The similarity between the outcomes Mao described in 1927 and those recorded in Shuangcheng's victim registers was not mere coincidence. As mentioned in chapter 1, at a provincial meeting in June 1947 discussing the summer campaign in which the victim registers were recorded, county officials were explicitly encouraged to review Mao's 1927 *Hunan Investigation*.[2] Perceptions of land reform events were no doubt influenced by what at that time seems to have already become the textbook for rural revolution. However, although this discourse affected the design of the registers and the verbal instructions handed down to village cadres, it was the village cadres and work teams, not county officials, who actually recorded the outcomes. It is unlikely that many of the authors of these registers had read Mao's classic. As I have argued throughout this book, traditional rural community norms and moral politics were equally as important in shaping events in both 1927 Hunan and 1947 Shuangcheng. Corrupt local elite and officials were a ubiquitous part of rural life, and given the chance,

Table 20. Land Reform Outcome Categories in Shuangcheng County, Summer 1947

Level 2	Persons	%	Level 1	Persons	%	Raw Text Examples
Killing	273	3.8	Execution	127	1.8	枪决; 枪毙; 人民公审枪决; 刀杀; 斗争后枪毙
			Beaten to death	116	1.6	打死; 群众打死; 群众过堂打死; 扫荡队打后死的; 联合斗争打死的
			Suicide/other death	30	0.4	吊死的; 冻死的; 自杀; 未看住跳井死; 自杀投井
Public Humili-ation	1,680	23.4	Parade/dunce cap	344	4.8	游街坦白; 带帽游行; 游街; 被分游街; 斗争游街
			Struggle meeting	1,190	16.6	斗争; 经过斗争; 被群众斗争; 上台坦白打他; 棒打坦白
			Public confession	112	1.6	坦白; 坦白改造; 坦白自新; 向群众坦白; 带二流子牌子上台坦白解放
			Confinement	34	0.5	扣押; 反省; 群众教育反省; 被押; 现在县政府反省
Escape	633	8.8		633	8.8	逃跑; 光复后逃跑; 去向不明; 全家跑了; 中央去了
Expro-priation/ Fine	4,580	63.9	Expropriation (generic)	3,991	55.7	被分; 未经斗争; 土地及浮物分劈; 净身出户; 土地房间被分
			Settle Accounts	42	0.6	清算; 经过清算
			Fine	16	0.2	赔款; 返还; 罚金; 罚洋炮一支
			Donation	531	7.4	自动; 自愿; 自愿动出; 自动分劈
Total	7,166	100.0		7,166	100.0	

Source: Author's calculations based on linked victim registers.

most villagers would bring them to justice through similar retributive means of forcing them to forfeit the property they illegitimately seized (expropriation), rectifying their behavior (public confessions and humili-ation), and taking revenge on violent criminals (execution).

Categorizing these outcomes involved searching through multiple fields of all the victim registers. The struggle and death registers contain a field for explicitly recording the method of punishment for each individual, but the expropriation and escape registers do not contain such a field. The instructions for filling in the expropriation registers tell the recorder to annotate individuals who were struggled against. The notes field of the expropriation registers records thousands of other events, but some expropriation registers are completely blank, suggesting incomplete recording. Other fields in the escape registers likewise record other events but to a lesser extent. Therefore, simply categorizing based on which register the person is recorded in would miss many important events. Through trial and error and manually checking individual records, I developed a program that extracts all event information and categorizes it according to the actual event, not according to the register in which it was recorded. As with the crime categories described above, the resulting data set contains multiple observations of individuals with multiple events, for which I rank events and assign each unique individual a single, highest-ranking event. Again, this ranking system somewhat biases the higher-ranked events by undercounting lower-ranked events, but again this bias is minimal—nearly 90 percent of individuals record only one event.

The ranking of actual events is somewhat more objective than the ranking of ascribed crimes. Table 20 lists the level 1 and level 2 outcome categories in rank order. The basic logic is as follows: Persons who escape will not worry about the expropriation of the property they abandoned. Public humiliation, often involving physical violence, implies that the person did not or could not escape and is a more severe punishment than expropriation—that is, violence against property (except of course for those victims who were struggled against in absentia). Finally, death is the most severe punishment. In terms of social or community logic, this ranking also holds true: expropriation of property might cause some grudges, but public humiliation was likely cause for vengeance, and killing a neighbor was no doubt the greatest shock to the community.

Within each of these categories, moreover, level 1 events are also ranked in similar terms of personal and social violence. Within the category of public humiliation, for example, confinement and public confession alone technically did not involve any physical violence, only psychological. Struggle meetings often involved beatings and other forms of physical violence carried out in front of a village crowd (not always, but the victim registers lack these details). Parading around the village then took this violent spectacle on the road in order to reach a wider audience. As shown in some of the raw text examples, these events often occurred together. It was not uncommon for a victim to be detained, forced to publicly confess, struggled against, and then paraded around the village (see chapter 6 for examples). In this sense, each category could also be considered inclusive of subordinate categories, even though actual data is lacking in most cases. Within "killings," I also consider a formal execution to be more serious than being beaten to death, which in some cases was unintentional. Suicides and other deaths, then, differed only in practice, not necessarily in principle. In Chinese society suicide almost always had an implicit killer: the person or group who caused the victim excessive physical or psychological stress.

Finally, a word about missing data and poor or biased recording. I do not in any way consider Shuangcheng's data to be absolutely flawless or complete, but I am confident that it is the most systematic and complete data on CCP land reform analyzed to date. As much as possible, I treat missing data as missing and unknowable, not as zeros. No escape registers exist for ten *cun,* and no struggle or death registers exist for about thirty *cun,* or one third of the county (see chapter 1, Table 3). One could assume that since all four victims registers were designed to be complimentary and distributed around the same time during the same campaign, and all ninety-one *cun* in the county have extant expropriation registers, it is possible that most of these places experienced "peaceful" land reform (at least up to the summer of 1947) without any violent struggle or deaths. The prevalence of "peaceful" land reform as mentioned in numerous work reports (see chapter 5) provides support for this assumption, but of course I cannot assume that no historical record means something did not happen. This is why, for example, I restrict my analyses of violence to villages with at least one record of violence.

The comprehensiveness of Shuangcheng's data also minimizes the chances of biased recording practices. One may think that because all of these data are official CCP records they must be biased and try to cover up the extent of land reform violence or other counter-narratives. On the contrary, however, looking at all six local land reform campaigns spanning two years provides multiple cross-checks that together produce a more objective view than previously possible. During several campaigns, like in the summer and winter of 1947, campaign objectives actually incentivized work teams and village leaders to report on violence as a measure of successful mobilization. Reports from these campaigns, therefore, may actually be biased toward over-reporting violence compared to other campaigns, like in the fall of 1946 and spring of 1948. Subsequent work team reports also regularly criticized the shortcomings of previous campaigns or particular work teams. As such, there is little evidence to suggest that the authors of the victim registers had any incentives to cover up land reform violence. The incredible detail and diversity of recorded victims, outcomes and reasons for violence further suggest that there was little "official" bias in the compilation of these administrative registers. Shuangcheng's work reports provide another source for cross-checking the recording quality of the victim registers. These work reports name a total of roughly one hundred victims of land reform violence, one quarter of whom are not recorded in extant victim registers. This may seem like a large proportion of unaccounted victims, but on the other hand there are several thousand more victims who appear in the victim registers and not in work reports. In the end, Shuangcheng's relatively complete data demonstrate that the selective sources of previous studies, like work reports, surveys and even personal memories, can be subject to many more biases. In other words, the more we learn about land reform, the more we realize how much we do not know.

Appendix E

Work Team Reports

The set of work reports used in this book comprise the complete collection of extant land reform work team reports dated between 1946 and 1948 currently held in the Shuangcheng County archives. Over two hundred thousand Chinese characters of their text have been transcribed into machine-readable format, representing the majority of the legible archival reports. For the seventy-one unique reports listed in Table 21, I have manually coded all of the villages they mention by name. All together, these reports mention seventy-two out of ninety-one unique *cun* (80 percent), and 208 out of at least 559 unique *tun* (37 percent). As discussed in chapter 4, however, only a small handful of villages in the county have detailed descriptions of land reform activities for more than one campaign. Most of these reports are set in one or two *tun* but often mention experiences and even just rumors from other neighboring villages. The number of villages a given report mentions is also illustrative of the nature of the report. Reports mentioning a small number of villages are more like classic descriptions of village mass mobilization (25/71 reports only report on a single tun), while reports mentioning tens of villages are higher-level campaign summaries or general investigations (11/71 reports, some of which only report on a week or two of work activity and mention on 10 or more tun).

Most of the reports are either dated or mention a date somewhere in the body of the report. In a few cases the date is implied based on the content (language and campaign terms) of the report. If only a month and day are mentioned, it is usually possible to infer the year based on the content of the report. Table 21 is sorted by the earliest month mentioned for each report. The earliest month mentioned includes the earliest date of previous work team activity, if any, as described in reports that mention other earlier work team visits in a given village (see chapter 1, Table 2 for a tabulation of the number of work reports per campaign period). After April 1948, the next extant work report is dated October 1948, which is after the compilation of the classification registers for the entire county. I exclude more than a dozen reports dated after this time, because they describe post–land reform issues such as collecting the grain tax after the harvest, land transactions, and veterans' affairs. Land reform, as defined by the equal redistribution of all village land, was completed in the summer of 1948, and there are no extant work reports describing the process of compiling the classification registers.

The periodization of land reform campaigns in this book is based on a combination of official policy directives and the dates of these work team reports. Reports from a given campaign often reference the campaign or other related jargon, and there is little overlap in such content across campaigns. For example, once the Eliminate Half-Cooked Rice campaign began in early 1947, no reports dated after this time talk about implementing Anti-Traitor and Settling Accounts except in the past tense. In this respect, within the county campaigns seem to have been highly organized and clear-cut or maybe just very limited in scope and effectiveness. Since in most cases each report describes a new village, campaign periodization shows that most villages experienced only one type of campaign. In the fall of 1947, for example, no work team talked about how they had to carry out the previous May Fourth Directive campaigns and policies in a given village before they could implement the new Outline Land Law policies.

Many of the reports follow a standard format that reveals their bureaucratic nature. The general format of reports, regardless of campaign, consists of an introduction to the subject village, a summary of the work team's implementation experience, and then a discussion of the problems and issues the work team or village faced in the process of mobilization. Within specific campaigns the format of different reports could also be very similar. Several reports of the Mop-Up campaign collected in the archival volume 129-1-15, for example, are divided into the same three sections: "How did the Mop-up begin and develop?," "The scale and patterns of the Mop-up," and "Some problems of the intensifying movement." Each report is written in a different style and describes a different area, but it is clear that the purpose of the various reports is the same and that they are all written for review by higher-level policy makers. The archival volumes of work reports also contain many duplicate reports. These are not like the distinct drafts of reports described in chapter 4 but word-for-word handwritten copies. Sometimes duplicates would contain extra markup like underlining and corrections. These duplicates were most likely created for the review of multiple administrators, perhaps at different levels, or perhaps for dissemination among several district governments, for example.

Table 21. Chronological List of Work Team Reports in Shuangcheng County, July 1946–April 1948

No.	Earliest Month Mentioned	Last Month Mentioned	Source	Pages	Districts Mentioned	# of *cun* Mentioned	# of *tun* Mentioned
1	7/1946	7/1946	129-1-3	65–67	4	2	3
2	7/1946	7/1946	129-1-3	68–77	4	2	3
3	7/1946	1/1947	129-1-3	142–67	9	5	10
4	7/1946	8/1947	129-2-3	1–34	8, 11	4	5
5	8/1946	8/1946	129-1-16	81–92	7	1	1
6	8/1946	8/1946	129-1-3	24–29	10	1	1
7	8/1946	8/1946	129-1-3	135–41	4	1	1
8	8/1946	8/1946	129-1-3	63–64	4	2	2
9	8/1946	8/1946	129-1-3	20–23	11	1	1
10	8/1946	8/1946	129-2-3	70–93	10	1	1
11	8/1946	8/1946	129-2-3	49–63	10	2	5
12	8/1946	11/1946	TDGGYD vol.1	68–70	2, 10	2	3
13	8/1946	1/1947	129-1-16	24–51	6, 8	3	4
14	8/1946	8/1947	129-1-16	155–61	10	5	7
15	9/1946	9/1946	129-1-16	77–80	10	2	2
16	9/1946	9/1946	129-1-3	108–121	Wuchang County	1	1
17	9/1946	9/1946	129-1-3	30–41	Wuchang County	1	10
18	10/1946	10/1946	129-1-3	42–50	9	4	15
19	11/1946	1/1948	129-1-68	48–60	2	6	10
20	1/1947	1/1947	129-1-16	73–76	5, 6	3	3
21	1/1947	1/1947	129-1-16	196–212	5	2	10
22	1/1947	1/1947	129-1-16	1–12	5	3	6
23	1/1947	1/1947	129-1-3	1–19	9	4	12
24	1/1947	1/1947	129-1-3	168–74	9	1	1
25	2/1947	11/1947	129-1-27	1–10	8, 11	5	7
26	5/1947	5/1947	129-2-3	41–48	6	1	1
27	6/1947	6/1947	129-2-1	70–78	3	1	2
28	8/1947	8/1947	129-1-16	132–37	2, 3	2	2
29	8/1947	8/1947	129-1-16	175–76	4	1	1
30	8/1947	8/1947	129-1-16	93–114	10	1	1
31	8/1947	8/1947	129-2-1	1–69	3	4	5
32	10/1947	12/1947	129-1-16	119–30	11	2	2
33	11/1947	11/1947	129-1-27	11–18	6	1	1
34	11/1947	11/1947	129-1-33	5	4	1	1
35	11/1947	11/1947	129-1-33	9	4	1	1
36	11/1947	11/1947	129-1-33	4–3	4	3	5
37	11/1947	11/1947	129-1-33	6–5	3	1	1

Table 21—*Continued*

No.	Earliest Month Mentioned	Last Month Mentioned	Source	Pages	Districts Mentioned	# of *cun* Mentioned	# of *tun* Mentioned
38	11/1947	11/1947	129-1-33	8–7	4	1	2
39	11/1947	11/1947	129-1-33	10	3	2	2
40	11/1947	12/1947	129-1-33	12–11	4	2	2
41	11/1947	2/1948	129-1-15	68–75	11	5	6
42	11/1947	2/1948	129-1-15	63–67	2, 3, 6, 7, 8, 10, 11	18	25
43	12/1947	12/1947	129-1-16	220–29	3	4	4
44	12/1947	12/1947	129-1-33	6	4	1	1
45	12/1947	1/1948	129-1-15	9–15	3	2	7
46	1/1948	1/1948	129-1-15	76–85	10	5	8
47	1/1948	1/1948	129-1-15	1–8	3, 9	6	7
48	1/1948	1/1948	129-1-15	16–30	3	4	4
49	1/1948	1/1948	129-1-15	87–91	3, 4, 6	6	6
50	1/1948	1/1948	129-1-15	43–50	11	5	11
51	1/1948	1/1948	129-1-15	51–62	10	6	11
52	1/1948	1/1948	129-1-16	52–68	2	1	1
53	1/1948	1/1948	129-1-16	216–19	9	2	5
54	1/1948	1/1948	129-1-16	149–54	9	1	1
55	1/1948	1/1948	129-1-33	2–1	4	5	10
56	1/1948	1/1948	129-1-68	75–82	2	3	3
57	1/1948	1/1948	129-1-68	96–97	2	1	1
58	1/1948	1/1948	129-1-68	23–32	2	1	1
59	1/1948	1/1948	129-1-68	39–47	2	1	1
60	1/1948	1/1948	129-1-68	86–89	2	3	4
61	1/1948	1/1948	129-1-68	83–85	2	1	1
62	1/1948	1/1948	129-1-68	98–122	2	1	1
63	1/1948	1/1948	129-2-3	64–69	9	1	1
64	1/1948	2/1948	129-1-15	103–121	5, 9, 10	5	6
65	1/1948	2/1948	129-1-68	17–22	2	5	8
66	1/1948	4/1948	129-1-68	123–67	2	1	5
67	1/1948	4/1948	129-1-68	2–16	2, 3	8	13
68	1/1948	10/1948	129-1-68	33–38	2	2	2
69	2/1948	2/1948	129-1-15	98–102	10	1	1
70	2/1948	2/1948	129-1-15	92–97	11	2	3
71	2/1948	2/1948	129-1-16	174	7	1	1

Notes

Chapter 1

1. Definition from Doreen Warriner, *Land Reform in Principle and Practice* (Oxford: Clarendon Press, 1969), xiv.

2. Peter Schran, *The Development of Chinese Agriculture, 1950–1959* (Urbana: University of Illinois Press, 1969), 20. Schran notes that the official figures "appear to be questionable in virtually every respect." See also Po Yi-po (Bo Yibo), "Three Years of Historic Achievements," *People's China* no. 20 (Oct. 16, 1952), 10; Sidney Klein, *The Pattern of Land Tenure Reform in East Asia after World War II* (New York: Bookman Associates, 1958), 166, 255; "Highlights of China's Achievements," *People's China* no. 1 (Jan. 1, 1953), 28, which states that land reform before 1949 was completed in areas containing 128 million people and between 1949–1952 was completed in areas containing 300 million people, making the total population affected by land reform 428 million, or 90 percent of the rural population. These figures imply that by 1953 the rural population of China was around 475 million and the total population close to 600 million.

3. See, for example, Karl Polanyi, *The Great Transformation: The Political and Economic Origins of Our Time* (Boston: Beacon Books, 1944); Douglass C. North, *Structure and Change in Economic History* (New York: Norton, 1981).

4. See William McNeill, *The Pursuit of Power: Technology, Armed Force, and Society since A.D. 1000* (Oxford: Basil Blackwell, 1982), esp. 21–23.

5. As quoted in Barrington Moore Jr., *Social Origins of Dictatorship and Democracy: Lord and Peasant in the Making of the Modern World* (Boston: Beacon Press, 1966), 6.

6. See, for example, Polanyi, *Great Transformation*, 33–42; Moore, *Social Origins*, 3–39. See also Kenneth Pomeranz, *The Great Divergence: China, Europe, and the Making of the Modern World Economy* (Princeton, NJ: Princeton University Press, 2000); Roy Bin Wong, *China Transformed: Historical Change and the Limits of European Experience* (Ithaca, NY: Cornell University Press, 1997).

7. McNeill, *Pursuit of Power*, 24.

8. Ibid., 50. See also William Guanglin Liu, *The Chinese Market Economy, 1000–1500* (New York: SUNY Press, 2015).

9. In contrast, "The key to the English situation is that commercial life in both town

and countryside during the sixteenth and seventeenth centuries grew up mainly though not entirely in opposition to the crown." Moore, *Social Origins*, 7.

10. Ping-ti Ho, *The Ladder of Success in Imperial China: Aspects of Social Mobility, 1368–1911* (New York: Columbia University Press, 1962), esp. 41–52; Moore, *Social Origins*, 170, 175, 187. Franz Michael's introduction to Chung-li Chang's *The Income of the Chinese Gentry* (Seattle: University of Washington Press, 1962), clearly states, "Under the influence of Marxist concepts of private ownership of the means of production by a ruling class, there has been introduced the concept of a gentry class in China which based its power and authority on the continued holding of large landed estates. This view . . . is contrary to the factual conditions in China. . . . The gentry landownership that existed was a result and not a precondition of the gentry's public power. . . . The Chinese gentry derived its position not from landed estates but from its educational monopoly" (xiv). More recent research has also begun to qualify the importance of the civil service exam system, at least in the Qing dynasty, by demonstrating that the highest levels of power continued to be dominated by a hereditary ruling class, and the mobility of degree holders was much more limited than previously believed. See, for example, Yuxue Ren et al., «清代缙绅录量化数据库与官僚群体研究清史研究», «清史研究» 2016 年11月第四期: 61–77.

11. See Etienne Balazs, *Chinese Civilization and Bureaucracy* (New Haven, CT: Yale University Press, 1964), 6, 13, 16–17.

12. See for example, McNeill, *Pursuit of Power*, 48–49, citing Ping-ti Ho.

13. See Tommy Bengtsson, Cameron Campbell, James Z. Lee, et al., *Life under Pressure: Mortality and Living Standards in Europe and Asia, 1700–1900* (Cambridge, MA: MIT Press, 2004), esp. 19.

14. For more discussion of lineage property, see David Faure, *Emperor and Ancestor: State and Lineage in South China* (Stanford, CA: Stanford University Press, 2007), where he writes, "In China, because the lineage ultimately was not justified in terms of business activities, private ownership of property was not an end but a means to furthering the focus of the lineage, which was the sustenance of its deceased ancestors and the continuation of its progeny" (7); James L. Watson, "Anthropological Overview: The Development of Chinese Descent Groups," in *Kinship Organization in Late Imperial China, 1000–1940*, ed. Patricia B. Ebrey and James L. Watson (Berkeley: University of California Press, 1986), esp. 277–79.

15. See Taisu Zhang, *The Laws and Economics of Confucianism: Kinship and Property in Pre-industrial China and England* (New York: Cambridge University Press, 2017).

16. Based on descriptions in Bengtsson et al., *Life under Pressure*, 19, 435. This concept is also somewhat analogous to "command systems" and "market-regulated behavior" in McNeill, *Pursuit of Power*. In many ways my argument can also be reduced to the concept of "bringing the state back in," in which the state and its political power are regarded as a central analytic variable for understanding social and economic change. Surprisingly, however, given the importance of the state in China, China is relatively understudied in this field of political science literature. See Peter B. Evans, Dietrich Rue-

schemeyer, and Theda Skocpol, eds., *Bringing the State Back In* (New York: Cambridge University Press, 1985), esp. 78–106, "The State and Taiwan's Economic Development," by Alice H. Amsden; Vivien A. Schmidt, "Putting the Political Back into Political Economy by Bringing the State Back in Yet Again," *World Politics* 61, no. 3 (2009): 516–46. For a similar view from the perspective of contemporary China, see Yongnian Zheng and Yanjie Huang, *Market in State: The Political Economy of Domination in China* (Cambridge, UK: Cambridge University Press, 2018).

17. This is perhaps one sense of what Balazs meant when he said, "The history of modern social development in the West (1500–1914), when reflected in the mirror of Chinese history, is seen to be the very reverse of what happened in China." Balazs, *Chinese Civilization,* 21.

18. See Eric J. Hobsbawm, *The Age of Capital, 1848–1875* (New York: Charles Scribner's Sons, 1975), 2–3.

19. See, for example, Joseph W. Esherick, *Reform and Revolution in China: The 1911 Revolution in Hunan and Hubei* (Berkeley: University of California Press, 1976); Moore, *Social Origins,* 178–201.

20. This increasing social fragmentation and disorder is well documented in the literature on Chinese state-building in the early twentieth century. See, for example, Prasenjit Duara, "State Involution: A Study of Local Finances in North China, 1911–1935," *Comparative Studies in Society and History* 29, no. 1 (1987): 132–61; Roy Bin Wong, "Opium and Modern Chinese State-Making," in *Opium Regimes: China, Britain, and Japan, 1839–1952,* ed. Timothy Brook and Tadashi Wakabayashi, 189–211 (Berkeley: University of California Press, 2000); Tony Saich, "Introduction: The Chinese Communist Party and the Anti-Japanese War Base Areas," *China Quarterly,* no. 140 (Dec. 1994): 1000–1006; Ralph A. Thaxton Jr., *Salt of the Earth: The Political Origins of Peasant Protest and Communist Revolution in China* (Berkeley: University of California Press, 1997). Compare with Mary C. Wright, *The Last Stand of Chinese Conservatism: The T'ung-Chih Restoration, 1862–1874* (Stanford, CA: Stanford University Press, 1957). On the incompatibility of such reforms, see, for example, Liang Shuming, «中国民族自救运动之最后觉悟» (上海: 中华书局, 1933), reprinted in «民国丛书» 第四遍, Vol. 14 (上海: 上海书店, 1992), esp. 117–62; Guy S. Alitto, *The Last Confucian: Liang Shu-ming and the Chinese Dilemma of Modernity* (Berkeley: University of California Press, 1979), 177–91.

21. For more discussion of a similar indigenous Chinese model, as theoretically expounded by Liang Shuming in the early twentieth century, see Alitto, *Last Confucian.*

22. See, for example, Theda Skocpol, *States and Social Revolutions: A Comparative Analysis of France, Russia, and China* (New York: Cambridge University Press, 1979), 48, where she writes, "The fundamental politically relevant tensions in all three Old Regimes [France, Russia, and China] . . . were centered in the relationships of producing classes to the dominant classes and states, and in the relationships of the landed dominant classes to the autocratic-imperial states."

23. See, for example, Lifeng Li, «经济的'土改'与政治的'土改'——关于土地改革历史意义的再思考,» «安徽史学» 2008 年第2期: 68–75. For more discussion of these

processes of hierarchy and entitlement in the PRC, see Felix Wemheuer, *A Social History of Maoist China: Conflict and Change, 1949–1976* (Cambridge: Cambridge University Press, 2019).

24. See Li Kang, «西村十五年: 从革命走向革命—1938–1952 冀东村庄基层组织机制变迁» (博士学位论文, 北京大学社会学系), 1999; Alitto, *Last Confucian,* 202–210.

25. See Philip C. C. Huang, "Rethinking 'the Third Sphere': The Dualistic Unity of State and Society in China, Past and Present," *Modern China* 45, no. 4 (2019): 355–91. Interestingly, this is also very similar to how Sarah Schneewind describes village policies at the beginning of the Ming dynasty in the fourteenth century. See Sarah Schneewind, "Visions and Revisions: Village Policies of the Ming Founder in Seven Phases," *T'oung Pao* 87, nos. 4–5 (2001): 317–59.

26. For more discussion of what people wanted or expected the state to do, see Wen-kai He, *Legitimating the Early Modern States: England, Japan, and China* (Forthcoming). For related examples from early China in which the people are portrayed as wanting a strong leader, see chapter 2, n57.

27. See Edgar Snow, *Red Star over China* (1938; New York: Grove Press, 1968).

28. See William Hinton, *Fanshen: A Documentary of Revolution in a Chinese Village* (New York: Vintage Books, 1966); Kathleen Hartford and Stephen M. Goldstein, eds., *Single Sparks: China's Rural Revolutions* (Armonk, NY: M. E. Sharpe, 1989), 3–33, citing landmark studies by Edgar Snow (1938), George Taylor (1941), Theodore H. White and Annalee Jacoby (1946), Chalmers Johnson (1962), Mark Selden (1971/1995), and Tetsuya Kataoka (1974).

29. E.g., Franz Schurmann, *Ideology and Organization in Communist China* (Berkeley: University of California Press, 1968); articles collected in Roderick MacFarquhar, ed., *China under Mao: Politics Takes Command* (Cambridge, MA: MIT Press, 1966).

30. Hartford and Goldstein, *Single Sparks,* 27–28, citing comparatists like Theda Skocpol (1979), Jeffrey Paige (1975), James Scott (1976), and Samuel Popkin (1979). See also Suzanne Pepper, *Civil War in China: The Political Struggle, 1945–1949* (Berkeley: University of California Press, 1978); Yung-fa Chen, *Making Revolution: The Communist Movement in Eastern and Central China, 1937–1945* (Berkeley: University of California Press, 1986); Joseph W. Esherick, "Ten Theses on the Chinese Revolution," *Modern China* 21, no. 1 (1995): 45–76; Pauline B. Keating, *Two Revolutions: Village Reconstruction and the Cooperative Movement in Northern Shaanxi, 1934–1945* (Stanford, CA: Stanford University Press, 1997); David S. G. Goodman, *Social and Political Change in Revolutionary China: The Taihang Base Area in the War of Resistance to Japan, 1937–1945* (Lanham, MD: Rowman and Littlefield, 2000).

31. E.g., Edward Friedman, Paul G. Pickowicz, Mark Selden, and Kay Ann Johnson, *Chinese Village, Socialist State* (New Haven, CT: Yale University Press, 1991); Keith R. Schoppa, "Contours of Revolutionary Change in a Chinese County, 1900–1950," *Journal of Asian Studies* 51, no. 4 (1992): 770–96; Joseph W. Esherick, "Deconstructing the Construction of the Party-State: Gulin County in the Shaan-Gan-Ning Border Region,"

China Quarterly 140 (Dec. 1994): 1052–79; Joseph W. Esherick, "Revolution in a Feudal Fortress: Yangjiagou, Mizhi County, Shaanxi, 1937–1948," *Modern China* 24, no. 4 (1998): 339–77; Philip C. C. Huang, "Rural Class Struggle in the Chinese Revolution: Representational and Objective Realities from the Land Reform to the Cultural Revolution," *Modern China* 21, no. 1 (1995): 105–143; Huaiyin Li, *Village Governance in North China, 1875–1936* (Stanford, CA: Stanford University Press, 2005); Huaiyin Li, *Village China under Socialism and Reform* (Stanford, CA: Stanford University Press, 2009); Yaohuang Chen, «统合与分化: 河北地区的共产革命, 1921–1949" (台北市: 中央研究院近代史研究所, 2012); James Kai-sing Kung, Xiaogang Wu, and Yuxiao Wu, "Inequality of Land Tenure and Revolutionary Outcome: An Economic Analysis of China's Land Reform of 1946–1952," *Explorations in Economic History* 49 (2012): 482–97.

32. E.g., K. Li, «西村十五年»; Runsheng Du, «中国的土地改革» (北京: 当代中国出版社, 1995); Chongji Jin, «转折年代——中国的1947年» (北京: 三联书店, 2002); Pinghan Luo, «土地改革运动史» (福建人民出版社, 2005); Kuisong Yang, «中华人民共和国建国史研究», 二卷, (南昌市: 江西人民出版社, 2009); Kuisong Yang, «革命: 杨奎松著作集», 四卷, (桂林: 广西师范大学出版社, 2012); Zhikai Dong and Tingxuan Chen, «土地改革史话» (北京: 社会科学文献出版社, 2011); Daoxuan Huang, "1920—1940 年代中国东南地区的土地占有——兼谈地主、农民与土地革命», «历史研究»第一期 (2005a): 34–53; Daoxuan Huang, «洗脸——1946–1948 农村土改中干部整改» «历史研究» 第4期 (2007a): 89–110; Daoxuan Huang, «张力与限界: 中央苏区的革命, 1933–1934" (北京: 社会科学文献出版社, 2011); Lifeng Li, «土改中的诉苦: 一种民众动员技术的微观分析», «南京大学学报 (哲学·人文科学·社会科学)" 2007.5: 97–109; Woyu Liu, «农村权力关系的重构: 以苏北土改为例 1950–1952," «江苏社会科学» 2012.2: 217–23; Yiping Zhang, «三十年来中国土地改革研究的回顾与思考», «中共党史研究» 2009.1, 110–19.

33. E.g., Xueqiang Zhang, «乡村变迁与农民记忆——山东老区莒南县土地改革研究 (1941–1951)" (北京: 社会科学文献出版社, 2006); Youming Wang, «解放区土地改革研究 1941–1948: 以山东莒南县为个案» (上海: 社会科学院出版社, 2006); Ronghua Huang, «农村地权研究 1949–1983: 以湖北省新洲县为个案» (上海: 社会科学院出版社, 2006).

34. E.g., Xiang Cai, *Revolution and Its Narratives: China's Socialist Literary and Cultural Imaginaries, 1949–1966*, ed. and trans., Rebecca E. Karl and Xueping Zhong (Durham, NC: Duke University Press, 2016); Brian Demare, *Land Wars: The Story of China's Agrarian Revolution* (Stanford, CA: Stanford University Press, 2019).

35. This collection has been carried out over the past couple decades by both individual scholars and institutions throughout China. Notable among these are the Shanxi University Research Center for Chinese Social History, which has collected village-level archives from over two hundred villages throughout Shanxi (for an early introduction see Long Xing and Weiqiang Ma, "Rural Grassroots Files from the Collectivization Era," *Modern China* 34, no. 3 (2008): 372–95); Shanghai Jiaotong University's "Chinese Local Historical Document Database," which contains approximately 350,000 documents primarily from Southeast China (see Shuji Cao, ed., «中国地方历史文献数据库» (上海:

上海交通大学出版社, 2015) http://dfwx.datahistory.cn/pc/ (Accessed Aug. 14, 2019); Letian Zhang at Fudan University, who has collected comprehensive Collectivization-era village-level archives from a single village in Zhejiang Province, including over 25,000 pages, 350 videos, and 800 audio recordings (see Letian Zhang, ed., «张乐天联民村数据库» (北京: 社会科学文献出版社, 2015) http://www.zltfieldwork.com/ (Accessed Aug. 14, 2019); East China Normal University's Center for the Study of PRC History, which has already published eleven volumes of contemporary archives from various villages and other organizations (see Gang Han et al., eds., «中国当代民间史料集刊», 九种十一册 (上海: 中国出版集团东方出版中心, 2011); and Si Zhang at Nankai University, who has collected comprehensive village-level archives covering virtually the entire second half of the twentieth century from Hou jia ying village in Hebei Province (see Si Zhang, «国家渗透与乡村过滤: 昌黎县侯家营文书所见», «中国农业大学学报 (社会科学版)" 第25卷第1期 (March 2008): 76–88.). One of the first English-language studies based on similar materials, from a village in Jiangsu, is H. Li, *Village China under Socialism and Reform*.

36. Esherick, "Ten Theses," 48.

37. See Friedman et al., *Chinese Village, Socialist State*, 101–107.

38. Since 1928 the CCP and KMT were the two main contenders for leadership of a unified central government in China. The KMT was the recognized ruling party on the mainland from 1928 to 1949, after which they retreated to Taiwan but continued to claim legitimacy. Throughout this book I will use the term KMT, an acronym for the Wade-Giles romanization of their Chinese name, Kuomintang (国民党). They are also commonly referred to as the Nationalists, or GMD, the standard pinyin romanization of the Chinese.

39. See, for example, John Service's descriptions of Nationalist politics in Joseph W. Esherick, ed., *Lost Chance in China: The World War II Despatches of John S. Service* (New York: Random House, 1974).

40. Parks M. Coble, Jr., *The Shanghai Capitalists and the Nationalist Government, 1927–1937* (Cambridge, MA: Harvard University Press, 1980), 46.

41. See Shuang Chen, *State-Sponsored Inequality: The Banner System and Social Stratification in Northeast China* (Stanford, CA: Stanford University Press, 2017). For more discussion, see Alitto, *Last Confucian*, 177–210, and see pp. 215–25 for a comparison between modern Confucianism and Maoism; Philip A. Kuhn, *Origins of the Modern Chinese State* (Stanford, CA: Stanford University Press, 2002), 80–113.

42. Balazs, *Chinese Civilization*, 17.

43. See also Marc Blecher, *China against the Tides: Restructuring through Revolution, Radicalism, and Reform*, 3rd ed. (London: Bloomsbury Academic, 2009).

44. For a similar argument in relation to the Qin dynasty unification of China in the third century BCE, see Charles Sanft, *Communication and Cooperation in Early Imperial China* (Albany, NY: SUNY Press, 2014), esp. 6.

45. Peter Hays Gries and Stanley Rosen, eds., *State and Society in 21st-Century China: Crisis, Contention, and Legitimation* (New York: Routledge, 2004), 3–5; Elizabeth Perry,

Challenging the Mandate of Heaven: Social Protest and State Power in China (Armonk, NY: M. E. Sharpe, 2002); Ane Bislev and Stig Thogersen, *Organizing Rural China—Rural China Organizing* (Lanham, MD: Lexington Books, 2012), 2.

46. Xing Ying, «农户、集体与国国家——国家与农民关系的六十年变迁» (北京: 中国社会科学出版社, 2014), 16–17.

47. See note 64 below for a relatively complete list of influential village narratives of land reform. See also Demare, *Land Wars*.

48. For more discussion of the importance of the county level in understanding Chinese political economy, see Marc J. Blecher and Vivienne Shue, *Tethered Deer: Government and Economy in a Chinese County* (Stanford, CA: Stanford University Press, 1996); Heng Hu, «皇权不下县?: 清代县辖政区与基层社会治理» (北京: 北京师范大学出版社, 2015).

49. Confucian moral economy has long stressed social equality and welfare. In the words of Confucius: "I have heard that the head of a state or a family does not worry about under-population, but about uneven distribution; not about poverty, but about instability. For where there is even distribution, there is no such thing as poverty; where there is harmony, there is no such thing as under-population; and where there is stability, there is no such thing as regime change." Translation adapted from Burton Watson, trans., *The Analects of Confucius* (New York: Columbia University Press, 2007), 115. In the Confucian state it is possible to conceive of the source of legitimate power as a kind of personal, moral benevolence or righteousness, as in Mencius's concept of the right to rebel against a corrupt ruler: "He who outrages the benevolence proper to his nature, is called a robber; he who outrages righteousness, is called a ruffian. The robber and ruffian we call a mere fellow. I have heard of the cutting off of the fellow Zhou, but I have not heard of the putting a sovereign to death, in his case." «孟子·梁惠王下», section 15, trans. James Legge, as quoted in Sturgeon 2011, https://ctext.org/mengzi/lianghui-wang-ii. See also Alitto, *Last Confucian*, esp. 213; Wenkai He, *Legitimating the Early Modern States*; Lily Tsai, *Accountability without Democracy: Solidary Groups and Public Goods Provision in Rural China* (New York: Cambridge University Press, 2007); Ying, «农户、集体与国家», 19.

50. Polanyi, *Great Transformation*, 34, for example, describes the integration of state and local *elite* interests that made enclosures possible in seventeenth-century England, in which the "formula appears to take for granted the essence of purely economic progress, which is to achieve improvement at the price of social dislocation. But it also hints at the tragic necessity by which the poor man clings to his hovel, doomed by the rich man's desire for a public improvement which profits him privately."

51. For cross-period comparisons, see, for example, Kung et al., "Inequality of Land Tenure"; Kuo-chun Chao, *Agrarian Policy of the Chinese Communist Party, 1921–1959* (Bombay: Asia Publishing House, 1960); Demare, *Land Wars*.

52. "Directive for Dealing with Agricultural Land in the Suburbs of Cities of Old Liberated Areas," New China News Agency Translation, *China Weekly Review*, March 4, 1950, 16. This was also the policy in suburban areas in South China, as noted in C. K.

Yang, *A Chinese Village in Early Communist Transition* (Cambridge, MA: MIT Press, 1959), 150.

53. «国有土地使用证», as illustrated in a photograph, "Uprooting the Feudal System of Land Ownership," in *People's China* 2, no. 2 (1950), 16–17.

54. Shao-chi Liu (Shaoqi Liu), "On the Agrarian Reform Law," *People's China* 2, no. 2 (1950), 5.

55. Ibid., 6. As may be expected, studies of 1950s land reforms tell a more complicated story.

56. See Appendix A, "Directive on the Land Question."

57. See Appendix A, "China's Outline Land Law," Article 1.

58. See Appendix A, "Resolution on the Chinese Communist Party Central Committee's Promulgation of China's Outline Land Law."

59. P. Luo, «土地改革运动史», 35–36. See also the original directive, «东北的形势和任务» (July 7, 1946), in Yun Chen, «陈云文选» (北京: 人民出版社, 1984), 1:307–313.

60. See the November 21, 1946, Northeast Bureau directive, «关于解决土改运动中«半生不熟»的问题的指示», in Dongbei jiefang qu caizheng jingji shi bianxie zu,«东北解放区财政经济史资料选编», 第一卷, (哈尔滨: 黑龙江人民出版社, 1988) (Hereafter DJCJZ), 293–96; and the Songjiang provincial meeting in December 1946, mentioned in «土地改革运动, 1945.9–1949.10» (哈尔滨: 黑龙江省档案馆编, 1983–1984) (Hereafter TDGGYD), 1:136, 152. See also a letter dated November 20, 1946, from a Northeast Bureau leader to Shuangcheng County and Songjiang provincial leaders that recommends to the same effect that land reform work is incomplete and needs to be reinvestigated, «张秀山关于双城五家区群运情况给海涛、鹏图、林诚的信», in TDGGYD, 1:68–70.

61. Other regions carried out similar campaigns in this period. See Hinton, *Fanshen*, 206–207; David Crook and Isabel Crook, *Revolution in a Chinese Village: Ten Mile Inn* (London: Routledge and Kegan Paul, 1959), 130–37; Zhongyang dang'an guan, ed., «解放战争时期土地改革文件选辑» (北京: 中共中央党校出版社, 1981) (Hereafter TGWX), 56–60.

62. Shuangcheng was one of fourteen counties in Songjiang Province, formerly Binjiang Province of Manchukuo, with its provincial capital in Harbin. Songjiang Province was incorporated into present-day Heilongjiang Province in 1954.

63. TDGGYD, 1:157.

64. "Order on investigating the county population for transmission to the province for the issuing of land deeds" (May 17, 1948), and "Announcement to have land deed fees collected in sorghum" (Oct. 25, 1948), in 129-2-11, 5–7, 16–18. However, the only actual land deed I have seen from this period in Shuangcheng is dated March 1949 (a land deed from District 9, photographed by the author in private folk museum in Shuangcheng).

65. These include a select mix of fiction and nonfiction accounts, as follows in order of publication:

Shangzhi County, Heilongjiang: Libo Zhou, 《暴风骤雨》 (1949; 北京: 人民文学出版社, 1952).

Huozhou shi, Shanxi: Jack Belden, *China Shakes the World* (1949; New York: Monthly Review Press, 1970), 174–89.

Zhuolu County, Hebei: Ling Ding,《太阳照在桑干河上》 (1956; 北京: 人民文学出版社, 2012).

Wu'an County, Hebei: Crook and Crook, *Revolution in a Chinese Village* (1959); David Crook and Isabel Crook, *Ten Mile Inn: Mass Movement in a Chinese Village* (New York: Pantheon Books, 1979).

Panyu County (district), Guangdong: C. K. Yang, *Chinese Village* (1959).

Lucheng County, Shanxi: Hinton, *Fanshen* (1966).

Guangzhou suburb, Guangdong: Anita Chan, Richard Madsen, and Jonathan Unger, *Chen Village under Mao and Deng* (1984; Berkeley, CA: University of California Press, 1992).

Xiamen, Fujian: Huang Shu-min, *The Spiral Road: Change in a Chinese Village through the Eyes of a Communist Party Leader*, 2nd ed. (Boulder, CO: Westview Press, 1998).

Songjiang County, Jiangsu: Philip C. C. Huang, *The Peasant Family and Rural Development in the Yangzi Delta, 1350–1988* (Stanford, CA: Stanford University Press, 1990).

Dongguan city, Guangdong: Sulamith Heins Potter and Jack M. Potter, *China's Peasants: The Anthropology of a Revolution* (New York: Cambridge University Press, 1990).

Raoyang County, Hebei: Friedman et al., *Chinese Village, Socialist State* (1991).

Shifang County, Sichuan: Stephen Endicott, *Red Earth: Revolution in a Sichuan Village* (New York: New Amsterdam, 1991).

Meishan city, Sichuan: Gregory A. Ruf, *Cadres and Kin: Making a Socialist Village in West China, 1921–1991* (Stanford, CA: Stanford University Press, 1998).

Mizhi County, Shaanxi: Esherick, "Revolution in a Feudal Fortress" (1998).

Ju'nan County, Shandong: X. Zhang, 《乡村变迁与农民记忆》 (2006).

Xinzhou County, Hubei: R. Huang, 《农村地权研究 1949–1983》 (2006).

Zhuzhou city, Hunan: Yiyuan Chen, 《建国初期农村基层政权建设研究, 1949–1957: 以湖南省醴陵县为个案》 (上海: 社会科学院出版社, 2006).

Jianchang County, Liaoning; Meizhou city, Guangdong: Jiangsui He, "Identifying Mistakes to Discipline a New State: The Rectification Campaigns in China's Land Reform, 1946–1952," PhD diss., Department of Sociology, University of California, San Diego, 2008.

Shangshui County, Henan: Teng Jia, 《土改背景下的乡村社会秩序重构——以河南商水县为个案的考察 (1947–1954)》 (华东师范大学, 中国近现代史博士论文, 2008).

Zhenjiang County, Changzhou County, Wuxi County, Wu County, Suzhou city, Jiangsu: Yiping Zhang, 《地权变动与社会重构: 苏南土地改革研究, 1949–1952》 (上海: 上海人民出版社, 2009).

Dongtai County, Jiangsu: Li, *Village China under Socialism and Reform*, 14–19. The CCP liberated this county in the fall of 1948 and appears in the pre–Land Reform Law area on the map, but according to Li, land reform did not start in the area until the winter of 1950 (16).

For a synthesis of a number of these narratives, see Demare, *Land Wars*.

66. On landlord compensation, see Kuisong Yang, «中华人民共和国建国史研究», 1:29–38; Jin, «转折年代——中国的1947年», 383–84. On targeting landlord descendants, see Hinton, *Fanshen*, 203; Crook and Crook, *Revolution in a Chinese Village*, 130–37.

67. The study of the model county, Ding Xian, and John L. Buck's farm surveys are some of the most notable examples of this style of research. See Sidney D. Gamble, *Ting Hsien: A North China Rural Community* (Stanford, CA: Stanford University Press, 1968); John Lossing Buck, *Land Utilization in China: A Study of 16,786 Farms in 168 Localities, and 38,256 Farm Families in Twenty-Two Provinces in China, 1929–1933* (New York: Reproduced by the Council on Economic and Cultural Affairs, 1956). See also Japanese social surveys introduced in Yoshiki Enatsu, 「中国東北地方における農村実態調査: 康徳三 (1936) 年度、満州国農村実態調査報告書にある統計資料について」 (Hitotsubashi University, Institute of Economic Research, Discussion Paper No. D97–23, Feb. 1998); Cao Xingsui, «满铁的中国农村实态调查概述» «中国社会经济史研究» 1991, no. 4: 104–109. For general discussion, see Tong Lam, *A Passion for Facts: Social Surveys and the Construction of the Chinese Nation-State, 1900–1949* (Berkeley: University of California Press, 2011), ch. 6, 142–70.

68. See, for example, Joseph W. Esherick, "Number Games: A Note on Land Distribution in Prerevolutionary China," *Modern China* 7, no. 4 (1981): 387–411.

69. Xiaotong Fei, *Peasant Life in China: A Field Study of Country Life in the Yangtze Valley* (New York: E. P. Dutton, 1939), is the preeminent example of a single village study, heavily influenced by leading anthropological methodologies like that of Bronislaw Malinowski. For a similar village-centric perspective in literary works, see, for example, Yi-tsi Mei Feuerwerker, *Ding Ling's Fiction: Ideology and Narrative in Modern Chinese Literature* (Cambridge, MA: Harvard University Press, 1982), 124. Largely inspired by methods of cultural and microhistory, current scholarship on rural China continues to focus on the village as the basic unit of investigation. See, for example, Long Xing, «走向田野与社会», 修订本 (北京: 生活·读书·新知三联书店, 2015).

70. William G. Skinner, "Marketing and Social Structure in Rural China: Part I," *Journal of Asian Studies* 24, no. 1 (1964): 3–43; "Marketing and Social Structure in Rural China: Part II," *Journal of Asian Studies* 24, no. 2 (1965): 195–228; "Marketing and Social Structure in Rural China: Part III," *Journal of Asian Studies* 24, no. 3 (1965): 363–99. See also Ying, «农户、集体与国国家», esp. 12–15.

71. For discussion of CCP organization, see, for example, Harry Harding, *Organizing China: The Problem of Bureaucracy, 1949–1976* (Stanford, CA: Stanford University Press, 1981), 1: "Under Communist Party rule, therefore, China has been transformed

from what Sun Yat-sen described as a 'sheet of loose sand' into one of the most highly organized societies in the world." Lyman P. Van Slyke, *The Chinese Communist Movement: A Report of the United States War Department, July 1945* (Stanford, CA: Stanford University Press, 1968), 7–8; Stephen I. Levine, *Anvil of Victory: The Communist Revolution in Manchuria, 1945–1948* (New York: Columbia University Press, 1987), chapter 3; Tetsuya Kataoka, *Resistance and Revolution in China: The Communists and the Second United Front* (Berkeley: University of California Press, 1974); Yung-fa Chen, *Making Revolution*.

72. «刘少奇关于彻底解决土地问题给晋绥同志的一封信», in Zhongyang dang'an guan, ed., «中共中央文件选集», 十八册, (中共中央党校出版社, 1991–1992) (Hereafter ZZWX), 16:487.

73. All of the original documents are preserved in the Shuangcheng district archives, accessed by the author over the course of three months in residence in the fall of 2011.

74. It is the intent of the author to have these data further cleaned and prepared for future release as a public data set.

75. The land expropriation registers include more than one thousand records of struggle. All of these victim registers together record a total of over seven thousand unique individuals.

76. Comparing with aggregate county statistics from 1946, 1947, and earlier in 1948, there was also little change in the population over the course of land reform:

Table 22. Aggregate County Statistics from 1946, 1947, 1948

Date	Households	Persons	Source
Jun. 1946	75,000	423,000	TDGGYD, 1:151
Sept. 1947	75,000	413,000	129-1-31, 2
Mar. 1948	66,000	360,000	129-1-75, 1 (rural population only)

Thus the total population remained around 420,000 (or 370,000 rural), and by July 1948 the number of households had increased to about 82,000 (or 71,000 rural), a 10 percent increase from previous counts. In contrast, national statistics suggest that the total number of households before and after land reform increased by over 50 percent, from 86.20 million in 1947 to 133.85 million in 1953. See Zhigang Guo, «当代中国人口发展与家庭户的变迁» (北京: 中国人民大学出版社, 1995), 12. Household divisions also played their own important role in the redistribution of wealth; see, for example, Hu Yingze, «土改后至高级社前的乡村地权变化——基于山西省永济县吴村档案的考察», «中共党史研究» 2014.3: 99–106.

77. See Appendix D for a table summarizing all recorded class labels.

78. See, for example, a series of district and village directives from District 2 from the end of May 1948, ordering villages to compile statistics of the number of households and each household's number of plots of land, in order to issue new land deeds (129-2-18, 48–61, see also discussion in chapter 4). These directives are dated shortly after District 2 completed the compilation of their classification registers.

79. «双城市解放战争时期公安史稿» (1945.11–1949.9) (双城市公安局, 1996) (Hereafter SCJZSGS), 97–106. I have seen only one original *hukou* booklet from this period, courtesy of Mr. Wang in Lequn Township, Shuangcheng, which was dated September 5, 1948, but the recorded date of investigation on the back was July 30, 1948. (Note that this booklet was registered in District 7, which completed compilation of their classification registers in mid-June.)

80. The classification registers were replicated in 1965, presumably as part of the Socialist Education movement. The emphasis on class and struggle in these titles also suggests they were heavily influenced by the rhetoric of this movement, which called for one of the largest mass mobilizations of class struggle since the land reform. For more details, see Richard Baum, *Prelude to Revolution: Mao, the Party, and the Peasant Question, 1962–1966* (New York: Columbia University Press, 1975).

81. One reason why I restrict analysis to the *cun* level throughout this study is because the recording of *tun* information is incomplete. Roughly one-third of all observations in the victim registers do not record the name of the *tun*, but in all cases the *cun* is either recorded or can be inferred.

82. Based on the forms in death register 129-1-22, 1–40. One notation in the escape registers also explains how one *cun's* summary list was lost and all they had left were scattered pages of the original *tun* investigations (129-1-21, 4).

83. However, only one *cun's* expropriation, struggle, and escape registers are filed together, including a cover page, demonstrating their simultaneous compilation. See land expropriation register 129-3-10, 38–44.

84. Records in death register 129-1-23, 13, correspond to events described in «双城文史资料», 政协黑龙江省双城县委员会文史资料研究委员会编 (双城县政府铅印室印刷, 1985) (Hereafter SCWZ), 2:11. Persons recorded in death register 129-1-22, 48, appear to be related to counterrevolutionary events described in SCWZ, 2:9, although the actual time of execution is unclear.

85. See 129-1-3, 21, 44, and corresponding expropriation registers 129-3-8, 129-3-9, and 129-3-10.

86. The three persons who were struggled against are recorded as serving in 1946 as the peasant association chairman and vice chairman and the *tun* head. See struggle register 129-1-25, 69.

87. See Zedong Mao, «毛泽东选集», (东北书店, 1948), 1:34–36.

88. TDGGYD, 1:156. See also an earlier directive from Zhu De and Liu Shaoqi that calls for the distribution of copies of the Hunan Investigation to cadres in Hebei, «朱德、刘少奇关于彻底完成冀东土改的指示» (May 6, 1947), in TGWX, 56–57.

89. See, for example, the land expropriation register in 129-3-1, 2.

90. Proportions are restricted to *cun* that have at least one record in each of the pairs of registers being compared. It is not clear what happened to the land of escapees, but presumably it was kept by family members who stayed behind or was redistributed later. For those who were killed, many of them were poor peasants with little land.

91. 129-1-24, 2

92. See D. Huang, «洗脸».

93. The district statistics record less confiscated land and persons overall compared to the victim registers. I prioritize the latter because they are more disaggregated.

94. This dating is based on the dates recorded in work reports describing these campaigns. See Appendix E.

Chapter 2

1. In 2014 Shuangcheng became a metropolitan district of Harbin, the provincial capital of Heilongjiang Province. Between 1988 and 2014 it was classified as a county-level city and before 1988 a county.

2. For more discussion of the social context of Shuangcheng in the Republican period, see S. Chen, *State-Sponsored Inequality*, chapter 8.

3. See also K. Li, «西村十五年».

4. For more details see S. Chen, *State-Sponsored Inequality*, chapters 2 and 3.

5. «双城县志», 双城县志编纂委员会 (北京: 中国展望出版社, 1990) (Hereafter SCXZ), 93–94.

6. Ibid., 122.

7. Ibid., 441.

8. 7-1-10-2, «省政府公粮公草征收指示», 松江省政府 (Sept. 3, 1946).

9. The distribution of crops sown in 1947 was similar to that in 1949 as well, suggesting that planting in 1947 was not significantly affected by the turbulence of civil war, land reform, or natural disaster (which came later in the summer of this year). See 129-2-56, 62, for a similar table from the summer of 1949. I use data from 1947 here because the administrative district divisions changed in 1948.

10. See, for example, Keating, *Two Revolutions*, 66–72.

11. See S. Chen, *State-Sponsored Inequality*, 70–71.

12. As Shuang Chen mentions, the 1890 figure no doubt excludes a significant number of unregistered households. See S. Chen, *State-Sponsored Inequality*, 83–85; SCXZ, 829.

13. SCXZ, 58.

14. North Chinese agriculture is typically characterized by low inequality of land and a high proportion of owner-cultivators, inactive rental market, and active labor market for households with surplus land. South Chinese agriculture, on the other hand, is typically characterized by high inequality of land, high rates of tenancy, and a relatively inactive labor market. See Kung et al., "Inequality of Land Tenure," 486–90; Levine, *Anvil of Victory*, 201–203; more discussion in chapter 5.

15. For more details, see Yuxue Ren, «清代吉林将军双城地区的身份制度与旗界、民界 (1815–1911 年)——兼论东北地区的封禁政策», «中国历史地理论丛» 第28卷第3辑 (2013.7): 115–23; S. Chen, *State-Sponsored Inequality*. A small number of

non-banner villages, especially in the southwest of the county, existed before the banner villages were settled in the early nineteenth century.

16. S. Chen, *State-Sponsored Inequality*, 15; SCXZ, 154. Before 1907 a wide range of unofficial land transactions took place, including conditional sales, mortgages, etc. See S. Chen, *State-Sponsored Inequality*, 148–57. For more general discussion of frontier political economy, see John R. Shepherd, *Statecraft and Political Economy on the Taiwan Frontier, 1600–1800* (Stanford, CA: Stanford University Press, 1993).

17. See Yoshiki Enatsu, *Banner Legacy: The Rise of the Fengtian Local Elite at the End of the Qing* (Ann Arbor: Center for Chinese Studies, University of Michigan, 2004). Especially in Northeast China, following the end of the Qing dynasty, many prominent Republican officials and elites were originally Qing bannermen or their descendants.

18. Cai Yunsheng, Zhai Wenxuan, and Yu Chencheng are recorded in Shuangcheng's land expropriation registers, and Cai's, Yu's, and Mo Dehui's real estate in the county seat are also recorded in registers of urban property that are not discussed in this book; see 129-2-51. As with many high-level elites, these persons were not subject to the violence of land reform, which primarily targeted low-level rural elites.

19. Around 1910 there were only about 48,000 metropolitan and rural bannermen in Shuangcheng, out of a total population of over 440,000. See S. Chen, *State-Sponsored Inequality*, 70–71, 83–85. The majority of landlords identified in both land reform work reports and contemporary interviews with elderly villagers share the same surnames as most of the founding banner families who originally immigrated to these villages in the early nineteenth century.

20. As mentioned in an interview with CDX, June 7, 2013. Bannermen continued to have privileged land rights as late as 1938; see SCXZ, 145; S. Chen, *State-Sponsored Inequality*.

21. Note also that the first CCP county head and other leading county cadres were also local bannerman descendants (and from landlord and rich peasant families).

22. For the larger implications of such property developments in North China, see Philip C. C. Huang, *The Peasant Economy and Social Change in North China* (Stanford, CA: Stanford University Press, 1985). Another implication is that in Shuangcheng the bannermen's initial endowments of land in the nineteenth century continued to help them accumulate disproportionate amounts of social and material wealth even after the end of the Qing. On some of the important effects of landed wealth on social outcomes in Shuangcheng, see Shuang Chen, James Lee, and Cameron Campbell, "Wealth Stratification and Reproduction in Northeast China, 1866–1907," *History of the Family* 15, no. 4 (2010): 386–412.

23. These figures were first quoted to legitimate the Outline Land Law on October 10, 1947 (see Appendix A), and then again by Liu Shaoqi on June 14, 1950, in «关于土地改革问题的报告», in Shaoqi Liu, «刘少奇选集» (北京: 人民出版社, 1985), 2:32.

24. See Dehong Guo, «中国近现代农民土地问题研究» (青岛出版社, 1993), ch. 1. See also Hu Yingze, «近代华北乡村地权分配再研究——基于晋冀鲁三省的分析», «历史研究» 2013.4: 117–36; K. C. Yeh, *Land Reform and the Revolutionary War: A Re-*

view of Mao's Concepts and Doctrines (Santa Monica, CA: Rand Corporation, 1971), 22–26; L. Li, «经济的 '土改' 与政治的 '土改'»; Kung et al., "Inequality of Land Tenure," 482–86. Kung et al., in particular, show that the distribution of land was significantly more unequal in South China than in the North.

25. These registers record a total of more than 6,600 households (land owners) owning over 175,000 hectares of land, while county statistics from around the same time (late summer 1947) record a total of more than 61,000 rural households and over 271,000 hectares of farm land.

26. SCXZ, 443–44; «海龙调查», in Dongbei ju xuanchuan bu, ed., «东北农村调查» (东北书店, March 1947), 213–14, 217–18

27. «海龙调查», 215–16.

28. Jihong Che, «试论伪满政权的地方基层统治机构», «齐齐哈尔师范学院学报» 1995 年第5期: 133–36. On the Manchukuo local police, see «海龙调查», 219–20.

29. See chapters 5 and 6.

30. See, for example, a story about how a CCP regiment was ambushed when returning along the branch line from Lalin to Zhoujia station in District 9. SCWZ, 2:28–30.

31. An official provincial report from June 1947 records Shuangcheng's population as just over 423,000, while the next most populous county in Songjiang province had a population of only 313,000, and the average population among all fourteen counties was only 160,000. See TDGGYD, 1:151.

32. See, for example, Kenneth Pomeranz, *The Making of a Hinterland: State, Society, and Economy in Inland North China, 1853–1937* (Berkeley: University of California Press, 1993); Susan Mann Jones, "Trade, Transport, and Taxes: The Decline of a National Medicine Fair in Republican China," in *Select Papers from the Center for Far Eastern Studies*, no. 4, 1979–1980, ed. Tang Tsou, 112–42 (Chicago: University of Chicago, 1981); Ramon H. Myers, *The Chinese Peasant Economy: Agricultural Development in Hopei and Shantung, 1890–1949* (Cambridge, MA: Harvard University Press, 1970); Ramon H. Myers, "How Did the Modern Chinese Economy Develop?—A Review Article," *Journal of Asian Studies* 50, no. 3 (1991): 604–628; P. Huang, *Peasant Economy and Social Change.*

33. Two summary tables dated September 1947 alternately record a total of 692 or 738 *tun* settlements but only 530 peasant associations. See 129-1-31, 2–3. Over the course of land reform and rural Collectivization, many of these separate settlements may have been physically consolidated into other villages and no longer exist.

34. Compare with Liang Shuming's rural reconstruction and "Confucian modernization," in Alitto, *Last Confucian.*

35. The middle group, labeled "middle peasants," were in limbo throughout land reform, sometimes being included in the list of enemies and sometimes being included in the list of peasant association members. See, for example, Daoxuan Huang, «盟友抑或潜在对手? ——老区土地改革中的中农», «南京大学学报 （哲学·人文科学·社会科学)" 第 5 期 (2007b): 82–96; Hui Bai, «试论1947年~ 1949 年华北土改运动中的中农政策», «中北大学学报 （社会科学版)" 2014 年第30卷第1期: 9–12.

36. Compare with Philip A. Kuhn, "Local Self-Government under the Republic: Prob-

lems of Control, Autonomy, and Mobilization," in Frederic Wakeman Jr. and Carolyn Grant, eds., *Conflict and Control in Late Imperial China* (Berkeley: University of California Press, 1975), 287–93; Stephen C. Averill, "Local Elites and Communist Revolution in the Jiangxi Hill Country," in *Chinese Local Elites and Patterns of Dominance*, ed. Joseph W. Esherick and Mary Backus Rankin, 282–304 (Berkeley: University of California Press, 1990).

37. See Appendix A, Article 7 of the "Directive on the Land Question" and Article 12 of "China's Outline Land Law."

38. 129-2-1 (Aug. 1947), 12–14.

39. 129-2-1 (Aug. 1947), 14–15.

40. «中共中央关于土地改革中各社会阶级的划分及其待遇的规定（草案),» in TGWX, 185. See also James Kai-sing Kung, "The Political Economy of Land Reform in China's 'Newly Liberated Areas': Evidence from Wuxi County," *China Quarterly*, no. 195 (2008): 675–90.

41. See Kuhn, "Local Self-Government," 287–95. In an October 1946 "Resolution on Land Reform," the Shandong provincial CCP government defined "evil gentry" (豪绅) and "evil bullies" (恶霸) as "those who gained excessive power over the peasantry through former government connections, and those who, as leaders or influential members of gangs, were able to intimidate the peasantry into submission." See "Resolution on Land Reform in Shantung Province," translation edited by Elizabeth Graham, *China Weekly Review* 105, no. 1 (1947): 18.

42. See TGWX, 184.

43. 129-1-16 (Aug. 1946), 138.

44. 129-2-3 (Aug. 1946), 75, 77.

45. 129-1-16 (Aug. 1946), 143.

46. On the original allotments of banner land and the position of village banner captain, see Chen, *State-Sponsored Inequality*.

47. 129-2-1 (Aug. 1947), 39–40.

48. Kuhn, "Local Self-Government," 291.

49. For example, Mencius' simple four-character statement, "protect the people and become a king" (保民而王), implies that the king's duty is to take care of the people and that the legitimacy of kingship depends on the people («孟子·梁惠王上», section 7, as quoted in Sturgeon 2011, https://ctext.org/mengzi/liang-hui-wang-i).

50. See also Cai, *Revolution and Its Narratives*, 103–112.

51. 129-1-16, 26.

52. 129-1-16, 27 (emphasis added).

53. See Appendix A, "China's Outline Land Law," Article 5.

54. See chapter 3; Kuisong Yang, «中华人民共和国建国史研究», 1: 69–70; «中共中央关于重发《怎样分析阶级》等两文件的指示» in TGWX, 90–91.

55. 129-1-33, 5.

56. However, as late as January 1948 an extant list from one village in District 2 records sixteen "poor peasants and hired laborers" who were not allowed to participate in the poor peasant and hired laborer assembly. Almost all of them are identified as opium

addicts, members of bandit armies, and former Manchukuo policemen and soldiers. See 129-1-68, 121–22.

57. Stuart R. Schram, ed., *Mao's Road to Power: Revolutionary Writings, 1912–1949* (Armonk, NY: M. E. Sharpe, 1994), 2:430; Mao, «毛泽东选集» 1:19–20.

58. For example, Mencius compares the heroic founder of the Zhou dynasty, King Wen (1112–1050 BCE), to the failure of the last ruler of the Xia dynasty, Jie (1728–1675 BCE), saying, "King Wen used the strength of the people to make his tower and his pond, and yet the people rejoiced to do the work, calling the tower 'the marvelous tower,' calling the pond 'the marvelous pond,' and rejoicing that he had his large deer, his fishes, and turtles. The ancients caused the people to have pleasure as well as themselves, and therefore they could enjoy it. In the Declaration of Tang it is said, 'O sun, when wilt thou expire? We will die together with thee.' The people wished for Jie's death, though they should die with him. Although he had towers, ponds, birds, and animals, how could he have pleasure alone?" «孟子·梁惠王上», section 2, trans. James Legge, as quoted in Sturgeon 2011, https://ctext.org/mengzi/liang-hui-wang-i. In other words, both King Wen and Jie exploited the people, but the crucial difference was their leadership style. Because King Wen was a benevolent leader, the people were happy to support him.

Another example that sounds identical to Mao's conception of the power of the masses comes from *The Annals of Lü Buwei* (吕氏春秋): "Day and night the people pray in vain that they will be used properly. Should they happen to be properly used by their superior, the people would run to him like a great reservoir of water pouring out of a breach into a ravine eight thousand feet below. Who would be capable of stopping them?" See Buwei Lü, *The Annals of Lü Buwei*, trans. and annotated by John Knoblock and Jeffrey Riegel (Stanford, CA: Stanford University Press, 2000), 19/5.1, 492–93.

59. Also known as lumpen-proletarians. See Philip C. C. Huang, "Intellectuals, Lumpenproletarians, Workers and Peasants in the Communist Movement: The Case of Xingguo County, 1927–1934," in *Chinese Communists and Rural Society, 1927–1934*, ed. Philip C. C. Huang, Lynda Schaefer Bell, and Kathy LeMons Walker, 5–27 (Berkeley: Center for Chinese Studies, University of California, 1978).

60. 129-1-16, 29–30.

61. 129-1-16, 38–40.

62. 129-2-3, 6–8.

63. 129-1-68, 58. See also chapter 5, n77.

64. Fang He, «从延安一路走来的反思» (香港: 明报出版社, 2007), 160.

65. See also Esherick, "Deconstructing the Construction of the Party-State."

66. See also Michel C. Oksenberg, "Aspects of Local Government and Politics in China: 1955–58," *Journal of Developmental Studies* 4, no. 1 (1967): 25–48; Jean C. Oi, *State and Peasant in Contemporary China: The Political Economy of Village Government* (Berkeley: University of California Press, 1989), 85.

67. 129-1-134; Matthew Noellert, "Land Reform and Local Government in China's Northeast: The Case of Shuangcheng County, Heilongjiang, 1947–1949," unpublished

paper presented at the International Conference on Land Reform and Rural Chinese Society, organized by Shanxi University, Research Center for Chinese Social History, in Jincheng, Shanxi, August 9–12, 2013 (in Chinese).

68. 129-3-11; Matthew Noellert, "Land Reform and Local Government."

69. SCXZ, 881–82.

70. 何方, «从延安一路走来的反思», 164–66.

71. Ibid., 169–70.

72. 129-1-27 (Nov. 1947), 1–3.

73. 何方, «从延安一路走来的反思», 169.

74. 129-1-3 (Jan. 1947), 44–45.

75. 129-1-3 (Jan. 1947), 9–10. Compare with Demare, *Land Wars*, 33–36, who focuses on work team intellectuals. The language and writing of most work team reports from Shuangcheng do not suggest that their authors, let alone other work team members, were highly educated.

76. 129-1-3 (Jan. 1947), 11–12.

77. Mao, «毛泽东选集», 1:20.

78. See Elizabeth J. Perry, *Rebels and Revolutionaries in North China, 1845–1945* (Stanford, CA: Stanford University Press, 1980); Lucien Bianco, *Peasants without the Party: Grassroots Movements in Twentieth-Century China* (Armonk, NY: M. E. Sharpe, 2001).

79. See Chalmers Johnson, *Peasant Nationalism and Communist Power* (Stanford, CA: Stanford University Press, 1962), 3; Ilpyong J. Kim, "Mass Mobilization Policies and Techniques Developed in the Period of the Chinese Soviet Republic," in *Chinese Communist Politics in Action*, ed. A. Doak Barnett (Seattle: University of Washington Press, 1969), 81.

80. For descriptions and summaries of the mobilization process, see Demare, *Land Wars*; Yung-fa Chen, *Making Revolution*, 154–56; Kim, "Mass Mobilization Policies and Techniques," 89–90; Gordon Bennett, *Yundong: Mass Campaigns in Chinese Communist Leadership* (Berkeley: Center for Chinese Studies, University of California, 1976); Lifeng Li, "Mass Movements and Rural Governance in Communist China: 1945–1976," *Journal of Modern Chinese History* 7, no. 2 (2013): 156–80.

81. This phrase, popularized later during the Cultural Revolution, was first mentioned by Mao in his 1939 speech "Speech at a Meeting of All Circles in Yan'an to Commemorate Stalin's Sixtieth Birthday" «在延安各界庆祝斯大林六十寿辰大会上的讲话». See Schram, *Mao's Road to Power*, 7:310. Despite Mao's claim to the contrary, China has a long tradition of justifying rebellion against corrupt rulers that can be traced back to Mencius, see chapter 1, n47.

82. See also Elizabeth Perry, "Moving the Masses: Emotion Work in the Chinese Revolution," *Mobilization: An International Quarterly* 7, no. 2 (2002): 111–28.

83. Mikhail Sholokhov, *And Quiet Flows the Don*, trans. Stephen Garry (1934; London: Putnam, 1970), 363.

84. 129-2-3, 73–86.

85. 129-1-16, 131–37.

86. 129-1-16, 35.

87. Compare with Alitto, *Last Confucian*, esp. 202–210.

88. 129-1-33, 5.

89. 129-1-16, 48; 129-2-3, 18.

90. See chapter 6 for more details.

91. Going back even further, Zhu Xi (1130–1200 CE) also wrote about how village associations could hold group criticism sessions to rectify village life. Cited in Kuhn, "Local Self-Government," 261. See also chapter 7, n7.

92. «拉林巩固工作中几点经验», in Dongbei ribao she, ed., «群众工作手册», (东北书店, 1947), 19. For more discussion of struggle meetings, see Perry, "Moving the Masses"; L. Li, «土改中的诉苦»; Yi Wu and Qi Chen, «'说话'的可能性——对土改'诉苦'的再反思», «社会学研究» 2012.6: 146–71.

93. See Kuhn, "Local Self-Government," on mobilization: "Somehow individuals and organizations must be stimulated to higher levels of activity in their own spheres of life and yet be more amenable than before to the interests of the larger society" (269). See also Johnson, *Peasant Nationalism*.

94. 129-2-1, 22–23.

95. 129-1-16, 44–45.

Chapter 3

1. See, for example, Kuhn, *Origins of the Modern Chinese State*; Moore, *Social Origins*, esp. 175–176; Yaohuang Chen, «统合与分化»; Prasenjit Duara, *Culture, Power, and the State: Rural North China, 1900–1942* (Stanford, CA: Stanford University Press, 1988); H. Li, *Village Governance in North China*; Lenore Barkan, "Patterns of Power: Forty Years of Elite Politics in a Chinese County," in Esherick and Rankin, *Chinese Local Elites*, 191–215; Saich, "Introduction," 1000–1006.

2. Kuhn, "Local Self-Government," 258.

3. Popular historical power abusers are the eunuch Wei Zhongxian (1568–1627), of the late Ming dynasty, and Emperor Qianlong's favorite, Heshen (1750–1799), in the mid Qing dynasty. The loyalty of local rebels can be seen, for example, in the classic novel *Water Margin* (水浒传) (ca. 14th century CE), in which a large organization of "108 outlaws" fight against corrupt officials all the way up to the central government and are then recruited to serve the emperor. The leader of the outlaws, Song Jiang, frequently expresses his loyalty to the emperor throughout the book. For other historical examples, see Joseph W. Esherick, *The Origins of the Boxer Uprising* (Berkeley: University of California Press, 1987), esp. 163; Perry, *Rebels and Revolutionaries*.

4. This feature acts as both a defining strength and a weakness of the Chinese political system. As a strength, it allows for the integration of diverse semiautonomous polities, but the autonomy of such polities can also tear apart the system from the inside. See also Jae Ho Chung, *Centrifugal Empire: Central-Local Relations in China* (New York: Columbia University Press, 2019); Jean-Laurent Rosenthal and R. Bin Wong, *Before and*

Beyond Divergence: The Politics of Economic Change in China and Europe (Cambridge, MA: Harvard University Press, 2011).

5. Oi, *State and Peasant*, 2–10.

6. Ibid., 9, 228. See also John Duncan Powell, "Peasant Society and Clientelist Politics," *American Political Science Review* 64, no. 2 (1970): 411–25; James C. Scott, "Patron-Client Politics and Political Change in Southeast Asia," *American Political Science Review* 66, no. 1 (1972): 91–113.

7. Other scholars have described similar rural political behavior during other periods of modern Chinese history, but as far as I know there are no such studies of land reform or the rise of the CCP. See Marc J. Blecher, "Leader–Mass Relations in Rural Chinese Communities: Local Politics in a Revolutionary Society," PhD diss., Department of Political Science, University of Chicago, 1978. http://search.proquest.com/docview/251727435/citation/4C87D8858CCF413FPQ/1. Blecher and Shue, *Tethered Deer*; Oksenberg, "Aspects of Local Government," 25–48; David Zweig, "Strategies of Policy Implementation: 'Policy Winds' and Brigade Accounting in Rural China, 1966–1978," *World Politics* 37 (1985): 267–93.

8. A social order that was further institutionalized over the course of the early PRC, as described in Wemheuer, *Social History of Maoist China*.

9. For more discussion, see David Kornbluth, "Ku Yen-wu and the Reform of Local Administration," in Philip A. Kuhn, ed., *Select Papers from the Center for Far Eastern Studies*, no. 1 (Chicago: University of Chicago, 1975/1976), 7–46; Philip A. Kuhn and Susan Mann Jones, "Introduction," in Susan Mann Jones, ed., *Select Papers from the Center for Far Eastern Studies*, no. 3 (Chicago: University of Chicago, 1979), v–xix; Franz Schurmann, *Ideology and Organization*, 404–425.

10. 《关于一九四八年土地改革工作和整党工作的指示》(May 25, 1948), in Dongbei renmin zhengfu nonglin bu, 《土地政策法令汇编》(沈阳, 1950), 61. See also Appendix A, Article 14 of the May Fourth Directive, for a vaguer but similar statement.

11. See Pepper, *Civil War in China*, 245; compare with Odd Arne Westad, *Decisive Encounters: The Chinese Civil War, 1946–1950* (Stanford, CA: Stanford University Press, 2003), 130; Levine, *Anvil of Victory*, 124–26.

12. SCXZ, 32.

13. TDGGYD, 2:24.

14. F. He, 《从延安一路走来的反思》, 167–68.

15. SCWZ, 1:12.

16. SCXZ, 33.

17. 129-1-16, 203.

18. 129-1-3, 67.

19. 129-1-3, 78.

20. 129-1-27, 2–3.

21. 129-2-3, 6.

22. 129-1-27, 8–9.

23. 129-1-15, 3.

24. 129-1-9, 42.

25. See especially Duara, *Culture, Power, and the State*.

26. For more detail, see H. Hu, «皇权不下县?»; Bradly Ward Reed, *Talons and Teeth: County Clerks and Runners in the Qing Dynasty* (Stanford, CA: Stanford University Press, 2000).

27. As cited in Kuhn, "Local Self-Government," 273.

28. SCXZ, 58. As state-sponsored settlers, the bannermen of Shuangcheng were subject to finer units of control through a separate banner administration from the early nineteenth century. See S. Chen, *State-Sponsored Inequality*.

29. Kuhn, "Local Self-Government," 279–87. See also Duara, "State Involution," 132–36; Li, *Village Governance in North China*, chapter 10, "Village Reorganization," 209–233; P. Huang, *Peasant Family and Rural Development*, 175–80.

30. SCXZ, 58–59. According to a central "self-protection" regulation following the Japanese invasion of North China in 1937, which transformed existing baojia organizations into districts and administrative villages (*cun*). See Che, «试论伪满政权的地方基层统治机构», 133–36.

31. See Duara, *Culture, Power, and the State*, esp. 64, 223–24.

32. In this respect, the Concordia Association, founded in 1932, bears some resemblance to the CCP in terms of its relationship to the state and its role in society.

33. The above summary is from Che, «试论伪满政权的地方基层统治机构».

34. As mentioned, for example, in 129-1-27, 1. See also Shuangcheng dang'an ke «双城县城乡新旧地名对照资料表» (March 12, 1980) (Hereafter DMDZ). Some *cun* were redrawn into neighboring counties, which accounts for much of the loss in *cun* numbers.

35. 129-1-68, 4.

36. 129-2-18, 3.

37. Compare with SCXZ, 61–62, which only mentions eighty-three *cun* instead of the ninety-one actually recorded in the classification registers.

38. F. He, «从延安一路走来的反思», 169–70.

39. The remaining ten members, including another district head, were sponsored by five other veteran cadres and work team captains.

40. F. He, «从延安一路走来的反思», 170.

41. 129-1-27 (Nov. 1947), 1–3. Compare with Joseph W. Esherick, "War and Revolution: Chinese Society during the 1940s," *Twentieth Century China*, 27.1 (Nov., 2001): 1–37, p. 4, where he writes that as a result of the 1942 Rectification Movement, "by the end of the war, party members were well schooled in the techniques of class struggle, the party's enemies were clearly on the defensive, and party control in the base areas was reasonably secure." While higher-level cadres may have been well-schooled in this respect, in practice they often had to rely on "less-schooled" personnel like this district leader to actually implement policies on the ground.

42. 129-1-16, 158; 129-2-1, 15; 129-1-15, 17.

43. 129-2-1, 71.

44. 129-1-10, 153-54.

45. The archival volume (129-1-10) only includes replies or transmissions from three other districts.

46. Needless to say, over 97 percent of these cadres were also originally from Shuangcheng or elsewhere in the Northeast.

47. SCXZ, 35.

48. The meaning of these two measures of social status was reversed sometime after 1949. In the PRC, *chengfen* (成份) more often referred to "personal background" (个人成份) and *chushen* (出身) more often referred to "family background" (家庭出身). I therefore use the actual information recorded under these two categories in this particular register to define them here.

49. The best example being Esherick, "Deconstructing the Construction of the Party-State."

50. Compare with Hong Yung Lee, *From Revolutionary Cadres to Party Technocrats in Socialist China* (Berkeley: University of California Press, 1991); Stephen Uhalley, *A History of the Chinese Communist Party* (Stanford, CA: Hoover Institution Press, 1988).

51. This expansion began as soon as March 1948 in Shuangcheng, with the election of administrative village people's congresses. See SCXZ, 35. See also an internal CCP central directive from May 1948 calling for the establishment of people's congresses and elections of government councils at the administrative village, district, and county levels. See Zedong Mao, *Selected Works of Mao Zedong* (Beijing: Foreign Language Press, 1961), vol. 4, "The Work of Land Reform and of Party Consolidation in 1948," 253.

52. 129-1-16, 131.

53. 129-1-3, 8.

54. 129-1-16, 84.

55. 129-1-3, 7.

56. 129-1-16, 11-12, 200-201. These more political aspects of Land Reform are discussed in more detail in chapter 6.

57. 129-1-16, 79-80.

58. Landlord revenge, including large armed assaults on village communities, was common during this period of land reform in any locality where the CCP's monopoly on violence could be contested. See an especially dramatic example in Libo Zhou, *The Hurricane*, trans. Xu Mengxiong (1955; Beijing: Foreign Language Press, 1981), 190-205.

59. 129-2-1, 31-35.

60. 129-2-1, 34-35.

61. See chapter 6 for more details.

62. Duara, *Culture, Power, and the State*, 218-23, shows that this problem with village leadership had already begun to develop in the Republican era as the demands of modern state administration increasingly burdened rural officials.

63. 129-1-16, 135-36.

64. 129-1-16, 136.

65. 129-1-27, 15-16.

66. 129-1-16, 121.

67. This aspect of land reform comprises the main focus of Hinton, *Fanshen*.

68. 129-1-16, 125–28.

69. The documents were not made "official" until May 24, 1948, by which time nearly three out of ten districts in Shuangcheng had completed recording their household classification registers. See «中共中央关于重发 «怎样分析阶级» 等两文件的指示», in TGWX, 90–91; «一九三三年的两个文件», in «群众»2.23 (June 17, 1948): 2–9; Levine, *Anvil of Victory*, 227.

70. Kuisong Yang, «中华人民共和国建国史研究», 1:69–70.

71. For more details, see, for example, D. Huang, «张力与限界»; Trygve Lotveit, *Chinese Communism, 1931–1934: Experience in Civil Government*, Scandinavian Institute of Asian Studies Monograph Series, no. 16 (Lund: Studentlitteratur, 1973), chapter 6.

72. 129-1-15, 16–17.

73. 129-1-68, 49.

74. 129-1-15, 92.

75. «土地改革中的几个问题» (Jan. 12, 1948), in Bishi Ren, «任弼时选集» (北京: 人民出版社, 1987), 413–37.

76. Bankrupt landlords, tenant rich peasants, and rich middle peasants are mentioned, sometimes indirectly, as subtypes of the major categories.

77. See Appendix A, the Northeast Bureau's "Letter to the Peasants," «中国共产党东北中央局告农民书», and "Supplementary Methods for Implementing the Outline Land Law," «东北解放区实行土地法大纲补充办法».

78. 129-1-15, 93–94.

79. For example, one village reported a three-day classification meeting, and even this appears to have been a relatively simple one. See 129-1-15, 19–20.

80. 129-1-68, 55.

81. 129-1-15, 98–102.

82. Ibid.

83. 129-1-15, 92. Not all villages were so successful, however. See, for example, 129-1-16, 149, in which the landlords and rich peasants knew better than to expose themselves any further.

84. 129-1-68, 97.

85. See chapter 5 for more details.

86. See also S. Chen, *State-Sponsored Inequality*; Wemheuer, *Social History of Maoist China*. Compare with Kung, "The Political Economy of Land Reform," who also hints at within-class inequalities in land allocation.

Chapter 4

1. For more discussion of Hinton, see Demare, *Land Wars*.

2. See, for example, some recent studies of county land reform experiences: Zhang,

«乡村变迁与农民记忆»; Wang, «解放区土地改革研究 1941–1948»; Yiyuan Chen, «建国初期农村基层政权建设研究».

3. Some of the members of work teams are introduced in chapter 2.

4. Compare, for example, 129-1-16, 155–61 and 129-1-15, 76–85; 129-1-27, 1–10, and 129-1-15, 63–67.

5. See L. Li, "Mass Movements and Rural Governance in Communist China"; Lifeng Li, «工作队: 一种国家权力的非常规运作机制——以华北土改运动为中心的历史考察», «江苏社会科学» 2010 年第3期: 207–214; Yaohuang Chen, «动员的类型: 北京市郊区农村群众运动的分析», «台湾师大历史学报» 第 50 期 （2013 年 12 月）: 155–98.

6. Charles P. Cell, *Revolution at Work: Mobilization Campaigns in China* (New York: Academic Press, 1977), 12–21.

7. For more discussion of the relations between leaders and led, see Blecher, "Leader–Mass Relations."

8. Dongbei ju xuanchuan bu, ed., «东北农村调查», 71–79.

9. 129-2-3, 49–63.

10. The following narrative is adapted from the various accounts in 129-1-16, 131, 138–45, 177–80; and 129-2-3, 70–93.

11. Moreover, the person who owned 72.5 hectares of land is recorded as *not* being struggled against in the 1947 land expropriation register. See 129-3-9, 19.

12. TDGGYD, 1: 68–70.

13. See Cell, *Revolution at Work*; Bennett, *Yundong*, on his concept of "mobilizational democracy"; Yung-fa Chen, *Making Revolution*; G. William Skinner and Edwin A. Winckler, "Compliance Succession in Rural Communist China: A Cyclical Theory," in *A Sociological Reader on Complex Organization*, ed. Amitai Etzioni, 410–38 (New York: Holt, Rinehart, and Winston, 1969); L. Li, "Mass Movements and Rural Governance"; Alan Liu, *Mass Politics in the People's Republic: State and Society in Contemporary China* (Boulder, CO: Westview Press, 1996); Vivienne Shue, *Peasant China in Transition: The Dynamics of Development toward Socialism, 1949–1956* (Berkeley: University of California Press, 1980), 69–72; Michel C. Oksenberg, "Policy Making under Mao Tse-Tung, 1949–1968," *Comparative Politics* 3, no. 3 (1971): 324. Li Huaiyin and others have also explored similar and more modern interpretations of such interplay between rural society and the central state, see H. Li, *Village China under Socialism and Reform*. On the efficacy of the campaign model, see Julia Strauss, "Morality, Coercion, and State Building by Campaign in the Early PRC: Regime Consolidation and After, 1949–1956," in *The History of the PRC (1949–1976)*, ed. Julia Strauss, 37–58 (New York: Cambridge University Press, 2007).

14. See Mao, «毛泽东选集», 1: 19; Schram, *Mao's Road to Power*, 2:429.

15. «在全国土地会议上的结论» (Sept. 13, 1947), in Shaoqi Liu, «刘少奇选集», 1:384.

16. 129-1-3, 46–47; Shue, *Peasant China in Transition*, 69–72.

17. F. He, «从延安一路走来的反思», 169–70.

18. 129-1-3, 12–13.

19. 129-1-68, 2–6. Compare with a similar account from District 4 in 129-1-33, 2.

20. See also Hinton, *Fanshen*, 250, 508; Zhou, *Hurricane*, 221 (Zhou, «暴风骤雨», 2:5); Yung-fa Chen, *Making Revolution*, 154–56; Kim, "Mass Mobilization Policies and Techniques," 89–90. In an interview with Shuangcheng resident TYX (male, age 80, interviewed Aug. 30, 2012), he also described how county cadres came to the district office to hold a meeting, and then some district cadres came to his village to appoint village cadres. For one of the most detailed studies of land reform implementation, albeit of the post-1950 national land reform, see John Wong, *Chinese Land Reform in Retrospect* (Hong Kong: Centre of Asian Studies, University of Hong Kong, 1973).

21. 129-2-11, 5–7; 129-2-18, 48–61. Although the original regional directive states that each household should get one land deed, this district head mistakenly requested one deed for each parcel of land, not each household.

22. For a similar analysis of early communist revolution in Hunan, see Roy Hofheinz Jr., "The Ecology of Chinese Communist Success: Rural Influence Patterns, 1923–45," in Barnett, *Chinese Communist Politics in Action*, 3–77.

23. Compare with 129-1-16, 27, 203; SCWZ, 2:28–30.

24. Compare with 129-1-27, 1–3; SCWZ, 1:15, 2:21–27; SCJZSGS, 4. See also 129-1-10.

25. See Hofheinz, "Ecology of Chinese Communist Success," 77.

26. Friedman et al., *Chinese Village, Socialist State*, 81–98.

27. 129-1-16, 31.

28. Extant work reports mention that District 7 was also a key test point for the Equalize Land campaign, but there is no direct evidence from this district in the county archives. See 129-1-15, 16.

29. See chapter 5, Map 13, for more discussion of socioeconomic correlations.

30. Note that in this period documents record the number of individuals physically beaten, in contrast to the number of struggles (meetings).

31. Cell, *Revolution at Work*, 73. See also Sebastian Heilmann and Elizabeth Perry, *Mao's Invisible Hand: The Political Foundations of Adaptive Governance in China* (Cambridge, MA: Harvard University Asia Center, 2011).

Chapter 5 Notes

1. See also T. Zhang, *Laws and Economics of Confucianism*, esp. 136–51.

2. See, for example, Kang Chao, *The Economic Development of Manchuria: The Rise of a Frontier Economy* (Ann Arbor: Center for Chinese Studies, University of Michigan, 1982); Ramon Hawley Myers, *The Japanese Economic Development of Manchuria, 1932–1945* (New York: Garland, 1982); David Wolff, "Bean There: Toward a Soy-Based History of Northeast Asia," *South Atlantic Quarterly* 99, no. 1 (2000): 241–52.

3. Jeffery M. Paige, *Agrarian Revolution: Social Movements and Export Agriculture in the Underdeveloped World* (New York: Free Press, 1975).

4. As described in Shitong Qiao and Frank Upham, "The Evolution of Relational Property Rights: A Case of Chinese Rural Land Reform," *Iowa Law Review*, Iowa City 100, no. 6 (2015): 2479–2506. See also T. Zhang, *Laws and Economics of Confucianism*.

5. See, for example, Friedman et al., *Chinese Village, Socialist State*, 86–89; Levine, *Anvil of Victory*, 210–11; H. Li, *Village China under Socialism and Reform*, 17–18.

6. See Duara, *Culture, Power, and the State*, 4–5; see also Michael Szonyi, *The Art of Being Governed: Everyday Politics in Late Imperial China* (Princeton, NJ: Princeton University Press, 2017).

7. See also Bianco, *Peasants without the Party*, 16–35.

8. S. Chen, *State-Sponsored Inequality*. For more discussion of this aspect of "power over property," see chapters 1 and 7.

9. See also Wemheuer, *Social History of Maoist China*: "Unlike a capitalist society, social hierarchies [in Maoist China] were determined less by wealth and private ownership than by a series of official classifications" (16).

10. For similar discussion, see William T. Rowe, *Crimson Rain: Seven Centuries of Violence in a Chinese County* (Stanford, CA: Stanford University Press, 2007).

11. State control over private wealth has a long history in China, one of the earliest recorded examples being that of Emperor Wu of the Han Dynasty (141–87 BCE). See chapter 7 for more details.

12. For related discussion in terms of class struggle, see C. Yaohuang, «统合与分化».

13. In Chinese, «关于土地问题的指示», «土地法大纲», and «土地改革法», respectively. Compare with Appendix A, and Albert P. Blaustein, ed., *Fundamental Legal Documents of Communist China* (South Hackensack, NJ: F. B. Rothman, 1962), 276.

14. See D. Guo, «中国近现代农民土地问题研究».

15. See, for example, Myers, *Chinese Peasant Economy*; Friedman et al., *Chinese Village, Socialist State*; Kung et al., "Inequality of Land Tenure"; and compare with P. Huang, *Peasant Economy and Social Change*.

16. See, for example, Bozhong Li, «中国的早期近代经济» (北京: 中华书局, 2010); Kung et al. "Inequality of Land Tenure"; compare with P. Huang, *Peasant Family and Rural Development*.

17. On Northeast agriculture see, for example, Levine, *Anvil of Victory*, 199–203; Ramon H. Myers, "Socioeconomic Change in Villages of Manchuria during the Ch'ing and Republican Periods: Some Preliminary Findings," *Modern Asian Studies* 10, no. 4 (1976): 591–620; Ramon H. Myers and Thomas R. Ulie, "Foreign Influence and Agricultural Development in Northeast China: A Case Study of the Liaotung Peninsula, 1906–42," *Journal of Asian Studies* 31, no. 2 (Feb. 1972): 329–50.

18. See 129-1-16, 131.

19. Friedman et al., *Chinese Village, Socialist State*; Kung et al., "Inequality of Land Tenure.." In the latter conception, therefore, violence appears as even more unnecessary and illegitimate.

20. See V. I. Lenin, *The Development of Capitalism in Russia: The Process of the For-

mation of a Home Market for Large-Scale Industry (1899; Moscow: Foreign Language Press, 1956); Karl Kautsky, *The Agrarian Question,* trans. Pete Burgess (1899; London: Zwan Publications, 1988).

21. 129-2-1, 14–15.

22. At least one report from District 4 also describes a resident strongman who used the money he extorted and embezzled from villagers to open a blacksmith shop in the county seat. See 129-1-3, 136.

23. See also Lynda S. Bell, "From Comprador to County Magnate: Bourgeois Practice in the Wuxi County Silk Industry," in Esherick and Rankin, *Chinese Local Elites,* 113–39. For a similar conclusion on late nineteenth-century rural elite, see Chang, *Income of the Chinese Gentry,* 125–47.

24. 129-2-3, 51.

25. See, for example, Paige, *Agrarian Revolution.*

26. In the words of Hung-chao Tai: "Ironically, in the context of history, the impact of land reform is not to enhance the economic and political value of land, but to reduce it." Hung-chao Tai, *Land Reform and Politics: A Comparative Analysis* (Berkeley: University of California Press, 1974), 479.

27. See ibid.; Farshad A. Araghi, "Global Depeasantization, 1945–1990," *Sociological Quarterly* 36, no. 2 (1995): 337–68.

28. 129-1-3, 2.

29. 129-1-9. According to SCXZ, 642, however, the county chairman whose name appears on this notice was one of the first three CCP county officials appointed to Shuangcheng by the Songjiang provincial working committee.

30. TDGGYD, 1:20–22.

31. «中共中央东北局关于处理日伪土地的指示», in DJCJZ, 1:264–65. See also P. Luo, «土地改革运动史», 34.

32. For example, the original opening line of one work report, later struck out, reads, "After the end of the war on August 15, 1945, nothing really changed here, except that the Japanese grain quota was no longer collected." 129-1-16, 131.

33. See «在全国土地会议上的结论» (Sept. 13, 1947), in Shaoqi Liu, «刘少奇选集», 1:386.

34. In addition, a directive issued by the CCP central intelligence department a little over a week after the May Fourth Directive, titled, "Central CCP Directive on Not Propagating the Liberated Area's Land Reform in Newspapers," ordered that nothing related to the May Fourth Directive should be printed in newspapers, in order to prevent scaring reactionaries. See TGWX, 10.

35. See Appendix A, Article 11.

36. See Appendix E for more details.

37. 129-2-1, 4–5.

38. See, for example, Szonyi, *Art of Being Governed.*

39. 129-1-68, 2–3.

40. From another report it appears that settling accounts was an activity often done

in the absence of the actual landlord; see 129-1-16, 144, and discussion in chapter 6. Settling accounts, the first method of political struggle mentioned in Mao's 1927 *Hunan Investigation*, typically involved adding up all the rents and other incomes that the landlord took from the people and calculating how much the landlord owed the people, and then reclaiming the debt by seizing the landlord's land. However, as Mao explicitly states in 1927, the main purpose of this activity was not to reclaim the debt, but to undermine the landlord's political status by exposing his wrongdoings. See Mao, «毛泽东选集», 1:34.

41. See land expropriation register 129-3-8, 34–35.

42. Escape register 129-1-21, 20.

43. Death register 129-1-22, 44.

44. 129-1-3, 3–4.

45. TDGGYD, 1:158.

46. See, for example, the villagers who decided to tear down the villa belonging to a corrupt village head, 129-1-16, 138–39.

47. Grain, as both seed and food, occupies a liminal place between movable property (means of production) and household belongings and appears in both modes of expropriation. In some accounts the only distinction between movable property and household belongings was whether or not it was hidden. See Xiaomin Zhi, «刘少奇与晋绥土改» (台北市: 秀威资讯科技, 2008), 173–74.

48. Robert C. Tucker, *The Marx and Engels Reader*, 2nd ed. (New York: Norton, 1978), 186. See also Weiwei Luo, "The Common Good: Property and State-Making in Late Imperial China," PhD diss., Department of History, Columbia University, 2019.

49. There is also evidence that this campaign was motivated by the need to extract resources during a critical period in the civil war. See, for example, a similar campaign in Daoxuan Huang, «查田运动: 理念、策略与现实», in Xiuli Xu and Zhenglin Huang, eds. 徐秀丽, 黄正林主编, «中国近代乡村研究的理论与实证» (北京: 社会科学文献出版社, 2012), 163–76.

50. See reports in 129-2-3, 1–34; 129-1-15, 25–26. These reports do not describe what this wealth actually consisted of, but it typically included grain, clothing and blankets, or simply cash.

51. 129-1-16, 156–57.

52. Interview with MDR (female, age 90, interviewed June 2, 2013).

53. TDGGYD, 1:154–61.

54. See Mao, «毛泽东选集», 1:24; Schram, *Mao's Road to Power*, 2:435.

55. Levine, *Anvil of Victory*, chapter 6; Odoric Y. K. Wou, *Mobilizing the Masses: Building Revolution in Henan* (Stanford, CA: Stanford University Press, 1994); Yongfa Chen, «内战、毛泽东和土地革命——错误判断还是政治谋略?» «大陆杂志»第92卷第1-3期 (Taiwan, 1996); Jin, «转折年代»; Dong and Chen, «土地改革史话».

56. «关于解决土改运动中«半生不熟»的问题的指示» (Nov. 11, 1946), in DJCJZ, 1:293–96; P. Luo, «土地改革运动史», 77–78; Other regional documents describe similar movements in this period. See TGWX, 56–60.

57. See, for example, Jin, «转折年代».

58. The correlation between the CCP's political position in the civil war and land reform policies is made explicit in Liu Shaoqi's September 1947 concluding speech at the national land conference where the Outline Land Law was drafted, «全国土地会议上的结论», in S. Liu, «刘少奇选集», 1:386.

59. 129-1-15, 1, 6.

60. 129-1-15, 4.

61. Mao, «毛泽东选集», 1:24.

62. «双城县粮食志», 双城县粮食志编纂委员会 (双城县: 双城县粮食局, 1994) (Hereafter SCLZ), 106–113.

63. No extant sources directly record the size of the 1947 fall harvest by district. For each district, I estimate the 1947 fall harvest by taking the recorded amount of land planted in 1947, minus the recorded equivalent amount of flooded land for which the harvest was completely lost, to calculate the amount of harvested land. For the amount of grain produced per hectare of harvested land, I use the productivity of district land in the fall harvest of 1948, which was a relatively average year, by dividing the amount of grain harvested by the area planted in that year. Then I multiply the amount of harvested district land in 1947 by the productivity from 1948 to calculate the size of the 1947 fall harvest. From this number I subtract the recorded state grain quota (both levied and purchased grain) to calculate remaining surplus grain. Dividing this surplus by the recorded population of each district then gives us the amount of surplus grain per person left over after natural disaster and state levies.

64. SCLZ, 94–95; reproduced from the original in 129-2-30, 13.

65. I have yet to find evidence that this violence correlated to any other typical land reform effects like the amount of property expropriated, proportions of landlords, tenancy patterns, etc. Compare with chapter 4, Maps 5-12.

66. 129-1-15, 108.

67. 129-1-15, 52.

68. 129-1-15, 70.

69. 129-1-15, 11.

70. 129-1-15, 70.

71. See chapter 6 for more details.

72. Compiled by the author based on records in 129-1-75 (March 1948).

73. See G. William Skinner, "Chinese Peasants and the Closed Community: An Open and Shut Case," *Comparative Studies in Society and History* 13, no. 3 (1971): 270–81.

74. For example, the Great Leap Forward Famine. For discussion of these issues of state, society, and famine, which here I can only hint at for 1947/48 Shuangcheng, see, for example, Ralph A. Thaxton Jr., *Catastrophe and Contention in Rural China: Mao's Great Leap Forward Famine and the Origins of Righteous Resistance in Da Fo Village* (New York: Cambridge University Press, 2010); the essays in Kimberley Ens Manning and Felix Wemheuer, eds., *Eating Bitterness: New Perspectives on China's Great Leap Forward*

(Vancouver: UBC Press, 2011); Felix Wemheuer, *Famine Politics in Maoist China and the Soviet Union* (New Haven, CT: Yale University Press, 2014).

75. 129-2-3, 15.

76. See also James C. Scott, *The Moral Economy of the Peasant: Rebellion and Subsistence in Southeast Asia* (New Haven, CT: Yale University Press, 1976), 157–60.

77. See Hinton, *Fanshen*, 578–92, for a similar story from North China.

78. 129-1-15, 16. See also chapter 2, n63.

79. See, for example, 129-1-16, 119, 216; 129-1-68, 4; 129-1-15, 17.

80. For an example of why counting household members was so difficult and contentious, see Hinton, *Fanshen*, 590–91.

81. (Grade 1 = red, grade 2 = blue, grade 3 = black). See 129-1-68, 96–97.

82. 129-1-68, 97.

83. See also Schran, *Development of Chinese Agriculture*, 21, 26; Endicott, *Red Earth*, 29.

84. Systematic data similar to that on land redistribution in Shuangcheng is not available for other property, but descriptive accounts suggest that this other property was also used to offset any remaining inequalities after the allocation of land.

85. For more discussion, see, for example, Takashi Maruta, 『革命の儀礼―中国共産党根拠地の政治動員と民俗』 (汲古書院, 2013); Scott, *The Moral Economy of the Peasant*.

Chapter 6

1. Mao, «毛泽东选集», 1:34; Schram, *Mao's Road to Power*, 2:441. See also Westad, *Decisive Encounters*, 130–36, who also emphasizes the importance of political campaigns alongside the confiscation of land.

2. See also Demare, *Land Wars*.

3. In general, these outcomes correspond to the four types of victim registers distributed by the Songjiang provincial government in the summer of 1947. Most of the deaths (outcomes 1–3) were recorded in the death registers, most of outcomes 5–7 were recorded in the struggle registers, and most of outcome 8 were recorded in the escape registers, but as mentioned in chapter 1, individuals could appear in multiple registers. Individuals have been linked within and across all four victim registers, and these outcomes thus represent each individual's most violent outcome recorded in any and all of the registers. See Appendix D for further discussion.

4. See, for example, the struggle meeting described in 129-1-16, 138–39, and 129-2-3, 76–77, in which both offenders had already fled the village, and further discussion in the section in chapter 6 on "Public Humiliation."

5. The escape registers have poor records of class status, but for purposes of comparison we could assume that most of the missing observations would have also been classed as landlords or rich peasants.

6. For related discussion of the roles of crimes and class in Land Reform struggles,

see D. Huang, «盟友抑或潜在对手?», 83–84: In the Ji-Lu-Yu liberated area (spanning parts of Hebei, Shandong, and Henan provinces), for example, a March 1947 directive calling for the intensification of struggle mentions that "some people even say that this landlord does not have any crimes, but actually being a landlord is a crime in itself."

7. See Appendix C for an explanation of recorded crime coding.

8. 129-1-16, 138–39.

9. Similar violent retribution against local leaders who abused their power for personal economic gain was also common in eighteenth- and nineteenth-century China, in part because such corruption by nonofficials was not covered in the Qing law code. See W. Luo, "Common Good."

10. See Appendix A.

11. See also K. Li, «西村十五年».

12. See Jeffrey Javed, "Land and Retribution: Morality, Mobilization, and Violence in China's Land Reform Campaign (1950–1952)," PhD diss., Harvard University, Department of Government, 2017. Yaohuang Chen, «统合与分化», 5–10; Fernando Galbiati, *Peng Pai and the Hai-Lu-Feng Soviet* (Stanford, CA: Stanford University Press, 1985), 338–40; Yung-fa Chen, *Making Revolution*, 176; Friedman et al., *Chinese Village, Socialist State*, 81–84; Rowe, *Crimson Rain*, 256–57.

13. For more discussion of settling accounts, see chapter 5, n38.

14. Levine, *Anvil of Victory*, 145.

15. Mao, «毛泽东选集», 1:35; Schram, *Mao's Road to Power*, 2:446.

16. Daoxuan Huang's study of out-migration in the Jiangxi soviet also demonstrates that the people fled the soviet area in response to radical CCP policies. See Daoxuan Huang, «逃跑与回流: 苏区群众对中共施政方针的回应» «社会科学研究» 第6期 (2005b): 124–32.

17. Xiaochun Ding, comp., «东北解放战争大事记» (北京: 中共党史资料, 1987), 292.

18. F. He, «从延安一路走来的反思», 167–68; SCJZSGS, 3; SCXZ, 360.

19. SCWZ, 1:11–19.

20. Ding,«东北解放战争大事记», 294.

21. Lionel Max Chassin, *The Communist Conquest of China: A History of the Civil War, 1945–1949* (Cambridge, MA: Harvard University Press, 1965), 114–15.

22. I have yet to find any evidence of significant land reform activity in or around Shuangcheng at these times.

23. Mao, «毛泽东选集», 1:21, 35–36; Schram, *Mao's Road to Power*, 2:431, 446.

24. Changchun, Jilin, was the national capital of Manchukuo (1931–1945), and Shenyang, Liaoning, had been the regional capital of the Northeast since the Qing dynasty. Harbin, Heilongjiang, became an important northern urban center after the opening of the Chinese Eastern Railway in 1903. See TDGGYD, 2:158.

25. Also note that within the county, in districts that bordered on Harbin, the provincial capital, escapees were more likely to escape there than to the county seat.

26. See, for example, 129-1-16, 145. Officially, any peasants who wanted to enter the county seat to seize a landlord or their property had to first get an introduction letter

from their local peasant association or district government and present it to the county public security bureau. See SCJZSGS, 115.

27. 129-1-68, 76.

28. For example, when a mop-up team arrived in one village in District 3, they found that all the landlords and rich peasants were gone, and a village cadre said they had all gone to a meeting in the neighboring village. The next day another mop-up team came to the village and were told the same thing. See 129-1-15, 13; 129-2-1, 38.

29. 129-1-15, 11.

30. Zhou, *Hurricane*, 14, 153–62. For cases in Shuangcheng, see, for example, 129-1-68, 2; 129-1-16, 49.

31. 129-1-16, 139.

32. Elderly interviewees today also recount that only some of the landlords in their village were struggled against during land reform and that every village had good and bad landlords; see FJX (male, age 82, interviewed June 4, 2013); GYB (male, age 66, interviewed May 31, 2013); WQF (male, age 77, interviewed June 7, 2013).

33. E.g., Hinton, *Fanshen*, and Frank Dikötter, *The Tragedy of Liberation: A History of the Chinese Revolution, 1945–57* (London: Bloomsbury, 2013), respectively.

34. See also Yuhua Guo and Liping Sun, «诉苦: 一种农民国家观念形成的中介机制», «中国学术» 第 12 期 （2003 年): 130–57; Huirong Fang, «无事件境» 与生活世界中的 «真实»—西村农民土地改革时期社会生活的记忆», in Yang Nianqun, ed., «空间·记忆·社会转型—«新社会史' 研究论文精选集» (上海: 上海人民出版社, 2001), 467–586.

35. At least one early report from District 4 suggests that poor lackeys were punished by parading around the village, because they did not have any housing or land that could be confiscated. See 129-1-3, 137; See also Rowe, *Crimson Rain*.

36. 129-1-16, 33–37.

37. 129-1-16, 37–40.

38. 129-1-16, 40–41.

39. 129-1-16, 42–43.

40. For a different perspective in which outsiders benefitted from Land Reform, see Yingze Hu and Aiming Zhang, «外来户、土改与乡村社会——以山西省永济县东、西三原村为例», «开放时代» 2017 年第1期: 154–69.

41. See Appendix C for more detailed discussion.

42. A standard *tun* in Shuangcheng had six democratically elected cadre positions—chairman and vice chairman of the PA, organization commissioner, propaganda commissioner, production commissioner, and commissioner of arms/militia captain. See 129-2-3, 37–40.

43. D. Huang, «洗脸», 90. See also Hinton, *Fanshen*, 238–39; Fangchun Li, "Mass Democracy, Class Struggle, and Remolding the Party and Government during the Land Reform Movement in North China," *Modern China* 38, no. 4 (2012): 411–45.

44. Lifeng Li, «党组织、党员与群众——华北土改期间的整党运动», «安徽史学» 2012.1: 66–76, 69.

45. Similarly, one page of county statistics from Shuangcheng records that between July and September 1947, 200 out of 549 activists (36 percent), 72 out of 288 new cadres (25 percent), and 176 out of 196 old cadres (90 percent) were "cleaned up," which averages out to a total of 43 percent of local leaders, a proportion similar to Huang's and Li's findings. See 129-1-31, 32.

46. See, for example, Philip C. C. Huang, "Intellectuals, Lumpenproletarians, Workers and Peasants," 5–27. In Shuangcheng, elderly villagers in one village still remember that their PA leader in 1948 was a kidnapper/bandit (绑票) during Manchukuo; see interview with ZQX (male, age 75, interviewed Aug. 27, 2012). For more general discussion on the issue of corruption in rural politics, see Oi, *State and Peasant*, 104–130; James C. Scott, "Corruption, Machine Politics, and Political Change," *American Political Science Review* 63, no. 4 (1969): 1142–58.

47. This example of a landlord making an emotional appeal for forgiveness could be understood as the inverse of what Elizabeth Perry describes in "Moving the Masses."

48. 129-1-16, 78–79. In this case, however, the landlord was eventually executed, but only after the work team took him to another village to be struggled against and found those villagers to be reluctant too. In the end, he was executed in what sounds like a somewhat secretive execution carried out by the local self-defense team (80). This sounds like an "undemocratic" execution, which would have been severely criticized in later campaigns but maybe not in the fall of 1946. Another similar story in which the landlord escaped but his lawyer was caught and executed can be found in 129-1-3, 20–29.

49. 129-1-27, 2. See also 129-1-3, 63; 129-2-3, 15; 129-1-16, 124.

50. On the historical development of public property, collective ownership, and moral accountability in China, see W. Luo, "Common Good."

51. 129-1-3, 36–37.

52. Based on linked victim registers in which the individual is also recorded as escaped or noted as not being present in the village.

53. See also Javed, "Land and Retribution"; Maruta, 『革命の儀礼』; Strauss, "Morality, Coercion, and State Building."

54. Peasant apathy toward land was a chronic problem throughout land reform. See, for example, 129-1-27, 8; 129-2-3, 6; 129-1-16, 31.

55. Dikötter, *Tragedy of Liberation*, 67, 73.

56. Hinton, *Fanshen*, xi.

57. SCWZ, 1:18.

58. 129-1-22, 2–4, 129-1-23, 28–40.

59. 128-1-15, 105–106.

60. 129-2-42, 8–9. The rumor says the village is located north of the county seat, but the name of the village corresponds to one south of the county seat in District 8.

61. It is therefore possible that the rumor refers to events that took place later during the Mop-Up campaign in early 1948, for which there are no extant records from this village.

62. 129-2-3, 22–24.

63. 129-2-3, 22–24, 31.

64. 129-2-3, 32–33.

65. See Perry, "Moving the Masses"; Li, «土改中的诉苦»; Wu and Chen, «'说话' 的可能性».

66. As represented, for example, by Dikötter, *Tragedy of Liberation*, and Friedman et al., *Chinese Village, Socialist State*, respectively.

67. See also Cai, *Revolution and Its Narratives*, 246–48.

68. See also 129-1-3, 22; 129-1-16, 144–45.

69. Perhaps they could also be justifiably categorized as reactionaries, for refusing to cooperate with the confiscation and redistribution of property, but throughout this book I try to maintain as broad a definition of class exploitation as possible. See Appendix C for more details.

70. 129-1-15, 82, 85.

71. Many other reasons for death involve persons freezing to death while running away to hide from mop-up teams in January 1948, when temperatures in Shuangcheng could reach minus 30 degrees Celsius. See also stories of people suffering from frostbite after hiding in fields and shacks overnight in 129-1-68, 25, 76; 129-1-15, 3.

72. 129-1-15, 6–7.

73. See, for example, P. Huang, "Rural Class Struggle in the Chinese Revolution"; Friedman et al., *Chinese Village, Socialist State*; Demare, *Land Wars*.

74. Compare with Virgil Kit-yiu Ho, "Butchering Fish and Executing Criminals: Public Executions and the Meanings of Violence in Late Imperial and Modern China," in Göran Aijmer and Jon Abbink, *Meanings of Violence: A Cross-Cultural Perspective* (Oxford: Berg, 2000), 141–60; Rowe, *Crimson Rain*, esp. 2–3.

Chapter 7

1. According to United Nations, *Land Reform: Defects in Agrarian Structure as Obstacles to Economic Development* (New York: United Nations Department of Economic Affairs, 1951), 3, nearly 1.3 billion people in the world, over 1 billion of whom lived outside Europe and North America (in the "developing world"), made their livings from agriculture around 1950. According to chapter 1, Table 1 of this book, there were nearly 400 million rural Chinese affected by land reform around 1950. According to 1953 census data, China's rural population was over 500 million (National Bureau of Statistics of China, "Basic Statistics on National Population Census in 1953, 1964, 1982, 1990, 2000 and 2010," http://www.stats.gov.cn/tjsj/Ndsj/2011/html/D0305e.htm (Accessed Sept. 10, 2019).

2. As quoted in Changqun He, «论两汉土地占有形态的发展» (上海: 上海人民出版社, 1957), 12–13. See also Yue Zhang, «汉武帝时期的垄断官营经济政策», «山西财经大学学报» 27, no. 1 (2005): 8–11. Thanks to Professor Li Bozhong for first hinting at this comparison with Emperor Wu, and apologies to him for taking so long to understand its importance.

3. C. He, «论两汉土地占有形态的发展», 1, 24–29. I loosely translate «中家或中

家以下的人» as "middle and lower classes." On the changing nature of the political elite during the Han dynasty, specifically in terms of the political struggle between wealthy hereditary aristocracy and middle-class literati, see also Martin J. Powers, *Art and Political Expression in Early China* (New Haven, CT: Yale University Press, 1991), esp. 82–96, 186–89.

4. He frequently refers to the state confiscation of land as a tool of oppression of «专制封建主义中央集权» or «专制封建主义的绝对君权» (both of which can be rendered as "centralized autocratic feudalism"), and characterizes the Imperial Chinese state since the early Han as the "highest and largest landlord," both very politically loaded terms that he obviously would not use to describe the new PRC state in the 1950s.

5. See Changqun He, «汉唐间封建的国有土地制与均田制» (上海: 上海人民出版社, 1958). This idea is also expressed in terms of the CCP revolution in Philip A. Kuhn and Susan Mann Jones, "Introduction," in Jones, *Select Papers*, No. 3, xii–xiii, where they write that "the very commitment to [revolutionary] equality implied as well the reconstitution of a highly centralized and powerful government authority, precisely to guarantee the extraction and redistribution of surpluses that would make equality possible."

6. «汉书·高帝纪上», paragraph 41, in Sturgeon, Chinese Text Project: «举民年五十以上, 有修行, 能帅众为善, 置以为三老, 乡一人». Note that the concept of the "masses" (众) also has a long tradition in Chinese politics. See also Kaidao Yang, «中国乡约制度», «村治» 3, nos. 2–3 (1933): 5.

7. See Kuhn, "Local Self-Government," 261. For more detailed discussion, see Kaidao Yang, «中国乡约制度, 第五章: 吕氏乡约的增损» «村治» 3, no. 5 (1933): 1–12.

8. Alitto, *Last Confucian*, 207. See also the rest of the discussion on pp. 206–215. Liang's village covenant system also included "cooperative societies" to organize economic production.

9. I also do not mean to suggest there is unending historical continuity of such traditions but that they continue to recur over time, more along the lines of what William Skinner describes in "Chinese Peasants and the Closed Community." See also the comparison between Liang Shuming's modern Confucianism and Maoism in Alitto, *Last Confucian*, 215–25, 283–91.

10. With a Gini coefficient of 0.64. François Bourguignon and Christian Morrisson, "Inequality among World Citizens: 1820–1992," *American Economic Review* 92, no. 4 (2002): 727–44.

11. United Nations, *Land Reform: Defects in Agrarian Structure.*

12. In the half century between the 1910s and 1960s, at least thirty countries around the world implemented significant agrarian reforms, including Mexico, Russia (Stolypin and Soviet reforms), Germany, Austria, Bulgaria, Estonia, Finland, Greece, Italy, Hungary, Latvia, Lithuania, Poland, Romania, Czechoslovakia, Yugoslavia, Philippines, Japan, Taiwan, North and South Korea, North Vietnam, India, Pakistan, Iran, United Arab Republic, Colombia, Bolivia, and Egypt. See Tai, *Land Reform and Politics*; Arthur Wauters, «欧洲农地改革» (彭补拙译. 商务印书馆, 1933); Elias H. Tuma, *Twenty-Six Centuries of Agrarian Reform: A Comparative Analysis* (Berkeley: University of Califor-

nia Press, 1965); Edwin E. Moise, *Land Reform in China and North Vietnam: Consolidating the Revolution at the Village Level* (Chapel Hill: University of North Carolina Press, 1983).

13. As stated in the first article of the PRC's 1950 Agrarian Reform Law. See Blaustein, *Fundamental Legal Documents*, 276.

14. China and East Asia in general are also identified as such in Bourguignon and Morrisson, "Inequality among World Citizens." See also Angus Deaton, *The Great Escape: Health, Wealth, and the Origins of Inequality* (Princeton, NJ: Princeton University Press, 2013); Thomas Piketty, *Capital in the Twenty-First Century* (Cambridge, MA: Harvard University Press, 2014).

15. See, for example, Hsiao Tseng, *The Theory and Practice of Land Reform in China* (Taipei: Chinese Research Institute of Land Economics, 1953), 40. Sun founded the Revolutionary Alliance Society a few years after returning from a tour of Europe, and some have claimed that he was strongly influenced by Henry George and like-minded German reformers. See also D. Guo, «中国近现代农民土地问题研究», 200; Michael Silagi, "Henry George and Europe: Precursors of Land Reform in Germany; Marx and the Land Question; the Beginnings of the Georgist Movement in the Empire," trans. Susan N. Faulkner, *American Journal of Economics and Sociology* 51, no. 2 (1992): 247–56.

16. See Lloyd E. Eastman, "Nationalist China during the Nanking Decade, 1927–1937," in *The Cambridge History of China*, vol. 13: *Republican China 1912–1949, Part 2*, ed. John K. Fairbank and Albert Feuerwerker, 116–67 (New York: Cambridge University Press, 1986, 151–52. KMT land policies are generally seen to have failed because of a lack of enforcement and the resistance of traditional elites both within the KMT and in local society, but as far as I know there is no specialized in-depth study of this issue. For more details see Dehong Guo, «南京政府时期国民党的土地政策与实践», «近代史研究» 1991.5: 169–91; Ming Cao, «南京国民政府初期 «土地法» 研究 (1928–1936)» （东北师范大学硕士学位论文, 中国近现代史, 2004年10月）, 30–38.

17. For details of Yan Xishan's program, see the detailed report of early experiments in northeast Shanxi, Zhijin Qi,"'土地村有' 下之晋北农村», «国闻周报» 第十三卷第十一期 (March 1936): 21–26. See also Donald G. Gillin, *Warlord: Yen Hsi-Shan in Shansi Province, 1911–1949* (Princeton, NJ: Princeton University Press, 1967). For Sichuan, see Zhongguo nong cun fu xing lian he wei yuan hui, "General Report of the Joint Commission on Rural Reconstruction (October 1, 1948 to February 15, 1950)" (Taipeh, Taiwan, China: Joint Commission on Rural Reconstruction, May 1950), 72–77; Deying Li, «民国时期成都平原的押租与押扣——兼与刘克祥先生商榷», «近代史研究» 2007 年第一期: 95–115. For more discussion, see Guy S. Alitto, "Rural Reconstruction during the Nanking Decade: Confucian Collectivism in Shantung," *China Quarterly* 66 (1976): 213–46.

18. See Peter Kolchin, *Unfree Labor: American Slavery and Russian Serfdom* (Cambridge, MA: Belknap Press, 1987). Kolchin describes how both of these systems of unfree labor emerged around the same time (seventeenth century), when growth, expansion, and a shortage of labor in America and Russia required that agricultural labor be made

compulsory. Then they also disappeared around the same time in the mid-nineteenth century when these institutions were no longer economically viable. See also Tuma, *Twenty-Six Centuries of Agrarian Reform*, 73–74.

19. See Henry George, *Progress and Poverty: An Inquiry into the Cause of Industrial Depressions and of Increase of Want with Increase of Wealth: The Remedy* (New York: Robert Schalkenbach Foundation, 1990). The issue of unproductive landowners freely collecting rents on private property would also become a central feature of the CCP revolution and its vilification of landlords. For more on the issue of poverty, see also Polanyi, *Great Transformation*, 111–29.

20. See, for example, Kevin Repp, *Reformers, Critics, and the Paths of German Modernity: Anti-Politics and the Search for Alternatives, 1890–1914* (Cambridge, MA: Harvard University Press, 2000), 75–76. Many of these reformers were also influenced by Henry George and were looking for solutions to the emerging social problems of industrialization, primarily manifested as socioeconomic inequality.

21. Lenin, *Development of Capitalism in Russia*; Kautsky, *Agrarian Question.*

22. See Lenin, *Development of Capitalism in Russia*, 172–183; Kautsky, *Agrarian Question*, 1:15–17, 168–75.

23. Lenin, *Development of Capitalism in Russia*, 51–54. The statistics Lenin uses originally group peasant households according to the amount of cultivated land. Here Lenin is perhaps one of the first to give these distributions of household land a social aspect by combining them to show that the bottom 40 percent of households possess about 12 percent of cultivated land and therefore constitute a poor group, while the top 20 percent of households possess over half of the cultivated land and therefore constitute a "well-to-do" group. Note, however, that Lenin does not mention the issue of landlords in his study.

24. Kautsky, *Agrarian Question*, 1:81–88. Compare with George, *Progress and Poverty*. In other words, it was the combination of increasing state control and increasing land rents that exacerbated the perceived discrepancy between landowners' social functions and economic remunerations. From these studies we can also see that this similar process took place in a wide variety of contexts, from Germany to the United States, and we can assume also in Russia, although in contrast to Kautsky and others, Lenin does not specifically talk about the rentier class.

25. Tuma, *Twenty-Six Centuries of Agrarian Reform*, 87–88, 92–93.

26. Ibid., 115–23.

27. Ibid., 135–39; R. P. Dore, *Land Reform in Japan* (1959; London: Athlone Press, 1984). For more examples from Europe, see Wauters, 《欧洲农地改革》.

28. For an alternative perspective, see Robert McC. Netting, *Smallholders, Householders: Farm Families and the Ecology of Intensive, Sustainable Agriculture* (Stanford, CA: Stanford University Press, 1993).

29. For more discussion, see Tai, *Land Reform and Politics*; Tsun-han Shen, *The Sino-American Joint Commission on Rural Reconstruction: Twenty Years of Cooperation for Agricultural Development* (Ithaca, NY: Cornell University Press, 1970).

30. See, for example, Moore, *Social Origins,* 20–29; Polanyi, *Great Transformation,* esp. 111–29.

31. Moore, *Social Origins.* See also Skocpol, *States and Social Revolutions.*

32. For more discussion of this issue, see, for example, Charles Tilly, *From Mobilization to Revolution* (New York: Random House, 1978); Jack A. Goldstone, "Toward a Fourth Generation of Revolutionary Theory," *Annual Review of Political Science* 4, no. 1 (2001): 139–87.

33. See Vivienne Shue, "Modern/Rural China: State Institutions and Village Values," in Bislev and Thogersen, *Organizing Rural China,* 229–30.

34. For more discussion of the Chinese alternative, see Alitto, *Last Confucian,* esp. 181–83; Blecher, *China against the Tides;* Zheng and Huang, *Market in State.*

35. For example, the early Ming as described in Schneewind, "Visions and Revisions." See also Weber's discussion of traditional authority in Max Weber, *Economy and Society: An Outline of Interpretive Sociology,* ed. Guenther Roth and Claus Wittich (Berkeley: University of California Press, 1978), 1:226–41.

36. Balazs, *Chinese Civilization,* 17. As Balazs himself wrote in 1964, "In spite of all the changes that have taken place in the world, the bureaucratic society of an empire that lasted for two thousand years is still with us as an extremely active force" (27).

37. See, for example, Wemheuer, *Social History of Maoist China.*

38. A clear manifestation of such "local totalitarianism" can be seen in the "local emperors" condemned in Shuangcheng's work reports. See also Blecher, "Leader–Mass Relations"; Blecher and Shue, *Tethered Deer.* Taking this argument a step further, Derk Bodde also writes, "*All* of Chinese society, from top to bottom was essentially authoritarian, the family as much so, or even more than, the governmental structure." In Ping-ti Ho and Tang Tsou, eds., *China in Crisis,* vol. 1, *China's Heritage and the Communist Political System* (Chicago: University of Chicago Press, 1968), 56.

39. Compare with Ying, 《农户、集体与国家》, who suggests the establishment of a qualitatively new hierarchy.

40. See, for example, chapter 2, n49.

41. Compare with Oi, *State and Peasant;* Shue, *Peasant China in Transition.*

42. Localism, often called "departmentalism" in the PRC context, means prioritizing the narrow interests of a single locality or unit over larger, national interests. For more discussion of related problems in other contexts, see, for example, Tilly, *From Mobilization to Revolution,* 1–4; and the discussion of feudalism in Kuhn, "Local Self-Government under the Republic."

43. Other notable regions for comparison include Shanxi, where Yan Xishan was also known for his progressive governance. See Gillin, *Warlord.*

44. See also Esherick, "Ten Theses," 7–48, for a similar view on other parts of China.

45. See, for example, other descriptions in Kuhn, "Local Self-Government"; Duara, "State Involution"; Duara, *Culture, Power, and the State,* H. Li, *Village Governance in North China.*

46. Kuhn, "Local Self-Government," 291. Partible inheritance has also been cited as

another factor; see, for example, Chang, *Income of the Chinese Gentry*, 125; Moore, *Social Origins*, 170.

47. For historical examples from Shuangcheng, see S. Chen, *State-Sponsored Inequality*. On the historical development of collective ownership norms, see W. Luo, "Common Good."

48. See, for example, chapter 1, n46.

49. See also W. He, *Legitimating the Modern States;* K. Li, «西村十五年»; Maruta, 『革命の儀礼』; compare with Ying, «农户、集体与国家», esp. 44–45.

50. Compare with Kuhn, "Local Self-Government," who might argue that such democratic village governance was conceptualized in ideas of self-government and feudalist thought no later than the late nineteenth century.

51. As described by Seymour Martin Lipset, *Political Man: The Social Bases of Politics* (Garden City, NY: Doubleday and Company, 1960).

52. Compare with Guo and Sun, «诉苦»; «无事件境» 与生活世界中的 «真实». For similar but more contemporary discussion, see Tsai, *Accountability without Democracy*.

53. 129-1-16, 135–36.

54. Even in contemporary Shuangcheng, where one might expect to find stronger private property rights, villagers negotiate planting and harvesting arrangements at the beginning of each year in terms of "buying" and "selling" their land, but such transactions often last for only a single harvest. See field notes, Sept. 6, 2011; Oct. 4, 2011; Jan. 19–20, 2013.

55. That is, S. Chen, *State-Sponsored Inequality*. For more discussion, see also Masayuki Tanimoto and R. Bin Wong, eds., *Public Goods Provision in the Early Modern Economy: Comparative Perspectives from Japan, China, and Europe* (Berkeley: University of California Press, 2019); C. He, «汉唐间封建的国有土地制与均田制»; W. Luo, "Common Good"; Wemheuer, *Social History of Maoist China*.

56. Similar to eminent domain, but in China the state uses this right much more actively and frequently than other modern states. See C. He, «汉唐间封建的国有土地制与均田制», who suggests land rights in China should be more accurately described as «占有权», or right of possession, not ownership. Elderly villagers in Shuangcheng that I have interviewed also describe how during land reform, land was "returned to the village (government)," who then allocated it to each household. See interviews with WCY (male, age 73, interviewed June 2, 2013); CDX (male, age 89, interviewed June 7, 2017); ZXY (male, age 82, interviewed June 1, 2013).

57. The whole concept of needing to encourage farmers to farm, mentioned in several Shuangcheng work reports, is at odds with common assumptions of private property rights and peasant interests.

58. For comparable discussion of Soviet Union collectivization, see Jenny Leigh Smith, *Works in Progress: Plans and Realities on Soviet Farms, 1930–1963* (New Haven, CT: Yale University Press, 2014).

59. See Hinton, *Fanshen*, ch. 21–29.

60. See Friedman et al., *Chinese Village, Socialist State*, 86-98.

61. See Ding, «太阳照在桑干河上»; Feuerwerker, *Ding Ling's Fiction*, 123-29.

62. On rumors, see also Demare, *Land Wars*, 27-28, 41.

63. When one village on the margin of District 3 received an order from the district government to send representatives to a district-wide meeting to discuss Outline Land Law implementation, they are reported to have said things like "What on earth can people accomplish by attending discussion meetings like this?" and "Anyway the district government requested this kind of person [to act as representative], so just tell him to go already!" See 129-1-17, 17.

64. Hinton, *Fanshen*, 508.

65. In the case of Shuangcheng, there is only one extant report of later rectification, a summary document from District 2 that describes implementation following the fall harvest in 1948. See 129-1-68, 33-38. For more discussion of general implementation in Lucheng county, see Weiqiang Ma, Hongqin Deng, and Lichao Yang, "The Pilot Land Reform Program and Land Reform in Pilot Villages: A Study of Pilot Land Reform and Party Consolidation in Lucheng, Shanxi," *Rural China* 16.1 (February 28, 2019): 9-37.

66. See interview with WQF (male, age 77, interviewed on June 7, 2013).

67. Compare with Javed, "Land and Retribution," who links retributive violence to state coercion rather than local interests.

68. For more discussion of the nature of Chinese governance, see Heilmann and Perry, *Mao's Invisible Hand*; Wong, "Opium and Modern Chinese State-Making"; Vivienne Shue and Patricia M. Thornton, eds., *To Govern China: Evolving Practices of Power* (New York: Cambridge University Press, 2017), 1-26. See also Harry Harding's conception of Chinese organizational policy as a "Chinese doll with a weighted base that wobbles when hit but never falls over," in which after each experiment central policies return to their own center of balance. Harding, *Organizing China*, ix. Similarly, Zhou Xueguang interprets such policy shifts as the result of "organizational failures" inherent in state socialism. See Zhou Xueguang, *The State and Life Chances in Urban China: Redistribution and Stratification, 1949-1994* (New York: Cambridge University Press, 2004), 16-20.

69. See Rosenthal and Wong, *Before and Beyond Divergence*.

70. In contrast to discriminatory policies in other modern nation-states, however, "out-groups" in China are often defined by subjective, political traits that are easier to manipulate than ascribed traits such as race, ethnicity, or religion.

71. See also S. Chen, *State-Sponsored Inequality*. In Qing dynasty Shuangcheng, the state focused on governing official bannerman settlers and acknowledged other groups in the settlement only when conflicts or demands appeared.

72. A number of stories recounting counterrevolution during the land reform period end with a note that the escaped culprits were later caught and executed in the early 1950s. See SCWZ 1:20-31, 37, 2:20, 30.

73. For more details, see Kuisong Yang, "Reconsidering the Campaign to Suppress Counterrevolutionaries," *China Quarterly* 193 (March 2008): 102-121.

74. The situation was different in parts of South China, where land reform and the Campaign to Suppress Counterrevolutionaries were carried out simultaneously.

75. See Roderick MacFarquhar, *The Origins of the Cultural Revolution*, vol. 1 (New York: Columbia University Press, 1974).

76. Baum, *Prelude to Revolution*, 22.

77. See William Hinton, *Shenfan: The Continuing Revolution in a Chinese Village* (New York: Random House, 1983), 337–60; Baum, *Prelude to Revolution*; Xiaobo Lin and Guo Dehong, «文革的预演——«四清» 运动始末» （北京: 人民出版社, 2013); Edward Friedman, Paul G. Pickowicz, and Mark Selden, *Revolution, Resistance, and Reform in Village China* (New Haven, CT: Yale University Press, 2005), 46–84.; Letian Zhang, «告别理想: 人民公社制度研究» (上海: 上海人民出版社, 2012).

78. Andrew G. Walder, *China under Mao: A Revolution Derailed* (Cambridge, MA: Harvard University Press, 2015), 200.

79. Compare with conceptions of such early policy fiat as a "tactical weapon" in K. C. Yeh, *The Chinese Communist Revolutionary Strategy and the Land Problem, 1921–1927* (Santa Monica, CA: Rand Corporation, 1970), iv.

80. The Four Cardinal Principles are Uphold the Socialist Road; Uphold the Dictatorship of the Proletariat; Uphold the Leadership of the CCP; and Uphold Marxism-Leninism-Mao Zedong Thought.

81. See Wang Feng, *Boundaries and Categories: Rising Inequality in Post-Socialist Urban China* (Stanford, CA: Stanford University Press, 2007); Wemheuer, *Social History of Maoist China*; S. Chen, *State-Sponsored Inequality*.

82. For more discussion, see, for example, Araghi, "Global Depeasantization."

Appendix B

1. See Mao, Zedong. *Report from Xunwu*, trans. Roger R. Thompson (Stanford, CA: Stanford University Press, 1990).

2. «怎样分析阶级» and «中华苏维埃共和国中央政府关于土地斗争中一些问题的决定» (Oct. 1933), "How to Analyze Classes," and "Decision Regarding Certain Questions in the Agrarian Struggle," in Schram, *Mao's Road to Power*, 1997, vol. 4, 546–67. Compare with also D. Huang, «张力与限界».

3. It is unclear which of Lenin's works the report is referring to here, but chapter 2 of *The Development of Capitalism in Russia* (1899) is one of the earliest analyses of rural classes.

4. 129-2-3, 52.

5. See chapter 5 on Shuangcheng's rural economy.

6. «任弼时选集», 人民出版社, 1987, 414–15. See also Kuisong Yang, «中华人民共和国建国史研究», 69–77.

Appendix C

1. For more detail, the programs to create these categories are also available upon request as Stata .do files.

2. See Matthew Z. Noellert, "New Perspectives on Communist Land Reform: Evidence from Northeast China, 1946–1948" (PhD diss., Division of Humanities, The Hong Kong University of Science and Technology, 2014).

3. Including in some cases crime information that is recorded on other parts of the register and not in the original form's "crime" field.

4. 129-1-16, 25–26.

Appendix D

1. See chapter 1, n86 and accompanying text.

2. Compare with chapter 1, n87.

References

Unpublished Archives

Note: Leading number refers to archive location in Shuangcheng district archives, (archive number 全宗号)—(index number 目录号)—(volume number 卷号).

129-3-1. «各村屯被分地主、富农、中农土地登记表». 双城县第二区政府. 黑龙江省哈尔滨市双城区档案局藏, 1947.

129-3-2. «各村屯被分地主、富农、中农土地登记表». 双城县第三区政府. 黑龙江省哈尔滨市双城区档案局藏, 1947.

129-3-3. «各村屯被分地主、富农、中农土地登记表». 双城县第四区政府. 黑龙江省哈尔滨市双城区档案局藏, 1947.

129-3-4. «各村屯被分地主、富农、中农土地登记表». 双城县第五区政府. 黑龙江省哈尔滨市双城区档案局藏, 1947.

129-3-5. «各村屯被分地主、富农、中农土地登记表». 双城县第六区政府. 黑龙江省哈尔滨市双城区档案局藏, 1947.

129-3-6. «各村屯被分地主、富农、中农土地登记表». 双城县第七区政府. 黑龙江省哈尔滨市双城区档案局藏, 1947.

129-3-7. «各村屯被分地主、富农、中农土地登记表». 双城县第八区政府. 黑龙江省哈尔滨市双城区档案局藏, 1947.

129-3-8. «各村屯被分地主、富农、中农土地登记表». 双城县第九区政府. 黑龙江省哈尔滨市双城区档案局藏, 1947.

129-3-9. «各村屯被分地主、富农、中农土地登记表». 双城县第十区政府. 黑龙江省哈尔滨市双城区档案局藏, 1947.

129-3-10. «各村屯被分地主、富农、中农土地登记表». 双城县第十一区政府. 黑龙江省哈尔滨市双城区档案局藏, 1947.

129-3-11. «县直机关、第三区（村)党支部共产党员登记表». 双城县. 黑龙江省哈尔滨市双城区档案局藏, 1947.

129-3-12 through 129-3-45. «土地改革时期划分阶级档案». 黑龙江省双城县. 三十六卷. 黑龙江省哈尔滨市双城区档案局藏, 1948/1965.

129-1-2. «拉林工作队一九四六年关于群众工作的报告». 中共双城县委员会办公室. 黑龙江省哈尔滨市双城区档案局藏, 1946.

129-1-3. 《工作队一九四六年向县委作的关于群众工作的报告》. 中共双城县委员会办公室. 黑龙江省哈尔滨市双城区档案局藏, 1946.

129-1-9. 《县政府: 关于各项工作训令通知国际资产报告》. 双城县人民政府办公室. 黑龙江省哈尔滨市双城区档案局藏, 1946.

129-1-10. 《县政府: 关于担架队工作的请示报告材料》. 双城县人民政府办公室. 黑龙江省哈尔滨市双城区档案局藏, 1946.

129-1-15. 《关于土改扫荡和排号站队运动深入的文件》. 中共双城县委员会办公室. 黑龙江省哈尔滨市双城区档案局藏, 1948.

129-1-16. 《一九四七年双城县十一区、韩甸在乡斗争地主活动的工作报告》. 中共双城县委员会办公室. 黑龙江省哈尔滨市双城区档案局藏, 1947.

129-1-20. 《二、三、四、五区: 各村屯土改时地主、富农外逃登记表》. 双城县人民政府办公室. 黑龙江省哈尔滨市双城区档案局藏, 1947.

129-1-21. 《六、七、八、九、十、十一区: 各村屯土改时地主、富农外逃登记表》. 双城县人民政府办公室. 黑龙江省哈尔滨市双城区档案局藏, 1947.

129-1-22. 《七、八、九、十、十一区: 在运动中对坏人处置情况登记表 （包括枪杀)." 双城县人民政府办公室. 黑龙江省哈尔滨市双城区档案局藏, 1947–1948.

129-1-23. 《二至七区: 在运动中对坏人处置情况登记表 （包括枪杀)." 双城县人民政府办公室. 黑龙江省哈尔滨市双城区档案局藏, 1947–1948.

129-1-24. 《二、三、四、五区: 各村屯对运动中的坏人斗争情况》. 双城县人民政府办公室. 黑龙江省哈尔滨市双城区档案局藏, 1947.

129-1-25. 《七至十一区: 各村屯对运动中的坏人斗争情况》. 双城县人民政府办公室. 黑龙江省哈尔滨市双城区档案局藏, 1947.

129-1-27. 《六、八区: 土评工作情况总结材料》. 双城县人民政府办公室. 黑龙江省哈尔滨市双城区档案局藏, 1947.

129-1-31. 《全县在土改运动中各种数字统计表》. 双城县人民政府办公室. 黑龙江省哈尔滨市双城区档案局藏, 1947.

129-1-32. 《全县各区村: 斗争果实统计表》. 双城县人民政府办公室. 黑龙江省哈尔滨市双城区档案局藏, 1947. 10.

129-1-33. 《一九四七年土改消息 （3、5、6、7期)." 双城县人民政府办公室. 黑龙江省哈尔滨市双城区档案局藏, 1947–1948.

129-1-68. 《二区: 划阶级定成份平分土地纠偏工作、站队排号、扫荡被斗问题总结》. 双城县人民政府办公室. 黑龙江省哈尔滨市双城区档案局藏, 1948.

129-1-74. 《各区各阶层人口、牲口、土地状况统计表》. 双城县人民政府办公室. 黑龙江省哈尔滨市双城区档案局藏, 1948.

129-1-75. 《各区: 没收地区生产资料和打、杀、押统计表》. 双城县人民政府办公室. 黑龙江省哈尔滨市双城区档案局藏, 1948.

129-2-1. 《一九四七年双城县三区正兰四屯势力群众斗争初步经验》. 中共双城县委员会办公室. 黑龙江省哈尔滨市双城区档案局藏, 1947.

129-2-3. 《一九四七年县委工作队在各区如何发动群众工作报告》. 中共双城县委员会办公室. 黑龙江省哈尔滨市双城区档案局藏, 1947.

129-2-11. 《关于发放土地执照的材料》. 双城县人民政府办公室. 黑龙江省哈尔滨市双城区档案局藏, 1948.

129-2-18. «二区政府: 有关工作方面的上级材料». 双城县人民政府办公室. 黑龙江省哈尔滨市双城区档案局藏, 1948.

129-2-42. «公安局社情报告». 双城县人民政府办公室. 黑龙江省哈尔滨市双城区档案局藏, 1949.

129-2-51.   «没收双城县大资产、官体、房产登记表、房权问题的报告及表报材料». 双城县人民政府民政科. 黑龙江省哈尔滨市双城区档案局藏, 1949.

129-2-56. «关于征收公粮工作». 双城县人民政府财政科. 黑龙江省哈尔滨市双城区档案局藏, 1949.

7-1-10-2. «省政府公粮公草征收指示». 松江省政府. 哈尔滨: 黑龙江省档案局, Sept. 3, 1946.

DMDZ. Shuangcheng dang'an ke 双城县档案科. «双城县城乡新旧地名对照资料表». 黑龙江省哈尔滨市双城区档案局藏, 1980.

SCJZSGS. 双城市公安局. «双城市解放战争时期公安史稿 (1945. 11–1949. 9)." 黑龙江省哈尔滨市双城区档案局藏, 1996.

Interviews and Fieldnotes

CDX. Chen, Dexi. Personal Interview. June 7, 2013.

FJX. Fu, Jingxiang. Personal Interview. June 4, 2013.

GYB. Guan, Yongbin. Personal Interview. May 31, 2013.

MDR. Ma, Dianrong. Personal Interview. June 2, 2013.

Noellert, Matthew Z. Field notes. 2010–2017.

TYX. Tong, Yuxue. Personal Interview. Aug. 30, 2012.

WCY. Wang, Changyin. Personal Interview. June 2, 2013.

WQF. Wang, Qingfu. Personal Interview. June 7, 2013.

ZQX, Zhao, Qingxiang. Personal Interview. Aug. 27, 2012.

ZXY. Zhao, Xingyuan. Personal Interview. June 1, 2013.

Published Primary Sources

Blaustein, Albert P., ed. *Fundamental Legal Documents of Communist China*. South Hackensack, NJ: F. B. Rothman, 1962.

Cao, Shuji 曹树基, ed., «中国地方历史文献数据库». 上海: 上海交通大学出版社, 2015. http://dfwx.datahistory.cn/pc/. Accessed Aug. 14, 2019.

Chen, Yun 陈云. «陈云文选». 三卷. 北京: 人民出版社, 1984–1986.

CHGIS. "CHGIS V5 DEM (Digital Elevation Model)." Harvard Dataverse, V8, 2015. https://doi.org/10.7910/DVN/E1FHML.

Chinese Academy of Surveying and Mapping—CASM China in Time and Space—CITAS—University of Washington, and Center for International Earth Science Information Network—CIESIN. China Dimensions Data Collection: China Administrative Regions GIS Data: 1:1M, County Level, 1990. Palisades, NY: NASA Socioeconomic Data and Applications Center (SEDAC, 1996). http://dx.doi.org/10.7927/H4C24TCF. Accessed Sept. 14, 2014.

Ding Xiaochun, comp. 丁晓春等编著. «东北解放战争大事记». 北京: 中共党史资料, 1987.

"Directive for Dealing with Agricultural Land in the Suburbs of Cities of Old Liberated Areas." New China News Agency Translation. *China Weekly Review*, March 4, 1950.

DIVA-GIS. Global country boundaries, 2011. http://www.diva-gis.org/Data. Accessed Sept. 14, 2014.

DJCJZ. Dongbei jiefang qu caizheng jingji shi bianxie zu 东北解放区财政经济史编写组. «东北解放区财政经济史资料选编». 四卷. 哈尔滨: 黑龙江人民出版社, 1988.

Dongbei ju xuanchuan bu, ed. 东北局宣传部编. «东北农村调查». 东北书店, March 1947.

Dongbei renmin zhengfu nonglin bu 东北人民政府农林部. «土地政策法令汇编». 沈阳, 1950.

Dongbei ribao she, ed. 东北日报社编. «平分土地文献». 东北书店, January 1948.

Dongbei ribao she, ed. 东北日报社编. «群众工作手册». 东北书店, 1947.

ESRI and Defense Mapping Agency. "Digital Chart of the World Files, China," 1990. Reprocessed and distributed by Penn State University, 1997. Released by CHGIS, Version 4. Cambridge: Harvard Yenching Institute and Fudan Center for Historical Geography, Jan. 2007.

Han, Gang 韩刚, et al., eds., «中国当代民间史料集刊». 九种十一册. 上海: 中国出版集团东方出版中心, 2011.

Liu, Shaoqi 刘少奇. «刘少奇选集». 二卷. 北京: 人民出版社, 1981–1985.

Lü, Buwei. *The Annals of Lü Buwei*. Translated and annotated by John Knoblock and Jeffrey Riegel. Stanford, CA: Stanford University Press, 2000.

Majia shi zupu. «马佳氏族谱». 四卷. 京华印书局, 1928.

Manshu 1:200,000 Zu. Tokyo: Rikuchi Sokuryobu, 1933. Made available by Stanford University Library at https://stanford.maps.arcgis.com/apps/SimpleViewer/index.html?appid=c1e874ab8bec4d6fa5b2e743a77d8ca9. Accessed July 30, 2019.

Mao, Zedong 毛泽东. «毛泽东选集». 六卷. 东北书店, 1948.

Mao, Zedong. *Report from Xunwu*. Trans. Roger R. Thompson. Stanford, CA: Stanford University Press, 1990.

Mao, Zedong. *Selected Works of Mao Zedong*. Beijing: Foreign Language Press, 1961.

National Bureau of Statistics of China. "Basic Statistics on National Population Census in 1953, 1964, 1982, 1990, 2000 and 2010." http://www.stats.gov.cn/tjsj/Ndsj/2011/html/D0305e.htm. Accessed Sept. 10, 2019.

Ren, Bishi. «任弼时选集». 北京: 人民出版社, 1987.

"Resolution on Land Reform in Shantung Province." Translation edited by Elizabeth Graham. *China Weekly Review* 105, no. 1 (1947).

Schram, Stuart R., ed. *Mao's Road to Power: Revolutionary Writings, 1912–1949*. 7 vols. Armonk, NY: M. E. Sharpe, 1992–2005.

SCLZ. «双城县粮食志». 双城县粮食志编纂委员会. 双城县: 双城县粮食局, 1994.

SCWZ. «双城文史资料». 政协黑龙江省双城县委员会文史资料研究委员会编. 二辑. 双城县政府铅印室印刷, 1984–1985.

SCXZ. «双城县志». 双城县志编纂委员会. 北京: 中国展望出版社, 1990.

Sturgeon, Donald, ed. Chinese Text Project. 2011. http://ctext.org.

TDGGYD. «土地改革运动, 1945.9–1949.10». 二卷. 哈尔滨: 黑龙江省档案馆编, 1983–1984.

TGWX. Zhongyang dang'an guan, ed. 中央档案馆主编. «解放战争时期土地改革文件选编». 北京: 中共中央党校出版社, 1981.

"Uprooting the Feudal System of Land Ownership." *People's China* 2, no. 2 (1950).

Zhang, Letian 张乐天, ed., «张乐天联民村数据库». 北京: 社会科学文献出版社, 2015. http://www.zltfieldwork.com/. Accessed Aug. 14, 2019.

Zhongguo nong cun fu xing lian he wei yuan hui. "General Report of the Joint Commission on Rural Reconstruction (October 1, 1948 to February 15, 1950)." Taipeh, Taiwan, China: Joint Commission on Rural Reconstruction, May 1950.

ZZWX. Zhongyang dang'an guan, ed. 中央档案馆编. «中共中央文件选集». 十八册. 中共中央党校出版社, 1991–1992.

Published Secondary Sources

Note: In alphabetical order by author, including Pinyin (Chinese sources) and Romaji (Japanese sources).

Alitto, Guy S. *The Last Confucian: Liang Shu-ming and the Chinese Dilemma of Modernity.* Berkeley: University of California Press, 1979.

Alitto, Guy S. "Rural Reconstruction during the Nanking Decade: Confucian Collectivism in Shantung." *China Quarterly* 66 (1976): 213–46.

Araghi, Farshad A. "Global Depeasantization, 1945–1990." *Sociological Quarterly* 36, no. 2 (1995): 337–68.

Averill, Stephen C. "Local Elites and Communist Revolution in the Jiangxi Hill Country." In *Chinese Local Elites and Patterns of Dominance,* edited by Joseph W. Esherick and Mary Backus Rankin, 282–304. Berkeley: University of California Press, 1990.

Bai, Hui 白卉. «试论 1947 年~ 1949 年华北土改运动中的中农政策». «中北大学学报 (社会科学版)» 2014 年第 30 卷第 1 期: 9–12.

Balazs, Etienne. *Chinese Civilization and Bureaucracy: Variations on a Theme.* New Haven, CT: Yale University Press, 1964.

Barkan, Lenore. "Patterns of Power: Forty Years of Elite Politics in a Chinese County." In *Chinese Local Elites and Patterns of Dominance,* edited by Joseph W. Esherick and Mary Backus Rankin, 191–215. Berkeley: University of California Press, 1990.

Barnett, Doak A., ed. *Chinese Communist Politics in Action.* Seattle: University of Washington Press, 1969.

Baum, Richard. *Prelude to Revolution: Mao, the Party, and the Peasant Question, 1962–1966.* New York: Columbia University Press, 1975.

Belden, Jack. *China Shakes the World.* 1949. New York: Monthly Review Press, 1970.

Bell, Lynda S. "From Comprador to County Magnate: Bourgeois Practice in the Wuxi County Silk Industry." In *Chinese Local Elites and Patterns of Dominance,* edited by Joseph W. Esherick and Mary Backus Rankin, 113–39. Berkeley: University of California Press, 1990.

Bengtsson, Tommy, Cameron Campbell, James Z. Lee, et al. *Life under Pressure: Mortality and Living Standards in Europe and Asia, 1700–1900.* Cambridge, MA: MIT Press, 2004.

Bennett, Gordon. *Yundong: Mass Campaigns in Chinese Communist Leadership.* Berkeley: Center for Chinese Studies, University of California, 1976.

Bianco, Lucien. *Peasants without the Party: Grassroots Movements in Twentieth-Century China.* Armonk, NY: M. E. Sharpe, 2001.

Bislev, Ane, and Stig Thogersen, eds. *Organizing Rural China—Rural China Organizing.* Lanham, MD: Lexington Books, 2012.

Blecher, Marc. *China against the Tides: Restructuring through Revolution, Radicalism, and Reform.* 3rd ed. London: Bloomsbury Academic, 2009.

Blecher, Marc J. "Leader–Mass Relations in Rural Chinese Communities: Local Politics in a Revolutionary Society." PhD diss., Department of Political Science, University of Chicago, 1978.

Blecher, Marc J., and Vivienne Shue. *Tethered Deer: Government and Economy in a Chinese County.* Stanford, CA: Stanford University Press, 1996.

Bo, Yibo (Po Yi-po). "Three Years of Historic Achievements." *People's China* no. 20 (Oct. 16, 1952): 10–15.

Bourguignon, François, and Christian Morrisson. "Inequality among World Citizens: 1820–1992." *American Economic Review* 92, no. 4 (2002): 727–44.

Buck, John Lossing. *Land Utilization in China: A Study of 16,786 Farms in 168 Localities, and 38,256 Farm Families in Twenty-Two Provinces in China, 1929–1933.* New York: Reproduced by the Council on Economic and Cultural Affairs, 1956.

Cai, Xiang. *Revolution and Its Narratives: China's Socialist Literary and Cultural Imaginaries, 1949–1966.* Edited and translated by Rebecca E. Karl and Xueping Zhong. Durham, NC: Duke University Press, 2016.

Cao, Ming 曹明. «南京国民政府初期 «土地法» 研究 (1928–1936)». 东北师范大学硕士学位论文. 中国近现代史. 2004 年10月.

Cao, Xingsui 曹幸穗. «满铁的中国农村实态调查概述». «中国社会经济史研究» 1991 年第 4 期, 104–9.

Cell, Charles P. *Revolution at Work: Mobilization Campaigns in China.* New York: Academic Press, 1977.

Central Intelligence Agency. *China: Provisional Atlas of Communist Administrative Units.* Washington, DC: US Department of Commerce, 1959.

Chan, Anita, Richard Madsen, and Jonathan Unger. *Chen Village under Mao and Deng.* Berkeley: University of California Press, 1992.

Chang, Chung-li. *The Income of the Chinese Gentry.* Seattle: University of Washington Press, 1962.

Chang, Yen. "China's Land Revolution: A Brief Review." *People's China* 2, no. 2 (1950): 10–11, 32.

Chao, Kang. *The Economic Development of Manchuria: The Rise of a Frontier Economy.* Ann Arbor: Center for Chinese Studies, University of Michigan, 1982.

Chao, Kuo-chun. *Agrarian Policy of the Chinese Communist Party, 1921–1959.* Bombay: Asia Publishing House, 1960.

Chassin, Lionel Max. *The Communist Conquest of China: A History of the Civil War, 1945–1949.* Cambridge, MA: Harvard University Press, 1965 [original French 1952].

Che, Jihong 车霁虹, «试论伪满政权的地方基层统治机构», «齐齐哈尔师范学院学报» 1995 年第5期: 133–36.

Chen, Shuang. *State-Sponsored Inequality: The Banner System and Social Stratification in Northeast China.* Stanford, CA: Stanford University Press, 2017.

Chen, Shuang, James Lee, and Cameron Campbell. "Wealth Stratification and Reproduction in Northeast China, 1866–1907." *History of the Family* 15, no. 4 (2010): 386–412.

Chen, Yaohuang 陈耀煌. «动员的类型: 北京市郊区农村群众运动的分析». «台湾师大历史学报» 第50期 （2013 年 12 月）: 155–98.

Chen, Yaohuang 陈耀煌. «统合与分化: 河北地区的共产革命, 1921–1949». 台北市: 中央研究院近代史研究所, 2012.

Chen, Yiyuan 陈益元. «建国初期农村基层政权建设研究, 1949–1957: 以湖南省醴陵县为个案». 上海社会科学院出版社, 2006.

Chen, Yongfa (Yung-fa) 陈永发. «内战、毛泽东和土地革命——错误判断还是政治谋略?». «大陆杂志» 第九十二卷第 1–3 期 (Taiwan, 1996).

Chen, Yung-fa. *Making Revolution: The Communist Movement in Eastern and Central China, 1937–1945.* Berkeley: University of California Press, 1986.

Chung, Jae Ho. *Centrifugal Empire: Central-Local Relations in China.* New York: Columbia University Press, 2019.

Coble, Parks M., Jr. *The Shanghai Capitalists and the Nationalist Government, 1927–1937.* Cambridge, MA: Harvard University Press, 1980.

Crook, David, and Isabel Crook. *Revolution in a Chinese Village: Ten Mile Inn.* London: Routledge and Kegan Paul, 1959.

Crook, David, and Isabel Crook. *Ten Mile Inn: Mass Movement in a Chinese Village.* New York: Pantheon Books, 1979.

Deaton, Angus. *The Great Escape: Health, Wealth, and the Origins of Inequality.* Princeton, NJ: Princeton University Press, 2013.

Demare, Brian. *Land Wars: The Story of China's Agrarian Revolution.* Stanford, CA: Stanford University Press, 2019.

Dikötter, Frank. *The Tragedy of Liberation: A History of the Chinese Revolution, 1945–57.* London: Bloomsbury, 2013.

Ding, Ling 丁玲玲. «太阳照在桑干河上». 北京: 人民文学出版社, 1956/2012.

Dong, Zhikai and Tingxuan Chen 董志凯, 陈廷煊. «土地改革史话». 北京: 社会科学文献出版社, 2011.

Dore, R. P. *Land Reform in Japan.* 1959. London: Athlone Press, 1984.

Du, Runsheng 杜润生. «中国的土地改革». 北京: 当代中国出版社, 1995.

Duara, Prasenjit. *Culture, Power, and the State: Rural North China, 1900–1942.* Stanford, CA: Stanford University Press, 1988.

Duara, Prasenjit. "State Involution: A Study of Local Finances in North China, 1911–1935." *Comparative Studies in Society and History* 29, no. 1 (1987): 132–61.

Eastman, Lloyd E. "Nationalist China during the Nanking Decade, 1927–1937." In *The Cambridge History of China.* Vol. 13: *Republican China 1912–1949, Part 2,* edited by John K. Fairbank and Albert Feuerwerker, eds., 116–67. New York: Cambridge University Press, 1986.

Enatsu, Yoshiki. *Banner Legacy: The Rise of the Fengtian Local Elite at the End of the Qing.* Ann Arbor: Center for Chinese Studies, University of Michigan, 2004.

Enatsu, Yoshiki 江夏由樹. 「中国東北地方における農村実態調査: 康徳三（1936）年度、満州国農村実態調査報告書にある統計資料について」. Hitotsubashi University, Institute of Economic Research, Discussion Paper No. D97-23, Feb. 1998.

Endicott, Stephen. *Red Earth: Revolution in a Sichuan Village.* New York: New Amsterdam, 1991.

Esherick, Joseph W. "Deconstructing the Construction of the Party-State: Gulin County in the Shaan-Gan-Ning Border Region." *China Quarterly* 140 (Dec. 1994): 1052–79.

Esherick, Joseph W., ed. *Lost Chance in China: The World War II Despatches of John S. Service.* New York: Random House, 1974.

Esherick, Joseph W. "Number Games: A Note on Land Distribution in Prerevolutionary China." *Modern China* 7, no. 4 (1981): 387–411.

Esherick, Joseph W. *The Origins of the Boxer Uprising.* Berkeley: University of California Press, 1987.

Esherick, Joseph W. *Reform and Revolution in China: The 1911 Revolution in Hunan and Hubei.* Berkeley: University of California Press, 1976.

Esherick, Joseph W. "Revolution in a Feudal Fortress: Yangjiagou, Mizhi County, Shaanxi, 1937–1948." *Modern China* 24, no. 4 (1998): 339–77.

Esherick, Joseph W. "Ten Theses on the Chinese Revolution." *Modern China* 21, no. 1 (1995): 45–76.

Esherick, Joseph W. "War and Revolution: Chinese Society during the 1940s." *Twentieth-Century China,* 27, no. 1 (2001): 1–37.

Esherick, Joseph W., and Mary Backus Rankin, eds. *Chinese Local Elites and Patterns of Dominance.* Berkeley: University of California Press, 1990.

Evans, Peter B., Dietrich Rueschemeyer, and Theda Skocpol, eds. *Bringing the State Back In.* New York: Cambridge University Press, 1985.

Fang, Huirong 方慧荣. "'无事件境' 与生活世界中的 '真实'—西村农民土地改革时期社会生活的记忆», in Yang Nianqun 杨念群, ed., «空间·记忆·社会转型—'新社会史' 研究论文精选集», 467–586. 上海: 上海人民出版社, 2001.

Faure, David. *Emperor and Ancestor: State and Lineage in South China.* Stanford, CA: Stanford University Press, 2007.

Fei, Xiaotong. *Peasant Life in China: A Field Study of Country Life in the Yangtze Valley.* New York: E. P. Dutton, 1939.

Feuerwerker, Yi-tsi Mei. *Ding Ling's Fiction: Ideology and Narrative in Modern Chinese Literature.* Cambridge, MA: Harvard University Press, 1982.

Friedman, Edward, Paul G. Pickowicz, and Mark Selden. *Revolution, Resistance, and Reform in Village China.* New Haven, CT: Yale University Press, 2005.

Friedman, Edward, Paul G. Pickowicz, Mark Selden, and Kay Ann Johnson. *Chinese Village, Socialist State.* New Haven, CT: Yale University Press, 1991.

Galbiati, Fernando. *P'eng P'ai and the Hai-Lu-Feng Soviet.* Stanford, CA: Stanford University Press, 1985.

Gamble, Sidney D. *Ting Hsien: A North China Rural Community.* Stanford, CA: Stanford University Press, 1968.

George, Henry. *Progress and Poverty: An Inquiry into the Cause of Industrial Depressions and of Increase of Want with Increase of Wealth: The Remedy.* 1879. New York: Robert Schalkenbach Foundation, 1990.

Gillin, Donald G. *Warlord: Yen Hsi-Shan in Shansi Province, 1911–1949.* Princeton, NJ: Princeton University Press, 1967.

Goldstone, Jack A. "Toward a Fourth Generation of Revolutionary Theory." *Annual Review of Political Science* 4, no. 1 (2001): 139–87.

Goodman, David S. G. *Social and Political Change in Revolutionary China: The Taihang Base Area in the War of Resistance to Japan, 1937–1945.* Lanham, MD: Rowman and Littlefield, 2000.

Gries, Peter Hays, and Stanley Rosen. *State and Society in 21st-Century China: Crisis, Contention, and Legitimation.* New York: Routledge, 2004.

Guo, Dehong 郭德宏. «南京政府时期国民党的土地政策与实践». «近代史研究» 1991.5: 169–91.

Guo, Dehong 郭德宏. «中国近现代农民土地问题研究». 青岛出版社, 1993.

Guo, Limin, and Wang Jianying 郭利民、王剑英, eds. «中国新民主主义革命时期通史地图集». 北京: 中国地图出版社, 1993.

Guo, Yuhua 郭于华, and Sun Liping 孙立平. «一种农民国家观念形成的中介机制». «中国学术»第 12 期 (2003 年): 130–57.

Guo, Zhigang 郭志刚. «当代中国人口发展与家庭户的变迁». 北京: 中国人民大学出版社, 1995.

Hao, Ping, and Yao Zongpeng 郝平、姚宗鹏. «老区土改与乡村社会——以太行革命根据地为中心的考察». 发表在 «土地改革与中国乡村社会» 学术研讨会. 山西大学, 2013 年8月9–12日.

Harding, Harry. *Organizing China: The Problem of Bureaucracy, 1949–1976.* Stanford, CA: Stanford University Press, 1981.

Harrison, James Pinckney. *The Long March to Power: A History of the Chinese Communist Party, 1921–1972.* New York: Praeger, 1972.

Hartford, Kathleen, and Stephen M. Goldstein, eds. *Single Sparks: China's Rural Revolutions.* Armonk, NY: M. E. Sharpe, 1989.

He, Changqun 贺昌群. «汉唐间封建的国有土地制与均田制». 上海: 上海人民出版社, 1958.

He, Changqun 贺昌群. «论两汉土地占有形态的发展». 上海: 上海人民出版社, 1957.

He, Fang 何方. «从延安一路走来的反思». 香港: 明报出版社, 2007.

He, Jiangsui. "Identifying Mistakes to Discipline a New State: The Rectification Campaigns in China's Land Reform, 1946–1952." PhD diss., Department of Sociology. University of California, San Diego, 2008.

He, Wenkai. *Legitimating the Early Modern States: England, Japan, and China.* Forthcoming.

Heilmann, Sebastian, and Elizabeth Perry. *Mao's Invisible Hand: The Political Foundations of Adaptive Governance in China.* Cambridge, MA: Harvard University Asia Center, 2011.

"Highlights of China's Achievements." *People's China* no. 1 (Jan. 1, 1953): 28–29.

Hinton, William. *Fanshen: A Documentary of Revolution in a Chinese Village.* New York: Vintage Books, 1966.

Hinton, William. *Shenfan: The Continuing Revolution in a Chinese Village.* New York: Random House, 1983.

Ho, Ping-ti. *The Ladder of Success in Imperial China: Aspects of Social Mobility, 1368–1911.* New York: Columbia University Press, 1962.

Ho, Ping-ti, and Tang Tsou, eds. *China in Crisis.* Vol. 1, *China's Heritage and the Communist Political System.* Chicago: University of Chicago Press, 1968.

Ho, Virgil Kit-yiu. "Butchering Fish and Executing Criminals: Public Executions and the Meanings of Violence in Late Imperial and Modern China." In *Meanings of Violence: A Cross-Cultural Perspective,* edited by Göran Aijmer and Jon Abbink, 141–60. Oxford: Berg, 2000.

Hobsbawm, Eric J. *The Age of Capital, 1848–1875.* New York: Charles Scribner's Sons, 1975.

Hofheinz, Roy Jr., "The Ecology of Chinese Communist Success: Rural Influence Patterns, 1923–45." In *Chinese Communist Politics in Action,* edited by A. Doak Barnett, 3–77. Seattle: University of Washington Press, 1969.

Hu, Heng 胡恒. «皇权不下县?: 清代县辖政区与基层社会治理». 北京: 北京师范大学出版社, 2015.

Hu, Yingze 胡英泽. «近代华北乡村地权分配再研究——基于晋冀鲁三省的分析». «历史研究» 2013.4: 117–36.

Hu, Yingze 胡英泽. «土改后至高级社前的乡村地权变化——基于山西省永济县吴村档案的考察». «中共党史研究» 2014.3: 99–106.

Hu, Yingze, and Zhang Aiming 胡英泽、张爱明. «外来户、土改与乡村社会——以山西省永济县东、西三原村为例». «开放时代» 2017 年第1期.

Huang, Daoxuan 黄道炫. «1920–1940 年代中国东南地区的土地占有——兼谈地主、农民与土地革命». «历史研究»第一期 (2005a): 34–53.

Huang, Daoxuan 黄道炫. «查田运动: 理念、策略与现实». In Xiuli Xu and Zhenglin Huang, eds. 徐秀丽、黄正林主编. «中国近代乡村研究的理论与实证». 北京: 社会科学文献出版社, 2012, 163–76.

Huang, Daoxuan 黄道炫. «盟友抑或潜在对手？——老区土地改革中的中农». «南京大学学报 (哲学·人文科学·社会科学)» 第 5 期 (2007b): 82–96.

Huang, Daoxuan 黄道炫. «逃跑与回流:苏区群众对中共施政方针的回应». «社会科学研究» 第 6 期 (2005b): 124–32.

Huang, Daoxuan 黄道炫. «洗脸——1946–1948 农村土改中干部整改». «历史研究» 第4期 (2007a): 89–110.

Huang, Daoxuan 黄道炫. «张力与限界: 中央苏区的革命, 1933–1934". 北京: 社会科学文献出版社, 2011.

Huang, Philip C. C., Lynda Schaefer Bell, and Kathy LeMons Walker. *Chinese Communists and Rural Society, 1927–1934*. Berkeley: Center for Chinese Studies, University of California, 1978.

Huang, Philip C. C. "Intellectuals, Lumpenproletarians, Workers and Peasants in the Communist Movement: The Case of Xingguo County, 1927–1934." In *Chinese Communists and Rural Society, 1927–1934*, edited by Philip C. C. Huang, Lynda Schaefer Bell, and Kathy LeMons Walker, 5–27. Berkeley: Center for Chinese Studies, University of California, 1978.

Huang, Philip C. C. *The Peasant Economy and Social Change in North China*. Stanford, CA: Stanford University Press, 1985.

Huang, Philip C. C. *The Peasant Family and Rural Development in the Yangzi Delta, 1350–1988*. Stanford, CA: Stanford University Press, 1990.

Huang, Philip C. C. "Rethinking 'the Third Sphere': The Dualistic Unity of State and Society in China, Past and Present." *Modern China* 45, no. 4 (2019): 355–91.

Huang, Philip C. C. "Rural Class Struggle in the Chinese Revolution: Representational and Objective Realities from the Land Reform to the Cultural Revolution." *Modern China* 21, no. 1 (1995): 105–43.

Huang, Ronghua 黄荣华. «农村地权研究 1949–1983: 以湖北省新洲县为个案». 上海社会科学院出版社, 2006.

Huang, Shu-min. *The Spiral Road: Change in a Chinese Village through the Eyes of a Communist Party Leader*. 2nd ed. Boulder, CO: Westview Press, 1998.

Information Office of the State Council of the People's Republic of China. "Fifty Years of Democratic Reform in Tibet." The Central People's Government of the People's Republic of China, March 2, 2009. Accessed Sept. 19, 2014. http://english.gov.cn.

Javed, Jeffrey. "Land and Retribution: Morality, Mobilization, and Violence in China's Land Reform Campaign (1950–1952)." PhD diss., Department of Government, Harvard University, 2017.

Jia, Teng 贾滕. «土改背景下的乡村社会秩序重构——以河南商水县为个案的考察 (1947–1954)». 华东师范大学, 中国近现代史博士论文, 2008.

Jin, Chongji 金冲及. «转折年代——中国的 1947 年». 北京: 三联书店, 2002.

Johnson, Chalmers. *Peasant Nationalism and Communist Power: The Emergence of Revolutionary China, 1937–1945*. Stanford, CA: Stanford University Press, 1962.

Jones, Susan Mann, ed. *Select Papers from the Center for Far Eastern Studies*. No. 3. Chicago: University of Chicago, 1979.

Jones, Susan Mann. "Trade, Transport, and Taxes: The Decline of a National Medicine

Fair in Republican China." In *Select Papers from the Center for Far Eastern Studies, No. 4, 1979–1980*, edited by Tang Tsou, 112–42. Chicago: University of Chicago, 1981.

Kataoka, Tetsuya. *Resistance and Revolution in China: The Communists and the Second United Front*. Berkeley: University of California Press, 1974.

Kautsky, Karl. *The Agrarian Question*. Translated by Pete Burgess. 2 vols. 1899. London: Zwan Publications, 1988.

Keating, Pauline B. *Two Revolutions: Village Reconstruction and the Cooperative Movement in Northern Shaanxi, 1934–1945*. Stanford, CA: Stanford University Press, 1997.

Kim, Ilpyong J., "Mass Mobilization Policies and Techniques Developed in the Period of the Chinese Soviet Republic." In *Chinese Communist Politics in Action*, edited by A. Doak Barnett. Seattle: University of Washington Press, 1969.

Klein, Sidney. *The Pattern of Land Tenure Reform in East Asia after World War II*. New York: Bookman Associates, 1958.

Kolchin, Peter. *Unfree Labor: American Slavery and Russian Serfdom*. Cambridge, MA: Belknap Press, 1987.

Kuhn, Philip A. "Local Self-Government under the Republic: Problems of Control, Autonomy, and Mobilization." In *Conflict and Control in Late Imperial China*, edited by Frederic Wakeman Jr. and Carolyn Grant, 257–98. Berkeley: University of California Press, 1975.

Kuhn, Philip A. *Origins of the Modern Chinese State*. Stanford, CA: Stanford University Press, 2002.

Kuhn, Philip A., ed., *Select Papers from the Center for Far Eastern Studies*. No. 1. Chicago: University of Chicago, 1975/1976.

Kung, James Kai-sing. "The Political Economy of Land Reform in China's 'Newly Liberated Areas': Evidence from Wuxi County." *China Quarterly*, no. 195 (2008): 675–90.

Kung, James Kai-sing, Wu Xiaogang, and Wu Yuxiao. "Inequality of Land Tenure and Revolutionary Outcome: An Economic Analysis of China's Land Reform of 1946–1952." *Explorations in Economic History* 49 (2012): 482–97.

Lam, Tong. *A Passion for Facts: Social Surveys and the Construction of the Chinese Nation-State, 1900–1949*. Berkeley: University of California Press, 2011.

Lee, Hong Yung. *From Revolutionary Cadres to Party Technocrats in Socialist China*. Berkeley: University of California Press, 1991.

Lenin, V. I. *The Development of Capitalism in Russia: The Process of the Formation of a Home Market for Large-Scale Industry*. 1899. Moscow: Foreign Language Press, 1956.

Levine, Stephen I. *Anvil of Victory: The Communist Revolution in Manchuria, 1945–1948*. New York: Columbia University Press, 1987.

Li, Bozhong 李伯重. 《中国的早期近代经济》. 北京: 中华书局, 2010.

Li, Deying 李德英. 《民国时期成都平原的押租与押扣——兼与刘克祥先生商榷》. 《近代史研究》 2007 年第一期: 95–115.

Li, Fangchun. "Mass Democracy, Class Struggle, and Remolding the Party and Government during the Land Reform Movement in North China." *Modern China* 38, no. 4 (2012): 411–45.

Li, Huaiyin. *Village China under Socialism and Reform*. Stanford, CA: Stanford University Press, 2009.

Li, Huaiyin. *Village Governance in North China, 1875–1936*. Stanford, CA: Stanford University Press, 2005.

Li, Kang 李康. «西村十五年: 从革命走向革命—1938–1952 冀东村庄基层组织机制变迁». 博士学位论文. 北京大学社会学系, 1999.

Li, Lifeng 李里峰. «党组织、党员与群众——华北土改期间的整党运动». «安徽史学» 2012.1: 66–76.

Li, Lifeng 李里峰. «工作队: 一种国家权力的非常规运作机制——以华北土改运动为中心的历史考察». «江苏社会科学» 2010 年第3期: 207–214.

Li, Lifeng李里峰. «经济的 '土改' 与政治的 '土改'——关于土地改革历史意义的再思考». «安徽史学» 2008年第2期: 68–75.

Li, Lifeng 李里峰. «土改中的诉苦: 一种民众动员技术的微观分析». «南京大学学报 (哲学·人文科学·社会科学)» 2007.5: 97–109.

Li, Lifeng. "Mass Movements and Rural Governance in Communist China: 1945–1976." *Journal of Modern Chinese History* 7, no. 2 (2013): 156–80.

Liang, Shuming 梁漱溟. «中国民族自救运动之最后觉悟». 上海: 中华书局, 1933. Reprinted in «民国丛书» 第四遍, Vol. 14. 上海: 上海书店, 1992.

Lin, Xiaobo 林小波, and Guo Dehong 郭德宏. «文革的预演——«四清» 运动始末». 北京: 人民出版社, 2013.

Lipset, Seymour Martin. *Political Man: The Social Bases of Politics*. Garden City, NY: Doubleday and Company, 1960.

Liu, Alan. *Mass Politics in the People's Republic: State and Society in Contemporary China*. Boulder, CO: Westview Press, 1996.

Liu, Shaoqi (Liu Shao-chi). "On the Agrarian Reform Law." *People's China* 2, no. 2 (1950): 5–9, 28–31.

Liu, William Guanglin. *The Chinese Market Economy, 1000–1500*. New York: SUNY Press, 2015.

Liu, Woyu 刘握宇. «农村权力关系的重构: 以苏北土改为例 1950–1952». «江苏社会科学» 2012.2: 217–23.

Lotveit, Trygve. *Chinese Communism, 1931–1934: Experience in Civil Government*. Scandinavian Institute of Asian Studies Monograph Series, no. 16. Lund: Studentlitteratur, 1973.

Luo, Pinghan 罗平汉. «土地改革运动史». 福建人民出版社, 2005.

Luo, Weiwei. "The Common Good: Property and State-Making in Late Imperial China." PhD diss., Department of History, Columbia University, 2019.

Ma, Weiqiang, Hongqin Deng, and Lichao Yang. "The Pilot Land Reform Program and Land Reform in Pilot Villages: A Study of Pilot Land Reform and Party Consolidation in Lucheng, Shanxi." *Rural China* 16, no. 1 (2019): 9–37.

MacFarquhar, Roderick, ed. *China under Mao: Politics Takes Command*. Cambridge, MA: MIT Press, 1966.

MacFarquhar, Roderick. *The Origins of the Cultural Revolution*. 3 vols. New York: Columbia University Press, 1974–1997.

Manning, Kimberley Ens, and Felix Wemheuer, eds. *Eating Bitterness: New Perspectives on China's Great Leap Forward*. Vancouver: UBC Press, 2011.

Maruta, Takashi 丸田孝志. 『革命の儀礼—中国共産党根拠地の政治動員と民俗』. 汲古書院, 2013.

McNeill, William. *The Pursuit of Power: Technology, Armed Force, and Society since A.D. 1000*. Oxford: Basil Blackwell, 1982.

Moise, Edwin E. *Land Reform in China and North Vietnam: Consolidating the Revolution at the Village Level*. Chapel Hill: University of North Carolina Press, 1983.

Moore, Jr., Barrington. *Social Origins of Dictatorship and Democracy: Lord and Peasant in the Making of the Modern World*. Boston: Beacon Press, 1966.

Myers, Ramon H. *The Chinese Peasant Economy: Agricultural Development in Hopei and Shantung, 1890–1949*. Cambridge, MA: Harvard University Press, 1970.

Myers, Ramon H. "How Did the Modern Chinese Economy Develop?—A Review Article." *Journal of Asian Studies* 50, no. 3 (1991): 604–28.

Myers, Ramon H. "Socioeconomic Change in Villages of Manchuria during the Ch'ing and Republican Periods: Some Preliminary Findings." *Modern Asian Studies* 10, no. 4 (1976): 591–620.

Myers, Ramon H., and Thomas R. Ulie. "Foreign Influence and Agricultural Development in Northeast China: A Case Study of the Liaotung Peninsula, 1906–42." *Journal of Asian Studies* 31, no. 2 (1972): 329–50.

Myers, Ramon Hawley. *The Japanese Economic Development of Manchuria, 1932–1945*. New York: Garland, 1982.

Netting, Robert McC. *Smallholders, Householders: Farm Families and the Ecology of Intensive, Sustainable Agriculture*. Stanford, CA: Stanford University Press, 1993.

Noellert, Matthew. "Land Reform and Local Government in China's Northeast: The Case of Shuangcheng County, Heilongjiang, 1947–1949." Unpublished paper presented at the "International Conference on Land Reform and Rural Chinese Society," Shanxi University, Research Center for Chinese Social History, in Jincheng, Shanxi, August 9–12, 2013 (in Chinese).

Noellert, Matthew, Byung-ho Lee, and James Lee. "Wealth Distribution and Regime Change in Twentieth Century China." Class lecture by James Lee, A New History for a New China, 1700–2000: New Data and New Methods, Part 1. Coursera. https://www.coursera.org/course/newchinahistory1. Released Aug. 12, 2013.

Noellert, Matthew Z. "New Perspectives on Communist Land Reform: Evidence from Northeast China, 1946–1948." PhD diss., Division of Humanities, The Hong Kong University of Science and Technology, 2014.

North, Douglass C. *Structure and Change in Economic History*. New York: Norton, 1981.

Oi, Jean C. *State and Peasant in Contemporary China: The Political Economy of Village Government*. Berkeley: University of California Press, 1989.

Oksenberg, Michel C. "Aspects of Local Government and Politics in China: 1955–58." *Journal of Developmental Studies* 4, no. 1 (1967): 25–48.

Oksenberg, Michel C. "Policy Making under Mao Tse-Tung, 1949–1968." *Comparative Politics* 3, no. 3 (1971): 323–60.

Paige, Jeffery M. *Agrarian Revolution: Social Movements and Export Agriculture in the Underdeveloped World.* New York: Free Press, 1975.

Pepper, Suzanne. *Civil War in China: The Political Struggle, 1945–1949.* Berkeley: University of California Press, 1978.

Perry, Elizabeth. *Challenging the Mandate of Heaven: Social Protest and State Power in China.* Armonk, NY: M. E. Sharpe, 2002.

Perry, Elizabeth. "Moving the Masses: Emotion Work in the Chinese Revolution." *Mobilization: An International Quarterly* 7, no. 2 (2002): 111–28.

Perry, Elizabeth J. *Rebels and Revolutionaries in North China, 1845–1945.* Stanford, CA: Stanford University Press, 1980.

Piketty, Thomas. *Capital in the Twenty-First Century.* Cambridge, MA: Harvard University Press, 2014.

Polanyi, Karl. *The Great Transformation: The Political and Economic Origins of Our Time.* Boston: Beacon Books, 1944.

Pomeranz, Kenneth. *The Great Divergence: China, Europe, and the Making of the Modern World Economy.* Princeton, NJ: Princeton University Press, 2000.

Pomeranz, Kenneth. *The Making of a Hinterland: State, Society, and Economy in Inland North China, 1853–1937.* Berkeley: University of California Press, 1993.

Potter, Sulamith Heins, and Jack M. Potter. *China's Peasants: The Anthropology of a Revolution.* New York: Cambridge University Press, 1990.

Powell, John Duncan. "Peasant Society and Clientelist Politics." *American Political Science Review* 64, no. 2 (1970): 411–25.

Powers, Martin J. *Art and Political Expression in Early China.* New Haven, CT: Yale University Press, 1991.

Qi, Zhijin 祁之晋. «'土地村有' 下之晋北农村». «国闻周报»第十三卷第十一期 (March 1936): 21–26.

Qiao, Shitong, and Frank Upham. "The Evolution of Relational Property Rights: A Case of Chinese Rural Land Reform." *Iowa Law Review*, Iowa City 100, no. 6 (Aug. 2015): 2479–2506.

Reed, Bradly Ward. *Talons and Teeth: County Clerks and Runners in the Qing Dynasty.* Stanford, CA: Stanford University Press, 2000.

Ren, Yuxue 任玉雪. «清代吉林将军双城地区的身份制度与旗界、民界 （1815–1911 年) ——兼论东北地区的封禁政策». «中国历史地理论丛» 第28卷第3辑 (2013.7): 115–23.

Ren, Yuxue 任玉雪, Bijia Chen 陈必佳, Xiaowen Hao 郝小雯, Cameron Campbell 康文林, and James Z. Lee 李中清. «清代缙绅录量化数据库与官僚群体研究». «清史研究» 2016 年 11 月第四期: 61–77.

Repp, Kevin. *Reformers, Critics, and the Paths of German Modernity: Anti-Politics and the Search for Alternatives, 1890–1914.* Cambridge, MA: Harvard University Press, 2000.

Rosenthal, Jean-Laurent, and R. Bin Wong, *Before and Beyond Divergence: The Politics of*

Economic Change in China and Europe. Cambridge, MA: Harvard University Press, 2011.

Rowe, William T. *Crimson Rain: Seven Centuries of Violence in a Chinese County.* Stanford, CA: Stanford University Press, 2007.

Ruf, Gregory A. *Cadres and Kin: Making a Socialist Village in West China, 1921–1991.* Stanford, CA: Stanford University Press, 1998.

Saich, Tony. "Introduction: The Chinese Communist Party and the Anti-Japanese War Base Areas." *China Quarterly* 140 (Dec. 1994): 1000–06.

Sanft, Charles. *Communication and Cooperation in Early Imperial China.* Albany, NY: SUNY Press, 2014.

Schmidt, Vivien A. "Putting the Political Back into Political Economy by Bringing the State Back in Yet Again." *World Politics* 61, no. 3 (2009): 516–46.

Schneewind, Sarah. "Visions and Revisions: Village Policies of the Ming Founder in Seven Phases." *T'oung Pao* 87, nos. 4–5 (2001): 317–59.

Schoppa, Keith R. "Contours of Revolutionary Change in a Chinese County, 1900–1950." *Journal of Asian Studies* 51, no. 4 (1992): 770–96.

Schran, Peter. *The Development of Chinese Agriculture, 1950–1959.* Urbana: University of Illinois Press, 1969.

Schurmann, Franz. *Ideology and Organization in Communist China.* Berkeley: University of California Press, 1968.

Scott, James C. "Corruption, Machine Politics, and Political Change." *American Political Science Review* 63, no. 4 (1969): 1142–58.

Scott, James C. *The Moral Economy of the Peasant: Rebellion and Subsistence in Southeast Asia.* New Haven, CT: Yale University Press, 1976.

Scott, James C. "Patron-Client Politics and Political Change in Southeast Asia." *American Political Science Review* 66, no. 1 (1972): 91–113.

Selden, Mark. *China in Revolution: The Yenan Way Revisited.* 1971. Armonk, NY: M.E. Sharpe, 1995.

Shen, Tsun-han. *The Sino-American Joint Commission on Rural Reconstruction: Twenty Years of Cooperation for Agricultural Development.* Ithaca, NY: Cornell University Press, 1970.

Shepherd, John R. *Statecraft and Political Economy on the Taiwan Frontier, 1600–1800.* Stanford, CA: Stanford University Press, 1993.

Sholokhov, Mikhail. *And Quiet Flows the Don.* Translated by Stephen Garry. 1934. London: Putnam, 1970.

Shue, Vivienne. "Modern/Rural China: State Institutions and Village Values." In *Organizing Rural China—Rural China Organizing,* edited by Ane Bislev and Stig Thogersen, 223–32. Lanham, MD: Lexington Books, 2012.

Shue, Vivienne. *Peasant China in Transition: The Dynamics of Development toward Socialism, 1949–1956.* Berkeley: University of California Press, 1980.

Shue, Vivienne, and Patricia M. Thornton, eds. *To Govern China: Evolving Practices of Power.* New York: Cambridge University Press, 2017.

Silagi, Michael. "Henry George and Europe: Precursors of Land Reform in Germany;

Marx and the Land Question; the Beginnings of the Georgist Movement in the Empire." Trans. Susan N. Faulkner. *American Journal of Economics and Sociology* 51, no. 2 (1992): 247–56.

Skinner, G. William. "Chinese Peasants and the Closed Community: An Open and Shut Case." *Comparative Studies in Society and History* 13, no. 3 (1971): 270–81.

Skinner, G. William. "Marketing and Social Structure in Rural China: Part I." *Journal of Asian Studies* 24, no. 1 (1964): 3–43.

Skinner, G. William. "Marketing and Social Structure in Rural China: Part II." *Journal of Asian Studies* 24, no. 2 (1965): 195–228.

Skinner, G. William. "Marketing and Social Structure in Rural China: Part III." *Journal of Asian Studies* 24, no. 3 (1965): 363–99.

Skinner, G. William, and Edwin A. Winckler. "Compliance Succession in Rural Communist China: A Cyclical Theory." In *A Sociological Reader on Complex Organization*, edited by Amitai Etzioni, 410–38. New York: Holt, Rinehart, and Winston, 1969.

Skocpol, Theda. *States and Social Revolutions: A Comparative Analysis of France, Russia, and China*. New York: Cambridge University Press, 1979.

Smith, Jenny Leigh. *Works in Progress: Plans and Realities on Soviet Farms, 1930–1963*. New Haven, CT: Yale University Press, 2014.

Snow, Edgar. *Red Star over China*. 1938. New York: Grove Press, 1968.

Strauss, Julia. "Morality, Coercion, and State Building by Campaign in the Early PRC: Regime Consolidation and After, 1949–1956." In *The History of the PRC (1949–1976)*, edited by Julia Straus, 37–58. New York: Cambridge University Press, 2007.

Szonyi, Michael. *The Art of Being Governed: Everyday Politics in Late Imperial China*. Princeton, NJ: Princeton University Press, 2017.

Tai, Hung-chao. *Land Reform and Politics: A Comparative Analysis*. Berkeley: University of California Press, 1974.

Tanimoto, Masayuki, and R. Bin Wong, eds. *Public Goods Provision in the Early Modern Economy: Comparative Perspectives from Japan, China, and Europe*. Berkeley: University of California Press, 2019.

Thaxton, Ralph A., Jr. *Catastrophe and Contention in Rural China: Mao's Great Leap Forward Famine and the Origins of Righteous Resistance in Da Fo Village*. New York: Cambridge University Press, 2010.

Thaxton, Ralph A., Jr. *Salt of the Earth: The Political Origins of Peasant Protest and Communist Revolution in China*. Berkeley: University of California Press, 1997.

Tilly, Charles. *From Mobilization to Revolution*. New York: Random House, 1978.

Tsai, Lily. *Accountability without Democracy: Solidary Groups and Public Goods Provision in Rural China*. New York: Cambridge University Press, 2007.

Tseng, Hsiao. *The Theory and Practice of Land Reform in China*. Taipei: Chinese Research Institute of Land Economics, 1953.

Tsou, Tang, ed. *Select Papers from the Center for Far Eastern Studies*, No. 4, 1979–1980. Chicago: University of Chicago Press, 1981.

Tucker, Robert C. *The Marx and Engels Reader*. 2nd ed. New York: Norton, 1978.

Tuma, Elias H. *Twenty-Six Centuries of Agrarian Reform: A Comparative Analysis.* Berkeley: University of California Press, 1965.

Uhalley, Stephen, Jr. *A History of the Chinese Communist Party.* Stanford, CA: Hoover Institution Press, 1988.

United Nations. *Land Reform: Defects in Agrarian Structure as Obstacles to Economic Development.* New York: United Nations Department of Economic Affairs, 1951.

Van Slyke, Lyman P. *The Chinese Communist Movement: A Report of the United States War Department, July 1945.* Stanford, CA: Stanford University Press, 1968.

Wakeman, Frederic, Jr., and Carolyn Grant, eds. *Conflict and Control in Late Imperial China.* Berkeley: University of California Press, 1975.

Walder, Andrew G. *China under Mao: A Revolution Derailed.* Cambridge, MA: Harvard University Press, 2015.

Wang, Feng. *Boundaries and Categories: Rising Inequality in Post-Socialist Urban China* Stanford, CA: Stanford University Press, 2007.

Wang, Hongbo, Shuang Chen, Hao Dong, Matt Noellert, Cameron Campbell, and James Z Lee. *China Multi-Generational Panel Dataset, Shuangcheng (CMGPD-SC) 1866–1914. User Guide.* Ann Arbor, MI: Inter-university Consortium for Political and Social Research, 2013.

Wang, Youming 王友明. 《解放区土地改革研究 1941–1948: 以山东莒南县为个案》. 上海社会科学院出版社, 2006.

Warriner, Doreen. *Land Reform in Principle and Practice.* Oxford: Clarendon Press, 1969.

Watson, Burton, trans. *The Analects of Confucius.* New York: Columbia University Press, 2007.

Watson, James L. "Anthropological Overview: The Development of Chinese Descent Groups." In *Kinship Organization in Late Imperial China, 1000–1940,* edited by Patricia B. Ebrey and James L. Watson, 274–92. Berkeley: University of California Press, 1986.

Wauters, Arthur. 《欧洲农地改革》. 彭补拙译. 上海: 商务印书馆, 1933.

Weber, Max. *Economy and Society: An Outline of Interpretive Sociology.* Ed. Guenther Roth and Claus Wittich. 2 vols. Berkeley: University of California Press, 1978.

Wemheuer, Felix. *Famine Politics in Maoist China and the Soviet Union.* New Haven, CT: Yale University Press, 2014.

Wemheuer, Felix. *A Social History of Maoist China: Conflict and Change, 1949–1976.* Cambridge: Cambridge University Press, 2019.

Westad, Odd Arne. *Decisive Encounters: The Chinese Civil War, 1946–1950.* Stanford, CA: Stanford University Press, 2003.

White, Theodore H., and Annalee Jacoby. *Thunder Out of China.* New York, NY: William Sloane Associates, Inc., 1946.

Wolff, David. "Bean There: Toward a Soy-Based History of Northeast Asia." *South Atlantic Quarterly* 99, no. 1 (2000): 241–52.

Wong, John. *Chinese Land Reform in Retrospect.* Hong Kong: Centre of Asian Studies, University of Hong Kong, 1973.

Wong, Roy Bin. *China Transformed: Historical Change and the Limits of European Experience.* Ithaca, NY: Cornell University Press, 1997.

Wong, Roy Bin. "Opium and Modern Chinese State-Making," In *Opium Regimes: China, Britain, and Japan, 1839–1952,* edited by Timothy Brook and Tadashi Wakabayashi, 189–211. Berkeley: University of California Press, 2000.

Wou, Odoric Y. K. *Mobilizing the Masses: Building Revolution in Henan.* Stanford, CA: Stanford University Press, 1994.

Wright, Mary C. *The Last Stand of Chinese Conservatism: The T'ung-Chih Restoration, 1862–1874.* Stanford, CA: Stanford University Press, 1957.

Wu, Yi 吴毅, and Chen Qi 陈颀. «'说话' 的可能性——对土改 '诉苦' 的再反思». «社会学研究» 2012.6: 146–71.

Xing, Long 行龙. «走向田野与社会». 修订本. 北京: 生活·读书·新知三联书店, 2015.

Xing, Long, and Ma Weiqiang. "Rural Grassroots Files from the Collectivization Era: Archives of the Chinese Social History Research Center of Shanxi University." *Modern China* 34, no. 3 (2008): 372–95.

Xu, Youchun, ed. 徐友春主编. «民国人物大辞典». 增订版. 河北人民出版社, 2007.

Yang, C. K. *A Chinese Village in Early Communist Transition.* Cambridge, MA: MIT Press, 1959.

Yang, Kaidao 杨开道. «中国乡约制度». «村治» 3, nos. 2–3 (1933): 1–28.

Yang, Kaidao 杨开道. «中国乡约制度,第五章: 吕氏乡约的增损». «村治» 3, no. 5 (1933): 1–12.

Yang, Kuisong 杨奎松. «革命: 杨奎松著作集». 四卷. 桂林: 广西师范大学出版社, 2012.

Yang, Kuisong. "Reconsidering the Campaign to Suppress Counterrevolutionaries." *China Quarterly* 193 (March 2008): 102–121.

Yang, Kuisong 杨奎松. «中华人民共和国建国史研究». 二卷. 南昌市: 江西人民出版社, 2009.

Yeh, K. C. *The Chinese Communist Revolutionary Strategy and the Land Problem, 1921–1927.* Santa Monica, CA: Rand Corporation, 1970.

Yeh, K. C. *Land Reform and the Revolutionary War: A Review of Mao's Concepts and Doctrines.* Santa Monica, CA: Rand Corporation, 1971.

Ying, Xing 应星. «农户、集体与国家——国家与农民关系的六十年变迁». 北京: 中国社会科学出版社, 2014.

Yunnan sheng wei dang shi yanjiu shi 云南省委党史研究室. «云南土地改革回忆录». 云南民族出版社, 2008.

Zhang, Letian 张乐天. «告别理想:人民公社制度研究». 上海: 上海人民出版社, 2012.

Zhang, Si 张思. «国家渗透与乡村过滤: 昌黎县侯家营文书所见». «中国农业大学学报 (社会科学版)» 第 25 卷第1期 (March 2008): 76–88.

Zhang, Taisu. *The Laws and Economics of Confucianism: Kinship and Property in Preindustrial China and England.* New York: Cambridge University Press, 2017.

Zhang, Xueqiang 张学强. «乡村变迁与农民记忆——山东老区莒南县土地改革研究 (1941–1951)». 北京: 社会科学文献出版社, 2006.

Zhang, Yiping 张一平. «地权变动与社会重构: 苏南土地改革研究, 1949–1952». 上海: 上海人民出版社, 2009.

Zhang, Yiping 张一平. «三十年来中国土地改革研究的回顾与思考». «中共党史研究» 2009.1: 110–19.

Zhang, Yue 张跃. «汉武帝时期的垄断官营经济政策». «山西财经大学学报» 27, no. 1 (2005): 8–11.

Zheng, Yongnian and Yanjie Huang. *Market in State: The Political Economy of Domination in China.* Cambridge, UK: Cambridge University Press, 2018.

Zhi, Xiaomin 智效民. «刘少奇与晋绥土改». 台北市: 秀威资讯科技, 2008.

Zhou, Libo 周立波. «暴风骤雨». 两册. 北京: 人民文学出版社, 1949/1952.

Zhou, Libo. *The Hurricane.* Translated by Xu Mengxiong. 1955. Beijing: Foreign Language Press, 1981.

Zhou, Xueguang. *The State and Life Chances in Urban China: Redistribution and Stratification, 1949–1994.* New York: Cambridge University Press, 2004.

Zweig, David. "Strategies of Policy Implementation: 'Policy Winds' and Brigade Accounting in Rural China, 1966–1978." *World Politics* 37 (1985): 267–93.

Index